Revelation in Christian Theologies of Religions

Revelation in Christian Theologies of Religions

Voices from across the Ages

Iain McGee

FOREWORD BY
Gavin D'Costa

☙PICKWICK *Publications* • Eugene, Oregon

REVELATION IN CHRISTIAN THEOLOGIES OF RELIGIONS
Voices from across the Ages

Copyright © 2024 Iain McGee. All rights reserved. Except for brief quotations in critical publications or reviews, no part of this book may be reproduced in any manner without prior written permission from the publisher. Write: Permissions, Wipf and Stock Publishers, 199 W. 8th Ave., Suite 3, Eugene, OR 97401.

Pickwick Publications
An Imprint of Wipf and Stock Publishers
199 W. 8th Ave., Suite 3
Eugene, OR 97401

www.wipfandstock.com

PAPERBACK ISBN: 979-8-3852-0251-5
HARDCOVER ISBN: 979-8-3852-0252-2
EBOOK ISBN: 979-8-3852-0253-9

Cataloguing-in-Publication data:

Names: McGee, Iain [author]. | D'Costa, Gavin [foreword writer].

Title: Revelation in Christian theologies of religions : voices from across the ages / by Iain McGee ; foreword by Gavin D'Costa.

Description: Eugene, OR: Pickwick Publications, 2024 | Includes bibliographical references.

Identifiers: ISBN 979-8-3852-0251-5 (paperback) | ISBN 979-8-3852-0252-2 (hardcover) | ISBN 979-8-3852-0253-9 (ebook)

Subjects: LCSH: Christianity and other religions. | Theology of religions (Christian theology). | Justin, Martyr, Saint. | Augustine, Saint, Bishop of Hippo. | Calvin, Jean, 1509–1564. | Edwards, Jonathan, 1703–1758. | Strange, Daniel.

Classification: BR127 M344 2024 (paperback) | BR127 (ebook)

VERSION NUMBER 05/21/24

Scriptures taken from the Holy Bible, New International Version®, NIV®. Copyright © 1973, 1978, 1984, 2011 by Biblica, Inc.™ Used by permission of Zondervan. All rights reserved worldwide. www.zondervan.com The "NIV" and "New International Version" are trademarks registered in the United States Patent and Trademark Office by Biblica, Inc.™

Some of the material in chapters 4 and 5 has been published previously in articles written by me:

"Revelation and Religions: Towards a more 'Harmonious' Jonathan Edwards." *Themelios* 46 (2021) 620–40.

"John Calvin: Logos-centric Theologian of Religions." *Journal of Reformed Theology* 17 (2023) 3–28 (extracts used in accordance with the CC-BY-4.0 licence).

"Reconsidering the Sensus Divinitatis in the Light of the Semen Religionis: John Calvin and Non-Christian Religion." *European Journal of Theology* 31 (2022) 215–39.

I would like to thank the publishers for permissions to include the material here.

Soli Deo Gloria

Contents

List of Tables | viii
Foreword by Gavin D'Costa | ix
Preface | xiii
Acknowledgements | xv

1. Introduction | 1
2. Justin Martyr | 21
3. Augustine | 53
4. John Calvin | 89
5. Jonathan Edwards | 123
6. Daniel Strange | 158
7. Conclusion | 193

Endnotes | 217
Bibliography | 331

List of Tables

Table 1. Light of Nature Knowledge in the Edwards Corpus | 149

Table 2. Implanted Knowledge in the Edwards Corpus | 152

Table 3. Synthesis of Theologies | 195

Table 4. The Role of Contextual Influences | 207

Foreword

THIS IS AN ORIGINAL book, important to the field, and very engaging due to McGee's elegant, sophisticated and accessible style. I commend it to all serious Christians reflecting on the relationship of Christianity to the religious and non-religious cultures within which we live.

The field of 'theology of religions' has been developed since the nineteenth century and led by Roman Catholic and Protestant theologians, with a lesser profile for Augustinian Reformed theologians. McGee corrects that way of viewing matters in two important ways.

First, he provides an in depth map of modern Reform theology of religions through the significant contemporary work of Daniel Strange, and McGee notes Strange's dependence on J. H. Bavinck and Cornelius Van Til—two giants of the modern period. McGee's mapping shows that the Augustinian Reformed contribution to theology of religions is significant. It poses a number of important challenges to mainstream theology of religions both in the method it adopts and the theology it develops, especially in its focus on the question of revelation.

But McGee goes much further. He draws the map back in time so as to assess the present, and through this, map out trajectories for the future. His second achievement, therefore, is in his tracing an earlier tradition upon which these authors are in variable ways dependent. McGee provides important studies of Justin Martyr, Saint Augustine, John Calvin, and Jonathan Edwards regarding their views about non-Christian religions. These chapters provide a contextualized historical perspective and McGee handles his primary and secondary sources artfully and insightfully—and often makes significant contributions to the study of these authors in arguments with secondary sources. These individual studies alone make the book an important historical-theological contribution to the field. McGee shows that the resources of theology of religions in the contemporary period lie in the past, and how through a creative retrieval of these sources in application to the modern context, the future opens up.

These two achievements alone would make this book a jewel. However, McGee goes even a step further in these individual studies through developing a framework for a Reformed theology of religions: a kind of list of questions that require clarification and can be played out very differently. Unlike many studies that focus on soteriology, McGee turns to the more basic and fundamental question of revelation. Is there any sense in which revelation could be said to operate in the religions? He thereby examines Justin, Augustine, Calvin, and Edwards asking this question and comes up with three seminal theological themes related to the question of revelation: Logos theology, the Prisca Theologia and the demonic. This theological and historical enquiry gives the study a further cutting edge in showing how the future development of the Reformed tradition requires a careful balancing of these three themes, and a recognition of how historical circumstances in the past have meant some themes were given more emphasis than others—while others were neglected. In this way, McGee also provides a framework by which to judge the work of the modern Reformed theologians he is inspecting, while also learning from them.

McGee draws his findings together to provide a road map for future Reformed theology of religions showing it to be resourceful, creative, intensely fruitful, faithful to the biblical tradition and to the great teachers in the Christian tradition—and is thereby biblical, traditional, fresh, and productive in the field of theology of religions. Most importantly, he grounds his position in the theological tradition and not in modern cultural assumptions that often sway many other scholars, but McGee is resourceful and able to tackle these latter assumptions critically and sensitively.

This book is destined to be a landmark showing both the rigorous theology and the open questions that remain to be explored in this field by theologians working out of the Reformed tradition.

McGee's writing style is envious. He is scholarly and rigorous but also accessible and conceptually clear. He is open to questions and keenly aware of critical problems as he advances through complex materials. He is at home with and sensitive to different historical periods and is both loyal to the Reformed tradition while seeking to develop it and further its range. I eagerly await his next book which will no doubt, build upon this, and advance his ambitious and important project.

As a Roman Catholic scholar working in this field, I've learnt greatly from McGee's work and insights. I say this to indicate the significant ecumenical import of the book. It will be a must-read for any Reformed theologian working in this field but also for any Christian theologian interested in these questions. Neglecting this work will impoverish the field. Reading this book carefully, promises to pay huge dividends.

Gavin D'Costa

Professor of Interreligious Dialogue, Pontifical University of St. Thomas Aquinas, Rome; Emeritus Professor of Catholic Theology, University of Bristol

December, 2023

Preface

THIS BOOK IS A lightly re-formatted and edited version of my PhD, awarded by the University of Bristol in 2024. My main goal in writing it is to make a Reformed Evangelical contribution to the theology of religions discipline and I do this by means of a wide-ranging historical theological study. Three of the five scholars studied in this work are Reformed Evangelicals and the two who existed before the early modern period are readily embraced by the tradition. The theologians studied are Justin Martyr, Augustine, John Calvin, Jonathan Edwards, and Daniel Strange.

There are two distinct, though related, foci within the theology of religions literature: soteriology and revelation. I note potential problems with a soteriological focus, and argue that a revelation-focused investigation should be central to the discipline. I suggest that three parameters (all relating in some way to God's revelation) have, in large part, dominated Christian theology of religions thought from the second right up to the twenty-first centuries, at least for the theologians whose works are considered in this thesis. These parameters are the *Logos*, the ancient theology tradition (*prisca theologia*), and demons.

For the first two of these (the *Logos* and the *prisca theologia*) I suggest two continua exist in the ideas of the five theologians studied. The first is the revelatory content and the second is the clarity of this (from fallen humanity's perspective). For the third, both the revelatory and anti-revelatory roles of the demonic are considered. The relationship between each parameter in each theologian's thought is examined, and a principled synthesis and comparison of the five different theologies is presented in the concluding chapter.

I argue that each rather different theology may well, for want of a better term, be considered a biblically-informed *contextually reflective* and *contextually reactive* attempt to explain the failures and shortcomings of other religions and religious expression, while seeking to demonstrate the uniqueness and superiority of the Christian faith.

Acknowledgements

BOTH OF MY PHD supervisors played an important role in helping me successfully complete the research which lies behind this project. From initial enquiry to final draft, Prof. Gavin D'Costa has been a model of enthusiastic engagement and critical feedback. I have learnt much from him and from his probing questions and nuanced critiques. I would particularly like to thank him for continuing supervision in an emeritus capacity, and also for providing a foreword to this book. I would also like to thank Dr. Jon Balserak for his sustained interest and support. From his initial detailed comments on my work on Calvin, to his patient engagement with the later work, Jon has exhibited scholarly care and a commitment to intellectual virtue. In discussing my supervisors with interested friends, I have described them, on more than occasion, as "The Dream Team": I feel privileged to have studied with them. I would also like to thank Dan Strange for agreeing to be interviewed on his work, and for giving of his time so generously for that, in addition to serving as the external examiner for the PhD viva. His gracious engagement has been much appreciated.

Once again, I find myself indebted to my wife and daughters for their patience while engaged in a large research project. Without their understanding, support and encouragement, I would have fallen at the first hurdle.

1

Introduction

1. Overview and Approach

IT IS NOT MY goal in this book to forward my own theology of religions, and neither is it to lend support to, or critique, an existing position or viewpoint. Rather, my goal is threefold: to seek to redress the paucity of methodologically grounded historical studies in the field; to compare and contrast five theologies, considered through the same revelation-focused lenses; and to consider what Evangelicals may learn from such a project, as we consider new questions and issues arising in theology of religions today.

It is generally acknowledged that Evangelical theologians[1] have been rather slow to arrive on the contemporary theology of religions scene.[2] Various possible explanations for this lateness have been suggested, one being that the defense of an exclusivist position has left Evangelicals on the back foot in some critical debates.[3] This book seeks to make a Reformed Evangelical contribution to the discipline and does so by means of a broad scope historical theological study.[4] Three of the five scholars whose works are examined in this study are Reformed Evangelicals and the two who lived before the early modern period are readily embraced by the tradition.[5] The book is written from the same tradition-specific viewpoint.[6]

While Evangelical Reformed theologians prize Scripture above tradition, creeds or confessions,[7] appeals to the past and appropriation of the church's historical wisdom are commonplace within Evangelical scholarly literature—both from the time of the Reformation to today.[8] I suggest, however, that for Evangelical theologians of religions the relevant history is located in something of a blind spot. Daniel Strange, a contemporary Evangelical scholar whose contribution to the discipline will be considered in more detail in chapter 6, rather quickly passes over the field's history before forwarding his own theology. He claims that the history of Evangelical theology of religions "has been ably done elsewhere."[9] I will argue below that Strange's rather sanguine assessment does not stand up well to the evidence. Indeed, I will suggest that the lack of serious engagement with the tradition's history may be part of the reason why Reformed Evangelicals have been so slow to arrive on the modern theology of religions scene. If one does not know one's tradition-specific history, one is left rather vulnerable when exposed to sophisticated theology of religions ideas and models developed by Roman Catholic, Pentecostal and other Christian thinkers. This being so, this book explores what Reformed Evangelicals might learn from their own "tradition" on this critical subject.

In this introductory chapter I explain the need for, the rationale behind, and the overall design of the book. In section 2, I document issues surrounding the development of a principled methodological approach to historical theology of religions research. In it I explain how I arrived at the research design employed in the study. This constitutes the bulk of the chapter. In section 3, I consider in some detail the issue of research focus and the value of identifying key parameters to guide theological enquiry. In section 4, potential problems with the research design are discussed, which I seek to address. I close by considering why the particular theologians have been chosen for inclusion in this study.

2. Christian Theology of Religions Method

2.1. Historical Appeals and the Problem of Method

I begin with the issue of method. Christian theologians of religions who have wished to demonstrate that their ideas are connected to the church's teachings recognize that their writings gain credibility through quoting and referencing the ideas of respected historical figures within the church—often from within their own religious tradition. So, for example, J. H. Bavinck makes numerous appeals to Calvin in his works;[10]

INTRODUCTION

Clark Pinnock believes the theology of religions he proposes follows in the footsteps of Justin, Erasmus and Wesley;[11] and Daniel Strange leans on the authority of Jonathan Edwards to support his contribution to the field.[12] Recognition of the need to understand and draw on the wisdom of the church's past in engaging with complex issues in theology of religions in the present is a commonplace.[13]

The appeal to the past is, however, fraught with difficulties, and I suggest that only some of these challenges are recognized in the Christian theology of religions discipline today. Starting with known obstacles, one of these, the need to acknowledge and respect historical distance and context, is a given. It is *de rigueur* to sensitively handle language meanings and the specific historical context of a theologian when interpreting historical texts. So, for example, Justin's *Logos* theory must be interpreted in its historical context and at the very least make reference to Stoicism and Philo; to understand Augustine's demonology one must consider his engagement with Apuleius and Porphyry, and so on.

Another issue which is largely respected within the field is the need to recognize that non-Christian religions are different for different theologians, not just in their definitions, but also in terms of the specific beliefs and practices a particular theologian has in view.[14] So, for example, Jonathan Edwards defines religion differently from Augustine; and false religion for Calvin (i.e., Roman Catholicism)[15] is different from non-Christian religion for Justin Martyr (i.e., Graeco-Roman paganism). A Christian theology of religions is never an abstract enterprise: it is either contextually grounded, or can readily be applied to actual religions.

The unacknowledged obstacle alluded to above is, I suggest, responsible for tripping up many theologians of religions in their appeals for credible historical support. This obstacle constitutes two separate, though connected, methodological issues. The first is the need to clearly define the subject matter focus of the discipline, and the second is the need to establish disciplinary parameters for the subsequent theological investigation. The methodological problem is a significant one and is directly related to the newness of the discipline.[16] In the absence of a focused exposition on the theme of theology of religions in the writings of figures from the church's past (which one would not expect given the acknowledged newness of the "discipline"), where does one look to find the relevant material?

Definitions of the discipline *Christian theology of religions* contain a number of different foci, and despite McDermott and Netland's assertion that there is "something of a consensus" surrounding the discipline's content and methodological approach,[17] I suggest that the evidence points against this judgment on both counts.[18] Regarding content, when investigating this subject area should a theologian's theory of revelation or soteriology be foundational?[19] Should Ecclesiology and Eschatology be considered? Which theological sub-disciplines should be primary, secondary and tertiary? Turning to method, where should the enquiry begin? Should one start with religions themselves (whether including or excluding Christianity),[20] religious consciousness,[21] the Bible, or Jesus Christ? Theology of religions is not just a new discipline, it is a new discipline which lacks a universally accepted central focus and an acknowledged theological framework for investigating and engaging with older, relevant work.

In the absence of a clear focus and the establishment of a manageable set of parameters to guide enquiry, the theology of religions researcher will, I suggest, be tempted to be satisfied by locating the more obviously present surface "nuggets" (i.e., clear relevant statements) in historical texts, and then go on to report such as being representative of the ideas of a particular figure. I would argue, however, that even when such statements are interpreted within their context (see the earlier points on the *known* historical challenges), the failure to recognize or understand the existence of a larger meaningful framework within which such quotable comments should be considered must be acknowledged. If not, the researcher is open to the charge of superficial treatment and even misrepresentation. I suggest that lack of consensus over focus and parameter identification is at least partially responsible for what may be considered the rather confusing appeal to the past within the discipline today—as I note in what follows.

2.2. Examples Demonstrating the Problem of Method

I provide two examples here, to illustrate the point that I am making: the first relates to Justin Martyr, and the second to John Calvin.[22] Gerald O'Collins, in a book outlining the Second Vatican Council's approach to religions and *Nostra Aetata*, states what he believes the role of the Johannine prologue to be within Justin's thought. He comments, "Justin had his eye on the revelatory and saving role of Christ for those who were not (or were not yet) Christians,"[23] and in contrasting Justin's partial and whole *Logos* idea (2 *Apol.* 10)[24] he believes this allows for and points to "the endless variety and modes not only in the presence of the *Logos* but also in the knowledge that he communicates."[25] Jacques Dupuis adopts a similarly positive interpretation of the *Logos* Christology of Justin in his respected book on theology of religions.[26] While recognizing the fragmentary nature of pre-incarnation knowledge of the *Logos* in Justin's thinking,[27] he states, "The patristic theme of the 'seeds of the Word' offers, today, a valid foundation for a positive approach to the 'religions' inasmuch as in them too, thanks to the active presence of the Word of God, justice and piety (*eusebia*) are not wanting."[28]

A very different conclusion about Justin and his contribution to the discipline is drawn by Gerald Bray—a Reformed theologian.[29] In contrast to O'Collins and Dupuis, Bray makes the following comment about second century apologists, including Justin, an interpretation which sets out a far less positive view of the role of the *Logos*: "However much they may have agreed that all human beings possessed something of the divine *Logos*, and even when they were prepared to commend a man like Plato for having made the best use of the *Logos* given to him, pagans were still the victims of demonic deception, with only a partial (and usually misleading) grasp of the truth."[30]

How can such starkly contrasting conclusions be drawn? While one may be tempted to refer to agenda, or presuppositions (with some justification), one indisputable reason is *method*. O'Collins does not consider other means of revelation in Justin's thought, and neither does he consider the strong *Logos*-demon counter-positioning in Justin's thinking on religions, when making his comments. Similarly, Dupuis makes no reference to Justin's demonology and opposition to idols when drawing his conclusions about *Logos* enlightenment in Justin's writings. Bray, on the other hand, demonstrates, at the very least, the rudiments of methodological sensitivity: he references Justin's anti-pagan religion polemic, his demonology and his view on the ancient theology tradition when considering Justin's *Logos* Christology. Solely on the basis of methodological approach, one would expect Bray's conclusions to be sounder, *if* he has correctly identified the parameters within which Justin's theology of religions is developed and *if* he has respected the known obstacles noted earlier.[31]

A second example illustrating the point I argue above is the interpretation of the contribution of John Calvin to the field. Veli-Matti Kärkkäinen, a well-known Pentecostal theologian, does not believe that Calvin thought religions to be only evil, arguing that he was also positive about non-Christian religiosity.[32] Bouwsma also argues for Calvin's appreciation of some religious phenomena, referencing a comment made by Calvin about the Greeks to support this viewpoint.[33] In contrast, Carlos Eire believes that for Calvin false religion is wholly explainable by recourse to fallen human nature, and only evil: "religion . . . springs from human nature itself,"[34] and "False religion, then, is embedded in the flesh itself, encoded in our genes."[35] While there are various possible reasons for the different conclusions drawn by Eire when compared to those of Bouwsma and Kärkkäinen, methodological approach is, once again, able to account for at least some of the confusion. In his treatment of Calvin, Kärkkäinen makes only passing reference to the seed of religion, and Eire barely touches on *Logos* enlightenment, focusing rather on the relegation of the role of demons in Calvin's understanding of religion when compared to that of the medieval church. Such, I believe, are not "rounded" methodological approaches. Turning to Bouwsma, I believe that on this particular occasion he represents well the position described earlier, namely the reporting of a surface-level "nugget" with little attention paid to the immediate or wider context and argument.[36] I suggest that the absence of a clear focus and the establishment of valid parameters to guide enquiry is, again, partly responsible for the different conclusions drawn. In the next section, I consider a way to develop a responsible method.

3. Theology of Religions: Focus and Parameters

3.1. Revelation as Central Focus

If, as Morali argues, the proper object of Christian theology is the study of God and his revelation, one must ask what overlap there is between Christian theology and non-Christian religions when the latter do not "contain" specifically *Christian* revelation.[37] A response to this viewpoint might be to argue that as part of the current reality of the fabric of God's creation, non-Christian religions must be "related" to God in some way through some *other* kind of revelation. Such indeed is the view of a number of Reformed theologians, this idea constituting the core of various definitions of religions from those writing within the Reformed tradition.[38] If the human religious response were a *total* suppression of this revelation, or if religions are a *wholly* human affair,[39] an argument could be made that the discipline Christian *Theology* of Religions is in fact an oxymoron, at least if one accepts Morali's argument for the need for the word *theology* to be used meaningfully within it. While non-Christian religions may be considered totally human creations by some Christian theologians, the view that God is "present" (in some way) in them has, I believe, been held throughout the history of the church.[40] At the same time, the view that such religions are non-salvific, essentially idolatrous and in many ways antithetical to Christianity has been held just as strongly, or even more strongly.

If one wishes to adopt a theological approach to the discipline, Morali's argument is that revelation should be central to this. I believe this to be a sound judgment call. There are two distinct, though related, foci within the theology of religions literature: soteriology and revelation. It would be fair to say that much more interest has been devoted to a consideration of the former compared to the latter within recent years.[41] A revelation-focused investigation is quite different to a soteriological focus, epitomized in Race's well-known, though also challenged, *Exclusivism, Inclusivism, Pluralism* typology.[42] From a methodological viewpoint it can be argued that the more common focus (soteriology) leaves the researcher vulnerable to a primary objection: namely, one starts with the goal or end in mind, i.e., salvation and then looks for a way to arrive there (even subconsciously) by appeals to revelation, rather than moving *from* revelation *to* salvation.[43] While there is a relationship between revelation and salvation, revelation in theology of religions should, I believe, take centre stage if a theological approach is adopted.[44]

Given this starting point, I now consider the vexed issue of methodological approach. Some approaches to the discipline advocate that, methodologically, one's engagement with people from other religions may take priority in the investigation: for example, John Hick seemed to suggest that judgments drawn from such encounters are of greater importance than the biblical witness.[45] Others have focused primarily on religious consciousness and psychology. I suggest, however, that a Christian *theological* understanding of religions must start with biblical-theological attempts to understand and explain first revelation, and then religion as a response to that revelation.[46] As noted earlier, Scripture is, for Evangelical Reformed Christians, the starting place for this enquiry.[47]

Biblical historical examples of religion (e.g., religions devoted to Ishtar, Baal or Chemosh in the OT or mystery religions in the Roman world)[48] and statements about them within Scripture are critically important for the Christian theologian.[49] However, I suggest that such comments cannot simply be lifted from the pages of the Bible to explain other religions today, for example, Islam or Buddhism.[50] It is not doubted that the Apostle Paul, while making reference to *universal* principles of revelation and religion in Romans 1, also had in mind *particular* religious beliefs and practices with which he was familiar when making the statements he did. The same can be said of the Apostle's approach on the Areopagus in Acts 17, in his engagement with the Athenians.[51]

If a Christian theology of religions seeks to be contextually grounded (in the sense that it tries to understand a particular instantiation of religion/s in time and space),[52] the identification of the appropriate biblical principles which can be brought to bear upon and then explain a particular religion is, arguably, the central concern of a distinctively *theologically* driven approach to understanding religions. But even here, there is disagreement among Evangelicals about which biblical passages are the relevant ones on draw on.[53] Furthermore, starting point is arguably more complex than being *either* theological *or* observational, because even a distinctively theological attempt to understand a particular religion will, consciously or subconsciously, need to "read back" *from* a religion *to* the biblical material, as well as move *from* the Bible *to* a religion to understand aspects of it. Indeed, such interaction between revelation and humankind's response to it can be understood to mirror, in some ways, the drama of the biblical record itself. Today, one can easily imagine this backwards and forwards movement when a Christian theologian tries to understand Islamic ethics or Buddhist views of salvation: while the Bible informs, how it does so requires a right reading of the phenomenon itself.[54]

This to and fro movement, occurring within its historical context, is, no doubt, the real locus of interest and challenge within the discipline for those who value a Christian theological approach. The danger of misreading what is going on in a religion, misapplying relevant biblical principles or even employing irrelevant principles to aid the enquiry are serious challenges for a tradition which has a high regard for Scripture. Furthermore, the very real possibility of an agenda-driven, opportunistic use of Scripture by a theologian to serve polemical purposes must be recognized at the outset.

As will become clear throughout the chapters that follows, four of the five theologians studied in this book have developed their theologies of religion *theologically* (i.e., looked for biblical and theological principles which can guide thought on revelation and religions) as they have *observed* the different religious answer(s) around them, whether fairly or unfairly, polemically or amicably, and within very different contexts.[55]

3.2. The Choice of Parameters

Above, I have argued for the need to define the core of the discipline and added my support to Morali's theological revelation-based approach. At the same time, I have noted that theologians need to observe and try to understand religions to ensure that their ideas are not abstract.[56] The next consideration to be addressed is the identification of appropriate parameters to govern a historical theological approach in this area, with revelation at its center. I believe two key criteria need to govern the choice of these parameters.

The first criterion relates to the scope of the investigation. The parameters chosen should facilitate a broad-brush investigation of revelation. How God reveals himself outside of the people of Israel in the Old Testament, outside of Christ as witnessed in the New Testament, and outside the ongoing witness of the Bible and the church in the world is the major guiding principle to adopt.[57] All the theologians studied within this book argue for the reality of such revelation. The relationship between this revelation and its human reception and religion (rather than between revelation and human psychology, or culture for example) should be the central focus.

The second criterion relates to historical sensitivity. As much as possible, parameters need to be fairly obviously present in the writings of the theologians whose works are considered. The idea that the *same* parameters might actually be present within, or at least *satisfice* to facilitate a comparative historical theological study spanning two millennia, might seem, *prima facie*, wholly unrealistic given the very different contexts within which these theologies have been developed. The danger of forcing the thought of historical figures to fit the moulds of modern paradigms and agendas is obvious. This being so, the second key criterion for the identification of a guiding parameter is sensitivity to historical voice.

After some detailed investigation, and with an eye to these two criteria, I arrived at the conclusion that three parameters (all relating in some way to God's revelation—criterion 1) have, in large part, dominated Christian theology of religions thought from the second right up to the twenty-first centuries, at least for the theologians whose works are considered in this book.[58] These parameters are the *Logos*, the *prisca theologia* (i.e., the ancient theology tradition), and demons. I provide a basic overview of what I mean by these terms at the outset, leaving detail to the chapters that follow. It should be stressed, before proceeding further, that these terms and the ideas associated with them are, at times, understood *very* differently by those who used them.

By the *Logos*, I primarily refer to life and light references to the pre-incarnate Son of God in the Johannine prologue (especially verses 4–5 and possibly verse 9). It should be noted that for Justin Martyr what he actually knew of this text is very difficult to establish;[59] nevertheless, his *Logos* theory is regularly referenced within the discipline, and hence also discussed in some detail along with the other theologians who explicitly reference this text.

The *prisca theologia* (or ancient theology tradition) needs more explanation because the term has been understood and used in very different ways.[60] At the risk of simplification, it is a *historically grounded* explanation for the presence of truth in non-Christian religion and philosophy or at least certain ideas and practices within them. As Walker notes, there are two quite distinct versions of this tradition.[61] It is the first of these that is held by some of the theologians whose ideas are studied in this book. This particular version posits Jewish (or Noahic, or even Adamic) revelation primacy for all "true"[62] religious knowledge in the world.[63] That is, a unilinear view of revelation is posited:[64] God's (special) revelation as documented in the biblical narrative (or memory of God's works) is considered to be the source of truth in other traditions, who have *borrowed* from it, or at the very least been informed by it.[65] It is commonly argued that the material so borrowed has "deteriorated" over time, being corrupted to a greater or lesser extent, with the consequence that non-Christian religions contain both a mixture of (ancient theology) truth alongside falsehood.[66] The second version of the ancient theology theory is that there are, in Walker's words, "pre-Christian revelations"[67] in history *outside* Judaism, these being responsible for what accords with Christianity in other religions or philosophies, having their origin in the same God.[68] This second version of the ancient theology, which can be termed multilinear,[69] is not espoused by any of the theologians studied in this book, though at times hints of this idea are expressed, as will be documented.[70]

Turning to the third focus—demons—this may appear, at first glance, to be a strange inclusion alongside the other two parameters, given that I have argued that an understanding of God's *revelation* should be at the core of the discipline. There are two distinct relevant roles here. The first is a *truly* revelatory role. For some scholars in this study demons can speak truth.[71] They can, accordingly, be called mouthpieces of God at times. More commonly, however, the idea that demons mimic, counterfeit, and pervert God's revelation is present in the different theologies examined. Accordingly, the inclusion of demons is essential both because of their revelatory role, and also their anti-revelatory activities, which take on various forms.

While the demonic can, in broad-brush terms, be considered both positive and negative, the other two parameters noted above may be considered "ambiguous" but in very different ways. *Logos* enlightenment is not always as positive as the ideas of life and light in the Johannine prologue might initially suggest, largely because of what is revealed and what is not. For Calvin, for example, what is revealed by the *Logos* is dreadful (to fallen humankind), not positive as in the thought of Dupuis, noted earlier, because in his thinking we are condemned by this light.[72]

Turning to the ancient theology tradition, while generally considered to be positive (in the sense that there are remnants of truth present in religious systems or philosophies around the world), such influences might be considered of doubtful value if truth, being mixed with error, leads solely to confusion—especially if all truths are corrupted by idolatry.[73]

For each of these three "carriers" or bearers of revelation, I believe two continua exist in the ideas of the theologians to be studied. The first is revelatory content,[74] and the second is the clarity of this content (from the human perspective). I suggest that employing these three parameters aids the researcher in understanding a theologian's understanding of religions: each mode or channel can reveal God, or reveal an aspect of his character. From the sinful human perspective, what is revealed may be obscure, or suppressed in varying degrees. Different relations between the three parameters need also be considered. Whether these various revelations are "captured" within religions (i.e., become part of religious texts or traditions) or influence humankind directly *outside* religions is another key issue which I discuss in chapter 6 and the conclusion. I will suggest that a methodological focus on revelation (rather than salvation) has significant implications for the scope of the discipline.

Before proceeding further, it is helpful to pause to make a key observation in the light of an earlier comment regarding the authority of

Scripture for Reformed Evangelicals. Put bluntly, there is a very slim amount of biblical material which can be appealed to regarding these three parameters. For *Logos* enlightenment, as noted, there are just a few verses (whose interpretation is highly contested). Importantly though, a number of theologians in this study have connected these verses to Romans 1:18–32—what is perhaps the "core" text informing Reformed theology of religions thought. For the ancient theology tradition, there are no specifically relevant biblical passages, although some have inferred such a tradition to be responsible for Melchizedek's (and others') knowledge of the true God.[75] For the demonic, there are, likewise only a few possibly relevant verses.[76] As such, all three parameters leave considerable scope for theological interpretation. I will return to this important observation in the concluding chapter.

Do these three parameters satisfy the two criteria noted earlier? Concerning the first criterion, that a parameter cover the broad bases of thought concerning revelation, while I believe that this requirement is satisfied with the choices noted above, this does not mean that additional parameters might not also be present in some theologians' thinking. When such is the case these other means of revelation are also discussed.[77] However, while some other relevant ideas exist, and will be mentioned, I will argue that consideration of the three parameters provides satisfactory broad-brush coverage of the various theological religious engagements discussed in the chapters that follow.

Concerning the second criterion governing parameter choice, I argued earlier that the language and ideas of the theologians should determine the parameters for this study, rather than these being imposed from outside. I believe that the three parameters outlined above satisfy this criterion, as all of the theologians examined in this book refer to at least two of them explicitly. Indeed, I will demonstrate in the chapters that follow that none of the theologians studied argues that the *first* step to "false" religion lies outside of these three parameters.

4. Alternative Methodological Approaches and Justification for the Approach Adopted

4.1. Alternative Approaches

Those theologians who have made revelation central to their theology of religions have often considered it alongside two other factors. Peter

Beyerhaus writes of these in the following way: "The evangelical view of non-Christian religions takes into account three constituent elements in them: the divine, because of general revelation; the human, because of human beings as (distorted) image of God; and the demonic."[78] Netland adopts a similar approach. He comments, "I suggest that human religiosity or religion in general, should be understood in terms of the following three interrelated biblical themes: (1) creation and revelation, (2) sin, (3) satanic and demonic influence."[79] The first focus in this taxonomy is the work of God (and would, I suggest, be wide enough to include *Logos* revelation and the ancient theology tradition); the second is the response of humans to this; and the third is the wholly negative influence of Satan and demons.[80]

It is clear that my own approach focuses primarily on the divine (i.e., the two primary means of revelation), excludes sin (or at least appears to do so),[81] and orients the investigation of demons not only to the negative, but also the positive: demons being bearers of truth, as well as opponents to it. A final observation is that the term *general revelation* used by Beyerhaus is not present in my research design.

4.2. Justification for the Approach

The idea of religions being a *sinful* response to *general revelation* is something of a common place in the Reformed tradition.[82] This being so, the absence of both in the proposed research design may raise questions and hence requires some justification.

Starting with sin, given that my approach is *theo*logical (as outlined earlier), with a primary focus on revelation, sin is not present as one of the key guiding parameters. Having said this, as will be made clear throughout this study, humankind's sinfulness plays a significant role in all of the theologians' views of non-Christian religions (more obvious in some, than others). The idea of pride, suppression of truth, and humanity exchanging knowledge of the true God for idols in response to revelation will be discussed in every chapter. This being so, sin is *not* excluded from consideration, though it is not one of the three key parameters governing the framework of the study.

Two distinct effects of sin need to be differentiated—and this is where I offer a slightly more refined viewpoint to that of Netland, outlined above. The first, and more obvious effect, which Netland notes, relates to humankind's *response* to revelation. Using my own taxonomy for a moment, the human response to *Logos* enlightenment is strongly influenced by a particular theologian's understanding of sin, and the same will be the case for responses to *prisca theologia* revelation or the human response to the varied roles of demons in non-Christian religions. None of the theologians studied in this book speak of revelation without consideration of the human response, affected by sin. The less obvious, and yet equally important influence of sin relates to the understanding of revelation itself. By this, I mean a theologian's view of sin impacts their view of revelation, not just the human response to it. This may not always be explicitly stated, but can, nonetheless, be identified with some degree of confidence. For example, Jonathan Edwards's view concerning the effects of sin on reason undoubtedly influenced his suggestion that some philosophers may have been *inspired* to speak the truths they did. Edwards refused to allow *reason* to be responsible for their insights, given his view of the noetic effects of the fall. Accordingly, he had to explain the presence of truth using a revelation channel which he believed *could* deliver such knowledge.

Moving now to general revelation, its absence may seem more problematic, given the focus on revelation in this book. The term *general revelation* is widely used in Evangelical circles to refer to the revelation of God known to all, in contrast to special revelation, typically understood to be more closely related to God's redemptive activity in human history (supremely the incarnation) and the record of it in Scripture, and Scripture itself.[83] The distinction between special and general revelation, and the importance of general revelation in Reformed thinking on religion is plain to see.[84] Why then is general revelation not one of the main parameters of the study?

There are two reasons why, and these can be traced to the criteria governing the choice of parameters discussed above. As stated, a parameter should be present in the thinking of the theologians themselves (rather than being externally imposed)—criterion 2, and should be central to their arguments concerning revelation vis a vis religion—criterion 1.

At times, I will suggest that there is a kind of identification of *Logos* revelation and what is normally termed general revelation—or at least a part of what typically falls under this term. As Braaten notes, historically, the way in which theologians differentiated what we might today call general revelation and special revelation today, was by reference to the Logos *asarkos* and the Logos *ensarkos*.⁸⁵ The more recent terminology (general and special revelation) does not necessarily accurately capture or reflect the historical data, language, or focus.⁸⁶ As noted above, the Johannine Prologue and Revelation 1:18–32 (one of the "classic" general revelation texts) have been connected on more than one occasion. However, for other theologians, a distinction between general revelation and *Logos* enlightenment has been made. In what follows, I discuss this identification or differentiation in a little more detail for the theologians whose ideas are studied.

For Justin and Augustine, I suggest that the idea of general revelation is largely subsumed into or under their *Logos* theologies. Augustine related parts of Romans 1 to Johannine prologue enlightenment and he weaved the two texts together, stressing the idea of *Logos* illumination and the resulting knowledge and mis-knowledge. For Justin, it is part of the *Logos* that is known by Socrates, not part of creation. The enlightenment he describes is from the eternal Son and of the eternal Son.

Calvin, like Augustine, also related the Johannine prologue to Romans 1. However, I believe his understanding is rather different to Augustine's. While Calvin's references to the *sensus divinitatis* are often quoted (and commonly interpreted as human awareness of God, experienced through general revelation), it is the *Logos* who gives humankind a working sense of conscience and the seed of religion in his thinking. Accordingly, religion springs from *Logos* gifting. The relationship between this gifting and the sense of the divine is complex, and I discuss this in more detail in the relevant chapter. Suffice to say here, I believe Calvin differentiates the *semen religionis* from the *sensus divinitatis*, and I argue that the role of the *Logos* is more central in his explanation for the phenomenon of non-Christian religion than the *sensus divinitatis*.⁸⁷

Jonathan Edwards made multiple references to the light of nature (what might be considered a puritan pre-cursor to the more modern term *general revelation*). He seemed to identify this light with shadows of the eternal Son, and yet was very wary of equating this with *true Logos* enlightenment. For Edwards, there is no *spiritual* enlightenment received by humankind from the *Logos*. However, the light of nature (the shadow of the eternal Son) is still experienced by humans; indeed, it is clear enough to condemn false religion, as will be noted. Edwards believed much was known of God (at least nominally) from the light of nature.

Daniel Strange's view fits least comfortably into the distinction noted by Braaten above. Strange explicitly rejects the relevance of Logos enlightenment to the discipline, but does use the term *general revelation*, and has advocated its value in understanding religions, to a certain extent. While Strange argues that the Son is behind general revelation, this revelation is not *of* the Son. While general revelation is present in his thinking on religions, it is not dominant: it is one of four revelations, and not the most significant of these.[88]

Given this brief overview, I believe using the terms *Logos revelation/enlightenment/illumination*[89] to be preferable to the use of the term *general revelation* in a study of this nature. At the same time, I recognize that on occasion a distinction may need to be made between general revelation and *Logos* enlightenment (particularly in the works of Calvin, Edwards and Strange) and endeavor to capture such distinctions, when needed.

5. The Choice of Theologians

Above, I have alluded to the names of all of the theologians whose works I consider in this book. In what follows, I provide a brief justification for these choices. To reiterate a point made earlier, while covering the historical span of the church, the particular tradition considered is Evangelical Reformed and the choice of theologians reflects this. A comparable Roman Catholic study, would, I believe, begin to diverge on the third choice,[90] and possibly diverge from individual contributions to authoritative documents such as those from Vatican II.

I suggest that Justin Martyr is the most obvious starting place for the broad historical overview which follows. He writes as the most important apologist in a socioreligious context which is far from sympathetic to Christianity. His influence on the church's thinking in this area is regularly noted.[91] Calvin, and other Reformed theologians, embraced his writings.[92]

Augustine, standing on the other side of the church's relationship to paganism (the side of ascendency), provides a helpful new perspective (when compared to Justin). His influence on the church's thinking is considered to be significant, and his influence on the Reformers universally acknowledged.[93]

Given that this study focuses on the Evangelical Reformed tradition, Calvin is the most obvious figure to consider from the early modern period.[94] Though not normally considered a theologian of religions, I suggest he makes a significant contribution.

Moving forward, into the post-Reformation era, Jonathan Edwards stands out as being the most significant Reformed thinker on non-Christian religions during the enlightenment years. The deist context in which he wrote, the greater awareness of non-Christian religions present in the world at that time, and his local geographical proximity to native-American religions make him an obvious candidate for detailed investigation.

In the twentieth century, H. Kraemer and J. H. Bavinck are clear contenders for inclusion, being outstanding Reformed missionary theologians who engaged with religions both first hand, and in the academy. However, I have chosen to focus on Daniel Strange and his contribution, rather than either of these. There are at least three reasons for this choice. The first is that he makes numerous appeals to the far more widely referenced Kraemer and Bavinck; he also states that he follows their ideas.[95] This means that the thought of Kraemer and Bavinck is discussed within the book. Indeed, Strange's dependencies and departures from their thinking is considered in some detail. The second reason is that Strange has done more than anyone from the Reformed tradition to engage the current generation of Evangelical Reformed Christians with the theology of religions discipline. He has written two relevant monographs: a published PhD critiquing inclusivism, and another in which he presents his own theology of religions.[96] He has also engaged with alternative positions within the discipline.[97] Strange's work is, in many ways, the current terminus of conservative Reformed thinking within the discipline.[98] The third reason for choosing to focus on Strange is that there is very little secondary literature referencing his thought or engaging with it to date.[99] This being so, its place within the Reformed tradition has not yet been seriously considered, a state of affairs I seek to redress in this book.

Such are the reasons for the choices of the theologians included in this study.

6. Mapping the Methodological Approach

6.1. Chapter Approach

While the three parameters (The *Logos*, the *prisca theologia* tradition and the demonic) are explicitly treated in the following chapters, I go about the engagement somewhat differently from one chapter to the next. There are two reasons for this. A key reason is my desire to be sensitive to an individual theologian's wider thought when considering the theology of religions contribution. A second factor influencing the approach adopted within a particular chapter is the state of the relevant secondary literature. For example, in considering Justin Martyr, I engage in some detail with Mark Edwards and his views because of their direct relevance to the subject matter. Accordingly, Mark Edwards's work influences, to a certain extent, the approach and avenues of thought pursued when treating Justin. The role of secondary literature in influencing the particular approach adopted is also present in the other chapters: the interaction with John Marenbon in the chapter on Augustine is a good example of this, and my engagement with Carlos Eire in the chapter treating Calvin. The impact of Gerald McDermott's research in affecting my engagement with Jonathan Edwards is also readily apparent. Concerning Strange's work, there is very little secondary literature engaging with it to date. Accordingly, I spend time considering the twentieth century influences on his work, examining the key choices he makes, and documenting some of the tensions that result from his Reformed eclectic approach.

Where one of the three parameters of the study is not given particular attention by a theologian this, of necessity, means that there is less discussion of that point. When this is so I try to consider reasons for this (e.g., Calvin's rejection of the *prisca theologia* tradition or Strange's rejection of *Logos* enlightenment). In doing so, I engage with historical context, and look for possible explanations for such "downgradings."

I do not provide any biographical sketches of the theologians at the beginning of the chapters as these are myriad and widely available;[100] however, I do seek to provide necessary historical background and context for each contribution considered.

6.2. Methodological Challenges

I believe that there are potential strengths and weaknesses with a study that spans the history of the church, as this book seeks to do. In what follows, I outline what I consider these to be and the ways in which I have sought to mitigate the possible weaknesses.

Starting with the first potential weakness, fine granularity and exhaustive treatment is not possible because of the approach I adopt. Some research has focused on one or two theologians' ideas on non-Christian religions.[101] Other studies have compared the ideas of a group of theologians within a similar time frame, comparing and contrasting their ideas. Good examples of this latter approach would be chapters 5–8 of McDermott's *God's Rivals*,[102] and Saldanha's *Divine Pedagogy: A Patristic View of Non-Christian Religions*.[103] Both of these research efforts have made it clear that even within roughly the same period of church history clearly different views have been held by theologians.[104] While recognizing the loss of detail and fine granularity in this book due to the number of theologians studied, and the range of history covered, I will argue below that this loss is compensated for by the gain of broad perspective.

Another potential weakness in my approach is its seeming lack of sensitivity to change, whether religious, theological, political, or societal, across centuries, cultures and nations. One obvious difference is the influence of Christianity on the world across the different eras. The world of second century Rome (Justin Martyr) is quite different to twenty-first century life in the North of England (Daniel Strange). Another challenge might be that the thought of theologians from classical antiquity, the early modern, modern, and post-modern eras cannot meaningfully be considered alongside one another. A final objection could be to point to potential insensitivities to developments in theology: comparing pre-Chalcedon Justin to post-Reformation Edwards, for example, might be considered a questionable research approach. Is it not, in some ways, *meaningless* to compare the ideas of theologians living and thinking in such different times and places?

While accepting the basic premise of this concern, I believe two constants in the study mitigate the potential problems associated with it. The first is that I am considering the *Christian church* response[105] (to non-Christian religion) and limiting my focus to just one "tradition"[106] within it. The second is that my focus is *theological*. As stated above, in my understanding essentially the *same* set of *theological* parameters has been employed by these theologians (although understood and used in very different ways) in their approaches. I believe that these two constants make the current study meaningful, while acknowledging the important contextual differences influencing the development of each particular theology.

7. Conclusion

While this book is historical-theological in focus, in the final chapter I consider what the contemporary Evangelical Reformed church might learn from the analyses, as she considers her own understanding of and engagement with non-Christian religions. I begin the Conclusion by synthesizing the five treatments discussed in the earlier chapters. This constitutes a principled attempt to compare and contrast five Christian theologies of religions investigated through the use of the same contextually grounded methodological framework.[107] As part of the discussion that follows this synthesis, I consider whether the various theologies may best be considered as biblically-informed *reflections* on and *reactions* to various contextually significant religious, doctrinal, ecclesiastical, and sociopolitical issues. I will cautiously suggest that there is much to be said in favor of such an understanding.

I do not overtly appreciate or challenge the approaches or ideas of the theologians in chapters 2–6. My goal within them is to understand and faithfully represent their thought within its context.[108] However, within the chapters, and also in the conclusion, I document some of the tensions and challenges which I perceive to be evident in the various handlings of the three parameters, including the connections that have been drawn between them, and the role of external influences in affecting which particular biblical passages have been appealed to. I finish by suggesting a number of possible areas of study for future research which naturally arise from this study, and which Evangelical scholars may wish to explore further.

2

Justin Martyr

Background

JUSTIN MARTYR (C. 100–165) is widely acknowledged to be the most important apologist of the second century.[109] He is also considered by some to be the first real theologian of the church.[110] In this chapter I focus on Justin's contribution to Christian theology of religions, a discipline in which his name and ideas are regularly referenced.[111]

Justin's pioneering engagement with pagan philosophy, pagan religion and Judaism in the early church context is widely acknowledged.[112] Justin lived at a time when the NT canon was not yet formally recognized,[113] and his writings have been termed innovative, unique and creative.[114] His ideas are particularly significant in that his initial steps in this engagement with religions and philosophy were to become, in time, a well-worn path traveled by later apologists and church fathers.[115] This is not to say that Justin's ideas were not challenged, or developed, rather that his general approach was largely accepted—at least for the first few centuries AD.[116]

1. Overview of Justin's Writings

As I will be considering wider co-text and readership in a number of the points to follow, I provide a brief overview of Justin's writings here.

Eight texts were, historically, attributed to Justin by Eusebius.[117] However, of these only three are now considered to be genuine: *Apology 1*, *Apology 2*, and the *Dialogue with Trypho*.[118] Turning first to the Apologies, various readerships have been suggested.[119] My own position is that an important intended audience of the two Apologies may well have been pagan-background Christians, in addition to interested pagan readers. I believe one convincing piece of evidence supporting this position to be the prevalence of demon references (as opposed to Satan references) in the *Apologies*.[120]

Turning to the addressees, there is considerable disagreement over whether the petition should be taken at face value or not.[121] If taken at face value,[122] *Apology 1* is an appeal to Antoninus Pius, Verissimus, and Lucius[123] against the unjust persecution of Christians[124] and a plea for toleration[125] and a fair trial when such are brought to court.[126] Whether or not the appeal ever entered the corridors of power, it is clear that Justin made it on the basis of some kind of shared values of justice and right dealing.[127] The structure of *Apology 1* has been variously understood.[128]

In the second *Apology*, as Buck notes, Justin states his reason for writing it four times—twice to inform the recipients of the unjust proceedings against Christians, and twice to inform and convert the Roman public.[129] The relationship between *Apology 1* and *Apology 2* is a contentious subject, and a number of possible relationships between the two documents have been suggested or argued.[130] The second *Apology* is approximately one quarter the length of the first. Whether or not one comes to the conclusion that the second is independent of the first, a number of key differences between the two texts have been noted. Thorsteinsson (who argues for independency) documents these.[131] In terms of the key themes covered in the second *Apology*, Ulrich states these to be: martyrs, enmity of demons, Christian eschatology and punishment, and the *Logos* doctrine.[132]

Turning to the *Dialogue with Trypho*, there is considerable disagreement regarding Justin's purpose in writing it. Key to a correct interpretation is identification of the audience, and scholarship is greatly divided over whether this was primarily Jewish, non-Christian gentile or Christian, or a mixture.[133] My own position is that it assumes a Hebrew background—and so is either written primarily for Jews and/or Christians.

Concerning the overall structure of the *Dialogue*, Allert suggests that chapters 10–142 can be considered to address "the explanation of the truth that Justin has found,"[134] terming chapters 31–118 "the

Christological section" within this.[135] He suggests that Justin's main aim in using Scripture is to convince Trypho that Jesus is the New Testament/New Law and also the *Logos* of God.[136] He believes that the bulk of the dialogue is taken up with objections to the claim that Jesus is the promised messiah.[137]

2. Justin's Contribution to an Understanding of Non-Christian Religion—Overview

Moving from general background information to specific theological emphases, Justin's contribution to a Christian theology of religions is typically understood to embrace three key ideas.[138] The thought for which he is best known, and most frequently quoted, is his *Logos* Christology, which I consider here to be: God's revelation within or to humankind, outside the medium of Scripture, of, or mediated by, the eternal Son of God—partly or exclusively in his role as *Logos Spermatikos*.[139] From where Justin "borrowed" his *Logos* theology and his intention/s in using it have become major points of discussion and contention among Justin scholars.[140]

Justin's second contribution to the field is in the area of demonology. Justin is considered to be the first Christian to have developed a historical explanation for the creation of demons, equating these with the Greek/Roman gods of his day.[141] There is a two-fold role for demons in Justin's thought. In general terms, demons are considered to be at war with the *Logos*, those who follow Him, and humanity in general. In relation to his thought on the presence of truth in non-Christian religions, Justin believed the demons to be responsible for inspiring the poets to incorporate mimetically perverted Christian truths (e.g., ideas of virgin birth) into their myths and poetry. The rationale given for this activity, Justin argued, is to camouflage the coming of Christ.[142]

With regard to his final major contribution to a theology of religions, Justin has been considered the first Christian to have appealed to the loan or theft theory, the idea that Plato and other philosophers (and even some poets) obtained their true ideas from Moses and the Prophets.[143] The idea that non-Christian philosophical and religious thought contains elements of truth, due to ancient "borrowing" from Israel, had been espoused by Jewish scholars before Justin.[144] For example, it was advocated by Aristobulus of Alexandria[145] and a version of it was also forwarded by Philo.[146]

There are various significant disagreements in the literature concerning how the three ideas described above are to be interpreted within Justin's thought. In this chapter I will focus on two of these disagreements. The first concerns whether there are indeed three separate channels of revelation. Mark Edwards has subsumed the *Logos* theory under the loan theory, arguing that seemingly direct *Logos* and "seed of *Logos*" revelation references in Justin's writings be understood within the context of and in reference to the loan theory alongside the exercise of human reason.[147] Such a reading has considerable implications for Justin's legacy for a Christian theology of religions, given that the *Logos* theory has traditionally been considered his major contribution to it.[148] A significant part of this chapter will consider whether Edwards's argumentation against an 'independent' *Logos* revelation source is warranted, and the implications of this for understanding Justin.

The second area of tension I wish to examine in more detail is the relative importance and specific content of the different truth sources in Justin's thinking. Did he consider them to be of comparable importance? Did Justin believe they worked together in series, in an enforcing or complementary way, and for the same purposes? Scholars are greatly divided over how to answer these questions.[149] I suggest differences of opinion can, in many cases, be traced to different interpretations of the meaning of *Logos* revelation in Justin's thinking. For this reason, I spend a considerable part of this chapter focusing on this subject.

In order to make the flow of the chapter clearer to the reader, I will state my conclusions before proceeding further. I will argue (contra Edwards) for separate *Logos* and loan sources of truth in Justin's thinking. I will make the case that Justin's idea of humankind partaking in the *Logos* and the idea of the seed of the *Logos* sown in humankind, while probably influenced by Stoic and middle platonic thought, is thoroughly invested by Justin with Christ and his ethical teaching. Specifically, I will argue that this revelation of the *Logos* is best interpreted (from the human perspective) as a vague awareness of the eternal Law of Christ (rather than the decalogue) and even Christ himself. Concerning the loan theory, I will posit that Justin used it to explain the presence of correct teaching in various schools of philosophy (especially Platonic) as well as in myths, these truths relating to aspects of creation, God and eschatology. However, I will argue that Justin excluded moral and ethical ideas from what was borrowed in the loan theory (contra Nyström).[150] In addition, I will suggest that the loan theory is *not* a significant emphasis in the apologist's thought. Finally, I will contend that the idea of demons speaking truth is a distinct idea in Justin's thinking (similar, to a certain extent, to the loan theory),[151] but that its importance should not be overstated. While downplaying the positive pedagogical role of this particular aspect of his thought, I will make the case that Justin's wider demonology is of critical importance in grasping his understanding of the role of the *Logos* and the seed sown by the *Logos*: without *Logos* revelation, Justin's view of demonic opposition makes little sense. In a number of places in the chapter I will argue (contra Edwards and Pretila) that *Logos* revelation plays a (indeed *the*) foundational role in Justin's argumentation and in his theology of philosophy and religions.

Having provided this overview, the outline of the rest of the chapter is as follows. In section 3 I examine Justin's thought on the demonic. I then provide a brief outline of interpretations of *Logos* revelation before critiquing Edwards's rejection of the *Logos* revelation theory. After summarizing Edwards's position, I go on to provide three arguments for an interpretation of *Logos* awareness being primarily ethical. These arguments are, firstly, the general tone of the *Apologies*, with a specific reference to lawmakers, and natural law in *2 Apology*; secondly, Justin's view of *Logos* law, Mosaic Law and Christ, as documented in the *Dialogue with Trypho*; and finally Justin's Christianizing of Socrates. While engaged in discussing these three points, I will point to support, where appropriate, for a Christo-centric eternal law understanding of *Logos* revelation in Justin's thinking. Discussion on the *prisca theologia* is embedded in the above, rather than treated separately.

3. Justin's Demonology

3.1. An Overview

Demons played an important role in Graeco-Roman religion and philosophy.[152] In second century thought, there were various types of demon, ranging from guardian angels to gods who were responsible for various activities, only some of these malevolent.[153] However, in the *Apologies* the demons (as a class) are evil,[154] and the demonic is a theme which runs through the *Apologies*.[155] Justin explained the existence of demons as being due to the intercourse of the angels and the daughters of men (Gen 6:4).[156] He believed the goal of the demons' activities to be the alienation of humankind from God and Christ,[157] and to keep humankind subject to their influence through religious devotion and practices, stimulated by fear.[158] Justin ascribed many evil actions to the demons, including: disrupting the order of the cosmos,[159] engendering many sins,[160] defiling women and corrupting boys,[161] persecuting those who are against them,[162] claiming sacrifice and veneration,[163] ensnaring by dreams and magic,[164] producing and assisting heretics,[165] and stopping the reading of certain (good) books.[166] To the bad angels he ascribed the creating of iniquitous laws.[167]

Of particular importance for our inquiry here is the claim that the demons inspired the poets.[168] The mechanism for this in Justin's thought is that the demons heard what the prophets said concerning the coming of Christ. Because they did not fully understand and also because they wanted to deceive humans and confuse them, they created fables—through the instrumentality of the poets. Justin did not believe that the poets were aware that they were being led astray by demons.[169] The demonic rationale behind this "inspiration" was the camouflaging of truth.[170] The specific truths which were mimicked include virgin birth, healing, raising from the dead, and ascension to heaven.[171] In an extended discussion, Justin drew multiple parallels between pagan myths and biblical stories, without specifically mentioning demonic mimesis, though it can be assumed.[172] Once he became aware of the camouflaging of true doctrine by this means, Justin stated that he laughed, finding the demonic strategy pitiable.[173] He argued that a similar mimetic counterfeiting to that seen in myth is also witnessed in certain religious activities in pagan temples: washings and taking off sandals,[174] in addition to Eucharistic-type practices,[175] together with the setting up of a statue.[176] He specifically documented the exclusion of crucifixion from mimesis.[177] Justin did not allow for the possibility that demons could confuse humankind concerning the reality of just punishment, or thwart attempts to spread the gospel.[178] It should be noted that the former relates to ethical knowledge and accountability—a key point to which I will return. A major achievement of Jesus Christ, in Justin's thinking, is his defeat of the demons.[179] Justin claims the demon-possessed are subject to Christian exorcism,[180] and this fact is given as evidence of the new reality which the demons now face in the light of Christ's victory over them.

Justin appealed to the activity of the devil, the fallen angels and the demons not only to explain what had gone on in the ancient world,[181] but also to understand what was happening in the Graeco-Roman religions of his day.[182] In addition to this, he spoke of their role in the contemporary animosity and persecution of Christians from both Romans[183] and Jews.[184] Furthermore, in his mind, the demons were also behind the work of heretics.[185] To say that demons loomed large in Justin's thinking about the world is, arguably, to understate his view of the demonic in the affairs of humankind.[186]

A key issue I wish to stress here is the idea of tension between order and disorder and the disruptive role of the demons (and bad angels) in the latter in Justin's thinking. I suggest that Justin's demonology makes no sense unless the *Logos* is considered active in the history of the world (not just the AD world) and with humankind. If the *Logos* is not, the demons would have no work to do. As Reed notes, "In a precise inversion of the activity of the Logos in human history demons promulgate irrational beliefs and behavior."[187] I believe that the active *Logos* is the necessary presupposition for the activity of the demons in Justin's thinking—a key point which I will develop later.

3.2. Demons as Conveyers and Twisters of Truth

What might be termed the "traditional" interpretation of Justin's thought concerning religions and philosophy is that religious myth was the domain of the demonic, and is wholly negative, whereas his views on philosophy could at times (or indeed often) be positive.[188] However, the problem with this view is that Justin sometimes approved of some of the poets' teaching. On five occasions, Justin specifically brought together the ideas of philosophers and poets (as generic groups) in a positive way.[189] A specific example is in *1 Apol.* 20 where Justin moves from positive approval of Plato to Stoic teaching and then on to Menander.[190] Pretila comments, "So while Justin selected Socrates as his model philosopher who came to champion monotheism through the enlightening of the *Logos* (*2 Apol.* 10), the apologist made Menander his representative from amongst the poets to serve that same exact purpose."[191] Such references to Menander do not, at face value, sit comfortably with occasions when Justin openly attacked the poets/mythmakers.[192] Accordingly, some scholars have argued either that Justin was contradictory in his handling of myth,[193] or ambivalent as to its value.[194]

A more recent argument, forwarded by Pretila, has built on some earlier more nuanced attempts to account for Justin's varied treatment of myth and the associated false religion.[195] He notes that while the references in *Apology 1* appear contradictory (both pro and against myth-makers), Justin's approach can be considered principled, but only if one appreciates Justin's rationale for the varied use.[196] Pretila argues that as Justin proceeds through *Apology 1* he moves through various developmental stages in his treatment of myth. The first is the appeal to myth, or "incorporation" of myth using Pretila's term, in the first 21 sections. The second is to question the value of myth (i.e., to begin a stage of "separation") in sections 22–29. This is followed by a mix of separation and incorporation in sections 30–53. The final stage is the outright rejection of the value of myth, what Pretila terms a decisive separation of myth, in the last sections (54–56).[197] The overall rationale for this shift in perception and understanding, he argues, is pedagogical. He believes that the pagan background Christians (the intended audience of the apology in his thinking),[198] like philosophers and their Roman peers, would have known of the myths, and their rather unique status as "lies containing truths."[199] He argues that Justin, initially at least, wanted to create a (positive) link between these myths and the Christian faith, on the grounds that such a connection could be of help to Christian believers who were tempted to return to their pagan past. In Pretila's opinion, in taking on this interpreting role vis a vis myth, Justin was following a well-known function of a philosopher.[200]

Critically important for our discussion, Pretila states that the demonic influence in myth is (somewhat paradoxically) the richest of the different "truth channels" in what it shows of God and redemption, though in a somewhat perverted sense.[201] Furthermore, and in a converse relationship to it, he argues that "direct" *Logos* mediated truth is both the rarest, and the vaguest in Justin's thinking.[202] He argues this on the basis of what truths are attributed to which of these two sources in Justin's writings—drawing on traditional general/special revelation terminology in so doing.[203] What Pretila does not do, when making the above distinction, is consider the relative *importance* of each in Justin's thinking. Even when considered solely in terms of the content value, placing mimesis above "borrowing" can be considered questionable in that the latter is clear, while mimesis truth is shrouded in error—even though typically considered to be more distinctively Christian.

Having stressed that Justin was putting himself in his readers' sandals in what he was saying (rather than speaking from personal conviction),[204] one might have expected Pretila to have offered a reduced role for the content value of demonic mimesis, particularly given the final stage of Justin's argumentation as noted above (i.e., rejection).[205] Given this "anomaly," while in broad agreement with Pretila's argument concerning Justin's pedagogical strategy, I am more inclined to adopt a middle ground position between his more positive evaluation of its value, and Saldanha's extremely negative conclusion concerning the importance of demon-transferred truth in Justin's view.[206] Accordingly, I do believe Justin to have advocated a demonic source truth theory[207]—but to have severely curtailed its value, as evident in the limited pedagogical apologetical function it serves in his thinking.

4. Interpretations of the Seed of the *Logos* and Direct *Logos* Revelation

Before considering Edwards's rejection of the idea of *Logos* revelation outside of Scripture, I provide some brief background to the *Logos* theory in this section and outline some different views concerning what the "seed of the word" is, in Justin's thought. The word *Logos* and its derivatives appear on multiple occasions in the two *Apologies*. The difficulty in translating the term, and the potential ambiguity of meaning, has been noted by a number of scholars, some of whom believe Justin may have capitalized on this fact.[208] The key *Logos* references in the Justin corpus, identified by Holte[209] (an important advocate of the independent *Logos* revelation theory), are: *1 Apol.* 5[210] and 46[211] and *2 Apol.* 8,[212] 10,[213] and 13.[214] References to the *Logos Spermatikos* are only found in the second apology. It should be noted that Holte does not refer to *1 Apol.* 44, *1 Apol.* 59, and *1 Apol.* 60—the clear (undisputed) borrowing loan references in the Justin corpus, in his argument. Knowledge from the borrowing in *1 Apol.* 44 is termed "seeds of truth" rather than "seed of the *Logos*." Holte does not conflate these expressions.

Various possible influences on Justin's thinking on the *Logos* have been hypothesized: John's gospel, Stoicism, Platonism, Middle Platonism, and Philo are the most common.[215] Nahm provides a helpful historical overview of trends and interpretations.[216] As noted earlier on, I will suggest that Justin may have borrowed his *Logos Spermatikos* terminology, and a few, but certainly not all of his ideas from Stoicism. However, following Jackson-McCabe, I will argue that Justin thoroughly Christianized these ideas in his theology of religions and philosophy.[217]

Holte sees no difficulty in believing Justin transformed the meaning of philosophical terminology (specifically *Logos* terminology and the *Logos Spermatikos* term), and he argues the underlying meaning of the *Logos Spermatikos* to be "Paul's doctrine on natural revelation."[218] He comments:

> The Logos Spermatikos theory is not intended to grant a character of revelation to religious or philosophical systems in their entirety. It is strictly limited to a few conceptions, i.e., certain ideas on God and on the falsity of idolatry and also certain basic moral conceptions. Justin can scarcely be said to have essentially extended the content of St. Paul's thoughts on a natural revelation.[219]

Elsewhere, Holte states Justin's idea of the *Logos* is "a principle for natural revelation, i.e., for the ethical and religious knowledge implanted in creation, on account of which Man can be held responsible to God."[220] Holte notes how the Stoic *Logos* was considered materially: "the principle for both physical and spiritual life," and *spermatikos* was associated with development. He describes how Philo used the term symbolically, and believes that Justin took it one step further in connecting it to the knowledge described by Holte above.[221] Barnard also argues that the key terminology was borrowed and adapted: "it may be that the most obvious solution is the correct one, viz. that in working out the logos spermatikos idea St. Justin took over the well-known Stoic term without taking over the Stoic connotation." A number of rather different interpretations have also been forwarded covering the range of knowledges that result from this revelation.[222] In what follows, I will argue for a rather more specific focus to that argued by Holte, namely that the seed of the *Logos* is the Eternal Law of Christ, who is, in some ways, Christ Himself. In terms of approach, I do not engage in detailed textual analysis of the key passages (for such studies see Holte, Saldanha, and Edwards), but rather approach the discussion from Justin's wider thinking, and the importance of theological ethics in his view.

4.1. Summary and Critique of Edwards's Rejection of Direct *Logos* Revelation

Edwards believes that Justin's *Logos* idea is primarily biblical, rather than Greek, and that the "womb" of the *Logos* doctrine is in the *Dialogue* (rather than the *Apologies*).[223] Edwards does not think that the OT supports a natural revelation of God: "the revelation of deity in the heavens is accessible only to those, who, like the Psalmist, know the Maker through his Law."[224] Edwards believes Holte (his main antagonist in his rejection of the *Logos* theory) to have understood Justin to maintain that "the knowledge of God [is] ubiquitous by nature."[225] He criticizes this interpretation, as he believes it fails to connect with the claim in the *Apology* that this knowledge (in his understanding) is from the Scriptures alone, i.e., due to loaning or borrowing.[226] Edwards criticizes the idea that the apologist be understood to have held to "the theory of a congenital intuition of sacred truth,"[227] calling this "an alien principle"[228] for Justin. Pointing to the content of *Dialogue* 4 he states that there is "no innate communion with God."[229] Concerning Justin's view of human nature, Edwards comments, "Nothing is granted to human beings by nature but their vices."[230] Further, he argues that there is no evidence of divine truths being "inborn" in Justin's thinking.[231] Edwards's most significant claim, in terms of the current focus, is:

> Justin nowhere shows himself aware that he holds two theories [logos revelation and loaned biblical revelation], or adopts the simple measures that would suffice to reconcile them. Both charity and economy should dispose us to conclude that he intended to state, not two—not even two complementary—theories, but one.[232]

This theory, he argues, is the loan theory.[233] Concerning philosophers' notions of the idea of the immortality of the soul, together with other doctrines known by them, Edwards comments, "Not nature, but the written text, is the vehicle of enlightenment."[234] In a book touching on the same subject, Edwards states, "When he [Justin] speaks of a distribution of 'seeds of truth to all' at 1 *Apol.* 44.10, he is not alluding to any act of direct insufflation, but to a custom of plagiarism from the Hebrew prophets."[235] Concerning Justin's famous Christianization of Socrates (to be discussed further in section 4.2.3), Edwards combines the loan theory with reason to explain it. He writes, "if, with Heraclitus and the sages of barbarous nations, he [Socrates] can be reckoned as a Christian before Christ (1

Apology 46.3), it is because, like other Greeks, he employed his reason upon the teaching of the prophets (1 Apology 44–45)."[236]

Having provided a brief overview of Edwards's thinking, I now engage with it. Firstly, it is important to note that in the quotations provided above, Edwards, at the very least, hints at times that clear loan references have been misappropriated by advocates of the *Logos* theory. However, Holte—who is the only named antagonist with whom Edwards argues—did not call upon the "seeds of truth" reference in *1 Apol.* 44 in support of the *Logos* theory: he clearly attributed what is known there to the loan theory.[237] Accordingly, Edwards makes an effort to exclude what Holte never tried to include within the non-loan *Logos* theory.

I believe there are two errors in Edwards's comments, and one major oversight. The first of the errors is that Justin did speak, albeit vaguely, of an innate awareness of God.[238] This though, is not "communion" (and Justin nowhere argued it was). What Edwards does not do is consider the relationship between ethical knowledge and the knowledge of God in Justin's thinking, and I will explore this relationship further in section 4.3.3.4. The second error concerns human nature. I suggest that Edwards's argument that Justin allows nothing to human nature but their vices to be a misinterpretation of Justin's thought.[239] Justin admits a universal awareness of natural law in reference to sexual ethics.[240] In addition to this, he recognizes that humans follow such universally acknowledged laws, for example in the enactment (and indeed following) of good laws (a point I elaborate on, below).[241] Being that it is commonly argued that Justin did not hold to a doctrine of original sin, this reference, at the very least, has the potential to weaken Edwards's strong "vices" claim concerning Justin's anthropology.[242]

Turning to what I consider to be the significant oversight in Edwards's argument, apart from one passing reference (and a quote mentioning the demons),[243] Edwards does not consider the relationship between the *Logos* theory or the loan theory and the demons in his key paper. If, as I am arguing here, there is a fundamental antithesis and hostility between the *Logos* and demons in Justin's thinking—a point argued for by a number of scholars (e.g., Holte, Skarsaune, Reed, Harnack)[244]—it seems imperative that the one be understood and interpreted in relation to the other (even if this is solely "*Logos* borrowing," as it is for Edwards). However, Edwards is silent on this relationship.

For Justin, genuine choice is essential to fair judgment.[245] If humankind has no choice to make (being only led astray by the demons, without reference to the position from which they are led), Justin's demonology makes no sense. Similarly, the idea that our rational faculties constitute the sum of what we are led astray from sets a *faculty* in opposition to (demonic) *activity*—a questionable juxtaposition. I will argue below that all of humankind, rather than just some philosophers, are aware of ethical norms in Justin's thinking. I believe Allert captures Justin's position more realistically, "man is a sinner [in Justin's thinking] because he allows the demons to lead him into rebellion against the Law of God which every man has within him as a part of the divine equipment in life."[246]

4.2. Evidence Supporting an Eternal *Logos*-Law Revelation

In what follows, I will argue, against Edwards (and following Holte), that Justin is best understood to argue for a distinct *Logos* revelation (in addition to making a separate appeal to the loan theory). Unlike Holte, whose main approach was textual, I will appeal to the natural law/eternal law theme in the Justin corpus to support the argument. Specifically, I will point to evidence supporting the idea of a sharp distinction in Justin's thought between ethical awareness (which I will argue is derived from human awareness of eternal *Logos* law) and knowledge of specific doctrinal truths (borrowed from the OT prophets). Secondly, I will argue that for Justin, Christ should be understood (primarily, though not exclusively) as the personification of the eternal law: revelation and the seeds sown should not be equated with awareness of the decalogue, per se.,[247] but rather a dim awareness of Christ and his summary of the eternal law.[248] In addition, I will posit that the loan theory is not as significant in Justin's thinking as Edwards believes. This is because what is loaned, in Justin's thinking, is not what Justin understood the heart of the Old Testament to be—the prophecy of Christ's coming—but rather truths about God and creation (alone).

4.2.1. The "Natural Law" Atmosphere of the Apologies

My intention in this section is to argue, pace Edwards, that Justin allowed more to humans than their vices, and that the most reasonable explanation for Justin's position is that he understood humankind to possess a vague awareness of the good, alongside the very occasional ability to follow the good, which I believe Justin attributes to the *Logos*.

It is generally acknowledged that the proof from prophecy (of Christianity's truth claims) section is the largest part of the first *Apology*.[249] The subject matter of the other six sections is essentially moral or ethical in appeal: illegality of Christian prosecution, Christian moral life (and its contrast with paganism), and the ethical teachings of Jesus. Justin's focus on a deeper understanding of law from his comments on the sermon on the mount is particularly noticeable in 1 *Apol.* 15 and 16. Justin supports his Apology, in part, by going to considerable lengths to show that the Christians were law-abiding and exemplary in their morals and ethics.[250] The presupposition behind this polemic is that the pagan world can recognize justice and morality.[251] In addition to the appeal to what is right, Justin stresses the readers' accountability to God for their actions.[252] At the same time, he discusses the difficulty his readers might encounter in seeing and judging rightly because of the subversive influence of the demons—whose role in this subterfuge he highlights.[253] If the demons are somehow kept at bay, Justin seems convinced the authorities will see the truth and reasonableness of what he argues.[254]

Chadwick considers the second Apology to be a Christian manifesto, written for gentiles (Christian or non-Christian) and to serve as a kind of commentary on two biblical passages (Romans 1–2 and Acts 17) which he believed Justin to have studied deeply.[255] If Chadwick's position is correct, this can be seen to add support to the position argued for here, concerning natural law awareness being foundational to Justin's polemic. Below, I focus on two issues, both from 2 *Apology*, which I believe point to Justin's belief in a kind of natural law (not a loan-informed law). These are legislator knowledge and a specific natural law reference.

4.2.1.1. Legislators in the *Apologies*

Like the philosophers (and even the poets) legislators are sometimes commended for some of their ideas which are "according to *Logos*" in Justin's writings.[256] Legislators are mentioned in three sections in the *Apologies*: 2 *Apol.* 7, 2 *Apol.* 9 and 2 *Apol.* 10.[257] In the first and last Justin combines legislators and philosophers together in his comments. A key issue I wish to address here is the source of the good legislation of the legislators: did they "borrow," or did they receive their ideas from the *Logos* directly?[258]

Legislators are not listed in the important borrowing statements made by Justin.[259] This, of course, does not mean that they may not have learned from the philosophers so listed—a point suggested by Minns and Parvis who keep their options open concerning the source/s for the enactments of legislators in their commentary on 2 *Apol.* 9.[260] I believe context helps narrow the options.

In the first reference (2 *Apol.* 7), there is a general appeal to humankind knowing what is right and just and what is not, evidence of this being that legislators and philosophers (everywhere) echo and enforce this in their commendation and prohibition of certain actions. The pattern of argument seems to proceed from an appeal to a universally accepted natural law rather than a loan theory reference: proof and evidence of societal natural law awareness is seen in the (right) statements of philosophers and legislators.

In the second reference (2 *Apol.* 9), in a section dealing with God's punishment of sinners, Justin argues that this idea is not unreasonable because humanity accepts the rightness of legislators carrying out a similar role: they do not unjustly punish. Further, Justin argues that the just laws they enact are in some way related to the *Logos* of the Father: "their Father instructs them through the Word [Logos] to do as He Himself does."[261] Not only does Justin draw an analogy between God and the legislators in law making and execution of these laws, he also attributes just laws to the *Logos*. Is this a reference to borrowing? As noted above, Minns and Parvis are open to this possibility. However, I would question this, as Justin immediately proceeds to discuss confusion about what is good and bad in the realm of laws. If borrowing was the source, I believe there would be less confusion.

In 1 *Apology* 27, Justin attacks specific bad laws, which, at the very least, are connived at by the addressees of the *Apology*,[262] and in 2 *Apol.* 10 he mentions the confusion that abounds (more generally) concerning what is good and bad in human laws. The language of confusion and contradiction used by Justin in this section is reminiscent of Justin's language about the disagreements between philosophers on true teaching and doctrine in *Dial.* 2, 2 *Apol.* 13, and 1 *Apol.* 44 (an important borrowing reference). Just as there was one original philosophy which later splintered, evidenced by contradiction between different schools of thought,[263] it seems that for Justin the *Logos*-law also became, over time, "many-headed," the evidence of this being the presence of both good and bad laws being enacted. For Justin, the reasons for the splintering and departure from universal law are attributable, in part, to the malevolent role of bad angels.[264]

I believe another argument supporting the idea that it is humankind's confused perception of the eternal law *behind* the decalogue, rather than borrowing *from* the decalogue that Justin has in mind in the above references is found in Justin's reservations concerning the mosaic law and the decalogue and his belief that the Mosaic law was for the Jewish people alone, containing both eternal and temporal injunctions (see section 4.2.2). I believe this important distinction swings the balance in favor of the "eternal law" awareness I am arguing for here. Because confusion concerning right and wrong has (in principle at least) been dispelled at Christ's coming,[265] Justin contrasts bad laws and bad living with the results of the first advent of Christ: Christians living in total accord with the perfectly good law teaching of the whole *Logos*.[266] The incarnation clarified what was good and bad, because the whole *Logos* came.[267] Human perception of part of the law—the eternal law—confused in part because of our limited capacity and sinfulness, and in part due to the demonic and bad angels, is contrasted with the author and perfect embodiment of that law—Jesus Christ. Justin stresses the importance of the ethical teaching of Jesus[268] and as noted by a number of scholars, Jesus's role as teacher is constantly emphasized by Justin.[269] Justin points to the exemplary lives of Christ's followers as part of the proof of his argument.[270]

One final argument for the occasional close relationship Justin draws between human laws, the eternal law and Christ is found in 1 *Apol.* 10: "For, what human laws were unable to effect, the Divine Word would have accomplished, had not the evil demons enlisted the aid of the various utterly evil inclinations, which are in every man by nature, and scattered many false and ungodly accusations-none of which, however, applies to us."

Edwards notes that the "Divine Word" is, elsewhere in Justin's writings, a title for Christ.[271] However, as he observes, this is not an appropriate interpretation here—as Christ has the power to defeat the demons, and here the Divine Word fails in its object. Edwards argues that the reference is to "the commandments given to Israel."[272] However, I suggest this is unlikely, as the readers of the apology were, in all likelihood, from a pagan background (whether Christian or not) and hence unlikely to equate this term with the Torah or decalogue. Human laws are, in Justin's opinion, a mix—containing both good and bad (see earlier). The eternal law (what I consider to be the Divine Word here) is perfect. However, in Justin's view, before the coming of the whole *Logos*, humankind's awareness of the eternal law is vague and (largely) without the power to save.[273] I suggest that Justin was contrasting a vague perception of the eternal law with Christ's incarnation and teaching when he made the following statement (interpretations in square brackets): "For the seed of something and its imitation, given in proportion to one's capacity [the eternal law perceived by humankind, not able to grow], is one thing, but the thing itself [Christ incarnate embodying the eternal law], which is shared and imitated according to His grace, is quite another."[274] Given the arguments above, I believe the reference to legislators enacting good laws in Justin's thinking to be due to occasionally correct responses to the eternal law, rather than due to borrowing.

4.2.1.2. The Natural Law Reference in 2 *Apology*

Moving on to the second argument I wish to forward in support of my interpretation of Justin's view of the *Logos*, I turn to Justin's use of the term "natural law."[275] This occurs in the case stated at the beginning of 2 *Apology* (of a Christian woman who had filed for a divorce from her worthless husband, and the resulting execution of the person who had taught her the Christian faith, along with others). Not only is the right reason (i.e., Christian restored reason) of the woman set in contrast to the un-natural behavior of the man, but as Jackson-McCabe points out, the law of nature and the teachings of Christ are equated.[276] While Edwards makes passing reference to this section of the Apology, he chooses to use it to argue that it does not refer to innate knowledge.[277] Such a response, focusing on mechanism rather than knowledge, per se., fails to address the appeal to natural law. As Holte notes, one does not have to, indeed should not, consider Justin's mechanism for such knowledge to be Platonic: Justin is vague on the mechanism.[278] What Justin seems to say here is that (all) humans know what is right and not right—and that what is right is equivalent to the teaching of Christ. Edwards fails to engage with the ethical knowledge that Justin assumes his addressees share with him in his comment.

I now turn to the *Dialogue*, and discussion of the law within it.

4.2.2. Law in *The Dialogue with Trypho*

4.2.2.1. JUDAISM AND ITS RELATION TO NATURAL LAW IN THE *DIALOGUE*

Justin differentiated the parts of the Mosaic law which were given in response to the Jews' hardness of heart with universally acknowledged good precepts.[279] Bates goes so far as to term the Mosaic law "bipartite" in his thinking: containing specifically Jewish laws, intended for Jews alone and "imposed" because of proneness to idolatry, and what he calls "universal laws."[280] There is however more support for a tripartite division: those elements foreshadowing Christ, those given because of the Jews hardness of heart and finally, the "precepts . . . given for the worship of God and the practice of virtue."[281]

As in the *Apologies*, Justin makes references to natural law ideas in the *Dialogue with Trypho*. The most important of these is in *Dial.* 93: "God shows every race of man that which is always and in all places just, and every type of man knows that adultery, fornication, murder, and so on are evil."[282] Does he explain this knowledge via a mechanism of borrowing from the Old Testament? This seems unlikely, given the universal appeal, specifically the language "every type of man," together with the fact that the particular sins noted are not specific to the decalogue.[283] Justin goes on to argue that the exceptions to awareness of these evil actions are to be found in the possessed or those corrupted in various ways and who have, as a consequence, "lost . . . their natural feelings of guilt."[284] Although Justin does not include the right worship of God in what God shows humankind—the focus is on ethics—he immediately follows this section by explaining that "all justice and piety" are found in Christ's summation of the commandments, suggesting that right worship cannot be separated from good ethics.[285]

In another section in the *Dialogue*, Justin wrote of those who have been justified not by following the mosaic law, but a set of higher principles: "those things which are universally, naturally, and eternally good are pleasing to God."[286] Justin notes that women of the OT, though excluded from the rite of circumcision, were justified by their piety.[287] As Goodenough comments, in his summary of sections 11–31 of the *Dialogue*, "Though God undoubtedly gave the law, justification throughout Jewish history has been a matter of moral integrity and purity of heart, not a matter of legal observance."[288] Justin seemed to argue that knowledge of what was right and wrong was "natural" and not learned from the Mosaic law, though such "natural" knowledge was contained within it.[289]

4.2.2.2. JESUS THE ETERNAL LAW

Justin terms Jesus the lawgiver on a number of occasions in the *Dialogue*.[290] Jesus is also called the "new law."[291] In context, these references are best interpreted in relation to the (old) Mosaic law: with Jesus contrasted to Moses.[292] However, arguably more important for Justin to show, (even) in the *Dialogue*, is Christ's identity as the eternal law.[293] Goodenough captures this important shift in emphasis, in stating: "The immeasurable superiority of Christianity to Judaism and heathenism alike lies in the fact that Christ is himself this everlasting law and everlasting covenant. Christ is the new law in a sense, but more correctly, He is the the [sic] Eternal Law."[294]

Philo believed the law of nature to be "higher" than the Mosaic law, which, in turn, can be considered a kind of copy of the law of nature.[295] The law of nature, for Justin, as suggested earlier, is Christ and/or his teachings. Indeed, in terming Christ the eternal law Justin suggests a kind of ontological identity rather different to Philo's thinking concerning the status of the Torah. As Jackson-McCabe notes, the "embodiment" of the natural law was a key issue of difference between Jews and Gentiles during this era:

> From at least the first century of the Common Era, some Jewish thinkers claimed that their nation's law, revealed to Moses by the creator of the world, was in act a written expression of the Stoics' natural law. Analogous claims would continue to be forwarded by Christians, who, however, more often asserted that it was rather the teaching of Jesus which gave verbal expression to natural law.[296]

Although Jackson-McCabe does not name Justin here, I believe the apologist exemplifies this Christian viewpoint. Holding the position he did (Christ as the eternal law) led Justin to have a lower view of the Torah than did Philo. Indeed, as noted earlier, I believe he held a considerably lower view of it.[297] A key reason for this is because Christ plays a critical hermeneutical role in Justin's understanding of the standing of the Mosaic law. As Wendel notes, "He [Justin] . . . explains that the new covenant and law (i.e., Christ) indicates which Mosaic precepts are 'eternal' and 'fit for every race' and which are suited for the hardness of the hearts of Jews (Dial. 67.10)."[298] Christ "sifts" the Torah and exemplifies the lasting and eternal within it, making it known "what precepts and actions God knows to be eternal and fit for every nationality,"[299] and which laws were just for the Jews.[300] For Justin, Christ not only fulfils, he also replaces[301] the obsolete law of Horeb "intended for you Jews only,"[302] with himself: "an everlasting and final law."[303] I suggest the replacement has both backward- and forward-looking aspects. It connects backwards to the eternal law before Mosaic law and forwards to Christ's universal proclamation to all. Justin's comments in *Dialogue* 43 make these points clearly:

> As circumcision originated with Abraham, and the Sabbath, sacrifices, oblations, and festivals with Moses (and it has already been shown that your people were commanded to observe these things because of their hardness of heart), so it was expedient that, in accordance with the will of the Father, these things should have their end in Him who was born of the Virgin, of the race of Abraham, of the tribe of Juda, and of the family of David: namely, in Christ, the Son of God, who was proclaimed as the future Eternal Law and New Testament for the whole world (as the above-quoted prophecies clearly show).

While Abrahamic circumcision and Mosaic law "had their end in Christ," Jesus's person and role extend far beyond this, as the universalistic language employed in the quotation above shows.[304] Rather than Christ's role being seen primarily as law observance fulfilment, Justin considered it to be embodiment of the eternal law elements of the Mosaic law leading to victory over the anti-law bad angels and demons. The OT's primary importance was, for Justin, its pointing to the coming of the *Logos* to achieve these ends. As Holmes observes, Justin's main interest in the Old Testament was prophecy, not law.[305] The main role of the prophets was to announce the coming of the *Logos*.[306] Skarsaune comments, "The prophets proclaimed in advance this victory of Christ. That is the central content of their message (e.g., *Dial.* 78:9). The prophets did not teach monotheism, virtue and eternal life in an abstract way. They proclaimed these truths by announcing the approaching defeat of the demons in the history of Jesus."[307] I believe the consequences of such an emphasis in Justin's teaching to be twofold: a lower view of the mosaic law (as discussed throughout this section),[308] and a less significant role for the loan theory in Justin's thinking than has sometimes been argued. This "downplaying" is because the doctrines that Justin specifically associates with borrowing are not those relating to the incarnation of the *Logos*.[309]

In closing this section, I suggest that Justin's view of the *Logos* as the natural law, embodied in Christ, creates an important bridge between Jew and Gentile. Both Jew and Gentile pre- and post-Moses were vaguely aware of this law. In the next section, I seek to consider the implications of this in greater detail—in Justin's labelling Socrates a Christian.

4.2.3. *Justin's Christianization of Socrates*

Justin's Christianization of Socrates (*1 Apol.* 46, *2 Apol.* 10, see also *1 Apol.* 5)[310] has attracted considerable attention among theologians of religion and Justin scholars. In what follows I will consider the feasibility of understanding the claim with reference to the previous *Logos*-Law revelation argument I am proposing, and also critique various alternative views of the appellation (including Edwards's interpretation). I will suggest that a literal reading of it is justified (when *Christian* is understood as a follower of part of the *Logos*), but that such an interpretation must be understood within Justin's wider thought (including his views on the demonic, his strong ethical righteousness view of salvation, and his "dispensational" view of history).

4.2.3.1. INTERPRETATIONS OF THE APPELLATION

In what follows I will outline four views of what Justin meant in labelling Socrates a Christian, After this, I forward an interpretation consistent with the view of the *Logos* Eternal-Law hypothesis discussed above.

Edwards's reading of the bestowal of the Christian label to Socrates is that Justin meant it literally, but only when the Christianization passages are understood in the light of the loan reference in *1 Apol.* 44, mentioned earlier. Only when so read, Edwards argues, are Socrates and Heraclitus listed as Christians among the Hebrews. Edwards states, "if, with Heraclitus and the sages of barbarous nations, he [Socrates] can be reckoned as a Christian before Christ (1 Apology 46.3), it is because, like other Greeks, he employed his reason upon the teaching of the prophets (1 Apology 44–45)."[311]

I believe there are two issues with Edwards's reading here. The first is that there is no reference in the Justin corpus to Socrates's dependence on Moses—indeed, there is very little reference at all to Socrates's beliefs or teachings.[312] Arguably, Edwards conflates Plato and Socrates in making the comment, and such a fusing, as Nyström, Daniélou, and Droge note is highly questionable.[313] Secondly, Edwards believed Socrates used his own reason (*logos*) on the scriptural revelation, and he differentiated this from direct revelation from *the Logos*. "Though some, like Socrates, lived *meta logou*, they did not live *meta tou logou*; they had their critical faculties by nature, but, except through plagiarism, no acquaintance with the Word."[314] That is, Edwards argues Justin differentiates *the Logos* (Christ) from *Logos* (reason) in support of this particular reading. Against such an interpretation, Baechle notes, in a detailed study,[315] that Justin does not always use the definite article to signal that he is speaking of Christ.[316] Further, Baechle considers the serious problems that ensue in the text if the meaning is not the same for both groups.[317] Accordingly, Edwards's interpretation can be challenged on linguistic and co-textual grounds.

In a rather different attempt to read the Christianization passages with the presupposition of additional revelation informing it, Paul Hacker appealed to "something like a private revelation"[318] being responsible for Socrates insights—a suggestion which would find support from those who believe Justin to have held the idea that some of the philosophers received special inspiration of some kind. Wolfson argued that Philo believed truth to be present in philosophy due to three reasons: theft, the use of reason (with God's help), and finally "it [philosophy] was God's special gift to them."[319] Immediately following this claim Wolfson comments, "Justin Martyr makes use of all these three Philonic explanations." As evidence of the third he provides Justin's reference to philosophy being "sent down" in *Dialogue* 2. However, the interpretation of Justin's meaning in that section of the *Dialogue* is contested. Holte, for example, believes that the reference to philosophy is "nothing but the Old Testament revelation."[320] Droge[321] concurs and Nyström believes Justin's comments in *Dialogue* 8 to indicate that the original philosophy is Christianity itself.[322] However Daniélou is more open to Wolfson's position. He argued that there is some support for the special gift interpretation elsewhere in Justin's writings, specifically in Justin's reference to an inspired Sibyl (*1 Apol.* 20 and 44).[323] I suggest, however, that there is nothing in these two references in the first *Apology* which do not permit them to be covered either by Justin's borrowing thesis or his demonic mimesis thesis.[324] Saldanha argues that Justin (mistakenly) believed these pagan texts to be Christian writings, but I do not think there is enough evidence to support this claim from the Justin corpus.[325] In sum, there appears to be a lack of support for the idea of private revelation or Greek inspiration in Justin's thinking.

Another group of scholars interpret the Christianizing label literally and argue that this suggests Justin was an early inclusivist, or at least sympathetic to such a position. Indeed, for some, the reference indicates that Socrates is a kind of pre-Rahnerian anonymous Christian.[326] Clark Pinnock stated, "Access to salvation for all was realized by a 'logos' doctrine which theologians like Justin Martyr . . . entertained."[327] Sanders[328] and McDermott[329] also reference Justin as sympathetic to the inclusivist cause or being an early inclusivist. I suggest that the most significant problem with the inclusivist view is that it isolates and focuses on the work of the *Logos* (without specifying what Justin meant by it) outside of a wider reading of Justin's thought: a serious oversight, as I hope to explain in what follows. In addition, it must be stressed that Justin believed Socrates rejected the religion (i.e., idolatry) of his day: he was saved by *not* following the popular religion.

I now turn to the final interpretation I will discuss here, by far the most popular among those who have argued against an inclusivist reading of Justin. This position advocates a non-literal reading/interpretation of the Christian label.[330] Specifically, it is argued that Socrates (and Heraclitus) are *Christian-like* (not Christians per se.), and they are so in that they, like Christians in Justin's time, were opposed to idolatry and rejected the demonic.[331] The textual support for this interpretation is the reference to atheists (i.e., being against the idols) in 2 *Apol.* 10 and in 1 *Apol.* 5. Further support for this understanding can also be found in the list of the Hebrews named. Apocryphal sources point to Abraham as being against idols,[332] and Daniel's friends likewise stood against idolatry; furthermore, Elijah is anti-Baal.[333] While I believe that the Christian-likeness explanation has a number of points in its favor (which I will note later), I suggest that there are three major problems with the simile/metaphor reading as currently presented.

Firstly, it can be argued that the non-literal interpretation of the appellation is only argued by some readers because of the "awkward" inclusion of the pagan names in the list. If understood metaphorically, this interpretation should, logically, be applied to both groups, and I believe such a reading risks saying too little for the Hebrew group, thereby driving a wedge between the pagans and Hebrews, whom it seems, Justin wishes to group together.

Secondly, from the wider co-text, I believe that the focus on idolatry and atheism, and the argument that these are primarily in mind here, to the exclusion of everything else in Justin's thinking, fails to take into consideration the introduction to *1 Apol.* 46, specifically the issue of accountability.[334] In the co-text preceding the reference to the pagan and Hebrew Christians, Justin argues for human accountability before the incarnation of the *Logos*. Read in this light, Justin is saying that before the *Logos* incarnate some were able to live according to the *Logos*—Christ is not totally "new." As Daniélou observed, "the incarnation represents only the high point of a permanent *oikonomia*" in Justin's thinking.[335] Those who lived according to the *Logos* are contrasted with those who did not. Importantly, the latter (who are mentioned after the pagan and Hebrew reference) are not termed idol worshippers, which would be the most expected designation if the atheist claim is dominant. Rather, they are termed useless people, enemies of Christ and murderers of his followers. Such, in context, must be understood to include both pagan and Hebrew.[336] Justin puts forward names which "prove" that accountability does not necessarily result in condemnation: both pagan and Hebrew have lived in accord with the pre-incarnate *Logos*.

Thirdly, from a theological perspective, I suggest that the metaphorical argument fails to look behind the implications of opposition to demons in Justin's thought. I will argue below that demon opposition and ethical virtue can be understood to be two sides of the same coin for Justin, and that this has not been recognized by those forwarding the metaphorical interpretation. More specifically, the failure to take into account Justin's wider beliefs concerning the relationship between the *Logos* and demons, and the full implications of what opposition to idols entails, weakens the plausibility of the Christian-*like* argument.[337] In the next section I will argue that an ethical Logos-Law revelation is best able to account for the Christian labelling of Socrates and Heraclitus.

4.2.3.2. Support for an Ethical *Logos*-Law Revelation

The first point I wish to make supporting an ethical *Logos*-law revelation reading, over against the interpretations outlined above, is that the focus in *1 Apol.* 46 is not right teaching or doctrine, but right living—living according to (the) *Logos*.[338] While Socrates's appeal to others to learn about God (this not being an easy task) is mentioned in *2 Apol.* 10, it is not teaching about this God, per se., that Justin focuses on in any of the relevant passages.[339] Turning to Heraclitus, the fifth century BC philosopher is also mentioned favorably by Justin in *2 Apol.* 8 (along with Musonius) in the context of Justin's praise of Stoic ethics, together with the importance of "avoiding evil," and his being persecuted.[340] Some scholars suggest that Justin believed Heraclitus to be a kind of pre-Stoic, whose ethics led him to reject idolatry.[341] Within the co-text of *2 Apol.* 8 this makes good sense.

To re-iterate the point being made here, while one needs to know what is right to follow it, it is not teaching that is in focus here. Chadwick's statement that Justin believed Socrates to have been "a genuine teacher of the way to happiness"[342] is not well-founded. Justin nowhere makes such a claim: a genuine follower of the *Logos*, yes, but not an instructor in the way of the *Logos*. In opposition to the argument of Goodenough, I do not believe it to be valid to argue that Justin had "faith" in mind in his references to Socrates and Heraclitus, for the simple reason that there is no mention of faith in these passages.[343] The men listed are not writers and not referenced as borrowers, instructors or teachers: rather, they are proffered to Justin's audiences simply as *followers* (of part of the *Logos*).[344]

There is a shift in focus in *2 Apol.* 10, where opposition to demons is central (Socrates's rejection of Homer and other poets, alongside his instruction to expel demons and evildoers). I consider the demonic—ethics relationship further in section 4.3.3.4. Suffice to say here, Justin seems to be arguing that exercise of right ethics (good deeds) is sufficient evidence of following the *Logos* in *1 Apol.* 46 and opposition to demons sufficient evidence in *2 Apol.* 10, *1 Apol.* 5 and *2 Apol.* 8. The relationship between the two has not, I suggest, been adequately considered in the literature to date.

At this point one might ask why Justin focuses on deeds (ethically righteous ones) and demon opposition in his "Christianization" passages, and not belief. To answer this, it is important to remember that Justin stated that all have a kind of knowledge of the true God (contra Edwards's point)[345] and in a critically important statement made in *Dial.* 1, Justin wrote that a wrong view of God, will, of necessity, result in ethical corruption.[346] Though unstated, I believe the opposite case should be understood as a given from this passage: a true view of God will lead to ethical righteousness. From where did Justin make this equation? As well as obvious biblical passages which he cited,[347] it may have been his initial contact with Christians that enforced the relationship in his mind.[348]

Another possible source for the connection made between right belief and right ethics may have been Stoic thinking in this area, particularly the Ciceronian idea that *nomos* is "the ethical expression of Logos."[349] As Jackson-McCabe notes, the gods were 'behind' rational belief and behavior in Stoic thought: "The possession of the ratio, according to Cicero, necessarily entails recognition of its ultimate source, and thus a belief in the existence of the gods."[350] If he was so influenced, Justin's adaptation of Cicero's idea here was twofold: to state that the eternal law consists of particular precepts which can be known,[351] and equating that law with Christ, who is the Son of God.[352] Justin describes the Christian God as "alien to all evil and . . . the Father of justice, temperance, and the other virtues."[353] Accordingly, those who exhibited such traits and virtues are, for Justin, Christians—followers of God and his *Logos*.

What though of the Hebrews mentioned? What effect does an accountability—ethical righteousness reading of the text have on the names provided? While Abraham's faith is often appealed to by Justin,[354] there are also references to his being "just" and "pleasing to God."[355] More importantly, Justin's choice of a pre-Moses figure should be considered significant. Turning to Elijah, while Justin does talk of Elijah's opposition to idols,[356] he also focuses on his fear (of God).[357] The three friends of Daniel are not mentioned elsewhere in Justin's writings, but in 4 Maccabees 16:21, Daniel and his friends are commended for their courage and endurance, not opposition to idols, per se.[358] Accordingly, I believe a case can be made that Justin specifically chose heroes of the Hebrew faith who lived according to the *Logos* (evidenced by their righteous deeds) outside of the normal operation of the cultic apparatus of Mosaic Judaism (whether pre-Moses, in exile or ostracized from Jerusalem). The clear waters of his *Logos* argument would, I suggest, only be muddied by bringing in complexities associated with the Mosaic law.[359]

4.2.3.3. Hebrew and Greek Similarities and Differences

In this section I consider how Justin could have grouped together both Jews and Greeks as living according to the *Logos*. As mentioned earlier, Justin was keen to differentiate the moral eternal law from the Jewish-only elements of the mosaic law. Harnack believed Justin to equate the decalogue with the natural law;[360] however, keeping the sabbath is one commandment that Justin clearly did not endorse, thus challenging Harnack's claim.³⁶¹ As noted earlier, Justin equated natural law with the teachings of Jesus, rather than the decalogue, per se.³⁶² Unlike the Apostle Paul, Justin did not consider the Hebrews to be particularly privileged compared to their Greek counterparts.³⁶³ Purves wrote:

> How did Justin regard the Hebrew dispensation? It must be admitted by all, we think, that at least in the apology, he gives no indication that he looked upon the relation of the Hebrews to God as having differed in any respect from that of other nations. He mentions Socrates and Heraclitus before Abraham, Elias and other Hebrews, as examples of men who lived conformably to truth before Christ came.³⁶⁴

Chadwick argues similarly.³⁶⁵ Further, Justin not only argues that *Logos* revelation is universal, but also that it is "effective"—hence the roll call.³⁶⁶ There is a shift, though only subtle, in the *Dialogue*. There Justin clearly states that the prophets are the only reliable conveyors of God's truth (*Dial.* 4 and 7) and in that sense the Jews were and are privileged. However, Justin argued that the Jews did not understand the Scriptures, as they were without the necessary enlightenment (and post-incarnation, the hermeneutical key of Christ) to understand their true intent.³⁶⁷ This being so, even taking into account the material in the *Dialogue*, Justin seemed to perceive Jewish advantage over the Greeks as, at most, negligible.³⁶⁸

Not only did Justin seem to minimize Hebrew privileges, at times he hinted that the pagan condition was, in some ways, more favorable to following the *Logos* than was the case for the Hebrews. I suggest Justin's aetiology of sin is responsible for this difference. Justin seemed to provide two rather different accounts for why there was sin in the world—relating Jewish sin to the Fall, and pagan sin to the demons.³⁶⁹ This can be termed Justin's disobedience versus deception understandings of the human condition.³⁷⁰ It has been argued that Justin did not subscribe to a doctrine of original sin;³⁷¹ at the same time, he characterized the Jewish condition as demonstrating a rebellious disposition, which showed itself in a positive attraction to the demons and rejection of God's law.³⁷² The pagans, on the other hand, were (simply) hindered by the demons from following the truth.³⁷³ While the bifurcated aetiology is present in Justin's thinking, it is important not to overstate it. As the tone of the *Apologies* makes clear, despite the significant role of the demons in the affairs of humankind,

Justin could still argue that those deceived by the demons were, ultimately, responsible and accountable: they could not blame the demons for their actions. If they could, the accountability context preceding the Socrates Christian claim would make no sense.

As noted above, Justin did at times speak of the privileges that the Hebrews had, which the Greeks did not—not least God's revelation and Scripture.[374] This being so, is there a need to differentiate *how* the *Logos* communicated to the two groups in *1 Apol.* 46, or indeed, *what* the *Logos* communicated? Holte differentiates the *mode* of *Logos* revelation, when he states that the Greeks mentioned in the key passage "obeyed the witness of their conscience," whereas the Hebrews "obeyed the prophetical revelation."[375] Importantly, Holte did not go on to argue that the two different modes of revelation (conscience and prophetic revelation) conveyed the same message. However, they proceed from the same *Logos*.[376] Holte writes this in unequivocal terms.[377]

But is the conscience/patriarchal revelation differentiation that Holte argues for here really so clear or evident in Justin's thinking in *1 Apol.* 46? Dupuis believes that a key idea present in the thought of Justin and the fathers in their *Logos* theology is the concept of "differentiated participation."[378] While this thought is certainly clear in the pre- and post-Christ eras,[379] I suggest it is far less clear when one considers the differences between the pagans and Jews in Justin's argumentation in his writings.

In sum, I believe there to be sufficient justification to argue that the two groups are treated essentially the same (though there are subtle differences between them) in the ethical accountability interpretation I am arguing for here. There are bigger and more important differences between the two groups in their knowledge of God's acts in history, and the plan of redemption. These were known by the Hebrews through Scripture. What was "borrowed" by the pagans, on the other hand, was not redemptive knowledge. These differences were, I believe, largely *irrelevant* to the argument that Justin is making in this section. To reiterate, this argument is that the eternal *Logos* law known universally, albeit vaguely, has been followed by a small minority of gentiles, alongside Jews who also knew more of God.

4.2.3.4. *Logos*-Law Revelation within Justin's Wider Thinking

Above, I have sought to argue for a literal view of Socrates's Christian appellation, challenging, among other interpretations, a Christian-like metaphorical reading. If we assume that Justin believed Socrates and Heraclitus to have followed a part of the *Logos* (i.e., obeyed the *Logos* and/or his law),[380] this would mean that they were exceptions to the Greek masses who were held captive by the demons. As opposed to the inclusivist reading, or the arguments which presuppose extra-revelation (Edwards and Hacker), Harnack argued that Socrates could not really have been understood to have been a Christian, because Socrates's ability to see truth (along with everyone else's) would have been limited by the demons in Justin's thought.[381] Harnack's point cannot be easily dismissed. Justin nowhere really explains how this is possible, but I believe that a correct understanding of the relationship between demons and ethics in his thought helps shed light on this difficult issue. Therefore, at this point, I wish to consider the relationship between demons and ethics in more detail, a point I have largely bypassed in the preceding discussion. In what follows, I will argue that ethical righteousness and idol opposition can legitimately be considered two sides of the same coin in Justin's thinking.

As noted earlier, there is a strong *Logos*-demon counter-positioning in Justin's thought—an issue which has been overlooked by some in their treatment of Justin as a theologian of religions.[382] What happens if the demons are rejected? Justin did not seem to allow for any "neutral" ground here. Although "Christian" heretics might be considered to have rejected idols in favor of a monotheistic God (their subsequent error being to subscribe to certain wrong doctrine), for Justin it was their bad ethical behavior which was evidence of their heresy and of their continued allegiance to demons.[383] Justin seemed not to allow the possibility that demons could be rejected and good ethics not result. The idea that idol opposition actually means that the law is (by default) obeyed is clearly present in some Rabbinic midrashes, for example: "Whoever acknowledges idolatry disavows the whole Torah, and whoever disavows idolatry acknowledges the whole Torah."[384] While there are various opinions concerning Justin's Rabbinic tradition knowledge,[385] it is clear that Justin saw a clear relationship between "right God" and "right behavior" in *Dial.* 1 concerning Philosophy.[386] He also argued that the opposite was the case with heretics (see earlier) and also with Jews.[387] One cannot live righteously if one does not know and love God. One possible objection to my argument here is where Justin approves of Stoic ethics, but disapproves of some of their other doctrines. I believe that this is less a problem than at first appears, if one remembers that "the original philosophy" has become corrupted in his thought, as has natural law: Justin was certainly prepared to allow (some) truth in both doctrine and (some) ethics in different systems, but nowhere did he suggest that these are ever pure or complete.

Accordingly, Socrates's anti-idolatry position (i.e., correct thinking about God) can be considered evidence of his keeping the law (i.e., having right ethics and behavior) in Justin's view—or vice versa. As noted by Nyström, Socrates (much more so than Plato) was a plausible "moral example" in the second century.[388] The argument of Sigountos that Socrates was not really a Christian, but that Justin "*merely* affirms that some throughout human history have stood up to the demonic deception of pagan religion [emphasis mine],"[389] fails to recognize what it means to actually oppose the demons for Justin. A similarly untenable one-sided reading is argued by Grant who states, "Justin . . . insisted that Socrates and Heraclitus were Christians, even if regarded as godless."[390] Such a claim, I suggest, is highly questionable, given the clear "right ethics-right God" argument present in Justin's thinking: good ethics cannot be understood apart from the rejection of demons and idols and basic commitment to the true God. In sum, the Christian metaphor reading of the Christian appellation of Socrates, while recognizing a key element of Justin's argument (his opposition to idols) has, by focusing on it exclusively, ultimately misinterpreted Justin's ideas.

Above I have argued that Justin understood the seed of the *Logos* as giving humans a vague awareness of the eternal law. Does this mean that Socrates had some awareness of Christ? Holte believes not, stating that "an analogous knowledge [is] gained through things reflecting and resembling Logos."[391] Barnard, on the other hand, is critical of Holte's view: "A close comparison of three passages in *2 Apol.* 8, 10 and 13 shows that St Justin assumed the presence in every man, before the coming of Christ, of part of the 'sowing logos' which is identical with Christ."[392] Daniélou[393] and Lilla[394] argue similarly to Barnard. This issue, whether the *Logos* is known, or gifts from the *Logos*, is a theme that will come up in most chapters of this book.

Given the preceding discussion, I would suggest that there are two key issues surrounding the analogous/direct object knowledge interpretations which need to be remembered. Firstly, there are occasions where Justin identified the eternal law with Christ. To know "the right" is to know Christ. Just as Stoic thought sometimes equated the law with God, and also separated it from him,[395] Justin seemed to do the same, at least at times. Accordingly, there does seem to be some kind of identification, which challenges the analogous reading.

However, Holte's reluctance to identify the seed of the Word with Christ, is, I believe, justified. It is helpful to consider Daniélou's comments in more detail on this point. He states that there is no difference in the object known, pre- or post-Incarnation:

> That which Socrates and Heraclitus knew is in fact the Word, who is Truth itself. They, however, only knew it obscurely. . . . Justin is not here envisaging any difference of content between the truth as known through the revelation of Christ and the truth glimpsed by participation in the Logos. The difference is solely one of fullness, certainty, clarity.[396]

While I would agree with the first part of Daniélou's statement, I do not think the content comment that follows it is valid. In line with the argument developed in this chapter, I believe the "part" of the *Logos* known to be ethical. While this is a critical part of Christ for Justin, it is not the sum of Christ.[397] While Christ's will is known (obscurely) by Socrates and Heraclitus, his full person is not. While the eternal law is Christ, Christ is not *only* the eternal law. Justin ascribes many other additional titles to Him, titles which I do not believe he could have allowed the Greeks to have been aware of, including: "Christ is spoken of as a King, and a Priest, and God, and Lord, and an Angel, and a Man, and a Leader, and a Stone, and a Begotten Son,"[398] and "Wisdom, the Day, the East, Sword, Stone, Rod, Jacob, and Israel."[399] Hence, I would suggest that the awareness is not analogous, but it would also be wrong to argue that the full *Logos* is apprehended—even though seen obscurely.

Conclusion

In this chapter, I have challenged Edwards's rejection of a distinct *Logos* revelation in Justin's theology by appealing to Justin's view of the demonic, his natural and eternal law comments in the *Apologies* and the

Dialogue, and through a re-consideration of his claim that Socrates was a Christian. I have argued that Justin's *Logos* theology is foundational to his view of religions and philosophy, and that it cannot be erased without misinterpreting his views.

Concerning his use of the loan theory, I have suggested that the doctrines that Justin traces to it are important, but more important in his apologetics are the prophecies of Jesus's coming—which are nowhere referenced in what is loaned. Although Horner believed the moral aspect of the law to have been transferred from Moses to Plato,[400] such a thought seems to be absent from Justin's loan theory references.

Turning to the demonic, as noted earlier, I suggest the demonic truth source to be a pedagogical tool only, and not to be considered on a par with the *Logos* theory and the loan theory in Justin's thinking. Justin's views on demonic disruption in the world and the counter-positioning of the *Logos* against the demonic is central to my interpretation. Justin's view of demons is critical to his view of false religion: those who follow the *Logos*, on the other hand, reject the demons and idolatry and embrace righteous living.

With the coming of Christ, Justin seems to have adjusted his expectations of what is required for salvation. Just as the Hebrew dispensation was ended, Justin seemed to believe that righteous living according to part of the *Logos*, was, post-incarnation, no longer an option either: two dispensations seemed to end with the coming of Christ.[401]

3

Augustine

Background

AUGUSTINE (354–430), TERMED BY Calvin "the best and most faithful witness of all antiquity,"[402] has much to say on non-Christian religion—testimony to this fact being a relatively recently edited volume dedicated to considering this aspect of his thought in the modern world.[403] While I draw on a number of texts from the Augustine corpus in the pages that follow, I highlight three here as being of especial importance. The first is the *City of God*,[404] which sheds significant light on Augustine's views on demons and the *prisca theologia*. Secondly, I engage in some detail with the first three homilies on the prologue of John,[405] and thirdly, I examine a section of Sermon 198—the *Sermon against the Pagans*.[406] I also refer to a number of other texts throughout the chapter, in part to gain wider perspective, and at times to engage with very specific aspects of Augustine's thought (e.g., demonic mediation, or Christ's mediatory roles).[407] While the treatment and analysis that follows can in no way be called exhaustive, I believe it provides sufficient coverage of the three major parameters and the revelation-religion interface, facilitating a basic understanding of Augustine's thinking on this subject. I give specific context for the key issues discussed throughout the chapter, rather than setting out a general context to Augustine—which is well documented elsewhere.[408]

The chapter begins by providing a summary of Augustine's thought on religion. In the second section I consider what roles demons played in his theology of false worship. Following this overview, I engage with his understanding of the religious knowledge of philosophers, whom Augustine differentiates from the religious masses. In doing so, I focus on two key areas. In section 3, I examine whether Augustine argued that philosophers learned what they knew of God from a version of the ancient theology (*prisca theologia*). I argue that Augustine did not really support this view, while he did not explicitly reject it. However, I note that his interpretation of the Erythraean Sibyl challenges his otherwise consistent rejection of multilinear channels of revelation from God outside Israel. Following this, in section 4, I provide a brief overview of Augustine's first three homilies on the Gospel of John, and consider whether Augustine believed philosophers to receive spiritual illumination from the Word of God, and what advantage, if any, this gave them compared to the masses. I consider what this illumination entails, along with its consequences. In section 4.3, I examine the relationship between philosopher illumination and religion in Augustine's thought. I engage in some detail with a particular claim of John Marenbon, who argues that Augustine had a different understanding of illumination and false religion to the Apostle Paul, as documented in Romans 1. I suggest that a close reading of a key text used to support Marenbon's interpretation (*Sermon 198, Against the Pagans*) does not support his interpretation. I believe discarnate *Logos* illumination to be the first step to idolatry among the philosophers in Augustine's thinking—a very different view to that of Justin, noted in the previous chapter.

1. Augustine and Religion

1.1. Religion in the Time of Augustine

As Wilken notes, religion in the ancient Roman world was less a matter of belief, than practice. Governing all aspects of life, religion was, in large part, concerned with the perpetuation of societal norms and expectations.[409] Adherence to requirements and the correct continuance of religious rights were considered to constitute piety;[410] scriptures, revelation and personal belief, on the other hand, were not part of the bedrock or foundation of Roman religion.[411] Strand notes that the ascent of the soul, given such a worldview, was to participate rightly in the established order.[412]

1.2. Augustine's Understanding of Religion

Augustine considered the etymology of the word *religio* in chapter 10 of *City of God*. He believed it to derive from *religare* (to bind)[413] and true binding to mean humanity directing itself to God and binding ourselves to him. The binding understanding of the word is the one that he preferred (over against the "choosing" interpretation he also employed).[414] Jones notes that Cicero's understanding of religion, derived from the verb *relegere* (to read again), involved engaging with, sifting and sorting to attain truth.[415] This interpretation differs from Augustine's understanding, namely: to acknowledge God, repent and turn to him.[416]

Augustine considers various religious terms in different languages in his consideration of the word *religio*, and the associated strengths and weaknesses of these in encompassing what true religion entails.[417] He notes that piety can be related to parents or God, and that *religio* can be said to exist between family members and friends. In a fuller definition of what he considered true religion to be, he comments, "And so, when one who already knows what it is to love himself is commanded to love his neighbour as himself, what else is being commanded than that he should do all that he can to encourage his neighbour to love God? This is the worship of God; this is true religion; this is right piety; this is the service which is due to God alone."[418] The close linking of the words worship, religion, piety and service in the above picks up the key ideas Augustine had discussed immediately prior to this statement, in his etymological overview of meanings of translations of *religion*.

In *True Religion*, Augustine also provides a "binding" understanding of the word *religio*, but adds an additional element to it. He outlines what true religion is *not*. This includes the worship of imagination, animals, parts of nature or even man's soul. He then arrives at his climactic statement that true religion is "binding ourselves tightly to him [God] alone (which is what religion is said to get its name from), so that we are quit of every superstition."[419] The exclusion of superstition, which, in context here should be understood to refer to the preceding list of what true religion is *not*, is the new element in the definition, and the part of it which I pay greater attention to in the next section. Jones believes grace to be at the heart of Augustine's understanding of true religion,[420] and describes this as being the "connective tissue" between humans and God.[421]

1.3. Two Continua in False Religions

As noted above, Augustine believed true religion to exclude superstition, a kind of derivative anti-religion in his thinking.[422] Within the category of superstition he included a great variety of non-Christian worship from idolatry to creation worship to magic (the latter particularly associated with the demonic).[423] Augustine's belief in a spectrum of false religious activity (from less bad to worse) has been noted by Jones[424] and is, I suggest, a critically important part of his thinking. A failure to take this into account can lead the interpreter into a number of errors, as I note later on in my discussion of Plato's religion in section 4.6.

In the *City of God* 7.27 Augustine differentiates the false worship of God (i.e., worship directed to the true God by false means) from the worship of a creature (i.e., worship directed to something other than God).[425] The worst type of religion, for Augustine, was the worship of a creature (even if not wicked) by inappropriate means. This was considered a twofold sin against God.[426] With these two category continua (object of worship and means of directing worship) governing his thinking, Augustine made numerous differentiations between various kinds of religions, suggestive that the distinctions are important to his thinking. For example, in *True Religion* 37.68 he provides a continuum of degrees of error in the object of one's worship (from less bad to worse), listing these as being from the world soul,[427] to procreative life, to animals and "mere bodies" (e.g., the sun). He also speaks of pantheism and worshipping one's own fancies.[428] Specific comparisons that Augustine made concerning points on the continuum include worship of part of creation being less reprehensible than that of an image,[429] original Roman religion being better than the worship of the Great mother;[430] and Egyptian worship of animal idols being worse than the worship of images of men.[431] Turning to the means, rather than object of worship, the religious cult involved could be more or less despicable (from the obscene to the more worthy), though a mitigating factor in evaluating the means is the actual object of worship: the obscene would be less reprehensible if it is directed to the correct object of worship.[432] Some (false) religion could more effectively contribute to the common good of society than other.[433] Indeed, Augustine attributed some good (a kind of virtue) to those involved in less reprehensible worship.[434]

2. Demons and their Place in Augustine's View of non-Christian Religions

Various opinions have been expressed concerning Augustine's demonology. For example, it has been described as being "highly integrated" into his theology[435] or essentially "ancillary"[436] to it. Augustine is not, typically, understood to have been an innovative or creative thinker in his demonology, and has been interpreted by Wiebe as (simply) giving intellectual rigour to existing ideas.[437] However, it has been argued that his theory of magic is innovative,[438] and his understanding of the fall of the angels is of great historical significance in the church's thinking. It is clear that Augustine's demonology developed over time, as documented by Burns, Wiebe and Ivanovska.[439] While making a couple of comments concerning this development, I focus primarily on Augustine's mature thought in what follows.

There are numerous references to and discussions on the existence and role of demons, and their interactions with humankind throughout the Augustine corpus, the most well-known of these being in the *City of God*.[440] It is not doubted that much of this engagement is highly polemical.[441] Ivanovska believes Augustine's demonology drew on three different sources: Scripture, Christian tradition (both orthodox and heterodox), and non-Christian religious and pagan religious philosophical thought.[442] I provide a brief overview of these influences in what follows (combining the first two).

2.1. Influence 1: Scripture and Christian Tradition

Augustine followed the Christian tradition that the gods of the nations were demons/devils,[443] appealing to Psalm 96 in support of this view.[444] The identification of demons with the pagan gods is a dominant theme in the *City of God*.[445] However, he moved away from the earlier Christian adoption of the Watcher's interpretation of Genesis 6:4 concerning the origin of demons.[446] While alluding to pagan stories supportive of the idea of the progeny of gods, he challenged the idea of the possibility of angelic offspring,[447] going on to reject the idea that fallen angels could be progenitors.[448] In so doing he broke with the earlier tradition (advocated by Justin and the later Methodius and Lactantius)[449] that the demons were the immortal spirits of the Nephilim, the progeny of fallen angels. While believing some of Enoch's writings to be authoritative, Augustine did not believe the Nephilim Watchers texts to be among these. Augustine may not have been the first to question the value or authenticity of the tradition: Bradnick believes Augustine's contemporary John Cassian (360–435) to have been the first to move away from it.[450] A key theological motivation for Augustine to adopt this position may have been his rejection of any creative power of demons and angels.[451]

Over many years Augustine developed an interpretation of the angelic fall based on the creation account, understanding the demons to be fallen angels.[452] As Bradnick notes, this view became the standard interpretation of the origin and identity of the demons thereafter in the church.[453]

Augustine endorsed a Euhemeristic understanding of the relationship between demons and idols, terming Euhemerus a "diligent historian."[454] In following Euhemerus's ideas, Augustine continued in the Christian tradition exemplified by Lactantius, Tertullian and Eusebius,[455] also making passing appeal to Varro[456] and to Hermes[457] to support the theory. In the *City of God* he states, "A more believable account is rendered of these gods when it is said that they were men, and that sacred rites and solemn festivals were established for each one of them, according to his genius, character, actions and circumstances, by those who chose to worship them as gods."[458]

Wiebe believes Euhemerism to be critically important to Augustine's thought on false religion.[459] The steps in his thought seem to have been as follows. Firstly, the recognition of some human achievement in society[460] resulted in the honoring of dead men in festivals.[461] The pagan artifacts/statues associated with these dead heroes, in turn, attracted demons who then possessed the associated artifacts.[462] Demons, in their turn, deceived people into thinking these statues or artifacts were gods.[463] The poets[464] contributed to the development of a particular religious cult perpetuating this false worship, as did certain rulers.[465] Following this, the demons re-directed the worship to themselves,[466] elevating their status and position, with no focus other than themselves.[467] In Augustine's thinking, the demons vie with each other to receive this worship,[468] all the while Satan as their head being pleased with the various deceptions being enacted.[469] As a consequence of this interaction, humanity is enslaved to its desires and the associated demons. Such enslavement is just punishment for such sin.[470]

As Wiebe notes, Augustine was not arguing anything new as he endorsed and propagated Euhemeristic thinking. However, what was perhaps new in his thinking is the totalizing approach he developed—one which was able to cover all the gods of the world.[471] Wiebe goes on to argue that Augustine's Euhemeristic explanation of idolatry is not just aetiological: it also helps explain the relationships (specifically resemblances) between peoples and their particular demons/gods.[472] When certain people choose to worship heroes revered for particular accomplishments, specific desires seem to be "enthroned" in the process. Demons play a significant role in the development of false religion among the masses in Augustine's thinking, and different kinds of worship can be explained because of the varied first steps towards idolatry.

Turning to other early church beliefs, Augustine agreed with the vast majority of the church concerning the corporeality of the demons,[473] and he appealed to Ephesians 2:2 concerning their habitat.[474]

2.2. Influence 2: Philosopher and Pagan Religion

Apuleius's[475] demonology has been considered a significant influence on Augustine, not just in the development of his demonology, but also in affecting his Christology.[476] Of particular importance is Apuleius's theory of demonic mediation, my focus in what follows.

A key difference between Augustine's demonology and that of Plato and the Platonists is that for Augustine, as for early Christians, the demons were not positive, or a mixed bag, but only evil.[477] They could hardly be otherwise, given Augustine's understanding of their being fallen angels, and his belief that the Bible only speaks of demons as evil.[478] He traced the etymology of the word *demon* to the Greek, with a root meaning knowledge, though stressing that such knowledge is without love.[479] In order to support his own argument for the evil character of demons, Augustine made much of the absence of reference to any positive moral characteristics in Apuleius's comments about demons.[480]

Augustine argued for the logical impossibility of Apuleius's demonic mediation theories. He believed that part of his problem was a misreading of Plato, namely misinterpretation of the idea that the gods have no dealings with men.[481] Location of the demons in spatial middle-ness (within the aerial between the aethereal and the earthly) does not facilitate mediation: this, Augustine argued, is one of the errors of Apuleius's theory.[482] Another error concerned the nature and qualities of these so-called mediators. These are all wrong: the mediators share the wrong natures or qualities (with the to-be-mediated parties) to effect mediation.[483] Augustine mocks the illogical argument.[484] Not being good themselves, being "governed by their passions,"[485] how could demons mediate between the good gods and sinful humanity? This all leads up to a powerful assertion explaining how Christ's mediation solves all the problems he believes to exist within the Platonist demonic schemes:[486] "But distinct from these [wicked angels] is the good Mediator, Who, in contrast to their immortality and misery, chose to be mortal for a time yet had the power to continue blessed in eternity."[487] And also: "Rather, we need a Mediator Who is united with us in our lowest estate by bodily mortality, yet Who, by virtue of the immortal righteousness of His spirit, always remains on high: not in terms of temporal location, but because of the excellence of His resemblance to God."[488] The movement from failed demonic mediation to the perfect mediation of Christ is striking, hence the point noted earlier concerning Apuleius's influence not only on Augustine's demonology, but also in affecting the development of his Christology.[489]

Before closing this section on philosophical influences, a brief comment on shared language between Augustine and Apuleius is warranted. Firstly, mediation in Augustine's thinking is between God and man. In Apuleius's thinking, on the other hand, it is between man and the gods, the supreme God being out of the picture.[490] Secondly, although Augustine agreed with Apuleius on the aethereal location[491] and bodily nature of the demons, he disagreed on the reasons for these being as they were: he believed the location to be a result of the fall,[492] and the bodily nature to be necessary, in part, to suffer hellfire.[493] While then, there is some kind of corresponding Apuleius-inspired framework in Augustine's thinking, not only is the content thoroughly Christianized, the framework itself is significantly adapted to the Christian faith.

2.3. Human-Demonic Interaction in Religions in Augustine's Thought

While the demons are, in some senses, omnipresent in Augustine's thinking,[494] they do not have the teeth that they may initially seem to.[495] There are, I believe, two main reasons for this. The first is Augustine's high view of the sovereignty of God: God is the Lord of the demons, who simply carry out his will.[496] Indeed, Ivanovska goes so far as to state, "one might argue, Augustine's common recourse to God's providential permission to explain the ultimate cause of each and every demonic act conceptually trumps over whatever theoretical demonology he had."[497] Augustine had no room at all in his thinking for the idea of demons striding throughout the earth and intercepting and molesting humans against their wills—a position that he could not tolerate given his strong opposition to the dualistic materialism of Manichaeism.[498]

The second reason for Augustine's disempowering of the demons (in their relation to humankind) is to be found in his view on the origin of evil. The angels fell because of a turn to self (rather than to remain fixed on God), the cause of this being pride.[499] In his more mature thought Augustine concluded that human sin is prior to any demonic deception or intervention, which simply facilitates and endorses what might be called *the fellowship of the proud*.[500] Augustine minimized, one could even go so far as to say excludes, any significant role of the devil in the fall of Adam and Eve.[501] While he certainly emphasizes the deception of demons, this is the deception of ends, what they can actually offer, rather than the deception of orientation, which in Augustine's thinking, is essentially already aligned with that of fallen humankind.[502] Demons can only deceive a human with a disposition to be so deceived, and the heart and root of this proclivity (both for humanity and fallen angels) is pride.[503] Of pride, Augustine comments:

> If instead [the mind] gets in its own way, so to speak, and it pleases it to imitate God perversely so that it wills to enjoy its own power, it becomes lesser to precisely the extent that it desires itself to be greater. And this is: "Pride is the beginning of all sin" [Sir. 10:15 (10:13 RSV)] and "The beginning of pride is when one departs from God" [Sir. 10:14 (10:12 RSV)].[504]

As Wiebe notes, "Despite their differing actions, Adam and Eve commit the same sin; despite their different natures, humans and angels fall with the same pride."[505] This being so, there is something of an alliance of common loves (away from God) between the fallen angels and humankind in Augustine's thought.[506] Indeed, as Brown states, humans attract the demons they want in Augustine's thinking.[507] Augustine comments on the alliance between the Platonists and demons in the following way: "For in their quest they have been lifted up by pride in their high culture, inflating their chest rather than beating their breast. Through an affinity in heart they attracted to themselves as associates and allies of their pride 'the powers of the air' (Eph. 2:2) who deluded them with magical powers."[508] The common love of self present within both demons and fallen humans results in human bondage to demons.[509] While Augustine was keen to place the origin of evil in the will,[510] he did not hesitate to speak of a resulting human slavery to demons.

In terms of the specifics of this relationship, Augustine portrayed it as one of interactive community,[511] operating through a common language of magic.[512] Community interactions were not just evident in temples, but through the theatre, and games, etc.[513] Humans would fulfill demonic demands, practice various rites, offer sacrifice and pray:[514] demons, on their part, would answer in non-miraculous oracles (see below),[515] and create illusions (facilitated in part, by virtue of their airy bodies).[516] Augustine considered this community, its language and signs, a demonic perversion or parody of true Christian community.[517] The consequences of engagement with such a community are not only negative for the individual, but also devastating for society.[518]

2.4. Explaining Demonically Inspired Prophecy

Augustine spent considerable time explaining how it was possible that through pagan divination (a key element of Graeco-Roman religion) the future could be foretold.[519] He did not challenge the basic facticity of such prophecy, but radically re-interpreted its mechanics from a Christian perspective.[520] Foundational to his theory was the exclusion of direct divine involvement.[521] Having established this, he argued that the bodily nature of demons enabled such prophecy to occur.[522] In Augustine's thought, the demons' bodies give them significant advantages over humans: speed, longevity and "acute senses."[523] Pagan prophecy was due either to demons foretelling their own plans, or due to their ability to read signs, or to their overhearing the plans of angels and God (by God's permission).[524] Such foretelling is, therefore, not miraculous in any way, and prophetic fulfilment in no way signals divine involvement or endorsement. Augustine also made the point that such foretelling was essentially uncertain: accurate foretelling could be thwarted or stopped.[525] When such was the case, the demons blamed the middlemen (e.g., soothsayers) in order to retain their standing.[526]

On the basis of the material discussed above, it is clear that demons play a significant role in false religion in Augustine's thinking. But did Augustine consider the above demonic involvement to be applicable to all humans and all human religion?

Dupont has argued that Augustine differentiated two types of men—the religious, who practice magic, and the philosophers.[527] There are occasions where Augustine speaks of such a distinction, as will be discussed later (in section 4.5). In the two major sections that follow, I consider this distinction and examine how the philosophers may have differed from the masses. I examine two different possibilities for such a difference. The first of these is whether Augustine considered philosophers or sages to be a special subset of humanity (outside Israel) who had learned truth of God through the ancient faith, and because of this knew more of God than the religious masses. The second is to consider whether the philosophers (or at least some of them) had, in fact, learned of God through Word of God (*Logos*) illumination.

3. The *Prisca Theologia*

Augustine engages with a number of the non-biblical sages or ancient theologians in his writings. In what follows I provide an overview and analysis of his engagement with Plato, Hermes and the Sibyls.[528] Before doing so, I outline his argument for a Hebrew-unilinear view of revelation.[529]

3.1. Augustine's Hebrew Unilinear View of Revelation

Augustine generally considered it necessary to argue against the legitimacy of the idea of the presence of other streams of religious wisdom and truth outside Israel.[530] To do this, he forwarded four arguments. The first was to advocate the historical primacy of Hebrew wisdom. In *City of God* 18:37 ff., he argued that Pythagoras was alive at the time of the Jewish deliverance from captivity (and not earlier). This being so, he believed the views of those who advocated the greater historicity of Pythagoras (whom he respected, to a certain extent) to Moses to be groundless. The theological poets—Orpheus, Linus, and Musaeus—are dated *after* Moses, whom Augustine calls "our true student of God." Having acknowledged that Moses learned from the Egyptians, he goes back to Abraham as the final appeal to Hebrew primacy of wisdom, dating Isis's mother to the time of Abraham's grandchildren (and not before).[531]

The historical argument was not, however, the only one that Augustine pursued, in his philosophical historiography. The second relates to fields of knowledge, and the need to differentiate these. Augustine admits of the presence of ancient Egyptian learning—and Moses's learning from it. However, he stated that this was primarily focused on astronomy (and other unnamed fields) which, he argued, is not true wisdom at all. He traces the beginning of meaningful wisdom in the Egyptian tradition to Hermes, whom he believes was the great-grandson of Atlas, who himself was a contemporary of Moses.[532]

Thirdly, in his uncompleted commentary on Romans, Augustine stated that Gentile writings are unreliable (even if they include some reference to the coming of Christ), because although they may occasionally contain truth, at the same time what they say is "so very full of superstitious idolatry."[533] In his own words, the different philosophers were "able to perceive a certain amount of truth in the midst of all their false opinions."[534] This included not only truths about God, but also about ethics. What was lacking in their thinking and knowledge was a complete picture of Christ: "Yet they knew not the end to which all these things are to be referred and the rule by which they are to be judged."[535] As Hooker notes, Augustine seemed to believe that the Apostle Paul limited the idea of inspiration to the Hebrew prophets in his comments on the beginning of the Epistle to the Romans.[536]

The fourth element of his argument for the veracity of the unique Hebrew stream of wisdom is the lack of agreement among (non-Hebrew) philosophers, in contrast to the agreement that is present among the various biblical authors.

3.2. Plato[537]

In *City of God* 8:11 Augustine alludes to the fact that previous Christian philosophers/theologians had appealed to the idea of the historical dependence of Plato on Jeremiah for the correct insights he had of God. Augustine had, at an earlier period of time, held this position, but corrected this in his *Retractions*[538] on the basis of a careful consideration of the dates involved—which he outlines in this section of the *City of God*.[539] However, rather than simply discarding the theory, he sought to rescue its plausibility by hypothesizing that it might have been possible that a later interpreter helped Plato study the Hebrew text, and he goes on to provide three justifications in support of this hypothesis. Referring to the *Timaeus* he notes similarities between its account of creation and the Genesis account and explains why parts of the former may look rather different from the Genesis account because of Plato's understanding of the elements. The second justification offered is Plato's description of the philosopher as the lover of God—which he considers correct. The final, and in his opinion the most significant support, comes from his understanding of Exodus 3:14. Commenting on the verse: "I am who am; and thou shalt say to the children of Israel, He Who is sent me unto you," Augustine argues that the truth present in this statement, namely that God is immutable, and created things are not, is a point that Plato also held and taught—and no one else but Plato.

Given the climactic point provided in this argument, the reader is surprised to find that in the next chapter of Book 8 of the *City of God*, Augustine begins with the thoroughly anti-climactic statement that it did not really matter what the source was for the knowledge that Plato had—whether by the explanation he had just argued, i.e., a somewhat modified dependence view, or through the witness of creation (referring in support of this idea to Rom 1:20). How to understand the language used by Augustine in this particular reference is contested. Haines's interpretation is that Augustine was indeed arguing for the latter case, and not Jeremiah dependence.[540] I suggest that support for this interpretation is found within the wider context (which Haines does not appeal to), specifically in *City of God* 8.9. After discussing the superiority of Platonic thought on the goal of man—to enjoy God—he closes the section by noting that not all who have thought similarly go by the name of Platonist—referring positively to those who follow Pythagoras. He then goes on to state that philosophers from different geographical areas may have been aware of and taught some Platonic truths. As O'Daly comments, "Any philosophers who held these views should receive the same accolade. It is the content of philosophy which counts. . . . Augustine is implying that there is a natural link between Christian beliefs and Platonist principles. *Other philosophers may have come to accept these principles or work them out independently* [emphasis mine]."[541] I suggest that this interpretation of "independent" awareness of God and the geographical spread of truth adds weight to the view that Augustine did not really support the traditional "borrowing" argument. Romans 1:20 was, for Augustine, able to account for the knowledge he believed to be present in Plato, while at the same time he seemed not to want to dismiss entirely a traditional Christian "borrowing" view.

3.3. Hermes

I suggest that Augustine's understanding and interpretation of Hermes is particularly helpful in getting to grips with his thought on false religion. As mentioned above, Augustine drew on Hermes in support of a Euhemeristic view of idolatry. However, Hermes was, in many ways, a problematic figure for Augustine, given his early Manichaeism and Hermes's favored status among this sect.[542]

Augustine does not totally dismiss Hermes and what he had to say: some of Hermes's statements can be useful "for the refutation of pagan error."[543] However, as Hooker notes, it would not have been in Augustine's best interests to have given much credibility to Hermes, given the more pressing pro-Old Testament polemic he employed in his engagement with Faustus.[544] Of particular interest here, is how Augustine believed Hermes, at times, to be "useful."

Augustine suggests that what truth there is found in Hermes, along with other basically unreliable extra-biblical authorities he refers to,[545] is because of divine compulsion.[546] He does not elaborate what he means by this in this particular context, but elsewhere he speaks of a very different source: he speaks of a "deceiving spirit"[547] and "evil spirit"[548] and the "grief of demons"[549] being responsible for the insights Hermes had.[550] Hooker has suggested other possibilities for the speaking of truth: namely a kind of inspiration, or knowledge gained through natural revelation.[551]

It is important to note that Augustine explicitly rejected the possibility of Holy Spirit inspiration for the true things which Hermes spoke.[552] While stating that the false part of Hermes's teaching (i.e., mourning the punishment of demons) was inspired by demons, he also stated that the true parts which he spoke, were, ultimately, from God.[553] This being so, it would seem best to interpret Augustine as saying that demons seem to speak truth (by compulsion of God) though typically they speak error (by their nature). This compulsion is differentiated from true inspiration. This interpretation seems to maintain the correct balance needed in handling the various comments.

Augustine believed Hermes to be an example of those whom Paul spoke of in Romans 1—knowing God, but not glorifying him as God.[554] He argued that the demonic strategy behind soothsayers speaking truth was to "win over even the faithful friends of God." However, what God actually achieved through this, was the opposite: "But God acted thus [i.e., compelled truth to be spoken] through those who did not know, in order that the truth might resound in every place, as a help to the faithful, and as a witness against the godless."[555] Accordingly, the idea of the demons being mouthpieces of God is clearly evident in Augustine's thinking—with two results ensuing: the strengthening of the church, and a testimony against those who were held in subjection to them. I will discuss the idea of truth within false religious systems in more detail in chapter 6.

3.4. The Sibyls

"Sibyls are always females, and always prophets: beyond that, they are very hard to pin down."[556] So states Hadas towards the beginning of his overview of the reception of the Sibyls in the early church. He notes their indeterminate locations, history and number, and questions whether any of the twelve books of Greek poetry within the *Oracula Sibyllina* contain any of the original prophecies, noting that many are probably Jewish and Christian forgeries.[557] In terms of their history, Hadas documents the loss of the Sibylline books in 83 BC,[558] and the subsequent efforts to gather versions of them from around the Mediterranean. What was gathered was subsequently checked and endorsed or rejected as forgeries by fifteen prominent men, the final accepted oracles placed in temples of prominence, being Roman state property. Consultation was typically required in crises and for religious guidance—though less so later on in the history of the Empire.[559]

While Augustine was fairly consistent in his suspicion and ultimate rejection of Hermes, he seemed to undergo a change of position concerning the Sibyls[560]—more accurately one of them—the Erythraean Sibyl.[561] Augustine was aware of the Christian reception of the Sibyls, and the tradition of the spoiling of the Egyptians (i.e., the idea of taking of what was good from the pagan world and claiming it for Christians), and the important role of Lactantius in propagating this "appropriating" viewpoint.[562] Augustine was, initially at least, cautious concerning the status of the Sibyls, grouping them together with Hermes in his engagement with Faustus and using similarly careful and suspicious language in his commentary on Romans and in *Letter 258*.[563] The specific language used there accords with other comments about how truth might be present in a pagan's writings (see above, section 3.3).

However, in *City of God* 18.23 Augustine seemed to adopt a far more positive stance to a particular Sibyl. He provides the reason for his about face in a quite lengthy biographical sketch regarding his first-hand engagement with a particular Sibylline poem. The actual poem contains references to judgment, righteousness, redemption, resurrection, and is anti-idolatry in nature, although, as Hooker notes, Augustine makes no reference to the content—only the somewhat hidden christological prophecy contained therein.[564] Of critical importance for Augustine is the unmixed nature of the poem (cf. his comments on Hermes and others, and the basic problem of inconsistency in pagan authors noted earlier). Given this fact, he concluded that the inspiration for the poem could only be from God:

> Now this Sibyl—whether the Sibyl of Erythrae or, as some prefer to believe, of Cumae—has nothing in the whole of her poem, of which this is only a very small part, pertaining to the worship of false gods, or of gods made by men. On the contrary, she speaks out against such gods and their worshippers so forcefully that she is, it seems, to be included among those who belong to the City of God.[565]

Following this claim, Augustine refers to additional prophecies about Christ from the Sibyls as documented by Lactantius, in support of his position.[566] What is particularly interesting to note is that on the basis of this one poem (albeit with some additional support from Lactantius), Augustine made such an unqualified claim, rather than suggesting occasional compulsion for the utterance (cf. the Hermes discussion above).

Though acknowledging a change in his stance on the Sibyls, Hadas is keen to show that Augustine is cautious in his about face, noting the language "seems to be" and also the indeterminacy of the identity of the Sibyl in Augustine's words, quoted above.[567] Hooker also notes that the endorsement does not extend to putting the text on the same level as Hebrew prophecy.⁵⁶⁸ Augustine seemed to be aware of the idea held in some pagan circles that the Sibylline oracles had been fabricated by Christians.⁵⁶⁹ Indeed, he documented the key advantage of Hebrew prophecy to be that it cannot be charged to have been changed by Christians—unlike the Sibyls.⁵⁷⁰ Accordingly, Hadas believes that Augustine would actually have been quite happy to relinquish appeals to the Sibyl, suggestive of a far more ambivalent relationship to this particular Sibylline text, despite the language used in embracing it.⁵⁷¹ The motivation for the claim may have been apologetic-polemic, but the reference, when considered alongside the wider thought of Augustine, remains puzzling.⁵⁷² Having provided an overview of the key ancient theologians and the *prisca theologia* tradition, I now turn to consider Word of God (*Logos*) illumination in Augustine's thinking and the relationship between it and religion.

4. Word of God Illumination

As noted earlier, Augustine suggested that Plato and other philosophers knew what they did about God either from borrowing, or from the testimony of creation—citing Romans 1:20 in support of this view. In section 3.2, I argued that the latter interpretation seems more plausible. As will be noted below, Augustine used Romans 1:20 to help him understand the Johannine prologue, which I consider in some detail in this section. It is important to highlight that Augustine's dependence on Paul in helping in the interpretation of other Scripture has been documented by a number of scholars.⁵⁷³

It would be naïve in the extreme to believe that there is consensus on what Augustine means by *illumination*.⁵⁷⁴ Much has been written on this subject and a number of different views have been proposed.⁵⁷⁵ Indeed, some have argued that the problem of illumination in Augustine's thinking is unsolvable, due to the presence of intractable ideas in his thinking.⁵⁷⁶ My own focus in this chapter is, however, much narrower than this much larger subject, being limited to the idea of philosopher illumination as documented in the first three homilies of John's Gospel, and specifically the idea of true wisdom, *sapientia* and knowledge of God from this illumination, rather than *scientia* knowledge.

4.1. Overview of the Johannine Prologue Homilies

While Augustine was strongly polemical at times, a case has been made by some scholars that the Johannine homilies seem to be relatively free from this.[577] This being so, a careful interpretation of the homilies is, I suggest, particularly helpful in understanding the relationship between illumination and religion in Augustine's thought.

The prologue is considered to play a significant role in Augustine's Christology and also his interpretation of John's Gospel.[578] Within the prologue, John 1:1 and John 1:14 are considered to be key verses for Augustine.[579] When discussing the incarnation, he stresses that the Word was already in the world,[580] but at the same time, he clarifies that the eternal Word is not a created being.[581] He argues that a new coming of the Word was needed, because his presence in the world was not noticed—because of stupidity, blindness and wickedness.[582] The darkness of the world is equated with "unbelievers, people who are without justice, wicked, rapacious, avaricious, lovers of the world!"[583] The fact that there is darkness (in humankind) does not mean that there is no light, but rather humans, "being darkness," do not recognize it.[584]

Augustine writes that the illumination of which John speaks in the early verses of this Gospel is of men rather than of cattle.[585] Specifically, the light is the possession of, "a rational mind, with which wisdom may be perceived."[586] Augustine differentiates the one light from the light of minds, "The light of minds is above minds and surpasses all minds."[587] There are then two lights in his thought—the human mind being a reflection of the divine.

In an extended reference to "some philosophers," Augustine states that they looked for the creator through creation, and he did not criticize them for doing so—as God can be found this way—referencing Romans 1:20–22 in support of this.[588] Indeed, Augustine stresses the reality of the knowledge that is then grasped.[589] However, he goes on, in the same vein as the Apostle Paul, to state that this knowledge does not result in true worship, but rather a turning away from what has been seen/touched. He attributes this movement to pride: "They saw where they were to go, but, being ungrateful to the one who set what they saw before them, they wanted to take all the credit for the sight themselves; and, grown thus proud, they lost what they saw and turned away from there to idols and images and to the cult of demons, worshiping a creature and disdaining the creator."[590]

For Augustine, the Word gives insight, but the error of the philosophers is to give themselves the credit for this. Where pride begins, idolatry results, and the initial seeing or grasping of the creator leads to a despising of the one initially seen. What, exactly, was grasped in this illumination? Part of what Augustine argued is the truth that creation was made by the Son. Augustine believed this teaching to be clearly present in some philosophers' books: "So then, those about whom he said, who though they had come to know God, saw what John says, because all things were made through the Word of God. In fact, they found such statements in the books of philosophers, as is the fact that God has an only begotten Son through whom all things are (Rom 11:36)."[591]

Augustine questions the ability of the philosopher[592] who can "touch that which is"[593] to actually attain the same. It is only the incarnation of the Word that enables steadfastness in the attainment of illumination: "Thus, so that we might also have the means to go, the one we were longing to go to came here from there. And what did he make? A wooden raft for us to cross the sea on. For no one can cross the sea of this world unless carried over it on the cross of Christ."[594]

Augustine believed it be a terrible irony that the Word which some of the philosophers saw from afar is the same (though incarnate) Word which can convey them across the sea separating them from the homeland, whom they reject:

> They refused to hold on to the humility of Christ, the boat in which they would safely reach what they were able to see from a long way off; and they were disgusted by the cross of Christ. The sea has to be crossed, and you disdain the cross? O proud wisdom! You mock the crucified Christ; he is the one you have seen from a long way off—In the beginning was the Word, and the Word was with God.[595]

Augustine references Paul (1 Cor 2:14) in stating that this illumination (being spiritual) is not properly apprehended by the non-spiritual.[596] While the vision of the homeland can be glimpsed by the philosophers, it may not actually be seen by Christians, who may just believe, and arrive there safely.[597]

In what follows I consider the *via-patria* distinction more closely, as well as the turn to religion for philosophers in Augustine's thought.

4.2. Considering The *Via* and the *Patria*

Augustine made references to the image of the homeland, the sea and the bark of Christ in other texts and I consider these in what follows, and how they help shed more light on this important issue raised in the prologue. In the *City of God* Augustine quotes Plotinus's paraphrase of the *Ennead.*, I, 6, 8 and I, 2, 3, going on to challenge his reader to recognize the need to be like God to arrive at God: "What has happened to that saying of Plotinus: 'We must fly, therefore, to our beloved fatherland, where dwells both our Father and all else. Where is the ship, then, and how are we to fly? We must become like God.'"[598] Miller believes that Augustine connected this idea of the need to become like God with aspects of Plato's famous cave metaphor (in particular, the "vision of the good, attained by the intellect alone"),[599] and that he went on to develop the image of the return to God (by way of the cross), present in the prologue homily, referenced earlier.[600]

I believe that there are three points of particular interest in the homeland analogy: the first is Augustine's dual illumination perspective. The second is that the focus is not on the vision, but on incarnational mediation: only Christ can heal the will.[601] The third is the opening of the way to the homeland to all—by faith. I consider each of these in turn, below.

Do the Platonists see the homeland? Do they have any true *sapiential* knowledge of God? Is there any unregenerate knowledge of God in Augustine's thought? Scholars are greatly divided on this question. Gioia[602] and Schumacher[603] do not believe that Augustine really allows for this, whereas Demarest,[604] Nash,[605] Haines[606] and Aucoin[607] do. The former group argue that a lack of love,[608] and faith[609] negate the possibility of such knowledge. Some of the latter group appeal to a kind of common grace to allow it,[610] while others have appealed to Augustine's doctrine of humans being made in the image of God,[611] or the theory of memory in his epistemology to argue for some real knowledge of God.[612]

What is clear is that in the metaphor Augustine speaks of three knowledges: a lack of knowledge or rejection of knowledge (of Christ the mediator); mis-knowledge or vague knowledge (e.g., seeing from afar) and finally knowledge (without qualification). While it is tempting (logically) to let the lack or mis-knowledge comments "overpower" the unqualified knowledge statements (especially given Augustine's understanding of the relationship between love and true knowledge),[613] he seemed keen to allow some true knowledge to stand.[614] This idea is not only present in this metaphor, but also in his attack on Platonists who should have known better, given what they *knew* as I discuss later in section 4.7. The charge of inconsistency levelled against the philosophers by Augustine, as noted by Cavadini,[615] Edwards,[616] and Ando,[617] makes little sense if all knowledge is mis-knowledge—though this is not to deny the fact that knowledge *becomes* mis-knowledge.

Cushman, who like Nash, Haines, and Demarest argues for some knowledge of God, differentiates two kinds of illumination in Augustine's thinking—that of the Eternal Word and that of the Incarnate Word.[618] Cushman argues that for Augustine the gentiles benefit greatly from Eternal Word illumination.[619] Miller also makes the same distinction as Cushman between two different *Logos* illuminations in Augustine's thinking.[620]

Helpful comment on the theological detail of these two illuminations is found in *Sermon 341*.[621] There, Augustine considered Christ to be described in three different ways in Scripture: firstly as God, secondly as the head of the church (as the human-God mediator), and thirdly, as the head and body of the church.[622] In Augustine's interpretation, Christ as God is the primary focus of the Apostle John at the beginning of the prologue.[623] In the role of God, the Eternal Word does not mediate; indeed, Augustine explicitly denies this possibility. In the *Confessions* he stated, "It is as man that he is mediator. He is not midway as Word; for the Word is equal to God and 'God with God' (John 1:1), and at the same time there is but one God."[624] In commenting on the word becoming flesh, Augustine recognizes that the Eternal Word continues his ruling of the world and his abiding presence with the Father (even at the incarnation).[625] In the homilies, Augustine clearly differentiated the incarnate Word's presence or absence in the world with the discarnate Word's omnipresence—indeed this distinction is fundamental to his homeland analogy.[626] This being so, while Augustine identified the way and the goal as the same (this often commented on in the literature), he also clearly differentiated the two—a point which is fundamental to the metaphor.

Returning once more to the ascent picture, and focusing now on the relationship between the will and reason in it, like Miller and Cushman, Brachtendorf argues that the homily vision suggests a dependence and adaptation of the Plato cave metaphor, noting a number of similarities between them.[627] He believes that placing the sea between the valley and the peak is Augustine's rather unique contribution, or adjustment, to existing ascent metaphors. In his reading, this additional obstacle (other than that of ascent) was added to reflect the distinction in Augustine's thought between "intellectual vision" and "willed adhesion to God."[628] Bractendorf points to passages in the *Confessions* in which Augustine speaks of the divided will, and the problem of the will.[629] Augustine was, in his own words, "too weak"[630] to enjoy the vision of God: in Augustine's thinking, the sinful will, pride and "the darknesses of . . .[the] soul,"[631] are not adequately taken into account in the Platonic vision of ascent.[632] Simply put, intellectual insight does not translate into living the blessed/happy life, because it has no "therapeutic competence"[633] in Augustine's thinking. In other words, one can know the truth (though fleetingly), but not love it.[634] For Augustine, true philosophy must do more than simply inform. In the words of Gilson, it must involve "an act of adherence to the supernatural order which frees the will from the flesh through grace and the mind from scepticism through revelation."[635] As LaChance suggests, Augustine may well be speaking from his own experience in his thinking in this particular homily,[636] and he certainly was in *Confessions* 7.20.26 where the same metaphor is alluded to. Accordingly, it seems that in employing this image Augustine was not averse to believing in some kind of (albeit transient) philosopher knowledge of the Word, the sinful will *not* precluding some knowledge of God, while at the same time, arguing that this knowledge is only transient and not enough for fallen man.

The second important element to note in this vision is the focus on the *via*—the mediator—who is the means of crossing the sea, namely Christ and his cross (an offensive means of achieving true beatific vision for the philosophers). A number of scholars have suggested that the incarnation, or certain aspects of it, is *the* hermeneutical key to Augustine's approach to John's Gospel.[637] Furthermore, a strong case can be made that the issue of mediation lies at the heart of Augustine's critique of Platonism: presenting a goal, but no effective means for arriving at it.[638] Cameron notes that Christ being *the way* became a significant leitmotif in Augustine's thinking (only) after 396 AD. He suggests that Augustine was initially reluctant to capitalise on this role of Christ due to Manichean misuse of it, but points to his increased employment of the mantra over time.[639] The incarnate mediator is able to achieve Plotinus's goal of flying to the country, being both human and divine, but he does this by means of crossing the sea, not through the air, as the incarnate mediator. As noted in section 2.2, this mediation is fundamentally different to

Augustine's understanding of the Platonic demonic mediation schemes, solving all the problems inherent within them.

The final significant departure from the Platonic ascent image is the way Augustine opens the ascent/way to God to all. Brachtendorf believes that the image Augustine paints is meant to reject intellectual elitism: those who do not apprehend the truths the philosophers know can still make the journey back to God—by means of embracing the cross.[640] Augustine was not impressed that the philosophers had no time for the masses—and specifically noted this neglect.[641] Augustine repeats, on numerous occasions, the universal reach of Christ's work.[642] Fiedrowicz contrasts the way of reason with the way of authority in Augustine's thinking. The latter kind of knowledge (the church's teaching) could simply be followed by the uneducated.[643]

While, in some places, Augustine stressed the knowledge the (Neo) Platonists had, at times he de-emphasized it. The most obvious way he does the latter in the prologue homilies is by making their knowledge extraneous for Christians to possess. This is made clear in his grouping of humanity into three categories: the great minds, the little ones and the proud philosophers.[644] Of the first, St. John is the exemplar—he sees the divine, and clings to the cross.[645] He is in the best position. In Brachtendorf's words "the great" are those who, "Through philosophy . . . possess the highest form of knowledge, and through religion their will is entirely oriented towards God."[646] The great have two things in common with the little—the vehicle of the cross as a means of crossing the sea, and the same destination. The little ones, however, do not see the vision.[647] The proud are the (Neo)Platonists. They see God, but do not have the humility to acknowledge the incarnation. While they grasp metaphysical truths,[648] they reject the incarnation, a historical fact which must be believed.[649] The overlap between the first and the third classes of humanity is the vision of the Eternal Word: the difference is the response to the Word made flesh. In *Confessions* 7, Augustine goes one by one through what the philosophers know and what they do not know.[650] The knowledge of God they have is ultimately made useless by the knowledge they do not have.[651]

Having considered the *via-patria* picture in some detail, I now focus on one other part of the Johannine Prologue homily, and the relationship between illumination and religion.

4.3. The Relationship between Illumination and Religion

Having noted the place for transient illumination of some philosophers in Augustine's thought, in this section I seek to examine the relationship between this illumination and religion, as documented in *Homily* 2.4. In speaking of the philosophers (without qualification) Augustine states, "They saw where they were to go, but, being ungrateful to the one who set what they saw before them, they wanted to take all the credit for the sight themselves; and, grown thus proud, they lost what they saw and turned away from there to idols and images and to the cult of demons, worshiping a creature and disdaining the creator."[652] Another translation of the latter part of this text is: "And having become proud, they lost what they saw and were turned from it to idols and images and to the cults of the demons to adore creation and to despise the creator."[653]

There are, I believe, three points of particular interest in this extract. The first of these is the turning. Why the turning occurs is not specified, although possibilities would include public opinion or pressure, pride (already noted in the sentence), demons, or the attractions of false religion. Augustine discusses all, in various places, and I provide a brief overview of the different possibilities in what follows.

Concerning the first (public pressure), Augustine notes this fear in *City of God* 10.3.[654] Commenting on similar texts (*Contra Faustus* 13.15 and *City of God* 10.11) Marenbon believes that Augustine did not really believe philosophers to be truly complicit with the masses in their polytheism: their response was purely expedient, due to a kind of pressure.[655] The problem in applying this particular interpretation to the passage in focus here is that it fails to account for the latter part of the statement: the philosophers *really* engage in false worship. I interact further with Marenbon's view in section 4.4, below.

The second possible factor that could be responsible for the turning is pride—already mentioned as a key factor at the beginning of the quotation. It is clear that pride plays a powerful role in Augustine's anthropology and demonology, as noted throughout this chapter. Turning to the role of demons, I have discussed this involvement in some detail in section 2. What should be remembered at this point is that particular demons would enthrone themselves and be enthroned by the particular vices of their adherents—and it is pride that is clearly in focus in this text. Indeed, Augustine makes this relationship explicit in his discussion of philosophers in *Confessions* 1.42.67: "For in their[656] quest they have been lifted up by pride in their high culture, inflating their chest rather than beating their breast. Through an affinity in heart they attracted to themselves as associates and allies of their pride 'the powers of the air' (Eph. 2:2) who deluded them with magical powers." In Augustine's thinking a very strong relationship holds between human pride and demons.[657]

One final possible reason for turning is the idea of the attraction of false religion. In discussing Augustine's engagement with Porphyry, Wilken argues that Augustine sees religion essentially as a distraction, and hence it could be considered responsible for the turning in the statement under consideration. Wilken believes that Augustine considered "material offerings and lesser gods" to have distracted Porphyry from his ascent to the true God.[658]

Having considered the idea of turning, the second major point of interest in this extract from *Homily* 2.4 is the new focus of philosophers, post-enlightenment, on creation, rather than the creator. As noted above, in section 1.3, in the discussion on false religions, the move from worship of the creator to creation (in various guises) forms a key part of Augustine's theology of religions. In Augustine's mind, different types of creation worship were more or less reprehensible. He does not specify the object in the passage under consideration—which could, theoretically, range from the world soul to animals.

The third comment of interest here in *Homily* 2.4 is the *means* by which creation is adored, namely demonic mediation. In the light of the distinction noted earlier (that of two fundamental errors in religion: the object worshipped and means employed in worship), what Augustine describes here is worship of a moderate evil, i.e., the creature or creation, by means which are singularly reprehensible to him (as discussed earlier), namely idols and the involvement of the demonic, although the particular cultus is not described. Whether this description covers all Platonic philosopher worship is a key issue I discuss further, in section 4.4, below.

In sum, this particular extract from *Homily* 2.4, when read in the wider context of the first three homilies, indicates the significant role of pride, and possibly demons and false religion in the loss of divine illumination and departure from the eternal Word. Pride is responsible for the turning away from true knowledge of God. False religion results from this, in an alliance with demons, and in a move to the worship of the created, away from the creator. Accordingly, there does seem to be some kind of relationship between illumination and religion—though not an immediately direct one, and certainly not a positive one—a point to which I return in section 4.7. It should be remembered that what Augustine describes above is the religion of philosophers, not the masses, who seem to live without any illumination at all in his thought.

4.4. Religion-less Philosophy?

In this section I consider whether false religion always results from transient philosopher illumination in Augustine's thought. I engage in some detail with Marenbon, who argues that this is not Augustine's main thought or concern.

Marenbon believes there to be three key elements to Augustine's understanding of the Platonists. The first is that they had some notion of the Christian God—a conclusion with which I concur, as noted above in section 4.2. The second is that "the best Platonists did not seriously and consistently believe in the polytheism they apparently indulged."[659] This idea was noted earlier in section 4.3, and is a key issue that I consider in more detail in what follows. Important to note here, before proceeding to the third element, is the distinction Marenbon makes between the Platonists as a class: some were guilty of polytheism, but another group were not—"the best Platonists." Thirdly, Marenbon notes the problem of pride and Augustine's constant references to it in discussing philosophers.[660] Such an emphasis also comes out clearly in the analysis of the prologue homilies above, and in earlier references in this chapter. It is the second of Marenbon's claims that I wish to focus on here, and the implications that Marenbon draws from it.

In support of his second point Marenbon refers to a number of statements from the Augustine corpus suggesting that there is a particular group of philosophers (in Augustine's thinking) who do not engage in false religion.[661] The idea that a distinction needs to be made between the religious polytheism of the masses and the essentially "non-popular religion" philosophers is not unique to Marenbon: Gioia and Dupont make similar comments.[662]

It is well known that Plato objected to aspects of pagan religion.[663] This is not the issue here. Rather, it is whether a certain sub-class of the philosophers were *essentially* monotheist and not *really* engaged in any kind of false worship in Augustine's thought, as Marenbon argues.[664] As described in the previous chapter, Justin certainly seemed to entertain this possibility.

Marenbon recognizes that the second element of his interpretation of Augustine's view of Platonism (one which, at the very least, minimizes the turn to false religion) is somewhat controversial. This is because it seems to oppose what he calls Augustine's "favourite text"[665] when discussing the philosophers—namely Romans 1:20-25—which ends with the fall into false religion. However, Marenbon believes there to be sufficient evidence to argue that Augustine modifies the focus and argument of Paul. His concluding comment on the discussion is as follows: "In short, when he considers Platonism, Augustine changes the emphasis of Paul's comment on natural theology, putting ideas of a reversion to polytheism into the background, and making a direct connection between pagan pride and the negative error of failing to see the incarnate Christ as the true mediator."[666]

It is worthwhile considering this statement carefully. Concerning the last part of it, as noted previously, the charge of rejection of the incarnate Christ is certainly part of the philosopher sketch which Augustine draws in the prologue homilies. But in stating this, Marenbon must be referencing AD philosophers—and so, logically, the focus here could be on figures such as Plotinus and Porphyry, rather than, for example, Pythagoras and Plato, indeed Marenbon states this clearly.[667] However, by adding Pythagoras and Plato as some of the exemplars of "best Platonists," alongside Porphyry,[668] Marenbon forms a group which on purely chronological grounds, cannot be considered to constitute those who reject the *incarnate* Christ. Had he limited the second part of the statement to Porphyry the argument would be valid—but he overextends the reference to Platonism. Augustine believes only some Platonists *reject* the incarnate Christ.

I now focus on the first part of Marenbon's interpretation, concerning the de-emphasis on polytheism in Augustine's thinking when considering some philosophers. Before considering it more carefully, it is helpful to step back from the claim to gain a little context. Marenbon's view seems to contradict material in the Johannine prologue homilies, in which pride leads to false religion for the philosopher (as documented above in section 4.1). Is Augustine inconsistent in his explanation of the steps to polytheism in the Johannine Homilies, when compared to what he says elsewhere? Did he develop in his thinking? Must we choose, can the difference be explained, or is Augustine actually just inconsistent? What evidence is there to support Marenbon's argument that there is a de-centring on the turn to false religion for philosophers (or at least a subset of them—specifically Pythagoras, Plato and Porphyry)?

In what follows I consider Marenbon's interpretation more closely, and I do so largely by returning to the key source text that he makes the most of, in support of the claim. To summarize my critique here, before providing the details for it, I will suggest that Marenbon fails to take into account three key issues in his argument. The first of these is Augustine's wider thought on continua in false religion, documented in section 1.3 above. The second is the polemical focus on contemporary popular demonic mediation which Augustine addressed in the *Sermon against the Pagans*. Third, I argue, contrary to Marenbon, that Augustine does not allow a philosophical natural theology monotheist position to stand, without it crashing down into polytheism. A critically important part of this argument is that the proud, apparently "mediator-less," philosophers still had their own mediators, but these were not the ones which Augustine needed to focus on or attack in his *Sermon against the Pagans*.

4.5. Considering *The Sermon against the Pagans*

In this section I consider the key text that Marenbon appeals to in support of his argumentation. This very long sermon, termed a filibuster by one scholar,[669] was delivered on New Year's day 404. The sermon contains sixty-three sections in Hill's translation. Approximately half way through it, Augustine seems to suggest a distinction between those who practice false religion and those who see no need for it:

> But of these people who hold down the truth of God in a lie there are two kinds. Some have entrusted themselves to their own virtue, have sought no helper, thinking their souls can be purified through philosophy, as though they needed no mediator. But we don't have to discuss these at present. What we are now going into action against is the sacrilegious sacred rituals of the pagans.[670]

Marenbon appeals to this, plus similar statements, to support his argument outlined in the previous section.

In considering this extract from the sermon, it should be noted that Augustine clearly has Paul's epistle to the Romans in mind here, in his language of suppression of truth (first sentence). Indeed, immediately prior to this quotation, towards the end of section 35 in the sermon, Augustine goes through a detailed exposition of Romans 1:25, focusing on the worship of the creature rather than the creator. This would suggest that Marenbon's use of this particular extract to support a movement away from Paul's theology to be, at face value, invalid. Furthermore, Augustine's reference to "these people" at the beginning of the section refers to those engaged in false worship of creatures and idols, in the previous section. While "these people" constitute two groups, the first should not be considered free of transferring false worship to creatures/creation. This co-textual evidence, I believe, begins to undermine Marenbon's argument.

While he recognizes the terrible sin of pride (as noted earlier), Marenbon, at the very least, suggests that the mediator-less class are in a somewhat *better* position than those who engage in sacrilegious acts in Augustine's thinking—at least in the implication that they are monotheists, and have not turned to multiple gods.[671] Even the expression "best Platonists" suggests this. There is some support for this view in this sermon. Augustine refers to a group, shortly after the extract provided above, who did not worship idols, nor involve themselves in Chaldean magic, stating that such must be understood and judged carefully, not discounting the possibility of genuine salvific revelation to them.[672] This certainly seems to be a significant distinction. However, to stop here (as Marenbon does) is problematic as those who depend on themselves, are not considered in a positive light at all by Augustine. In his thinking they are *also* being led astray by "that proud enemy of souls" though he does not mention sacrilegious rituals here. Augustine's final judgment on this group is that "It is indeed a great uncleanness of the unclean soul, thinking it can purify itself all on its own."[673] Contrary to the view of Marenbon, in some ways in Augustine's thinking, this "mediator-less" group are worse than those who seek some sort of mediation: the mediator seekers are not presumptuous and they want to be purified.[674] I suggest therefore, that while Augustine is indeed making distinctions, he is doing so solely in the area of false *religious* practice.

As is clear from the end of the quotation provided above from section 36 of *The Sermon against the Pagans*, Augustine focuses on the group who engage in sacrilegious (devilish) rites in the sermon. Indeed, Salzman categorizes the focus of the sermon to be anti-idolatry.[675] Some of those involved in these rites are philosophers.[676] The group that Augustine does *not* wish to focus on is, presumably, the one whose ideas are not so great a threat to his listeners. The exemplar of this group is Pythagoras.[677] Elsewhere in his writings, Augustine identified Pythagoras as a precursor to later Platonist philosophers.[678] Accordingly, we can say with some confidence that Augustine considers the seeming "non-mediating group" to be a subset of the Platonists, a set to be differentiated from other more modern Platonists who are severely compromised by their demonic mediation and theurgy.

Marenbon, as noted earlier, is keen to place Porphyry alongside Pythagoras and Plato in this particular subset of better Platonism. While recognizing Augustine's condemnation of Porphyry's engagement in theurgy,[679] Marenbon interprets Augustine to be saying that Porphyry (simply) went along with the crowds, but that he did not consider him a polytheist.[680] This interpretation of Porphyry and his grouping together with Plato and Pythagoras, is, I suggest, somewhat questionable, and I provide my justification for this judgment below.

It is true that Augustine appreciated elements of Porphyry's thinking, including his criticism of the reincarnation views of Plato,[681] the uselessness of sacrifices to the moon[682] and the idea of a universal way of salvation.[683] However, as I will note below, in the area of demonic mediation, while noting the vacillating and somewhat inconsistent nature of Porphyry's thinking,[684] rather than grouping him together with Plato and Pythagoras, he clearly paired him with Apuleius and those in the Chaldean demonology camp.[685] Why then did Augustine not deliver a knock-out blow on Porphyry? Simply, I suggest that such would have been counter-productive to his use of some of Porphyry's ideas to support his own positions elsewhere: Augustine's polemical approach was not inimical to such usage.

4.6. Platonic Religion in the *City of God*

To sum up the argument so far, I have suggested that a subset of the Platonists is indeed differentiated by Augustine from others (including some philosophers) who engage in sacrilegious rites. While Marenbon argues that these are not really polytheists, I have argued that the extract from the *Sermon against the Pagans* does not support such a reading: both the background context, and the comments that follow it do not seem to suggest the idea of the existence of a somewhat favored sub-set of religion-less philosophers in Augustine's thinking. I seek greater clarity on the subject of the religion of the "best Platonists" by turning to the most focused criticism of Platonism and its relationship to religion, as given in *City of God*, chapters 7–10. My goal in this section is to identify what Augustine understood the umbrella error of Platonic religion to be, while noting key distinctions within this.[686] In what follows I summarize some key points from this part of Augustine's works, before returning to the Marenbon claim.

As a group, the Platonists (and here the reference seems all embracing) are considered by Augustine to fit the pattern of behavior noted by Paul in Romans 1, namely that they worship creation rather than the creator.[687] Indeed in *City of God* 8:12 Augustine says that all Platonists (including Plotinus, Porphyry and Plato) "held that sacred rites should be performed in honour of many gods."[688] This is not the only time that he makes such a claim.[689] The general smear, however, is greatly refined as he proceeds to engage with a specific subset of Platonic philosophers.[690]

As he proceeds in his argument, Augustine clearly wishes to drive something of a wedge between Plotinus[691] and Plato on the one side, and Porphyry and Apuleius on the other when it comes to discussing demonic mediation.[692] At the same time, as the reference in the previous paragraph makes clear, he also wishes to keep them together, though for the sake of a different argument.

Of the two groups it is the latter pair (Apuleius and Porphyry) whom Augustine believes to be far from Plato in their demonic mediation beliefs, which he argues to be Chaldean rather than Platonic.[693] For Augustine, Chaldean religion is worse than Platonic religion. Apuleius and Porphyry search for demonic mediators; Plato is less perverse, but this certainly does not make him *just* a monotheist in Augustine's view, as Marenbon claims.[694]

In *City of God* 8.13 the issue of the *religions* of the Platonists is raised. In Augustine's thinking Plato considered the gods to be good,[695] and to have dealings with men.[696] He notes how Plato condemned the immoral gods of the theatre—a commendable action.[697] In observing this, he comments how far contemporary Platonists are from Plato on this point in their rejection of the idea that gods have dealings with men,[698] together with their acceptance of morally ambiguous demons to mediate between the gods and humans. Plato did not endorse such beliefs. The newer, illogical, and perverse turn to demons is contrasted with the older Platonism. This fact, I believe, is critical to remember, when considering Augustine's thinking in *The Sermon against the Pagans* referenced earlier.

Mediation was still there in Plato's thinking, as I note below, but is contrasted with Apuleius and Porphyry's more *overt* turn to the evil demonic and the practice of sacrilegious rites.

Augustine develops his argument as follows. He notes that some Platonists call angels demons while others might call them gods. He believes that if Plato's view is that the gods/angels are created, immortal, and blessed in their right relationship with God, then Plato agrees with Christians (and their view of the angels), despite the naming inconsistencies.[699] He goes on to discuss gods/good demons/angels, specifically addressing the question whether they need or would accept our worship, arguing that they would not.[700] The chapter heading for *City of God* 10.3 sums up the argument to this point: "Of the true worship of God, from which the Platonists deviated when, even though they knew that God is the Creator of the universe, they worshipped angels, whether good or bad, with divine honour." The reference "whether good or bad" is one that Augustine keeps open at this point, though he comes to a decisive conclusion later on in quite dramatic language, where he will state they do *not* worship good angels.

If the Platonists glorified the one God, all would have been well. But they did not. Angels worship God and do not want worship: "both the blessed immortal [i.e., angels] and we wretched mortals, if we are to be immortal and blessed, must worship the one God of gods Who is both our God and theirs."[701] Angels would never accept worship from humans.[702] Augustine believed that Plato thought the immortal part of man (i.e., the soul) to come from God, but not the mortal part (i.e., the body), this created by the gods.[703] Augustine argued that the theological error behind Plato's (and other Platonists') practice of directing their worship to the wrong object (angels/gods), is because of their wrong ideas of creation, specifically the idea that humans were not created by God, but by the gods (even if this were at the supreme God's bidding).[704] This is the error of Plato, which Plato could not resolve. Augustine states, "If these persons could only be rid of the superstition which causes them to seek to justify the offering of rites and sacrifices to such gods as though they were their creators, they would also easily shake off the error of this opinion."[705]

The angels/gods do not create;[706] they should not be worshipped: they are not mediators.[707] In worshipping these created beings, the supreme God is not worshipped by the Platonists.[708] It is at this point that a corner is turned in the argument. Augustine goes on to deny the possibility that it was good angels who were being worshipped by Plato: they would reject this, not being the creators of humans. In Augustine's thinking, therefore, it must be demons who are being worshipped by Plato and the *old school* Platonists. After working through the argument, Augustine comes to his damning conclusion on the object of their worship: "It follows, then, that those whom they would call gods, and whom they encourage us to worship as our parents and makers, are, after all, no more than the forgers of our shackles and chains. They are not our creators, but our jailers and warders, who bind us in a most bitter and grievous house of correction."[709]

Augustine therefore concludes that Plato's worship was not directed to God, or to angels, but to demons. This being so, it is not correct to argue that Plato had good theology but bad religion.[710] He had theology which contained good and bad points, and the bad points (especially concerning errors about creation) had devastating consequences for his religion. Returning to the earlier comment regarding the group smear of the Platonists, Plato was, by and large, put into the same boat as other philosophers by Augustine, though a less Chaldean demonically-infested part of it.[711] While Plato was praised for rejecting some of the popular religion of his day, in Augustine's view this did not actually lead to him being able to break free from *different* demonic adherence. The religion of the masses was replaced only by a different false mediatorial religion.[712] As Augustine noted in the *Sermon against the Pagans*, section 61, in a detailed discussion of the Johannine prologue homily ascent metaphor, it is not as if the philosophers just stay where they are, looking at the vision—they get lost in the woods trying to get to the homeland, woods where the devil offers *various* mediating possibilities to them. As Gioia comments, "Without Christ, even if in theory it is possible to know God because he is the creator and as such he is objectively immanent in his creation, we do not recognize him as the Lord and instead of being led to God through created realities, we transform them into idols."[713]

In his engagement with Varro's[714] discussion of the three types of theology,[715] Augustine rejected the value of the mythical theology and civil theology, but had time for natural theology. At the same time, while agreeing with Plato's rejection of the mythical/poetic religion, there was no such thing as pure natural Platonic theology in Augustine's thinking.[716] It would only lead to false religion—and he was keen to point this out, rather than sideline the conclusion, as Marenbon argues. Augustine did not try to make Plato an exception to engaging in false religion, and I believe one of the reasons for this is that he did not want to leave what limited natural theology he considered possible in an ambiguously "good" place: the associations he made between this and various religious practices in *City of God*, brought it crashing down.[717] In sum, I believe that false religion is as real for the best Platonists as it is for the masses in Augustine's thinking, though this religion is different. For Augustine, illumination *only* leads to idolatry.

4.7. Word of God Illumination and Philosopher Accountability

In this section, I consider Augustine's strong comments concerning philosopher accountability. I do so to highlight the idea of true knowledge in his thinking, and also to note the negative implications of the turn away from this knowledge in his thought.

Augustine takes the philosophers to task because of their choice: they should have known better.[718] For Augustine, they, unlike the masses, were able to use God-given reason, at least partially and dimly, to overcome the human bondage to the senses.[719] But what did this avail them? Nothing.[720] As a number of scholars have noted, Augustine was keen to point out, indeed emphasize, this inconsistency.[721] Marenbon's argument largely sidesteps the issue of inconsistency which is, in many ways, at the heart of the attack on the philosophers.

What are the implications for eternal Word illumination in Augustine's thinking? If the above argument is sound, Augustine seems to argue that knowledge of God (through *Logos* illumination, which he relates to creation in Romans 1:20) results in pride, which subsequently manifests itself in inappropriate religious responses to God, which can vary considerably in the specific details. Observing this, Corey suggests that there is a significant shift away from what might be considered a very positive view of eternal Word illumination (e.g., as seen in Justin) to what we might consider to be a "dangerous" Word illumination in Augustine's thinking. She comments, "While for previous philosophers in the Platonic tradition, the *Logos* and natural beauty of the world were beacons to the Divine eternal realm, now the natural world as a product of God, and endowed with the light from God, can entangle the soul in her ascent to God."[722] This, I believe, is a well-founded observation, in light of the discussion above. Such a view must be contrasted with Justin Martyr's, as provided in the previous chapter.

Like Corey, Cushman also argues for a *direct* relationship between awareness of God and idolatry in Augustine's thinking.[723] Similarly, Westerholm points out that while Augustine allows for the mind to appreciate theological truths, he believes the next response to be only idolatry.[724] A mediator is always sought (and worshipped). In Augustine's words, "they [the philosophers] could not but seek for some means whereby they might reach those sublime things which they had Understood."[725] If one did not know of or if one rejected the incarnate mediator, the devil was ready to take the role of mediator, in various guises.[726]

For Augustine, as noted earlier, the discarnate *Logos cannot* mediate God to man. Philosophers who appreciate this light of the *Logos* cannot respond to it appropriately, as such illumination cannot ultimately help. Earlier on, I suggested that it is necessary to acknowledge both knowledge and mis-knowledge of God in Augustine's thinking. True theological knowledge (e.g., metaphysical truths) results in pride in Augustine's thinking. On the other hand, theological mis-knowledge (not knowing *clearly* e.g., the facts of creation for Plato) results in false religion, which, for Augustine, always involves demons, who form an alliance with those with similar loves. The array of various alliances ensures a pluralism of religion.

Conclusion

I summarize the key findings of this chapter in conclusion. Regarding demons, I have documented a significant shift away from Jewish apocalyptic explanations for the existence of demons, a view that had been adopted by some in the early church (e.g., Justin). Augustine's belief that the demons were fallen angels would become the standard view of the church for centuries thereafter. Augustine believed in a significant role for demons in false religion; however, in highlighting human sinful culpability and co-operation with demons, along with an emphasis on God's sovereign reign, he somewhat mitigated their powers of deception. Having said this, it is clear that he genuinely believed in universal human slavery resulting from demonic deception. At the same time, demons could be compelled to speak truth.

Turning to the ancient theology tradition, I noted from a key passage in the *City of God* how Augustine downplayed the idea that Plato borrowed from the people of Israel. Furthermore, I considered how

Augustine thought it possible that truth could be present in the writings of pagans (e.g., Hermes), and his seemingly inconsistent explanation concerning the text of a particular Sibyl.

Augustine accepted that the Platonists (and only those following this tradition) had benefitted from revelation as documented in Romans 1:20. I noted how Augustine used this passage to help him understand *Logos* illumination in the first three homilies of John's Gospel. I have suggested that Augustine focuses on a certain knowledge and mis-knowledge of God resulting from *Logos* illumination. This transient knowledge seems to be of metaphysical truths, with little emphasis on ethical awareness (cf. Justin, in the preceding chapter). I concluded by arguing that Marenbon has not sufficiently established his argument that Augustine departed from the Apostle Paul's view of religions in Romans 1:20–25. I suggest that word of God illumination, not able to mediate between God and fallen man, is, indirectly at least, the first step to false religion for philosophers, in Augustine's thinking. The religion of the masses (who seem to experience very little *Logos* illumination) is, on the other hand, explained by an appeal to Euhemerism in a religious "system" that mimics Christianity.

4

John Calvin[727]

Background

CALVIN IS NOT TYPICALLY considered to be *a theologian of religions*. While a few scholars have considered the Reformer to have made a contribution to the field,[728] his lack of interest in Islam, in particular, has been noted, and this, doubtless, has contributed to the more commonly held viewpoint that he was uninterested in the subject of non-Christian religion.[729] This, however, is not the full picture. Despite his lack of engagement with Islam, Calvin engaged theologically with what he believed to be his own era's errant religiosity, in addition to various historical forms of false worship and false religion. As will be discussed below, he classified religions, forwarded his view of how they developed and also hypothesized what he considered to be the generic elements within them.

As Muller has noted, it is often hard to identify the specific influences on Calvin's thinking in any one particular area.[730] A significant impacting role from Calvin's humanist educational background has been argued by some,[731] and scholastic influences on his thinking have also been identified.[732] Calvin's use of ideas and writings from the church fathers is also well documented.[733] Of particular importance in considering his thinking on religion and humankind's religious nature is his use of Stoic thought and terminology, which I consider in some detail in section 4.2.

Turning to the Calvin corpus, It has been pointed out by more than one scholar that the *Institutes* should be read alongside the commentaries (and vice versa).[734] This advice has been followed in the approach adopted in this chapter. In passing, it should be noted that the different emphases present within these two text types are quite striking in the area of theology of religions. For example, while Calvin primarily focuses on the individual when considering God's revelation to humankind in the first few chapters of the *Institutes*, in the commentaries his ideas about the role of kings, individual "influencers," nations and societies in the formation of religions are expounded. The first has been examined in detail (though often outside the context of theology of religions discussion), the latter much less so, and rarely have the two been considered together. The lack of connection between the two treatments in Calvin's thinking is, at times, stark. Specifically, I do not believe Calvin to have given much thought to the relationship between the individual idolatrous response to revelation (as documented in the first five chapters of Book 1 of the *Institutes*) and religious life in a non-Christian nation as given in his commentaries. This is, arguably, due to his specific goals in writing the first chapters of Book 1 of the *Institutes*—to render humans guilty and accountable to God—rather than to consider the phenomenon of non-Christian religion, per se.

1. Calvin and Religion: Overview

1.1. Definition and Context

As Muller notes, religion—"the right worship of God"—was a fundamentally important idea for the Reformers.[735] Calvin defined religion in the following way: "Here indeed is pure and real religion: faith so joined with an earnest fear of God that this fear also embraces willing reverence, and carries with it such legitimate worship as is prescribed in the law."[736] Although not explicitly framed as such, Calvin's definition should be understood to be a Christian, more specifically Reformed Christian, understanding of religion, stressing an affective element and implicitly, a true knowledge of self.[737] Calvin understood worship, this unique human propensity, to be the first duty of humankind, the basis of life: "for the pure worship of God, we know, is ever to have the first place, and that justly; for on this depend all the duties of life."[738] This being so, it was of critical importance for Calvin that people understood of what "pure worship" consisted.[739] As Balserak argues, the establishment of true worship was, arguably, a major part of his life's goal.[740] Given this conviction, idolatry and the corruption of religion was a major focus of attack in his writings and sermons.[741] Calvin stressed the importance of obedience to God's will concerning right worship:[742] sacrifices and good deeds presented to God are not acceptable to him if they are not presented in accordance with his will, or if this worship is shared with others. A lack of understanding of God's will, or non-adherence to it would, of necessity, lead to false worship and such were his conclusions as he observed the beliefs and practices of the church of his day.

Given his context, Calvin's "applied" theology of religions focus was undoubtedly what he considered to be abuses within the Roman Catholic Church. What he perceived to be devotion to relics, images and statues he unashamedly termed idolatry. He referenced his early exposure to traditional folk Catholic ceremonies in his youth, and strongly rejected and repudiated the value of these in later life.[743] Calvin drew parallels between the idolatry of the church of his day with Israelite idolatry in the OT, seeing no real difference between the two.[744] He also drew parallels between Jewish idolatry and the practices of pagans,[745] and between pagan practices and the Roman Catholic Church.[746] In *A Treatise on Relics* Calvin mocks varied churches' claims to house essentially the same relics and bones, noting, *inter alia*, that the cross carried by one man was now so big that three hundred would struggle to carry it. While in some senses humorous, it is a scathing and sarcastic assault on what he openly terms idolatry in the church.

In writing of the medieval era, Eire references the idea that churchgoers experienced anxiety as they sought confirmation of acceptance by God: saint worship and devotion to relics developed to satisfy this need.[747] Calvin argued that such worshippers believed that their "gods" would keep them safe. One of the reasons for physical idols, he thought, was that people believed they would bring God closer,[748] and that this would "bring solace."[749] However, this was not the case: forgiveness could not be found in such a way.[750] He explained the attraction and lure of idolatry in the following way:

> For this is the origin of idolatry, that when the genuine simplicity of God's worship is known, people begin to be dissatisfied with it, and curiously to inquire whether there is anything worthy of belief in the figments of men; for men's minds are soon

attracted by the snares of novelty, so as to pollute, with various kinds of leaven, what has been delivered in God's word.[751]

The spirituality of true worship, in Calvin's mind, is a great obstacle to humankind's perverted tendency to bring God down to the human level. As part of this argument he also dismissed the idea within the Roman Catholic Church that pictures and images could help the illiterate worship aright.[752] What he perceived as idolatry he considered peculiarly "insulting" to God,[753] as it involved a transfer of honor due to God.[754] In Eire's words, for Calvin "idolatry is thus the most sinister parody of man's relationship with God and the boldest affront to the divine majesty."[755] Calvin constantly stood against idolatry, whether in the Roman Catholic Church of his time, or in his comments on Judaism, Islam and pagan religions.[756] The common thread he saw between these religions (i.e., idolatry) is indicative of his overarching theology of religions approach, and central to it.

1.2. The Origin and Classifications of Religions

Concerning the historical origins of false religion, Calvin challenged what he believed to be the prevailing ideas of the day, namely that ancestor worship was the initial kind of idolatry.[757] He suggested that there had been a chronological demise in the type of false religion practiced in the world: from worship of celestial bodies, to mortals, to a pantheon of gods or heroes.[758] While he mentioned Egyptian idolatry a number of times in his writings, he did not place the worship of objects within this particular overview. The Egyptians, however, came under special condemnation, Calvin believing them to have a propensity to idolize everything, including onions.[759] I will consider Calvin's understanding of the Egyptians in more detail, in sections 2.2 and 3.4. Suffice to say here, he differentiated them from the more noble Greeks, whom, he argued, were "above" the grosser Egyptian practices, including their worship of animals.[760] Bouwsma's comment that "Respect for the religious insights of the natural man, even after the Fall, is . . . implicit in Calvin's belief in the superiority of Greek religion to other expressions of ancient paganism,"[761] while correctly recognizing a distinction in Calvin's thought, overstates the idea of "respect" which Calvin showed for any false religions.[762]

There is no idea of a continuum in Calvin's thinking on religion, with Reformed Christianity occupying primacy of place in an evolutionary process, or being the exemplar of a genus: for Calvin, Reformed Christianity was true religion and everything else false.[763] It is fair to say that Calvin was not particularly interested in investigating the varieties found in non-Christian religions,[764] as he did not really consider polytheism any worse than a misdirected monotheism.[765] Having said this, he did, at times, hint at there being more "light" in some religions compared to others.[766] However, leaning on the authority of Augustine he believed the seemingly good present in some individuals (e.g., exhibited in friendship and temperance) to be of no value to God because such duties or acts are not correctly grounded in true faith or the right motivation.[767]

Calvin stated that the root cause of idolatry was lack of knowledge of the true God, together with a desire for illicit knowledge.[768] Capetz suggests that idolatry was just one of an unholy trinity in Calvin's thought on non-Christian religion, the other two elements being superstition and hypocrisy.[769] False worship, religious belief and practices which were not "pure and real" are called "superstitions" or simply "false religions" in Calvin's writings.[770] At root, these were all attempting, through human effort, to try to placate God with good works, rituals and sacrifices. Such delusional thinking, he believed, was inspired by Satan.[771]

In his commentaries, in particular, he reflected on the different players involved in false religions. Concerning the role of kings, Calvin believed that they could be tempted to deify themselves, and use religion for their own purposes.[772] Religious systems of three different broad classes[773] could be mandated by kings and imposed upon their people/s.[774] The first, "philosophical," was grounded in natural reason, the second, "poetic," related to enactments of fables in theatres, and the third, "political," was a more pragmatic approach which appealed to common consent to keep society cohesive. Calvin recognized that cities and nations could have their own gods and religions,[775] and that city patriotism could influence the commitment to a god.[776] He believed that particular belief systems could become entrenched in a society,[777] with members of a society influencing other members of the community (in a negative way) around commitment to a particular (wrong) idea of God.[778]

Calvin spoke of the role of some humans influencing others, leading them away from true to false religions, speaking of "many monstrous spirits who, to destroy God's name, do not hesitate to misdirect all the seed of divinity spread abroad in human nature."[779] In its context, this reference seems to be a purely human influence, without the involvement of supernatural agents. Alongside such comments, he noted group dynamics surrounding adherence to tradition, and the power of tradition in maintaining religious commitment.[780] In terms of the depth of commitment that could result from adherence to these false religions, referring to the confused reception of Paul and Barnabas in Lystra (Acts 14:12–15), he commented, "By which example we are taught what a mischief it is to be accustomed and acquainted with errors in youth, which can so hardly be rooted out of the mind, that even through the works of God, whereby they ought to have been redressed, they wax more hard."[781]

1.3. What Religions Have in Common and Why

Calvin opined that the common elements in religions were a sense of guilt, supplication for mercy, practice of sacrifice[782] and the doing of good works[783] to seek the god's pardon, or see the gods pacified, thereafter seeking for some sign of propitious reciprocal action from the god.[784] In Calvin's thought man "creates," or more commonly, "invents" gods, and also creates religions. Calvin describes gods as "false" and "fictitious."[785] He presented the logic for this argument in the following way:

> For the reason why an idol is nothing is, that it must be estimated according to the thing that it represents. Now it is appointed for the purpose of representing God: nay more, for the purpose of representing false gods, inasmuch as there is but one God, who is invisible and incomprehensible. The reason, too, must be carefully observed—An idol is nothing because there is no God but one; for he is the invisible God, and cannot be represented by a visible sign, so as to be worshipped through means of it.[786]

Calvin often describes idols as nothing.[787] The idea that gods are not real, but, "the figments of [people's] own brains,"[788] mirroring man's image, rather than God's,[789] is a dominant theme in Calvin's description of idolatry in pagan philosophy, the Old Testament, New Testament, and in the church of his era. In a rather pithy way, Calvin summarized the connection he believed to exist between false belief and the corresponding false worship in the following way: "Therefore the mind begets an idol; the hand gives it birth."[790] Actual practice could change, as new idols could be created; false (i.e., idolatrous) beliefs, on the other hand, are typically viewed by Calvin as deeply entrenched.[791] When Calvin speaks of human nature being "a factory of idols,"[792] he meant that everyone replaced the true God with his or her "accommodated" or domesticated alternative, typically built after the person's own image.⁷⁹³ It would be fair to say, however, that he did not really connect such comments to actual religions, as I noted earlier. Taken at face value, there would be as many gods as humans if one limited one's investigation of theology of religions in Calvin's thought to the first five chapters of Book 1 of the *Institutes*.

Idolatry, in Calvin's thought, did not necessarily involve the creation of images. For example, in discussing Islam and Judaism, though recognizing that Jews and Muslims claimed to be worshipping the creator, he nonetheless used the term "idol" for what they were worshipping, while acknowledging the absence of any physical image: "For the Heathen men did make sacrifice also, and some of them had no Idols, thinking that they offered to God the maker of heaven and earth: and yet whereto did all their Sacrifices serve them, but to their condemnation? For they had overthrown God's order, because they aimed not at our Lord Jesus Christ."⁷⁹⁴ "They who form their ideas of God in his naked majesty apart from Christ, have an idol instead of the true God, as the case is with the Jews and the Turks."⁷⁹⁵

Having provided some basic background to Calvin's thinking, I now proceed to consider his views on the demonic.

2. The Role of the Demonic in Calvin's Theology of Religions

2.1. The *Institutes*

Although Calvin argued that idols are nothing, he spoke of a personal devil and demons, and dismissed the idea that Satan was just an idea.⁷⁹⁶ In *Institutes* 1.14.3–19 he outlined his basic view of angels and demonology. In what follows I provide a brief overview of relevant discussion within the *Institutes* before investigating the subject in more depth.

In *Institutes* 1.14.3 Calvin states that angels are created beings, and believes that they are not mentioned in the creation account as they are not seen (referencing the Nicene Creed to support this view). He rejects the idea that devils are merely thoughts in *Institutes* 1.14.19. He notes the human propensity to ascribe divinity to angels, and condemns Mani's view of God and the devil.

Calvin calls the devil "a degenerate creation of God," noting that his nature is from his perversion rather than his created nature, describing the devils' origins in similar language.⁷⁹⁷ In terms of Satan's activities, the list he produces is quite dreadful: "For he opposes the truth of God with falsehoods, he obscures the light with darkness, he entangles men's minds in errors, he stirs up hatred, he kindles contentions and combats, everything to the end that he may overturn God's Kingdom and plunge men with himself into eternal death."[798]

Although the main focus of the human-devils interaction within this section of the *Institutes* relates to Christians, Calvin does make several comments which could be interpreted as being significant for his views on the role of demons in false religions. Following on from his statement about the degenerate nature of demons he states that they "became the instruments of ruin for others."[799] He also writes, after noting that demons cannot really hurt Christians, that "the wicked they subdue and drag away; they exercise power over their minds and bodies, and misuse them as if they were slaves for every shameful act."[800]

While documenting the dreadful activities of Satan and demons, Calvin dismisses any idea of real rivalry between God and the devils. In *Institutes* 1.14.7 he argues that Satan "can do nothing unless God wills and assents to it," going on to note that the same activity in Scripture is, at times, attributed to God and Satan—specifically the blinding of unbelievers. This, he argues, is documented for a specific reason, namely to show Satan's subservience.[801] Satan obeys God "whether he will or not" and is "compelled to render him service."[802] Calvin documents Satan's defeat by Christ in *Institutes* 1.14.18.

A dominant theme running throughout his treatment of angels and the devil in the *Institutes* is the danger of "empty speculations"[803] on the subject matter. In *Institutes* 1.14.4 he expresses his displeasure at the unhealthy interest of those who want to know on what day the angels were created, along with "the nature, orders, and number of angels." In *Institutes* 1.14.16 he criticizes those who want to know more than Scripture teaches concerning the fall of the devils. He argues that Scripture is silent on this matter as it "has nothing to do with us." Calvin defends the amount of information given in Scripture. While noting its paucity, it suffices: indeed, it is "more than enough to clear God's majesty of all slander."

2.2. The Commentaries

Some of the quotations cited above suggest, or hint at, a possibly significant role of demons in non-Christian religions. However, the fact that a major emphasis in *Institutes* 1.14 is on Satanic attacks on Christians and also God's rule over the demons makes it rather difficult to be sure of Calvin's convictions on the demons-religions interface. In what follows I argue that this ambiguity is cleared up, to a considerable extent, in the commentaries. I will show that Calvin downplays and limits an active role of demons in the creation or perpetuation of non-Christian religions. However, at the same time, I will point to examples where he argues that the end of all non-Christian religion is, in fact, worship of Satan. The demons are not very active players in religion, but they are active recipients of any worship not directed to God, according to his will. This important distinction in roles, I believe, helps manage some of the ambiguity at times present in Calvin's language.

Before proceeding further, it should be noted that in stark opposition to Justin's view (though not naming him), when commenting on Genesis 6:4, Calvin rejected outright the idea of demonic progeny, terming the idea "abundantly refuted by its own absurdity," expressing seeming amazement at how such an interpretation could ever have been considered possible within the church.[804]

Concerning the role of demons in non-Christian religions, generally speaking Calvin spoke of this role being parasitic, stressing human corruption *prior to* any demonic involvement:

> In short, idols teach naturally, and they teach through the artifice and delusion of Satan. They teach naturally; for by their silence they show that they are not gods, inasmuch as there is no strength in them. They teach, also, by the artifice of the devil; for they are made to claim a kind of divinity, and thus dazzle the minds of men, *who are already corrupted by their own delusions* [emphasis mine].[805]

This movement (from fallen sinful nature to alliance with the demonic) is similar to that noted in Augustine's thinking, as documented in the previous chapter. Satan's role is to add to the confusion, bewitching through means such as attractive modes of worship, and affording ways to gain illicit knowledge.[806] Related to this latter point, Calvin alludes to Satanic deception as a kind of echo of the event of the Fall, though does not make a connection to man's desire for illicit knowledge in this.[807] Even where a more active role of Satan is described, "depraved curiosity" precedes this: "the experience of all ages teaches us that men of depraved curiosity have often received from Satan, by means of magicians, a knowledge of things which could not have been obtained naturally."[808]

In his comments on Psalm 73 Calvin seems to allow for false religion being of three kinds: those religions which involve Satanic deception, those relating to a kind of self-deification, and finally a set relating to self-dependence.

> For those who are not beguiled by the former artifice of Satan, so as to be led to fabricate for themselves false gods, either deceive themselves by arrogance when confiding in their own skill, or strength, or prudence, they usurp the prerogatives which belong to God alone; or else trepan [entrap] themselves with deceitful allurements when they rely upon the favor of men, or confide in their own riches and other helps which they possess.[809]

Accordingly, Calvin seemed to suggest a kind of spectrum of demonic involvement in false religion, though never arguing that the role is dominant.

A "test case" affording potentially valuable information on Calvin's thought on the role of demons in religion is his handling of references to the gods of Egypt. In Scripture, the gods of Egypt are said to be judged by Yahweh (Exod 12:12; Num 33:4). While Calvin notes the conquering of these gods[810] and states that they had power,[811] he also states that they are non-existent. He calls them "mere fictions,"[812] "fictitious,"[813] "false and invented by the imaginations of man,"[814] and "powerless."[815] On Moses's exclamation of praise in Exodus 15:11 "Who is like you, O Lord, among the gods?," Calvin argues that these gods were purely human inventions:

> Moses (as has been said) is professedly contrasting the one true God, whose religion and worship existed among the children of Abraham, with the delusions of the Gentiles. The word "sanctitas," holiness, expresses that glory which separates God from all His creatures; and therefore, in a manner, it degrades all the other deities which the world has invented for itself.

On the basis of this brief overview, it is clear that Calvin's interpretation leans more towards the gods being non-existent delusions: not active gods or demons.

But this is not the full story. At times, Calvin calls some gods "demons" or "devils" or the devil,[816] and as noted in the reference to the gods of Egypt above, on occasion he alluded to some kind of power associated with them.[817] While he did on at least one occasion, state that the gods of the heathens are demons,[818] unlike Justin and Augustine, Calvin seemed very reluctant to make this equation. Significantly, he believed that the gods referred to in Psalm 96:5 (a key text in this debate) to be either angels or idols (rather than demons): honoring *angels* is wrong.[819] The intention of the Psalmist, he argues, is to show that ascription of glory to such, away from God is wrong: "the gods of the heathen are vanity and nought, for such is the meaning of the Hebrew word, elilim."

In contrast to Augustine, Calvin struggled to accept the idea that demons could become agents of revelation. In his commentary on the demon calling Christ "the Holy one of God," in Mark 1:21–28 and Luke 4:31–36, he argues that the statement was made to confuse the hearers, and to insinuate a kind of alliance between Christ and the devil. The rebuke of Christ, Calvin argues, is to dispel the insinuation. However, at the same time he seems to reluctantly admit the possibility that the confession was forced from the demon (by God). While the demon was "forced to yield to the power of Christ," he prefers to call the title ascribed to Jesus an empty one, because the demon does not *truly* acknowledge Christ's lordship in submission.[820] While Calvin does not hesitate to acknowledge God being the source of all truth, including pagan "wisdom" cited approvingly by Paul,[821] he seemed more reticent to call what might be considered true statements "truth" if uttered by demons.

The overview provided above suggests there to be much less of an idea of active demonic involvement in religions in Calvin's thinking than is the case for Justin or Augustine. However, as I note below, for Calvin demons are the recipients of false worship within false religions.

For Calvin, while there may be more or less Satanic involvement in religions, when considering the ends or consequences of worship not directed to God in the appropriate way, he believes it is transferred, by default, to Satan. This is how Calvin interprets 1 Corinthians 8:4 and 1 Corinthians 10:19 and 20. In commenting on 1 Corinthians 8:4, Calvin argues that an idol is "an empty figment of the human brain, and must therefore be reckoned as nothing." He also states, "An idol is nothing because there is no God but one; for he is the invisible God, and cannot be represented by a visible sign, so as to be worshipped through means of it.

Whether, therefore, idols are erected to represent the true God, or false gods, it is in all cases a perverse contrivance."

This statement fits well with previous discussion—what may be considered the dominant theme in Calvin's thinking on idols. However, in his comments on 1 Corinthians 10:19 and 20 he refers back to the above verse and explains the idea that sacrifices are actually offered to demons (rather than idols which are nothing). He dismisses the idea that the Apostle Paul has in mind the good heroes of Roman religion or the "good" demons in Plato in his comments, and seeks to reconcile the idea that idols are nothing and demons are worshipped as stated in this particular text of Scripture, in the following way:

> I answer, that the two things [the worship of imaginary deities and worship of idols being the worship of demons] are quite in harmony, for when men become so vain in their imaginations (Romans 1:21) as to render divine honor to creatures, rather than to the one God, this punishment is in readiness for them—that they serve Satan. For they do not find that "middle place" that they are in search of, but Satan straightway presents himself to them, as an object of adoration, whenever they have turned their back upon the true God.[822]

In this sense, therefore, all idols or false gods or imaginary deities can, in a roundabout way, be identified with or called demons or devils as the latter receive worship when false gods are worshipped—though this is not the intention of the worshipper.

Eire believes that Calvin repudiated Augustine's view on the active role of demons in religions, suggesting that he may have followed Bullinger and Zwingli in adopting this position.[823] Eire terms the rejection of the demonic as the starting place of false religion, together with what he believes to be Calvin's anthropologically-oriented focus on the origin of religion, "a giant step away from Catholic Tradition."[824] He goes on to qualify this understanding somewhat, in stating that Calvin still admitted a smaller role for Satan and the demonic in religion, namely that of tempter of humans and attempted disrupter of God's plans.[825] While Eire provides very little support for his argument concerning the relegated role of demons within the Calvin corpus, the overview given above supports Eire's general conclusions, though I will return to, and also challenge the anthropological follow up claim he makes, in the conclusion of this chapter.

2.3. Calvin's Relegation of the Involvement of Demons in False Religions

Why did Calvin give Satan a much less prominent role in his theology of religions, compared to the early and mediaeval church? One reason may be Calvin's understanding of the Fall, and his interpretation of the subsequent religious history of humanity.[826] Calvin famously rejected the Platonic idea of sin as ignorance and viewed sin as involving culpable guilt.[827] In many ways Calvin's anthropology sufficed to explain religion, without the need for third party demonic involvement. As Eire notes, "Banning the devil from the scene heightened human responsibility."[828]

Another possible reason why Calvin did not want to give Satan and the demons a significant role in his thinking on religions is that, as noted earlier, they were under God's authority, and in no way uncontrolled. Satan's power, including his power to deceive, is given him by God: Satan can only follow God's decrees.[829] Calvin did not want to endow demons with more power than he believed they really had. When they seemed to have power, he downplayed this. One piece of evidence supporting this interpretation is that he preferred to explain what appeared to be demonic miracles in the court of pharaoh to sleight of hand and deception rather than the working of supernatural evil.[830]

A final important observation here, is that Calvin seemed very speculation-averse on this subject. Calvin had no place for the kind of "developed" demonology present in Justin's and Augustine's thought. While with Augustine he shared a high view of God's sovereignty, and a profoundly negative view of sin, he did not and would not connect or relate his thought on angels and demons to elaborate structures which he considered to have no precedent in the Bible. Calvin very much played down, rather than played up, the active role of demons in his theology of religions. I suggest he did so, in part, because he believed the biblical evidence to be largely silent on this involvement.

3. Calvin and the *Prisca Theologia*

3.1. Background

Although the traditional Mosaic primacy version of the *prisca theologia* tradition was still appealed to by theologian scholars during Calvin's lifetime (most notably by Bucer and Champier,[831] as noted below) the fifteenth and sixteenth centuries witnessed interest in various new versions of the ancient theology tradition. Walker believes increased interest in Platonism to have been responsible for this change during this period.[832] Each of the three elements foundational to the ancient theology theory referenced by Justin and Augustine were challenged:[833] alternative accounts to Hebrew historical primacy were advocated;[834] appeals to the adequacy of reason in religion were made;[835] and hints at, or outright advocacy of, multilinear versions of the ancient theology tradition began to appear.[836]

Malusa documents three schools of thought explaining the historiography of philosophy in the renaissance era, which he labels: "philological-humanistic" (as advocated by Marsilio Ficino), "Platonic-concordistic" (represented in the ideas of Giovanni Pico della Mirandola), and the sceptical (as argued by Gianfrancesco Pico della Mirandola).[837] A common goal of Marsilio Ficino (1433–99), Giovanni Pico della Mirandola (1463–94), and the later Agostina Steuco (1496–1548) was to seek harmonization of thought between numerous religious and philosophical beliefs and Christianity.[838] Giovanni Pico's nephew, Gianfrancesco, a key mouthpiece of the sceptical school, was a significant opponent of this shift towards syncretism. He rejected outright his uncle's attempts at synthesis, and stressed disunity and disharmony between various philosophical and religious systems and the beliefs of Christianity, stressing the uncertainty of the former.[839] In what follows I provide a brief outline of the first two schools mentioned by Malusa. I make reference to the third in sections 3.3 and 3.4.

3.2. Ficino and Pico's Ancient Theology Arguments

Like some of the church fathers, Ficino was eager to show the ancient heritage of the *prisca theologia*. He was also keen to align some of his views, particularly his Platonist ones, with the early Augustine.[840] Ficino translated Plato[841] and also the *Corpus Hermeticum*,[842] which he and many others believed to indicate pre-Platonic "Christian" insights. Only later were these writings discovered to be fraudulent by Casaubon and others.[843] The quest for the discovery of the unity of philosophical thought[844] in monotheism, creation ex-nihilo, Trinty, end-time resurrection, and final judgment[845] occupied much of Ficino's attempts at harmonization, with his belief in the eternity of the soul foundational to this project.[846] Ficino believed that Plato built on and perfected[847] the earlier wisdom of (in chronological order) Zoroaster,[848] Hermes Trismegistus, Orpheus, Aglaophemus, and Pythagoras.[849] The admittance, indeed promotion, of Zoroaster into the line of pedigree, was, in Idel's view due to the influence of Plethon[850] on Ficino.[851] Ficino's interpretation of Plato, as Screech notes, was a Christianizing one.[852]

Van Gelder believed Ficino to have argued for two truth traditions: one philosophical and one religious, both leading to felicity, but by different routes.[853] Kristeller understands Ficino to have argued that these two ways (the Hebrew religious and the Hermetic-Platonist philosophical) are related, as sisters, running in parallel over time, neither subservient to the other:[854] rather, the relationship is one of complementation.[855] Ficino wanted to tie philosophy, religion and politics together,[856] and he held an expansive view of what religion entailed.[857] Religions of all times were, to some extent, legitimate in his thought,[858] though Christianity was the pinnacle of religion.[859] Edelheit believes that the ancient theology tradition argued for by Ficino was essentially a natural theology—not based on *direct* inspiration, as opposed to the biblical revelation which was.[860] At the same time, he points to references suggesting occasional direct inspiration.[861] Howlett, on the other hand, traces Ficino's understanding of the ancient theology tradition to original revelation, this being passed on.[862] Whether through reason, inspiration or ancient revelation, what could be known and attained from this knowledge was "participation in truth." As Ficino himself stated, "they brought themselves as near as possible to God's ray by releasing their souls, and since they examined by the light of that ray all things by uniting and dividing through the one and the many, they too were made to participate in the truth."[863]

Given comments such as these, it is not particularly surprisingly that Ficino has been understood by some to have been an early kind of deist, expressing his commitment to a universal religion.[864]

Ficino's various statements on the ancient theology tradition are difficult to reconcile: some are traditional, others not.[865] Different interpretations of his work, and critiques of these, have been discussed by Idel.[866] Idel himself believes Ficino wrote differently for different audiences, the reason being that some of his more radical views would not have been appreciated by more conservative elements within the church.[867] Idel also argues for the legitimacy of interpreting Ficino as holding to a view of two independent truth traditions: philosophical and Jewish religious.[868] More recently, Howlett has appealed to the idea of continent-specific truth streams in Ficino's thinking (Persian, Egyptian, Greek and Jewish).[869] No matter which of these theories best represents his thought, it is clear that Ficino's ancient faith tradition bore little resemblance to that propounded by Justin or Augustine: it involved a far more ambitious all-embracing, and non-judgmental view of philosophy.

Turning now to the "Platonic-concordistic" school, Giovanni Pico took the idea of synthesis to a new level, both in trying to reconcile Platonic and Aristotelian thought, and in expanding the number of materials to be so unified—bringing in cabbalistic material, among others, into the picture.[870] Pico is famous for developing his 900 theses based on multiple sources, which, he believed, showed a unified understanding of God within them[871] (at least when the correct hermeneutical key was applied,[872] and even then, the presence of error was also acknowledged).[873] This search for unity was, Sudduth believes, a Christocentric syncretistic search.[874] Compared to Ficino, Pico allowed for a more propaedeutic role for philosophy, leading to religion.[875] Unlike Ficino, he did not elevate Plato to a pinnacle, nor develop a (rather small) historical chain of ancient sage witnesses: rather, he emphasized all philosophies as having a common source.[876] Agostino Steuco echoed this latter conviction in his own work, while differentiating two ways to attain this key knowledge: through historical study or intellectual application. This unity of knowledge he termed "perennial philosophy."[877]

3.3. Erasmus and the Reformers on the *Prisca Theologia*

That Erasmus was influenced by some aspects of Italian humanism is not doubted, but Walker, Boyle and Wallace all believe Erasmus repudiated any version of the ancient theology tradition.[878] While Erasmus's comments on the possible salvation of the heathen were ambiguous, he seemed to be clear on the idea of revelation of the *Logos* to all and was interested in making links between Christianity and various philosophies.[879]

Luther was aware of some of Pico's writings and at times he appreciated certain insights from philosophers.[880] However, he did not believe their insights to be of any spiritual value.[881] Williams, on the basis of analyzing Luther's comments on Jonah 1:5, believes that Luther held to a kind of Adamic version of the *prisca theologia*, containing vestiges of "light and reason" which were transmitted through posterity.[882] However, in analyzing the same passage, Boyle argues that Luther's main emphasis is on revelation from reason and nature, and its insufficiency.[883] Ziegler interprets Luther in a similar way to Boyle.[884]

Bucer clearly argued for the traditional version of the *prisca theologia*, holding to the view of Plato's dependence on Moses.[885] According to Kok, Bucer found in pagan literature a "lower grade form of revelation" to that of Scripture, and his argument why pagan literature was, at times, useful was because of this borrowing.[886] Kok believes a clear difference emerges between Bucer and Calvin on the status of pagan literature on this point.[887]

3.4. Calvin's View of the *Prisca Theologia*

Was Calvin aware of the ancient theology tradition and the newer versions of it developed during the renaissance? It is, I believe, fairly safe to assume that Calvin would have been aware of the "traditional" view held by Justin and Augustine, and of Bucer's holding to it, as he knew him well, along with his commentary on Romans. But what about the newer versions of the tradition? Muller believes that Calvin's attack on "Epicureans" involved "a debate with proponents of a revived ancient philosophy," which is suggestive of awareness.[888] It is also possible that Calvin was aware of the ideas of Ficino and Pico because of their influence on French humanists who, in turn, developed their own versions of the *prisca theologia*.[889] His rejection of Cicero's opinion that religion improves over time could also be interpreted as an implicit criticism of an important element of newer ideas.[890] Further, he may have had in mind Pico's cabbalistic interpretation of Scripture in his comments concerning questionable etymological exegesis.[891]

Given the above tentative suggestions, I turn now to Calvin's entanglements with Servetus which I believe are the clearest evidence of his awareness of newer variants of the *prisca theologia* and the uses to which they were being put. Walker suggests that Servetus was probably introduced to the tradition by Champier, such a position clearly present in *Christianisti restitutio*—particularly the Hermetic appeal.[892] Walker traces a specific heretical belief in Servetus's thought (the Father's temporal priority to the Son) to Orpheus, and also points to significant Hermetic influence regarding Servetus's pantheistic tendencies.[893]

In the *Institutes* 4.16.31 Calvin pours scorn on Servetus's appeal to Hermes Trismegistus (and the Sibyls) calling the former, a key figure in the newer *prisca theologia* schemes, as noted above, a heathen, contrasting his ideas with "the authority of God."[894] An additional strand of evidence indicative of a clear rejection of the *prisca theologia* is Calvin's dismissal of Egyptian wisdom. Calvin went out of his way to exhibit what can only be described as utter disdain for the wisdom of Egypt, and he flatly rejected the possibility of any transmission of light via Egypt. Indeed, he used the idea of Egyptian proximity to the people of Israel as reason for greater blame for their folly, rather than to argue for positive influence one way or the other.[895]

Calvin held a number of views which, when compared with Ficino and Pico, indicate starkly divergent positions. These would include his animosity to the idea of philosophy being a propaedeutic tool;[896] his narrow definition of acceptable worship;[897] Christianity being totally distinct from other religions (because of his commitment to a binary view of religion); there being one (not two or more) streams of salvific revelation;[898] the state of the human condition,[899] and the significance of the cross.[900] Calvin, would, I suggest, have agreed with the repudiation of Pico's views by his nephew. Gianfrancesco, in opposition to the ideas of his better-known uncle, believed the project of seeking religious and philosophical harmony to be a false reading of earlier thought, in essence a pipe dream.[901] Calvin stressed the certainty to be found in the Christian faith and emphasized the contradictions and absurdities present in philosophical thought—especially religious thought.[902]

3.5. The Rationale for Calvin's Position

Dewey Wallace Jr.'s interpretation of Calvin's position on the *prisca theologia* is that he "ignored" it.[903] In Wallace's opinion, Calvin believed that the truth known by the pagans was obtained through creation.[904] While his ignoring explanation is possible, given the wider historical context, I believe it more likely that Calvin more purposefully rejected the tradition and for two main reasons.

The first of these reasons is Calvin's relationship with Philosophy, aptly termed "complex" by Nuovo.[905] Calvin's criticism of some of Plato's ideas and of Augustine's early Platonism is well known.[906] At times he sought to distance himself from Platonism, indeed condemned Plato.[907] At the same time, the Reformed turn to Plato, from Aristotle, cannot be denied.[908] It has been argued by a number of scholars that Calvin was essentially eclectic (rather than syncretistic) in his approach: keen to use Plato's thought when it suited him, and not averse to dismiss his thought when it did not.[909]

It is clear that Calvin differentiated religious insights from earthly wisdom in the writings of the philosophers. He was (very) generous in what he admitted of some philosophers' ideas in matters in science and worldly knowledge,[910] insights which he attributed to the work of the Holy Spirit.[911] Concerning the knowledge of God and his fatherly care in salvation, however, he termed pagan understanding and insight into the heart of religion as being "blinder than moles."[912] In reality, however, he admitted some knowledge here as well.[913] McNeill believes that Calvin "frequently recognises the *discernment* by pagan philosophers of elements of *religious* truth [emphasis mine]."[914] In support of this claim he refers to Calvin's use of Cicero's awareness of God idea in *Institutes* 1.3.1, and his approving reference to Aristotle's mention of man as being a microcosm of God in *Institutes* 1.5.3. Is this a fair reading of Calvin? I suggest it is somewhat problematic, and I suggest why in what follows. In an oft-cited passage Calvin commented:

> Certainly I do not deny that one can read competent and apt statements about God here and there in the philosophers, but these always show a certain giddy imagination. As was stated above, the Lord indeed gave them a slight taste of his divinity that they might not hide their impiety under a cloak of ignorance. *And sometimes he impelled them to make certain utterances by the confession of which they would themselves be corrected* [emphasis mine]. But they saw things in such a way that their seeing did not direct them to the truth, much less enable them to attain it! They are like a traveler passing through a field at night who in a momentary lightning flash sees far and wide, but the sight vanishes so swiftly that he is plunged again into the darkness of the night before he can take even a step let alone be directed on his way by its help. Besides, although they may chance to sprinkle their books with droplets of truth, how many monstrous lies defile them! In short, they never even sensed that assurance of God's benevolence toward us (without which man's understanding can only be filled with boundless confusion).[915]

Of particular interest in this quotation is the idea that some of the divine insights, or "droplets of truth" that Calvin recognized to be present in pagan thought, were *in spite of* the overall views of the philosophers (note highlight), a clear (gracious) revelation of God, fundamentally inconsistent with the views of the recipient.[916] The compulsion to speak truth is not because of the Devil's involvement, but because of God's temporary enlightenment. McNeil's comment noted above, considered in isolation, can be misunderstood: "discernment" suggests careful consideration—quite the opposite of the picture that Calvin paints in the quotation above. Calvin recognized, at times with explicit approval,[917] the occasional glimmers of *religious* truth within philosophers' and orators' ideas (though he would, at times note their limitations[918] or re-interpret them—e.g., the *sensus divinitatis*—see section 4.2.2.). However, I suggest that these were considered to be only divine flashes, and were certainly not due to the "discernment" of the thinker: lightning is not a suitable metaphor to suggest ratiocination, being both unexpected and transient. As Bouwsma observed, Calvin, by and large, scorned philosophers' religious ideas.[919]

While recognizing some religious insight, Calvin emphasized key doctrines *not* known by the philosophers, and hence the total inadequacies of their belief systems.[920] Unlike some of his contemporaries, he rejected outright a multilinear view of revelation, and an independent Gentile revelation tradition.[921] Given such a position, Calvin did not admit a "second level" authority of revelation into his thinking.[922] As noted earlier, there was patristic warrant for the traditional *prisca theologia* scheme; however, Calvin made it clear that he did not consider himself bound to follow the fathers blindly, when he considered they had strayed.[923] Speculation was a serious weakness in any methodology, and ancient theology theories were, I believe, dangerously speculative in his thinking.[924] Calvin was extremely wary of the "penetration" of philosophical thought into Christianity.[925] As Stengel has noted, the cross was out on the periphery of much ancient theology thinking,[926] and the worry that heresy could often be traced to the penetration of philosophical thought into Christianity was clearly present.[927] Calvin consistently minimized the significance of what religious truth he deemed to be present in the thought of philosophers. Like Gianfrancesco Pico,[928] Calvin sought to stress discontinuity, rather than continuity between the philosophers and Christianity.

I turn now to a second reason in support of the view that Calvin may have more purposefully rejected various ancient theology traditions. While Calvin did make comments on the history of religions (as he understood the field, and as documented in section 1.2 above), he was more intent on establishing individual human accountability to God, as opposed to considering the societal outworking of such idolatry, and what this meant for different individuals born within and participating in these societies in history.[929] As noted above, while there are occasional forays into discussion of historical-sociological religiosity in his writings, a strong connection is not made between the two. Preus has rightly noted a significant difference between Zwingli and Calvin in this regard.[930] Preus differentiates a historical or empirical approach to the field to one focused on a natural or essentialist understanding. He placed Zwingli in the first camp, and Calvin in the second. He comments, "rather than tracing the origin of religion, Calvin discussed its basis in human nature, apart from the question of historical beginning."[931] It is undoubtedly right to acknowledge that Calvin adopted an essentially ahistorical approach to his theology of religions, especially in the first five chapters of Book 1 of the *Institutes*—in some ways similar to that of the Apostle Paul in Romans 1.[932] However, I believe there is sufficient material (see section 1.2) to soften the idea that he was *totally* disinterested in this history.

4. The *Logos* of God in Calvin's Theology of Religions

In this section I analyze Calvin's commentary on the first few verses of chapter 1 of St. John's gospel within its historical context. I consider what the Reformer said about the *Logos* and his understanding of one role of the *Logos* in relation to non-Christian religions.

4.1. Background

Calvin completed the Latin version of his commentary on John in 1552,[933] after having written and revised his Pauline commentaries, and having finished work on the catholic epistles.[934] Larsson believes Calvin wrote the commentary with the understanding that the reader would have already read the *Institutes*.[935] He argues the polemical orientation of the commentary to be twofold: against Roman Catholic interpretation (especially its metaphysical emphases),[936] and secondly, with an emphasis on reprimands, both those in the text, and in his own application.[937] He believes Calvin's guiding hermeneutical approach to John's gospel to have been anthropocentric, focusing on humankind not obscuring God's glory, rather than this glory itself.[938] Larsson sees such an approach as having been developed, in part, in response to challenges in Geneva.[939] Pitkin also believes that "theological anthropology" is a key guiding principle for Calvin in his approach to and understanding of John's gospel.[940] She believes that Calvin built on Melanchthon and Luther's view of John's gospel, namely one emphasizing faith in Christ and its consequences.[941] She endorses the view of Farmer that there is a shift in focus from the Christological issues that dominated early and mediaeval church thinking, towards truly knowing one's self before one can be saved,[942] together with a "concern for the moral implications of the Gospel."[943]

4.2. Analysis of the Treatment of the Johannine Prologue

Like Erasmus, Calvin chose to use the French equivalent of *speech* rather than *word* for the translation of *Logos* in John 1, commenting that "the speech" (*sermo*) creates humankind and also preserves us. He then distinguishes humankind from animals on the grounds of our understanding and ability to reason (v. 4). Despite these special human endowments, Calvin states that they are diminished after the Fall: the darkness of verse 5 in the prologue is the darkness of the sinful human mind: reason is powerless to lead us to God. The Speech, however, still mediates two lights to humankind: "The light which still dwells in corrupt nature consists chiefly of two parts; for, first, all men naturally possess some seed of religion; and, secondly, the distinction between good and evil is engraven on their consciences."[944] Calvin goes on to contrast the light received by humankind with the response to it: "But, what are the fruits that ultimately spring from it [the light], except that religion degenerates into a thousand monsters of superstition, and conscience perverts every decision, so as to confound vice with virtue?"[945]

Calvin differentiates two "powers" of the Son of God in the Johannine prologue: the first evident in "the structure of the world and the order of nature," and the second in its renewal and restoration.[946] The two-fold light that humankind now receives from "the grace of the Son of God" is mediated by the Word in the first (and only the first) of these roles or powers.[947] The second role is necessitated by human blindness to the initial gifting. New aid is given in the incarnation.[948] While Calvin uses the term "blindness" to describe the human condition, he acknowledges that sparks remain,[949] and while he initially condemns conscience as defunct, in verse 9 he acknowledges that it works (at least to a certain extent) suggestive of a rhetorical emphasis earlier on. His overall intent seems to be that reason (enlightened by the *Sermo*) can no longer guide humans back to God, although he acknowledges that it is sufficient to regulate life and develop society. This, however, is ultimately of no lasting spiritual value.[950]

On verse 9 Calvin rejects the idea that the light being referred to is the Gospel, preferring to understand it as a universal enlightening of humankind—all of whom receive this light. He downplays what this light can achieve for fallen humans, differentiating it from the light of faith, calling it "the common light of nature, which is far inferior to faith." The shift from the *Logos* in verse 1 to the focus on humankind's reception of *Logos* light in John 1:4, is, Pitkin believes, a good example of Calvin's desire to make pertinent anthropological points when he could.

Pitkin notes that for Aquinas and the fathers, life and light in the Prologue "refer to the Divine word."[951] She notes that the light, for Erasmus, is Christ.[952] For Calvin, however, this is not the case. This shift in focus, Pitkin argues is quite unique:

> Calvin seems to have departed entirely from the traditional view that the Word or Speech itself is the light. The Speech as agent of creation and providence is rather the source of the light that exists in human minds in order to lead them to acknowledge God; "light" is not the Speech, but a mirror in which the divine power of the Speech can be beheld.[953]

Pitkin goes on to say, "Calvin completes the shift from christological to anthropological focus in his comments on verse 5. Here the light that shines in the darkness is not Christ or the Word or even the gospel but rather the seed of religion and the distinction between good and evil still engraved on the fallen human conscience."[954]

While Calvin is known to have respected Chrysostom, he did not follow him on his understanding that the shining of verse 9 is the light of the Gospel.[955] Calvin's division of the *Logos* roles in this passage is not developed in his thinking, and neither are its implications. The difficulties in making sense of the twofold mediation of the eternal Son in Calvin's thought have been recognized and discussed by a number of scholars.[956] I submit that the work to which he put the division in the prologue is of great significance for his view of religions.[957] I believe his approach allowed him to avoid pantheism, while at the same time enabling him to connect humankind to God by natural law, thereby allowing him to argue for both the presence and the inexcusability of false religion.

Concerning his rejection of pantheism, while Backus terms Cyril's influence on Calvin's treatment of the prologue "omnipresent,"[958] I suggest this claim needs to be qualified due to Calvin's significant shift away from Cyril's emphasis on humankind's participation in the *Logos* in this passage.[959] While there is life dependence in Calvin's comments on fallen humankind in this passage, there is no real participation.[960] Participation occurs pre-fall and for redeemed humanity, but not in humankind's fallen state in Calvin's thought.[961] Calvin may have adopted this interpretation to consciously steer clear of a kind of stoic *Logos* pantheism or Stoic *logos spermatikos* idea.[962]

Turning to the first part of the light—the *semen religionis*—the seed of religion is referred to a number of times in the *Institutes* and in Calvin's commentaries, with slightly different emphases.[963] Why did Calvin use the seed metaphor? Horowitz notes it is one of the images commonly used to depict the source of virtue in Stoic thought (alongside "Reason," "common notions," and "sparks").[964] Horowitz believes that these "unit ideas" as she terms them, show the connection between man and God's law in Stoic thought.[965] Calvin's use of three of these terms in his exegesis of the Johannine prologue is suggestive, at the very least, of influence and Eire specifically contrasts Calvin's borrowing of the Stoic universal dissemination of the seed of religion idea, with Zwingli's rejection of it.[966] However, on closer examination, the borrowing is more of the shell of the seed, rather than its kernel (to extend the metaphor reference). For Calvin, there was no possibility that reason (or the seed or indeed the spark) could guide anyone to righteousness as the Stoics believed possible.[967] Unlike Stoic thought, where the seed metaphor indicated a potential for growth, typically developed through education, for Calvin *post lapsum*, the seed of religion produces dreadful fruit.[968] In Stoic thought man develops through training: in Calvin's he slides into a thousand monstrosities of religion.[969] While Calvin mentioned the *semen religionis* in his discussion of the soul,[970] his language stands in sharp contrast to the idea of man containing divinity within himself, an idea he explicitly rejected.[971] Overall, as Williams notes, the Stoic view of humankind was essentially that of pre-lapsarian Adam, not fallen man, and therein lay their error in Calvin's view.[972] Wolterstorff believes Calvin speaks of the seed of religion as both a disposition and also innate knowledge of God.[973]

Like Augustine, Calvin linked John 1:5 with Romans 1:21.[974] In his exposition on 1 Corinthians 1:21 he states that the philosophers were no exception to those who knew, but did not know God. He states, "For there will not be found one of them [the philosophers], that has not from that first principle of knowledge, which I have mentioned, straightway turned aside into wandering and erroneous speculations, and for the most part they betray a silliness worse than that of old wives." The comment is similar to that found in Augustine's thought—though lacking the idea of falling in with demons, following the turning away. In his remarks on 1 Corinthians 2:11, Calvin also refers to John 1:5, noting that it is the Spirit who can open blind eyes.[975]

4.2.1. The Sensus Divinitatis in Context

At this point in the discussion a necessary diversion away from the Prologue commentary text is required, in order to give essential context to a point I will be developing in the pages that follow. The particular issue I wish to focus on is the *sensus divinitatis*, and its relation to the *semen religionis* in Calvin's thinking.

Calvin's use of the term *sensus divinitatis*, commonly translated as *the sense/awareness of the divine*, has been referenced and appealed to by various apologists, theologians, theologians of religion/s and missiologists to serve a number of (often conflicting) purposes. Typically, the rather "simple" appeal to the *sensus* has been made solely with reference to the first few chapters of Book 1 of the *Institutes*, where the term is used. It does not occur elsewhere in Calvin's writings, but any failure to take into account relevant and related thought found elsewhere in the Calvin corpus, which may help understand his purpose(s) in using it, would obviously be a concern.[976]

Notably absent in discussion on the *sensus* to date has been how the term should be understood in relation to the *semen religionis* and how the two terms (together) should be understood in relation to the phenomenon of non-Christian religion. More commonly the *sensus* has been discussed alone and in the context of epistemological and/or apologetical concerns.[977] In what follows I provide some broader textual context before considering this relationship.

In Calvin's theology as developed in the first five chapters of Book 1 of the *Institutes*, there are three ways in which God reveals himself to all: through creation (this being perceived through the senses of the individual); through providence (in history, society and in an individual's life); and by internal revelation to the individual.[978] The first "channel" can be understood as God's manifestation in everything that is in this world, though excluding humankind's creations. The second centers on God's ongoing engagement in the world: namely, the maintenance of his creation, his ordering of society, and his directing of history. The third is some kind of "innate" knowledge of God—a quite controversial subject in the Calvin literature.

Calvin's treatment of God's universal revelation in the first few chapters of Book 1 of the *Institutes* focuses primarily on the negative consequences of this revelation for humankind after the fall and its ineffectiveness in producing reconciliation. He stresses the need for special revelation (in particular Scripture, together with the enlightenment of the Holy Spirit) to address the condition of the *post-lapsum* sinner.[979] Calvin's treatment of Scripture in chapters 6–10 of Book 1 of the *Institutes* contrasts the clarity of its message with universal revelation (as documented in chapters 1–5). Further, his discussion of the Trinity in chapter 13 follows his condemnation of idolatry in chapters 11 and 12, namely humankind's failed attempts to "bridge the gap" documented in the first five chapters of the *Institutes*. Such is the wider context within which Calvin's usage of the *sensus* occurs.

Turning now to the idea of the *sensus divinitatis*, and focusing on what he said of it, Calvin called the innate,[980] "God-endowed" revelation to know God and to receive and interpret his revelation an "awareness of divinity."[981] Possible synonyms are "sense of deity"[982] and "impression of a divine being."[983] Calvin believed that "there is within the human mind, and indeed by natural instinct, an awareness of divinity."[984] Commenting further on this awareness he stated, "God himself has implanted in all men a certain understanding of his divine majesty."[985] Because of humankind's fallen nature and sinful choices, Calvin maintained that we fight with and struggle with this awareness of the divine. However, the awareness is tenacious: were it to be blotted out, humankind would lose its humanness.[986] According to Calvin, "a sense of divinity . . . can never be effaced,"[987] and a function of the *sensus* is a means of goading humankind to seek God.[988] Part of the reason for the "indestructibility" of the *sensus* in Calvin's thought is that "it is fixed deep within, as it were in the very marrow."[989] For Calvin, the conviction that there is some God "is naturally inborn in all."[990]

The comments above suggest some kind of knowledge of God, but Calvin also speaks of human awareness of God in ways which seem to weaken the import of some of these statements. For example, he states that atheists extinguish "the light of nature"[991] and that humankind imagines God according to its own presumptions.[992] Further, he states that "it appears that if men were taught only by nature, they would hold to nothing certain or solid or clear-cut, but would be so tied to confused principles as to worship an unknown god."[993] Outside the *Institutes* Calvin argues that the idea of God can be buried[994] and that "true doctrine" can be extinguished.[995] In his exposition of Hebrews 11:3, he talks about the "knowledge" of God that the heathen have as "an opinion" which is "evanescent," describing this as "a mere shadow of some uncertain deity, and not the knowledge of the true God."

Much has been written about the *sensus divinitatis*, especially whether it is knowledge, a disposition for knowledge, possible but not real knowledge, or something of a red herring—an insignificant part of Calvin's thinking.[996] My own position is that there is some kind of knowledge, as I will explain in what follows. I will also argue that it was important for Calvin to maintain this knowledge in his war against idolatry, and to differentiate it from false religion—the corrupt fruit of the *semen religionis*.

4.2.2. The *Semen Religionis* and the *Sensus Divinitatis*

What is the relationship between the *semen religionis* and the *sensus divinitatis* in Calvin's thinking?

Though observing small differences between the two, Dowey believes Calvin to have used the two terms to mean basically the same thing.[997] Dowey is not alone: Parker, McNeill, Bavinck, Jones, Hoitenga, Eire, and Potgieter also understand the two terms as roughly synonymous.[998] There is ample justification for adopting such an interpretation, not least because some of Calvin's own comments strongly suggest this.[999]

However, the understanding that the two terms are basically the same, or used in a very similar way by Calvin, is not universally accepted. Capetz, for example, states that the two terms "emphasize differing aspects of the same reality."[1000] He suggests that the *semen religionis* is the source for the religious response, *based* on the awareness of God. A rather different view is held by Woolford, who argues that the *sensus* refers to awareness of God and the *semen religionis* the awareness of the worship he should be given.[1001] Gootjes, on the other hand, interprets Calvin to say that the *semen religionis* includes external revelation, whereas the *sensus* refers to just innate knowledge.[1002] He believes the *semen religionis* to be "the source of man's religion, his faith, obedience and worship."[1003]

Preus goes a step further than the scholars noted above, in interpreting the *sensus* as a kind of common grace brake upon the activity of religion. He states, "It is only the persistence of the sense of divinity in man that prevents religion from degenerating completely."[1004] I do not think Calvin went so far as Preus argues here, but I do suggest that the tension at which Preus hints in this comment can be of considerable help in getting to grips with Calvin's thought. Generally speaking, the *sensus* refers to an awareness of God and his revelation (which Calvin stresses at times and minimizes at other times). On the other hand, his treatment of the *semen religionis* (*post lapsum*) focuses primarily on human religiosity which is negative and inappropriate. I suggest that the different focus and stress may be significant, and that employing an idolatry hermeneutic key may be of significant assistance in interpretation—as I explain in what follows.

Within the historical context outlined in section 1.1, above, it is clear that Calvin viewed idolatry as *a* or indeed *the* key religious challenge of his times. What light might this fact shed on his use of the terms *sensus divinitatis* and *semen religionis*? An important element of his anti-idolatry polemic, as hinted before, is his emphasis on the dishonesty, duplicity and hypocrisy in humankind's idolatrous religious behavior. On a number of occasions, the Reformer suggests that "deep down" there exists a tension between false religious practice and the ongoing sense of the divine.[1005] In the two quotations below I note this tension. In the first, Calvin explicitly contrasts the corrupt fruit of the seed[1006] with the ongoing awareness of the true God: "And though so soon as they begin to think upon God, they vanish away in wicked inventions, and so the pure seed doth degenerate into corruptions; *yet the first general knowledge of God doth nevertheless remain still in them* [emphasis mine]."[1007] In the second he states:

> When, therefore, men invent for themselves various gods, and when everyone is led here and there without any judgment, it is a monstrous thing; *for when the subject is pressed on the attention of the rudest, they confess that there is some supreme deity, and are at length constrained to allow that there is but one true God* [emphasis mine]; whence then is it that there is such a multitude and variety of gods in the world? How is it that they who hold this principle—that God ought to be worshipped—fall

away, and adopt many gods, and never can determine who the true God is, or how he is to be worshipped?[1008]

In both of these extracts (the first written in relation to Athenian idolatry, the second being a more general indictment of humankind's religious behavior), Calvin states that false religious practices, i.e., the corrupt fruit of the *semen religionis*, can co-exist, though not peacefully, with some sort of ongoing testimony of the *sensus divinitatis*, the knowledge that a supreme God exists, a God the adherents *know* they do not worship when pressed on this issue, or which they confess to worship along with other gods.[1009] The belief that some kind of knowledge continues in the midst of irreligious practice, and the idea that idolatry substitution operates at the level of the mediator not at the knowledge of God himself, should be noted.[1010] Mediation is, I believe, central to his argument against false religion. Calvin argues that a reason for idolatry is the absence or rejection of a merciful mediator, and this is consistent with his distinction of the two roles of the *Logos* in the Johannine prologue, discussed in section 4:

> For even if many men once boasted that they worshiped the Supreme majesty, the Maker of Heaven and Earth, yet because they had no Mediator it was not possible for them truly to taste God's mercy, and thus be persuaded that he was their Father. Accordingly, because they did not hold Christ as their Head, they possessed only a fleeting knowledge of God.[1011]

The substitution of honor that occurs in idolatry in Calvin's thought is the creation of a set of intermediate gods, not actually a rival God. He makes this point clearly in the following comment on Hosea 2:8, concerning the Roman Catholic Church of his day:

> It is the same with the Papists of the present day; they have their Baalim; not that they regard their patrons in the place of God: but as they dread every access to God, and understand not that Christ is a mediator, they retake themselves here and there to various Baalim, that they may procure favour to themselves; and at the same time, whatever honour they show to stones, or wood, or bones of dead men, or to any of their own inventions, they call it the worship of God.[1012]

Calvin believed the tendency to "install" a set of patron sub-deities, or a pantheon of deities, between humankind and the supreme God to have been a common activity since the fall.[1013] Such being the case, I suggest he is able to contrast the ongoing *sensus divinitatis*, an awareness of the true God, with the fruit of the *semen religionis*, evidenced in the creation of demi-gods and idols.

I suggest, therefore, that Calvin employs the *sensus* neither to prove the existence of God nor to challenge claims to atheism,[1014] but rather to highlight religious hypocrisy and culpability. If there were not some ongoing real knowledge of God, his anti-idolatry polemic could not be meaningful or effective. The kind of knowledge he allows for is not just limited to a stimulus to religion, but an ongoing testimony. The idea of war with God, of some kind of internal religious conflict among adherents of false religions that Calvin speaks of,[1015] makes no sense if the awareness or knowledge of the true God has actually been replaced, or is so dimly perceived as to almost not be there.

I believe that this interpretation not only fits Calvin's comments on religions (largely overlooked by those discussing the term within its immediate context alone) but also supports, in part, Capetz' view on Calvin's primary goal in writing the first few chapters of Book 1 of the *Institutes*. Capetz states that "the purpose of the introductory chapters [of the *Institutes*] is to convince us that false religion in its various manifestations is at odds with the essential or 'created' character of human existence."[1016]

Having spent some time on this important excursus concerning the *semen religionis* and its relation to the *sensus divinitatis*, I now return back to the commentary on John, to consider the second part of the light mediated by the *Logos*—conscience: "the distinction between good and evil is engraven on their consciences."[1017]

4.2.3. Conscience

Very briefly, it can be said that Calvin spoke of the conscience executing certain functions, and also having cognitive content too.[1018] At any one time in the *Institutes*, or elsewhere, Calvin could focus on a particular function (and call this function *conscience*), or a particular cognitive element, and do the same. He could also use conscience as a rough synonym for the mind.[1019] Accordingly, the term *conscience* has a remarkable elasticity/non-specificity in Calvin's thought.

Although the Reformer does not discuss to what conscience refers in making differentiations between right and wrong in his comments here, it cannot be doubted that it is God's will for humankind, i.e., natural law, that he had in mind.[1020] For Calvin, the conscience and natural law interface seems to be as follows: The *Logos* implants the natural law in man's heart/soul/conscience which, in turn, serves as the guiding star to conscience, also part of the soul of man. Conscience, in turn, having reference to God's standards and "spying on man" accuses humankind when we fall short of these standards, making us feel guilty. In the final step of the cycle, conscience brings us to the judgment bar of God, where the voice of conscience throughout life is endorsed by God. A complete circle is important to maintain, as Calvin stressed the ultimately Godward orientation of conscience.[1021] While Calvin does say, occasionally, that the conscience judges,[1022] this role is rather carried out by God himself. In Calvin's thought, conscience is spy, witness and court convenor: one might say it pronounces a "preliminary" (informal, though informed) verdict on our actions. Being put there by God, God's executor becomes, in the final judgment, fallen humankind's executioner.[1023]

Calvin interpreted the natural law known by humans in different ways (less or more, first table versus second table knowledge) depending on his focus.[1024] I would suggest that in the Johannine prologue he must have in mind both first and second table, because of the twinning with the *semen religionis*. Elsewhere, he explicitly links conscience with idolatry (that is, first table awareness),[1025] and suggests that pagan magistrates know of their need to regulate religious piety (not just human relationships).[1026]

The law only (*lex nuda*) gift, mediated by the *Logos* is dreadful in Calvin's view.[1027] This is because the bare law is only condemnatory, having no propaedeutic role, unlike the fuller mosaic law (containing promise).[1028] Calvin equated Christ and the Law,[1029] emphasized the unity of the Old and New Testaments,[1030] and stressed that Christ was the fulfilment[1031] and substance of the law[1032] as well as its interpreter[1033] and mediator.[1034] The law with promise—the mosaic law—foreshadows Christ incarnate and crucified. However, the accomplishment of redemption is the second role of the *Logos*, a role that Calvin explicitly rejected as being present in enlightenment of the *Logos* in the prologue.[1035]

While the influence of Stoic thought on Calvin's view of natural law is well documented, and generally acknowledged, the influence in his treatment of the prologue exhibits both dependence and rejection.[1036] In Calvin's view the *Logos* mediates the natural law to all through conscience, rather than the Stoic channel of reason.[1037] Another difference is that natural law is a gift in Calvin's thinking, and as noted earlier this does not signify participation, as it does in Stoic thought.[1038] Unlike in Stoicism, in Calvin's view it is God who gives and informs the conscience.[1039] A number of scholars have noted the critical role of conscience as part of God's revelation to humankind in Calvin's thought.[1040] While it may well pervert some decision making (as Calvin notes in the first part of the passage—though not the latter part), Calvin could also term it a terror, and it seems to be an aspect of God's revelation that, even post-fall, Calvin considered to be still functioning, though not always perfectly.[1041] If natural law were really so vague to conscience, or if conscience did not function appropriately, it could not be such a terror to humankind. Calvin makes numerous references to conscience being a merciless accuser, having a power which cannot be overcome/suppressed.

While not wishing to seek precision in Calvin's thinking where it should not be sought, I suggest it is reasonable to equate conscience here with part of what Calvin meant by the *sensus divinitatis*.[1042] Such an interpretation would strengthen my earlier argument, concerning a difference in focus in this term, compared to the *semen religionis*.

Returning to the idea of the dual roles of the *Logos*, I suggest that in Calvin's thinking fallen humankind seeks the fruit of the second role or part of the *Logos* (the renewal and restoration role) through its own idolatrous responses to the first, to pacify conscience troubled by the *lex nuda*, with the goal of seeking forgiveness.[1043] As noted earlier, the seeking of forgiveness is a common thread in his idea of false religions. The idea that idolatry is, in essence, the creation of false mediators, rather than substitution of the true God, is, I believe, clearly present in Calvin's thought.[1044]

Conclusion

In summarizing the conclusions of this chapter, I refer to two claims, noted in passing above, which I engage with in more detail here.

Carlos Eire argued that Calvin is best understood as being an anthropological theologian of religions, stating that for Calvin "religion springs from human nature,"[1045] and that "false religion ... is ... encoded in our genes."[1046] Preus makes a similar comment: "Calvin discussed the source for religion in completely anthropological terms."[1047] Nuovo seems to concur with these views.[1048] In what follows, I will suggest that these evaluations seem to miss an important element of Calvin's thought.

Calvin's demotion of the role of Satan, and rejection of the ancient theology traditions in his understanding of religions seem reasonably clear. I have suggested that his aversion to speculation and worries over the penetration of philosophical thought into true religion may be behind these responses. Enlightenment from the *Logos*, when considered alongside his understanding of sin, enabled Calvin to account for both sparks of truth and error in non-Christian thought and religion.[1049]

I suggest that the problem with an anthropological reading of Calvin's idea on religions is that it suggests an innate tendency without sufficiently recognizing that religious activity is, for Calvin, a reaction or reflection (largely, though not totally, inappropriate) of gifts mediated by the *Logos* in his creating and sustaining capacity. When Eire states, "As Calvin saw it, whatever springs from the *semen religionis* comes from within the human self, not from any divine source, much less from the *Logos Spermatikos*," this claim minimizes or overlooks the fact that the ultimate source of the *semen religionis* and natural law is the *Logos* in Calvin's thought.[1050] Humankind is involved in a continuous response to God's ongoing gifts: conscience, and religiosity are not simply one-off deposits in Calvin's thinking: they are part of God's ongoing engagement with his creation, together with our response to him. Kraemer, I believe, accurately portrays this tension: "Calvin evinces in his words an awareness that there is in the religions, despite their utter failure and reprehensibleness, a confused discourse with God, the Father of Jesus Christ."[1051]

I submit that for Calvin religions are an inappropriate response to a partial revelation from the *Logos*, who mediates the *lex nuda*, God's will to humans who are made in the image of God to be in communion with God. This being so, one would expect non-Christian thought and religion to contain "sparks" of order and creation in Calvin's thinking, reflecting to some extent the sustaining role of the *Logos*. Such indeed seem to be Calvin's conclusions in his praise of the this-worldly wisdom evident in some philosophies and religions. In this limited sense, therefore, false religions (or perhaps more accurately elements of them) may be considered to be of some *earthly* value in Calvin's thought—though I am not aware of Calvin ever having said this.[1052]

Rather than fanning the sparks of truth present outside the church so that they would combine into a larger, harmonious flame (cf. Ficino and Pico) Calvin believed these sparks were extinguished mid-flight. Further, he considered them very insignificant sparks when compared to the glory of the light of Christ—the heart, rather than the hands and feet of the *Logos*.[1053] His rejection of the idea of redemptive christological mediation, and the absence of actual spiritual enlightenment in his commentary on St. John's prologue, explains why Calvin was so negative about religions in terms of their *spiritual* ends and goals.

5

Jonathan Edwards[1054]

Background

JONATHAN EDWARDS (1703–58) HAS been termed "arguably America's greatest religious genius."[1055] Part of that label carries with it some ambiguity as to whether he was primarily a philosopher, churchman, philosopher-theologian (or vice versa), or an apologist.[1056] In terms of his relationship to the Reformed tradition, while Edwards was happy to take on the Calvinist label, he stressed that he was so in principle, rather than being a follower of Calvin.[1057] He has been interpreted by some as seeking to clothe these Reformed convictions in appropriate Enlightenment garb,[1058] valuing the freedom to innovate and speculate.[1059]

Regarding his engagement with the theologians discussed in chapters 2, 3, and 4, he called Justin Martyr "an eminent father in the Christian church,"[1060] and referred to Calvin a number of times.[1061] However, he made very little reference to Augustine ("Austin").[1062] Reformed theologians who have been deemed to have played a role in his thinking include John Owen,[1063] Francis Turretin[1064] and Peter van Mastricht.[1065] In addition to these Reformed theological influences, other people considered to have shaped Edwards's thought include (in alphabetical order): Bishop George Berkeley,[1066] his father,[1067] Locke,[1068] Malebranche,[1069] Henry More[1070] (and other Cambridge Platonists), Newton,[1071] and physico-theologians.[1072]

It is not uncommon for the same writer (e.g., Calvin or Locke) to have been considered a significant influence in one area, while specifically disregarded or not followed in another.[1073] Crisp and Strobel describe him thus: "he was a lifelong intellectual magpie who promiscuously gathered into his nest ideas and arguments from many different sources."[1074] This view echoes the earlier appraisal of William Morris.[1075]

As noted above, it is commonly understood that Edwards did not like to follow the ideas of a particular authority slavishly.[1076] While this is undoubtedly true in some areas, it is less so in others. As will be noted below, his readings and engagement with scholars who documented their views on the sources for and teachings of non-Christian religions showed considerable, one might say uncharacteristically uncritical, dependency. This is important to note, as this particular area of his work is in primary focus in this chapter.

1. The Works of Jonathan Edwards

Before focusing on Edwards's thought on non-Christian religion, it is important to make brief reference to the materials in the Jonathan Edwards corpus. Edwards was not a systematic theologian, in terms of his approach to discussing theology, although some of his theological treatments were more systematic than others.[1077] The material in the Jonathan Edwards corpus includes his sermons, publications, letters, and notebook entries. Concerning the latter, there are a large number of references to the *miscellanies* in what follows (volumes 13, 18, 20, and 23 of the *Works of Jonathan Edwards Online*). These are notebook entries of varying lengths. The status of these documents is somewhat contentious, and hence requires some comment before proceeding further.

Some scholars have contrasted the *miscellanies* with what Edwards taught publicly, and argued for a tension between the two: the public face conservative, the private more speculative.[1078] Others have strongly argued against the legitimacy of this interpretation.[1079] It has been suggested by some that the *miscellanies* are incomplete musings, and therefore should be considered less representative of his final thoughts, and as such not be given equal status to the work published in his lifetime.[1080] While there may be some validity to these arguments, Ava Chamberlain has forcibly demonstrated that the *miscellanies* not be considered merely private musings, in part because of the way they are written.[1081] Marsden believes them to be the source material for the great magnum opus Edwards planned to write, but never did,[1082] and the fact Edwards was willing to let colleagues borrow journals of *miscellanies* also supports the argument that they were not just private notes.[1083] Further, as Waddington observes, it is clear that he transferred ideas from the *miscellanies* into his public material.[1084] Accordingly, my approach in this chapter has been to give material from the *miscellanies* equal standing with other writings in the corpus—evidencing as they do conservativism at one time and more speculative leanings at another. However, where the hypothetical or speculative nature of an idea is actually flagged by Edwards in a particular *miscellany* I note this, and treat it as such. Before engaging with Edwards's historical context, I summarize his view of religion, and a key distinction he made between notional and sensible religion.

2. Religion and the Knowledge of God

2.1. Definition of Religion

Edwards believed that religion is "the great business . . . for which we are created," and in which our true happiness consists.[1085] He defines religion as "an intercourse between ourselves and our Maker," grounded in true knowledge of self and God.[1086] Edwards stressed the involvement of the affections in true religion,[1087] stating that "true religion, in great part, consists in holy affections."[1088] Love being foundational to his definition, religion not based on this is called "hypocrisy and a vain show."[1089] Following in the steps of Calvin[1090] and the Westminster divines[1091] he distinguished notional (or speculative) religious knowledge from "sensible" knowledge of God, the latter being experiential, spiritual and true.[1092]

2.2. Speculative versus Sensible Knowledge of God

Speculative or notional knowledge of God includes implanted knowledge, light of nature/reason (see below) as well as knowledge through revelation.[1093] Notional knowledge of religious truth was understood by Edwards to function on the same plane as scientific knowledge—being essentially "natural," and more or less competent.[1094] He believed that the Holy Spirit could enhance both religious or scientific knowledge, assisting reason and conscience, without communicating himself.[1095]

Edwards differentiated notional knowledge from sensible knowledge, a head versus a heart knowledge of God.[1096] While he stressed the importance of a sensible knowledge of religious things, notional knowledge gained from implanted knowledge, the light of nature and revelation is fundamentally important because without this there could be no sensible knowledge.[1097] The latter is direct (not mediated)[1098] and involves real "apprehension," rather than engagement with "signs" alone.[1099] A "new sense" is required for there to be sensible knowledge, this sense raising the mind above its natural earth-bound orientation and response to the light of nature or revelation.[1100] The provision of this new sense is by a work of God in the heart, not due to the attainment of new knowledge, per se. The consequence of this heart change is a new perspective on what has been previously known, whether in revelation or nature. This new sense enables the person to view revelation or the light of nature appropriately, not simply as facts.[1101] Sholl summarizes Edwards thought thus: "When a person receives grace through the work of the Holy Spirit, argues Edwards, God instills a new principle that transforms the sense of the heart. The transformed state enables a person to have a 'new simple idea,' a novel apprehension of the reality already experienced that leads to a new habit."[1102] He also states, "God's illumination, for Edwards, synthesizes internal reflection about the world and the external sensation of it."[1103]

For Edwards, the effect of the new sense is not only to restore the supernatural principle lost at the fall so that the Spirit now guides the natural faculties, but also to sanctify (natural) reason as well.[1104] I discuss Edwards's thought on reason and the noetic effects of the fall in more detail in section 6.1. I do so because of the need to understand how his thinking in this area impacts his thought on reason and the light of nature.

2.3. Common Grace

As mentioned above, Edwards believed the Holy Spirit could be at work, non-salvifically, in unbelievers. Common grace could, for Edwards, lead to a heightened awareness of God's communication (through the light of nature or revelation), without the bestowal of true grace. He stated: "Natural men may have common grace, common illuminations and common affections, that are from the Spirit of God, as appears by *Hebrews*

6:4,"[1105] and: "Natural men may have convictions from the Spirit of God, but 'tis from the Spirit of God only as assisting natural principles, and not infusing any new and supernatural principle."[1106] In the *Religious Affections* Edwards distinguished insights of philosophers from the work of the Spirit in the church, by calling the former enabling "a more than ordinary, though not special and saving assistance of the Spirit."[1107] A key reason why "illumined" philosophers (i.e., those who received "great illuminations" and "elevations of mind") were not considered "truly gracious" (i.e., Christians) was the absence of humility, this attribute an essential indicator of true knowledge and an internal work of the Spirit in Edwards's thinking.[1108] Developments in arts, science, war and peace associated with these thinkers were contrasted with their religious growth, termed on one occasion "an uncultivated desert."[1109] Having noted this, the consequence of the Spirit's "external" work may, in certain cases, include the attainment of a kind of moral virtue,[1110] and the possible fruits of this are considerable, including a generous charitable giving.[1111] However, the key ingredient missing from such virtue was the critical element which only an *internal* operation of the Spirit could effect—love.[1112]

3. Historical Background and the Enlightenment Context

The Arminian "threat" was traditionally understood to have been the key foil to Edwards's writings and sermons.[1113] That this was a serious concern to be addressed head on by Edwards is beyond dispute.[1114] However, in a newer analysis of his thought, taking into account a much wider range of his writings, McDermott, Zakai, and Zhu, among others, have persuasively argued that Edwards perceived deism to be the key challenge of his day.[1115] Embodying as it did a whole range of issues which Edwards felt strongly about, he spent considerable time and effort preaching and writing against it.

As Harrison has noted, deism is probably far more nuanced than is typically understood.[1116] Historians generally agree that there was no singular unified deist movement; indeed the idea that there was a movement at all has also been called into question.[1117] Barnett argues that the main thrust of the "movement" was anti-clericism (i.e., was focused against clerical abuse) rather than being anti-revelation in orientation.[1118] Harrison, on the other hand, believed that the real issue for the deists was the *relationship* of natural religion to revelation,[1119] reason being viewed as a type of revelation by Toland[1120] and Locke.[1121] Other historians, as noted by Hudson, believe deism was, at heart, focused on the establishment of natural religion,[1122] due to the belief that reason was seen to be competent and sufficient.[1123] The sparks of truth identified by Calvin, were, in such a viewpoint, not just sparks, but sound foundations for "natural" religion.[1124]

A key subject of contention and interpretation taken up by some deists in this era to support their arguments was their understanding of Chinese religion.[1125] Jesuit missionaries reported Christian-like elements in Chinese culture and religion. How were these to be understood? Deists adopted two main positions. The first was to appeal to natural religion and reason to explain what was being observed.[1126] The second was to argue that Egyptian wisdom was the source of such civilization and culture.[1127] The main argument of those who opposed deist writers (including Edwards) was that it was Christianity (more specifically the Old Testament, or parts of it) which was the source of all religion and possibly all wisdom also—whether in Chinese religion or other non-Christian religious expression.[1128] References to religions within this debate were far from disinterested: interpretations of reports of these "exotic" religions were the key munitions used in the war for and against certain deist positions. Edwards's engagement with religions was, accordingly, highly polemical.[1129]

It is fair to say that Edwards recognized the diversity present within deist writings and he undoubtedly read some deists' works including those of Toland, Chubb[1130] and Tindal.[1131] In a sweeping summary of what he believed deists to stand for, he understood their position to be: anti-Bible, anti-revelation, anti-Christ, anti-miracles. He also believed that some deists argued for the sufficiency of reason and the light of nature, and some questioned the reality of an afterlife.[1132] Concerning the idea of the sufficiency of reason in religion, he wrote, "They [deists] deny any revealed religion, or any word of God at all, and say that God has given mankind no other light to walk by but his own reason."[1133] The last part of the quotation is, I believe, of fundamental importance in understanding Edwards's thought. The place of reason in religion, and its limitations was, arguably, the central focus of Edwards's attack on deism. There were a number of different aspects to this attack, as will be made clear in what follows. One element of Edwards's assault on deistic thought was to assert that there was no such thing as pure reason.[1134] He argued that ancient theology revelation (see sections 4 and 4.1) typically informed reason.[1135] The irony in the last line of the quotation below is deliberately aimed at what Edwards perceived to be the "irrationality" not only of deist belief, but also poor logic:

> Now amongst all the religions hitherto known or heard of, there never was one, which did not require to be taught and learned. The deists say their religion is that of nature, and universally known without teaching. Yet the world hath been always trusting to real or pretended revelations, and knew nothing of an untaught religion, till about a century ago, that some deists began to set up a new one, which, if we may believe themselves, needed not to have been taught, because everybody knew it before.[1136]

Given this position, Edwards could boldly state that "all the right speculative knowledge of the true God, which the deists themselves have, has been derived from divine revelation."[1137]

In the section that follows, I consider his view of the *prisca theologia* tradition, this being the key starting point for all non-Christian religious expression in his thought.

4. The *Prisca Theologia* and Inspiration

The *prisca theologia* plays an important role in Edwards's thought on revelation and reason. Indeed, I believe it is the cornerstone of his theology of religions. While in other chapters I have started with the demonic as the first subject in focus, in this chapter I start with the ancient theology tradition because of a particular interpretation of the demonic which I will discuss in section 5.4., and which only makes sense within the context of Edwards's view of the tradition.

Edwards drew on, and supported the traditional, but also newly updated and revived ancient theology tradition. He enthusiastically, and rather uncritically, copied, commented upon and endorsed the observations and explanations of Chevalier de Ramsay, Ralph Cudworth, Theophilus Gale, Hugo Grotius, Edward Stillingfleet, and others on Chinese (and other) religions, and the Adamic/Noahic/Hebrew source theory, referenced above, and explained below.

4.1. The Single Source Theory Attack on Deism

Brown has argued that Gale was probably the most important influence on Edwards in developing his own ideas of the *prisca theologia* and non-Christian religion.[1138] Gale expended considerable energy examining materials from around the world in order to make sense of various philosophies, belief systems and religions, and he interpreted this material in order to defend a particular theological position. Gale summed up his key thesis thus: "the wisest of the Heathens stole their choicest Notions and Contemplations, both Philologic, and Philosophic, as wel Natural and Moral, as Divine, from the sacred Oracles."[1139] In other words, he argued that *whatever* was good and true in the world (religious or otherwise) had as its basis God's original revelation, meaning Adamic, Noahic, and Judaic revelation. Edwards copied numerous sections of Gales's "findings" in his *miscellanies*, and it is clear that he wholeheartedly embraced and endorsed Gale's thesis, recommending Gale as a reliable authority.[1140] After transcribing extracts from Gale about the dependence on Judaism for the "purer wisdom" and knowledge found around the world, he stated:

> These things also confirm that human learning and all useful and noble knowledge, and not only knowledge in things divine and spiritual, was originally from the church of God in all ages of the world, as the light of the gospel has most evidently been the occasion of all such knowledge since Christ, so that [no] barbarous nation has received so much as civility, but from the church of Christ.[1141]

In Miscellany 350 Edwards explained that "natural religion" known in various parts of the world before the coming of Christ was practiced because of what had been passed down by tradition,[1142] preserved (in part) because of its "agreeableness to reason."[1143] Part of the need for new revelation in the history of redemption was not only to ensure that the older revelation to Israel was maintained and developed, but also so that it could be disseminated outside its borders.[1144] Not only religious and philosophical knowledge, but also ethical knowledge and religious practice (specifically sacrificing), were considered to have been borrowed from Judea.[1145] In Miscellany 969, citing Gale and then Prideaux, Edwards gives credence to the idea that Zoroaster was a key link between Jewish religion and Greek philosophy.

Edwards believed that much was known of God from the ancient theology tradition. In Miscellany 953, he states:

> That the HEATHEN PHILOSOPHERS had their notions of the unity of God, of the Trinity, of the immortality of the soul, the last judgment, the general conflagration, etc. by tradition, from the first ages of the world and from the Jewish nation, is manifest by their own testimony. And many things they say show that they suppose that they had these things by tradition, from those that were divinely instructed and inspired of God [capitalization in original].[1146]

In a later summary statement, he commented:

> Many other things are there cited by Ramsay from many other philosophers that show that all the chief philosophers placed virtue primarily in devotion, spiritual knowledge, and union with God; and believed God to be the Creator, universal orderer and moral governor of the world; and [believed in] the immortality of the soul and spiritual happiness of heaven.[1147]

Edwards also argued, at the same time, that the various fables and stories that existed in different religions and areas *confirmed* the historicity of the Bible.[1148]

But how reliable were the observations and conclusions of Gale? Levitin is highly critical of his work, terming it scholarly backward because of its attempt to serve theological ends.[1149] While recognizing some of the problems in Gale's work (documented by Levitin and others) McDermott notes various redeeming features of his scholarship, including some of his comments on Plato.[1150] It should also be stressed that Levitin himself notes Gale's partial dependency in some areas on Georg Horn, a highly respected historian of his time.[1151] In fairness to Gale, he was not the only agenda-driven writer of the period: theological or ideological agendas were primary, not secondary in the debate (as noted earlier). As Brown notes, "Both sides [deist and non-deist] mined classical sources with remarkable credulity, grasping onto any shred of evidence, no matter how tenuous, in favor of their theory of cultural priority."[1152] As a result, almost everyone found what they were looking for in an appeal to their particular version of the tradition. Brown succinctly, and with some irony, summarizes the resulting positions as follows: "Thus Toland argues for the Jewish mythologizing of pagan history; Voltaire sees Moses as a Jewish translation of the Bacchus myth. Where Edwards seizes on the fact that

Indian Brahmans have a tradition about Adam as proof of Semitic priority and influence, Voltaire takes this Vedic figure of Adimo as proof of the opposite."[1153] This summary statement is helpful in highlighting a point noted earlier concerning the larger context within which religions were discussed and "used" by Edwards and others. It also highlights the fact that the debate could not easily be resolved.

Given his astuteness elsewhere, it is fair to say that Edwards displayed a certain amount of naivete in his handling of material related to this subject. Indeed, a number of Edwards's commentators have noted his uncritical dependence on second-hand sources in this regard.[1154] The possible problems of chronology[1155] and the rather forced interpretations (often quite fanciful Christianisation of the data)[1156] did not seem to have raised questions in Edwards's mind as they should have done. This is no doubt due to what Edwards considered the bigger issue to be: the need to dispel the notion that reason was an adequate basis for religion, as he believed some deists to argue.

4.2. The *Prisca Theologia* and Its Demise

One of the possible problems in appealing to the Judaic primacy view of the *prisca theologia* was that if other religious traditions contained enough revealed truth within them which the Spirit could use to lead to salvation, then Protestant Christianity as proclaimed in the eighteenth century was not necessary. Edwards tried to balance two principles to offset such a conclusion. Firstly, addressing the Deist objection that God would have been unfair if he had not revealed himself universally,[1157] Edwards argued that revelation (*supplementing* the light of nature) did not occur in just one corner of the world, but was spread around the globe. For Edwards, if people were interested in attaining truth, it was there.[1158] On the other hand, the second principle he held was that the tradition had actually become of little or no value.[1159] Accordingly, alongside the transmission of revelation, Edwards was keen to document its deterioration and corruption, spiralling downwards to end in the practice of human sacrifice among other religious perversions.[1160] Departures from revealed truth in distant geographical areas of the world were explained in a number of ways: because of a preference to resort to reason rather than revelation,[1161] a losing sight of the original revelation of God,[1162] or a confusing of signs to what they pointed.[1163] Edwards seemed to adopt a variety of positions concerning how quickly this deterioration occurred. These need not necessarily be considered contradictory, given the earlier comment concerning ebbs and flows of revelation in the History of Israel, and possibly parallel experiences outside Israel as a consequence. On occasion he was agnostic about the speed at which the revelatory tradition was corrupted, or he argued for a quite rapid descent into idolatry.[1164] He also seemed to suggest that the tradition only deteriorated slowly,[1165] and that up to the time of Moses and then Christ, useful ancient theology knowledge still existed: "even till Christ's time, there remained by tradition many scraps of truth among the heathen, that would greatly have served well-disposed inquirers as a clue in their search after truth."[1166] In seeming opposition to such an observation, on occasion Edwards also argued that some countries and peoples had never actually known any ancient theology revelation.[1167]

The attempt at achieving a right balance between these two positions is not only evident in comments Edwards made on preservation and deterioration, but also in his appraisal of non-Christian religious thought. While he occasionally made unqualified positive comments,[1168] he typically "balanced" such with more negative observations.[1169] For example, in considering Socrates, Plato and Xenophon, he writes, "And if they really discovered the Truth themselves They meanly encouraged Idolatry instead of boldly testifying against it."[1170] On the idea of monotheism in Socrates and Plato, he balances the rightness of the notion with their polytheism.[1171] In a similar vein, he contrasted their good principles with their criminal practice.[1172] While Socrates, Plato and Cicero had some valid ideas about a future life beyond the grave, their arguments for it are weak and uncertain.[1173]

In his own time, Edwards believed non-Christian religions to be full of error due to humankind's "degenerate nature."[1174] Whether or not Edwards's balancing acts were successful or convincing is open for discussion. Suffice to say here, I do not believe Edwards gave sufficient consideration to the possibility that the deterioration of the tradition weakened, or even defeated, the potency of his appeal to the universal spread of such revelation in his argument against the deists.

4.3. Inspiration outside Israel

Before closing this section discussing the *prisca theologia* tradition in Edwards's thinking, I engage with a particular comment he made concerning pagan inspiration. I do so because of its apparent contradiction to a number of his views about the *prisca theologia* tradition.

As discussed above, Edwards endorsed Gale's main thesis concerning the *prisca theologia*. Accordingly, he believed that "wise men of all nations,"[1175] learned from the "wise men of the church of God,"[1176] as part of his argumentation, and he stated that what knowledge the heathen had was due to this contact, passed down over time.[1177] Indeed, he suggests that those who gained this knowledge second-hand were actually aware of the divine source of their learning.[1178]

Edwards believed inspiration to be one of four ways in which God revealed himself to humankind before the close of the canon.[1179] Examples of men who were inspired include Elihu,[1180] Job and Melchizedek.[1181] Given this context, Miscellany 1162 opens with what may be described as a bolt from out of the blue (italics and capitalizations in original): '*It may be worthy of consideration whether or no some of the* HEATHEN PHILOSOPHERS *had not, with regard to some things, some degree of* INSPIRATION *of the Spirit of God, which led 'em to say such wonderful things concerning the Trinity, the Messiah, etc.*'[1182] The critical "new" issue raised in this miscellany is that those who may have been so inspired were not Biblical characters (in context, the heathen philosophers are Socrates, Plato and unnamed others). After starting the miscellany thus, Edwards goes on to argue that the gift of inspiration does not mean that the person is in a right relationship with God, citing Balaam, King Nebuchadnezzar, Pharoah, and his officials, along with the devil as examples.[1183]

Edwards closes the miscellany by noting the benefits of such inspiration. He argued that there were three reasons for this kind of inspiration: to create a kind of bridge between other nations and Israel, as a preparation for the gospel, and as a post-conversion corroboration tool. He also added a fourth comment in which he more conjecturally opined whether "benefits to the soul" may have accrued to those who received such inspiration.[1184]

Edwards seems to offer a different explanation for heathen inspiration than his hypothesis in Miscellany 1162 in an earlier Miscellany (953). There he downplays the notion that philosophers were inspired (though affecting to be so), stating that this was no more than borrowing from the (truly) inspired.[1185] As Plantinga Pauw argues, the line of argument adopted in Miscellany 953 is consistent with his support of the ancient theology borrowing argument: "The apologetic argument in these entries [Miscs. 953, 959, 962, 986] was that the truths of the ancients were derivative of the church's revealed wisdom, not an independent, competing source of knowledge."[1186]

I believe it is reasonable to postulate that the issue which Edwards was struggling with, and which was behind the hypothesis of Miscellany 1162, was how Plato could have known so much of the Christian faith (at least as interpreted by Gale and others) as he did.[1187] Given the deist context, Edwards could not permit the kind of knowledge Plato and others possessed to be obtained through the light of nature/reason alone. The bigger issue with which Edwards was engaged was the place of reason in religion—not the issue of inspiration, per se. Inconsistency of apologetic (whether that be contradiction or unnecessary redundancy—which seems to be present here) was arguably less important to Edwards than excluding revelation truths from the realm of reason.[1188] I believe this to be the most satisfactory way of understanding the hypothesis.[1189]

5. Edwards on the Demonic

5.1. Influences

As observed by McClymond and McDermott, Edwards's thought on angels and devils has not attracted much attention.[1190] At the same time, Edwards's interest is clearly evident—both in sermons and the more recently available *miscellanies*.[1191] While there is certainly overlap in existing research concerning the possible sources for and influences on Edwards's demonology, there are interesting variations too. Reaske perceives there to be three major influences on his thought in this area—the Bible, Flavel and Milton—believing the Bible to be the most significant of these.[1192] Juchno has suggested a notable influence from Cotton Mather (while not discounting the influence of Flavel and Milton).[1193] Minkema emphasizes the influence of Milton,[1194] (while also recognizing some dependency on the Mathers). Seah notes the significance of the book of Revelation for Edwards's ideas, but also raises the question whether Milton's influence may, overall, have been more significant than Scripture's.[1195] In what follows, I provide a brief outline of Edwards's view of angels and devils, before considering the devil-religions interface in more detail.

Edwards believed that angels were God's ministers, and were means of dispensing grace, supporting Christ in his work on earth and in assisting believers.[1196] Satan and the devils were equally real, and active.[1197] In

Edwards's thought humans are in the hands of the devil.[1198] In a sermon preached to Indians at Stockbridge in 1753, he documents this belief clearly.[1199] After discussing the sinful state of humankind and the abhorrence of this before God, Edwards goes on to speak of humankind's relationship to the devil. He makes three points concerning this: humans are the devil's children, his captives, and our souls are the devil's habitation.

While making comments such as these, Edwards, like others from the Reformed tradition, was also keen to balance, perhaps more accurately minimize, the idea of Satan's power, compared to God's.[1200] No matter what Satan's plans were, God ultimately overcame them, for his own glory. For example, the Roman Empire—part of Satan's plan to overcome the Messiah—was, in actuality, used by God to facilitate the spread of the Gospel.[1201] Edwards stated that all Satan's efforts against God only resulted in greater glory to God.[1202]

As noted by Minkema, and McClymond and McDermott, Edwards was not averse to speculation on the subject of angels and devils,[1203] though at times leaning on church authority to support such flights of fancy.[1204] One such speculative idea was that a third of the angels fell,[1205] the reason being that they refused the idea of worshipping a human—Jesus Christ incarnate.[1206] Satan's pride was at the heart of this refusal,[1207] rejection of God's sovereignty being behind this temptation.[1208] Minkema suggests an influence of Milton in Edwards's description of how the angels were cast out of heaven by Christ,[1209] and also in the naming of Satan as Lucifer.[1210] Edwards believed that the fallen angels are to be replaced with the elect, and stated that Christ in his victory over Satan replaced him as head of the angels, now occupying this place of honor.[1211] While Satan plays a role in the fall of humans, Seay notes that for Edwards it is a somewhat diminished one.[1212]

5.2. The Devil and Religions

In terms of the role of the devil in false religions, there seems to be one dominant theme in Edwards's thought—that of counterfeiting deception:[1213] a favorite image utilized is Satan being an angel of light.[1214] Delusional ideas of receiving immediate revelation were one such tool which Satan used to lead astray Pythagoreans, Gnostics and heretics, among others.[1215] Edwards stated: "And a very great part of the false religion that has been in the world, from one age to another, consists in such discoveries as these, and in the affections that flow from them [inspiration and ecstasies]."[1216] Edwards believed human imagination to be the main route by which Satan can deceive. After discounting the possibility that Satan can actually influence the soul directly, Edwards stated, "it must be only by the imagination, that Satan has access to the soul, to tempt and delude it, or suggest anything to it."[1217] Rather than power being the key weapon in Satan's arsenal, subtlety and wile are considered to be the main means of achieving his ends.[1218] Edwards stated: "The devil in heaven thought to have overcome God by strength; but he was convinced by experience, by his being cast out down to hell, that it was in vain to oppose his strength to God's. Therefore in the next place, though he saw God was stronger than he, yet he thought to get the better of him by craft and subtlety."[1219] In the context of revivals, Edwards wrote, "Tis by the mixture of counterfeit religion with true, not discerned and distinguished, that the devil has had his greatest advantage against the cause and kingdom of Christ, all along, hitherto."[1220]

Mimicry is mentioned a number of times in the context of false religion, and seems to be an important characteristic of false religion in his thinking.[1221] However, as noted earlier, the deceit, wiles and mimicry do not (ultimately) succeed. Edwards believed Satan does not learn from his previous defeats: his craftiness is not so sharp that he can be a match for God. On the contrary, governed by malice and rage, the devils act like fools, and the devil is no more than a great "blockhead."[1222]

5.3. The Three Demonic Kingdoms (Roman Catholicism, Islam, and Heathenism)

In Edwards's thinking Lucifer, before his fall, was a type of Christ.[1223] Fallen, he rules a parallel kingdom set up over against Christ's. This kingdom contains three specific dominions.

The first is the Roman Catholic church, described by Edwards as "that part of the church that yielded to this rival of Christ, who had no right to her."[1224] The Roman Catholic Church was the worst exhibition of the devil's deceit because at one and the same time it professes and denies Christ.[1225] The period after Constantine and before the Reformation was, in Edwards's opinion, the darkest period of the church's history, the Roman Catholic Church of that era being characterized by superstition, idolatry, ignorance, worship of saints, and the abuse of political and religious power.[1226] While it was the masterpiece of Satan's strategy, the Roman Catholic Church was only one part of Satan's kingdom in Edwards's thought. The other two geographically distinct powers are Islam and Heathenism.[1227] He stated:

> All the false religion is supported by these three powers, viz., the power of heathenism, the power of hypocrisy, i.e., false Judaism and false Christianity, and the power of false prophecy [i.e. Islam]. And the whole of Satan's visible empire upon earth, is mainly divided into these three great kingdoms, viz., his antichristian or false Christian kingdom, which is the kingdom of the beast, his Mahometan kingdom, or the kingdom of the false prophet (for the Mahometan world follow and worship Mahomet as the great prophet of God), and his heathen kingdom, or the kingdom of the dragon. 'Tis probable that all these will in some respect join together, and help one another at that time, as the enemies of the true religion are wont to do when Satan's kingdom seems to be in eminent danger; though they differ and at other times have great dissension among themselves (*Isaiah 41:5-6*, with the rest of the chapter). There will probably be a great deal of confederacy, caballing and leaguing together to help one another between the heathen, Mahometan and antichristian powers.[1228]

All three parts of Satan's empire would, as noted in the last sentence of this quotation, unite against the church in the end times.[1229] While advocating the idea of a kind of Satanic triumvirate, at other times Edwards focused on just the two horns of the anti-Christ: Roman Catholicism and Islam, which between them sprang from the old Roman empire—Satan's initial attempt at overcoming Christ. The initial empire was, after the time of Christ, split down the middle into the Muslim East and Roman Catholic West.[1230]

Edwards considered Mohammed and Islam in a very dim light,[1231] believing Muslims to be apostates.[1232] He stated that what little light there was in Islam was due to borrowing from Christianity.[1233] He compared it to Pharisaism,[1234] and argued that its doctrines, rather than challenging humans, were adapted to our ideas and desires.[1235] McDermott believes that Edwards merely propagated the views of the era in his analysis and comments.[1236]

Heathenism is characterized in two modes: the first is that of old heathenism—the Roman Empire—with the modern form witnessed in Indian religion in the Americas, and other areas of the world. Concerning the old heathenism, Edwards recognized positive elements in Greco-Roman Religion—specifically moral virtues.[1237] At the same time, he noted the religious confusion in Plato and others, as documented earlier. Concerning the contemporary heathen world of his time, Edwards believed that the Americas were populated with people by Satan after the incarnation, Satan's intention being to move these humans away from the influence of the Gospel.[1238] Those who live in geographically distant places from "Christian" lands are, in Edwards's view, victims of this ploy of Satan. At the same time, Edwards believed the Chinese to be, in some ways, exceptional, attributing their civilization to the keeping of the teachings and traditions of Noah.[1239] China was something of an anomaly—praised at one time, but still in desperate need of true religion.[1240]

Regarding the relationship between Satan and the American Indians, Zakai believes Edwards was influenced by Mather in adopting the position of strong Satanic influence, together with the view of Puritans that the American settlers were the means God was using to conquer this territory of Satan.[1241] At the same time, Edwards equated the degeneracy of the Indians with that of Europeans,[1242] and he was essentially consistent in his view of *all* humankind being in the grip of Satan. Despite the overall negative view of Indian religion, McDermott points to references in Edwards's later writings which, he believes, indicate a softening of Edwards's position towards the Indians and their spiritual state in response to his personal engagement with them.[1243] McClymond and McDermott's evaluation of Edwards's differentiation of religions is this: "Greece and Rome, along with China, received favorable evaluation, while Islam and Native American religions came under censure."[1244] Given the overview presented above, I suggest that this appraisal is framed somewhat simplistically, while correctly recognizing the existence of a kind of spectrum of false religion in his thinking.

5.4. A Close Analysis of Miscellany 307

In what follows I will consider, in some detail, a key miscellany concerning Satan and religions, and Gerald McDermott's interpretation of it. I pay particular attention to this miscellany as it focuses in some detail on the devil's role in false religion in Edward's thinking. Before engaging with it, I provide some necessary background to Edwards's thought on types.

5.4.1. Typology and Types in Religions

Edwards used the term *type* in two distinct ways: as a hermeneutical tool in interpreting the Old Testament in the light of the New,[1245] and as a "vertical reality"[1246] tool to see spiritual reality in a concrete world.[1247]

Without doubt, Edwards expanded the conservative typological approach to Scripture.[1248] I focus here, however, on Edwards's second conception of types: to see aspects of the world (post-biblical history and nature) as types of their spiritual antitypes.[1249] Puritan writers such as John Flavel had mined the world—especially nature—for reflections of what it showed of God.[1250] One could argue that Calvin opened up the way for such an approach in the Reformation era;[1251] indeed, there were hints of such an understanding of the world in Augustine and Bonaventure.[1252] For Edwards, nature was replete in communicating God, containing as it does microcosmic images or reflections of God.[1253] However, in order to see these correctly "the book of Scripture" was needed to interpret "the book of nature."[1254]

Studebaker suggests that the types in creation are, for Edwards, related to creation truths as opposed to what is revealed in the *prisca theologia*—i.e., redemptive truths: "Nature possesses typological character because it is the product of the communication of the Word in creation. The *prisca theologia* is a communication of the Word in redemption."[1255] However, this neat classification does not adequately capture Edwards's thinking, as he clearly saw some redemptive truths in types in creation—e.g., the silkworm, or the sun.[1256] Historical events could also be typological, and at times were a type of redemption.[1257] For example, Edwards considered New England as a type of Israel,[1258] and he provided an extended analysis of how Rome's historic triumphs were typological of Christ's in *Shadows of Divine Things*, Image 81.[1259]

Why did Edwards believe God used types as a means of communicating himself? He stated that such a display was in accord with God's wisdom, where creation is seen to be "typical" of the real, unseen spiritual reality.[1260] The primary beauty (being invisible) could not be observed by humankind: its shadow could. The types were a potential communication to believers. Edwards scattered his sermons with types as he believed them to be a means of instruction that could be easily grasped.[1261] Sweeney believes that types were also there for the non-Christian, a clear parallel existing between these and the parables of Jesus: on the one hand types communicate, on the other, they hide truth for those who cannot "see" them.[1262]

A considerable number of Edwards's commentators have argued that nature types are *only* read aright by the (biblically-literate) regenerate.[1263] McDermott, while initially seeming to endorse this view, seems later on to have expanded the readership.[1264] I believe the strongest case which can be brought forward to support McDermott's more recent interpretation of the ability to read types is Edwards's reference to Ovid.[1265] As I have argued elsewhere,[1266] I do not think that this reference warrants the conclusions which McDermott draws from it. The type is not redemptive and the truth it points to could be seen by the light of nature.[1267]

5.4.2. A Critique of Gerald McDermott's Interpretation of Miscellany 307

Having provided some background to Edwards's typology, it is now appropriate to consider McDermott's claim that Edwards believed there to be a special category of types in Edwards's thought—types in religions. McDermott makes the following claims: "Others have shown that Edwards pushed beyond the boundaries of traditional Christian typology to include history and nature; I propose that he went even further to bring other religions into his system."[1268] He also stated:

> Edwards pressed those implications [that all the world was typical] even further by proposing that God had planted types of true religion even in religious systems that were finally false. God outwitted the devil, Edwards suggested, by using diabolically deceptive religion to teach what is true. In an early entry in the Miscellanies [Miscellany 307], Edwards suggested that the heathen practice of human sacrifice was the result of the devil's mimickry of the animal sacrifice God had instituted after the Fall.[1269]

In large part, the argument McDermott forwards is dependent on his interpretation of Miscellany 307. I provide the full *miscellany* below, as I will consider it in some detail.

> God prepared the Jewish world to receive the doctrine of satisfactory sacrifice by appointing the sacrifices of beasts; and the devil prepared the Gentile world for receiving the same by mimicking God in this thing of sacrificing, intending thereby

> the more effectually to promote his own interest. And they were the more prepared by the devil's going such lengths as to require human sacrifices, which were common among the heathen, and sacrificing of children (and sometimes only sons), [to] receive this human sacrifice, Jesus Christ. Their minds were hereby possessed with such sort of notions [as] the satisfaction and propitiation of slain sacrifices, that it was a great preparation. And so indeed was [the] heathenish doctrines of deities' being united to images, and the heathenish fables of heroes' being begotten [by] gods, a preparation for their receiving the doctrine of the incarnation, of the Deity's dwelling in a human [body], and the Son of God's being conceived in the womb of a virgin by the power and Spirit of [God].[1270]

In this *miscellany* Edwards documented how God had prepared the Israelites for the idea of satisfactory punishment through the OT sacrificial system. Edwards states that the devil had instituted sacrifice (including child sacrifice) for his own (unspecified) purposes, thereby mimicking God's work. However, Edwards believed that in God's providence, Satan's work could actually prepare people to accept the idea of Christ's sacrifice. He makes a similar point in relation to idolatry (divine and material substance combined) as also being preparatory, in some way, for the Christian doctrine of incarnation.

On the basis of his analysis of this passage, McDermott believes that for Edwards, "God had planted types of true religion even in religious systems that were finally false."[1271] He also stated: "God used false religion to teach the true."[1272] With McClymond, McDermott believed that the types pointed people in the right (spiritual) direction.[1273] In McDermott's view, these types point to Christ,[1274] and he considers them comparable to OT types.[1275] A shift in his view of who can read types[1276] opens up the possibility for McDermott that redemptive types in nature and religions can be used by the Spirit, possibly to save.[1277]

I critically consider McDermott's position in what follows. I do so, in the first instance, by a close examination of the miscellany.

Firstly, it should be noted that Edwards does not call the Satanically planted perversions "types." It is true that he compares the sacrificial system of Israel instituted by God to the sacrificial systems in parts of the heathen world. It is also true that the former are elsewhere called shadows or types by Edwards. There is a kind of parallelism in his argument. He does not say, however, as McDermott interprets him, that "God had planted types." The mechanism involved is different (the subject is the devil, not God). The devil mimics God in this activity.[1278] Further, Edwards implies (but does not state) that God permitted this Satanic work—rather than instituted the "type," per se. In light of the previous comments concerning Satanic deception in religion, and how God ultimately overcomes such devilish initiatives, Edwards's language here seems essentially consistent.

I believe that there are, at face value, two plausible interpretations of what Edwards meant in this miscellany. Turning to the first, it is possible (within the context of the miscellany alone) that Edwards understood the "type" implanted to be *independent* of the ancient theology tradition, and this appears to be McDermott's view. The implanting of religious types is quite distinct from the ancient theology in McDermott's thought, and on occasion he clearly disassociates implanted types from the tradition.[1279]

The second interpretation, not adopted by McDermott when interpreting Miscellany 307, would be to understand child sacrifice and idolatry as *perversions* of the ancient theology tradition. In support of this understanding are Edwards's own comments relating heathen sacrifice to the *prisca theologia* (rather than the light of nature).[1280]

As noted earlier, Edwards believed that the pristine original revelation broke down over time, and he saw various actors playing a role in this, including the devil. As McDermott himself states, "the original purity of divine truth is continually breaking down, corrupted by profane and demonic mixture."[1281] When McDermott writes that "they [pagan religious practices] were not merely human insights but developments (albeit twisted and broken) of original perceptions granted by Jesus Christ himself,"[1282] this suggests an ancient theology *dependency*, not independent type implantation.

I suggest that this second interpretation (not the one that McDermott applies to Miscellany 307, but one, nonetheless that he, along with McClymond, understood Edwards to believe) is better able to account for the existence of both truth and perverted truth in religions, and in Edwards's overall thought. Not only is the explanation simpler, it avoids the unnecessary complications that arise from the creation of a separate class of revelation, a class that Edwards nowhere specifically espoused.[1283]

The fact that a shadow of truth remains in a perverted truth can, of course, be used by God for his own purposes and glory, and Edwards clearly spoke of God's preparatory work here, but not "teaching" per se. (cf. McDermott's language). It seems to be more like the setting up of templates, which, though filled with error, stimulate certain expectations.[1284]

The idea of "broken types" being present in non-Christian religions seems to accord well with Edwards's generally negative view of religious beliefs and practices outside the church, as noted earlier. In a number of ways, Edwards's thought in this miscellany seems to mirror certain aspects of Justin's on demonic mimesis.[1285] As with Justin, however, I suggest that the limited pedagogical value is geared primarily to hindsight.

6. Reason, the Light of Nature, Conscience, and the *Logos*

6.1. Reason: Its Abilities and Limitations

Before considering *Logos* enlightenment and the light of nature, I provide a brief outline of Edwards's understanding of reason, building on some of the observations documented in section 2.2. Given his deist context, I believe this is particularly important to consider.

Edwards understood Adam and Eve to have possessed natural and supernatural faculties or principles, "implanted" by God.[1286] After the fall, he believed the supernatural faculties, namely "spiritual understanding, inclination, and action," together with love to God through the gift of the Holy Spirit[1287] to be lost.[1288] The "inferior" natural faculties (including reason), on the other hand, were not lost, but damaged.[1289] For Edwards, humans receive the faculty of reason from the Son of God and will from the Holy Spirit;[1290] these are a consequence of humans being made in the *imago Dei*.[1291]

According to Edwards, after the fall reason (along with other elements comprising man's natural faculties) lacks spiritual guidance or supervision (i.e., it is misdirected in orientation, not being sanctified by the Spirit, and therefore inclined to self-love). It is also corrupt in and of itself.[1292] Being doubly disadvantaged (not correctly guided by supernatural faculties and also darkened),[1293] Edwards was adamant that reason could in no way assist humankind to arrive at a right knowledge of God—even though it could know many things about God (as noted above in section 2.2, dealing with speculative and sensible knowledge).

Edwards defined reason as, "that power or faculty an intelligent being has to judge of the truth of propositions, either immediately, by only looking on the propositions, which is judging by intuition and self-evidence; or by putting together several propositions which are already evident by intuition, or at least whose evidence is originally derived from intuition."[1294]

Most Edwards commentators are in agreement that Edwards's definition of reason was influenced by Locke.[1295] However, he was certainly no slave to Locke, rejecting the view of reason's competence to know God, and also the notion of disinterested rationalism.[1296]

The classification of reason as a faculty in the definition above should be noted. Edwards believed that the deists had confused "faculty" with "rule," or spoke of reason in both ways, failing at times to discriminate the different meanings in their argumentation. In his view, the deists had elevated reason (the faculty) to be able to make judgments as to what was reasonable or not. This, of course, makes no sense.[1297] For Edwards, the true rule by which unfallen reason should be governed is the eternal law of nature.[1298] Edwards agreed with the deists about the perfection of this law of nature, but argued that they had confused this with the light of nature (that is, what humankind knows of this law), a totally different proposition after the fall.[1299] He described the law of nature being "exceedingly obscured and blinded" after the fall, though perfectly clear for Adam, and clear enough still to condemn.[1300] He spoke of the light of nature being dim,[1301] not equally distributed,[1302] and in places he believed it could be nearly extinguished,[1303] and could almost be obliterated.[1304] At the same time, Edwards contrasts the clarity of the light with the greatness of human darkness, resulting in "monstrous forms of religion."[1305] I discuss what the light of nature shows in Edwards's thought in more detail in section 6.2.

Toland, alluding to the language of the Johannine Prologue, suggested that reason was the light of the eternal Son, a true and reliable guide to humankind. He believed that "Reason is not less from God than revelation; 'tis the Candle, the Guide, the Judg he has lodg'd within every Man that cometh into this World."[1306] For Edwards, on the other hand, the light of nature is not clear to fallen humans, and even if the perfect law of nature could be known now, it can no longer help humankind in our sinful state.

Edwards went about establishing his argument concerning reason's impotence in spiritual matters in a number of ways. I summarize these below.

The first was to argue that reason is not the appropriate faculty to know God. While, as noted above, Edwards certainly acknowledged the importance and role of reason in knowing God "speculatively," he believed reason to be the wrong faculty through which true knowledge of God could be attained: in his view the function of reason is to "perceive truth" rather than to perceive excellence (i.e., God).[1307] The appropriate way to perceive excellence is through the heart: "Tis rational to suppose, that it should be beyond a man's power to obtain this knowledge, and light, by the mere strength of natural reason; for 'tis not a thing that belongs to reason, to see the beauty and loveliness of spiritual things; it is not a speculative thing, but depends on the sense of the heart."[1308] He also states, "There is such a thing, as a spiritual and divine light, immediately imparted to the soul by God, of a different nature from any that is obtained by natural means."[1309]

Reason, limited to effective operation on the natural plane alone, is engaged with "substance and logic" (alone) and not spiritual reality.[1310] Accordingly, "when fallen man sets himself to worship God through the employment of his natural faculties, he worships not the true God but idols."[1311]

Turning to a second argument against the competence of reason in religion, Edwards believed that while the facts of God's creation and implanted knowledge are communicated to humankind, reason cannot make sense of these facts and how they relate to each other: "Ratiocination, without this spiritual light, never will give one such an advantage to see things in their true relations and respects to other things and to things in general."[1312] He also stated: "This darkness is not that man is unable to see the facts, but that he does not know what to do with the facts once they are perceived."[1313] The problem of incorrectly relating ideas due to a lack of a true foundation[1314] has been summed up by Lee in the following manner: "the ultimate relational meaning of a given group of ideas can be apprehended only by seeing those ideas in their relationship with the meaning of the ultimate, God."[1315] Unregenerate and unsanctified reason cannot achieve a true apprehension of God, God being spiritual, and humankind's (fallen) reasoning operating solely at the natural level, unable to relate the light it has to the true God.

Thirdly, for Edwards, what reason apprehends is not the idea itself, but only the sign of the true idea.[1316] Because of its fallen state the mind confuses the one for the other—for example, in worshipping the sun, rather than God.[1317]

Fourthly, the problem of not interpreting facts correctly, or viewing things in their right relations is not, for Edwards, simply a "lack" or due to dullness, but because of a fundamental antithesis between the nature, or disposition of the receiver of revelation, and the revelation itself. As Edwards commented, "Tis not rational to suppose, that those whose minds are full of spiritual pollution, and under the power of filthy lusts, should have any relish or sense of divine beauty, or excellency; or that their minds should be susceptive of that light that is in its own nature so pure and heavenly."[1318] He also wrote, "The reason why natural men have no knowledge of spiritual things, is because they have nothing of the Spirit of God dwelling in them."[1319] Edwards believed it was "reasonable" to expect the mind to be confused in this matter, because sinful failings are also plain to see in other areas of human life.[1320]

The fifth point that Edwards employed against reason's religious competence was an empirical, historical argument. Rather than reason having solved humanity's religious problem, Edwards argued that its limited and confused functioning had merely exacerbated humankind's religious state. He stated: "Thus I think it is evident, that through mere unassisted nature, in its present . . . blindness and corruption, we can neither have a religion, nor a law, sufficient to answer the ends of society, or to render individuals good and happy."[1321]

Edwards found evidence for this not just in general observation, but specifically in the works of the philosophers, whose ideas were, on occasion, enthusiastically appealed to by some deists. If these Spirit-enabled (see section 2.3) Greek thinkers could not agree among themselves about God, or reform society, what did this signify concerning reason's competence?[1322] If their reason-dependent religious conclusions led only to "brutal stupidity" it had clearly failed.[1323] Indeed, Edwards highlighted the failure of reason to attain the chief good in the ancient world as the backdrop for the incarnation—God's solution to the problem.[1324]

Above, I have outlined five points forwarded by Edwards in his argument against what he believed to be the deist contention that reason could be depended on in matters of religion. Alternative attempts to classify his thought in this area include the analysis of Gerstner who believed there to be four limitations to reason,[1325] and Wainwright who condensed them to two: inattention to the ideas of God, and the lack of a notion of true beauty.[1326]

6.2. The Light of Nature

Edwards, on occasion, seemed to use *reason* and *light of nature* synonymously, and one might argue that in so doing he committed the same error he accused the deists of—confusing the faculty and its rule or guide.¹³²⁷ The light of nature was one of two ways in which God taught humans in Edwards's thought, the other being revelation. He stated:

> There is a two-fold light that God gives to the children of men to discover things to 'em that concern their true interest and happiness, viz. the light of nature, and the light of revelation. The light of nature is manifestation and evidence, that is given of these things to men's natural reason, from those works of creation and God's common providence, that all mankind behold. The other light is revelation, which is something above the light of nature. 'Tis that manifestation God has made of himself to the world by his word, or by his own immediate instructions, given in a miraculous manner by visions, miracles, and the inspiration of his Spirit.¹³²⁸

Neither of the lights referred to above are abstract: they are related to God's will.¹³²⁹ It is clear from this quotation that Edwards viewed revelation as supplementary and complementary to the light of nature. Edwards seems to have been particularly concerned to document and delimit both what was and was *not* revealed through this light, and this concern may well have been in response to his perceptions of the deist appeal to reason. At the same time, it should be remembered that another position he adopted was that there was actually no such thing as reason operating without the benefit of revelation—as described earlier in section 3. There is an evident tension between Edwards's desire to clearly define what the light of nature teaches and what it does not, as well as to challenge its distinct, discrete existence in the lives of men and women.

Edwards believed that the light of nature teaches "many truths concerning God and our duty to him."¹³³⁰ At the same time, he specifically excluded certain knowledge needed for salvation from this light: "for though there are many truths concerning God and our duty to him that are evident by the light of nature, yet no one truth is taught by the light of nature in that manner in which it is necessary for us to know it."¹³³¹ As Wainwright put it, for Edwards, "Natural reason is insufficient for constructing an adequate natural theology (although not for discerning *some truths* of natural theology)."¹³³²

In order to investigate what Edwards considered the light of nature to reveal, and also not show, I conducted a simple collocation framework search of the *WJE Online* corpus. In Table 1, below, I document the results from a "light of nature" search in the Edwards corpus, edited to exclude occasions where the material was copied from another author, referencing only clear indications concerning what was and what was not known by the light of nature.[1333] I provide some comments on the contents after the table.

Table 1—Light of Nature Knowledge in the Edwards Corpus

Known by the light of nature	Not known by the light of nature
Ought to obey God and not engage in vengeful acts[1334]	(true) religion[1342]
The evil of ingratitude[1335]	The general judgment;[1343] assurance of future rewards and punishments[1344]
Appropriate punishment for wrongdoing[1336]	Certain specifically Christian doctrines, relating to Christ (incarnation and mediation)[1345]
The need to keep one day in seven special[1337]	
(Hypothetical?) *would* teach? Belief in an afterlife[1338]	Anything positively useful to humankind concerning redemption (gospel and mediation)[1346]
God's justice[1339]	Assurance that repentance is sufficient or accepted; That God would accept repentant sinners[1347]
The being and certain attributes of God; that he cares for his creation, is inclined to display his glory, the appropriate human response of adoration to this, and the just punishment for failing to do so[1340]	Immortality of the soul[1348] (*almost unattainable*)
	Salvation through another's righteousness.[1349]
Various sexual sins[1341]	The need for sacrifice[1350]
The rightness of war and self-preservation[1351]	
The evil of blasphemy[1352]	
Man's superiority over woman[1353]	
That we are in a state of fallenness and displeasing God, in need of reconciliation[1354]	
The terror of hell[1355]	
Holiness of God and need for holiness for salvation[1356]	
The ability to discern wickedness in False religion (heathen and Catholic)[1357]	
The need for righteousness to obtain God's favor[1358]	

As can be seen from the items in the left-hand column, it is clear that Edwards gave considerable scope to this light, and he gave examples of those who benefited from it, responding to it as well they could—including Stoic philosophers and Socrates.[1359]

I believe that there are two main reasons why Edwards stressed what could be known through the light of nature. Firstly, and on a practical level, such light was a necessary antidote to atheism. If a part of humanity received no ancient theology revelation, and *only* received the light of nature—a possibility he seemed to countenance at times—then there needed to be enough communication from God through the light of nature "channel" to establish humankind's accountability. Secondly, as noted earlier, in Edwards's thought there was no *true* knowledge of God without this notional knowledge, in the sense that knowledge in the right-hand column is not contrary to, but supplementary to that on the left—even though what is on the left only becomes "real" once the right-hand column knowledge is known and a new sense of the heart is given by the Holy Spirit. When this is the case, the light of nature becomes spiritually valuable to the believer: "The light of nature teaches that religion which is necessary to continue in the favour of the God that made us; but it cannot teach us that religion which is necessary to our being restored to the favour of God, after we have forfeited it."[1360] While nature did not hold out redemptive truths for the unregenerate, the believer could read the book of nature correctly with the Bible in hand, once given a new sense of the heart.

Turning back to Table 1, the first item in the right-hand column (the absence of true religion) in some ways totally diminishes the positives in the left-hand column. In dismissing the *spiritual* value of this light, Edwards echoed John Owen, and the puritan tradition.[1361] Edwards, like Calvin, drew on Cicero to argue for the insufficiency of the light of nature.[1362] He also stressed that in our state as sinners what is *not* communicated by the light of nature is what is most needed, namely revelation of God's redemption.[1363] This revelation, for Edwards, is very much tied to historical events, not reason, or nature.

Considering the items in the left-hand column as a group, the bulk of what is revealed through the light of nature seems to be quite disconcerting in what it shows about the creator-creature relationship (cf. "The wrath of God is revealed from heaven," Rom 1:18). While the majority of references are distinctly religious (i.e., first table of the law items, including duty to God, blasphemy, Sabbath keeping) others are second table (e.g., sexual sins). In Edwards's thought, the light of nature seems to be like law, leading to a guilty awareness of self and God, with little indication of evangelical truths. Indeed, on occasion, Edwards seems to equate the light of nature with OT law, suggesting that the latter was a clear documentation of the former.[1364]

It is interesting to note non-moral law items in the column as well: male-female relations, self-preservation and war. With regards to true and false religion, it should be observed that the light of nature, in Edwards's view, is distinctly (Protestant) Christian with humankind having sufficient light to discern between false religion (i.e., Catholicism or heathenism in context) and the true, on the basis of this light. In stating this, Edwards seemed to suggest that those involved in non-Protestant Christian worship are actually aware, or at least can be aware (because of what is known from the light of nature), that this worship is misdirected. I discuss this point further in chapter 6, section 3.2.

Concerning possible inconsistencies in the listings, the issue of justice and punishment is in both (general judgment is not known, but appropriate punishment, justice and the terror of hell is known). A possible explanation for this is that, on occasion, Edwards allowed for some truths to be known through both channels. At other times he stated he was not sure which channel was responsible for certain knowledge.[1365]

6.3. The Light of Reason

Edwards made far fewer references to what the *light of reason* shows to humankind, compared to the *light of nature*, though the references seem largely synonymous.[1366] The idea that the light of reason could ascertain that God was triune was,[1367] in Plantinga Pauw's words, a claim displaying "worrisome bravado."[1368] However, she goes on to provide some evidence that Edwards altered his view on this over time.[1369] As noted earlier in the discussion of Miscellany 1162, the fact that inspiration was hypothesized as being the source for such knowledge should also be remembered.

As is clear from Table 1, the light of nature seems to be primarily related to the external witness of the created world in Edwards's thinking.[1370] Edwards also spoke of some knowledge which was implanted. I document this below in Table 2—showing the results from a search of "implant*" in the corpus.

Table 2—Implanted Knowledge in the Edwards Corpus

Awareness of causation[1371]

Regard to and duty to God[1372]

A sense of desert relating to justice, proportion, harmony and agreement[1373]

Natural and superior principles—the natural remaining,[1374] the superior lost in the fall, but regained in conversion[1375]

The affections[1376]

A relish of moral beauty—though this is not true virtue[1377]

A desire to live for ever and to attain this—a stimulus to do good[1378]

The soul[1379]

Sexual desire/family upbringing[1380]

Expectation of reward/punishment according to actions[1381]

Affections relating to fear/dread[1382]

Pity—to help preserve humankind[1383]

Conscience[1384]

Gratitude[1385]*

Love for society[1386]**

Natural/family affection—for the preservation of humankind[1387]***

   * "though it be true" suggests some hesitation here.
   ** note this is a "may"
   *** phrased somewhat hypothetically

Some of this implanted knowledge is similar to certain light of nature references provided in the first table above (e.g., the sense of desert/proportion and also duty). Other implanted knowledge is not deemed to come from the light of nature (specifically: awareness of causation, affections, a desire to live for ever, and conscience, plus references to various instincts). This suggests that Edwards may have used the term *light of nature* more generally for what is known of God through creation and providence. The stronger social fellow-man (second table of the law) references seem more dominant in the implanted list, when compared with the light of nature list, particularly natural instincts necessary for society to function effectively. Before leaving this section it is important to consider conscience in more detail, given its inclusion in Table 2, and implied inclusion in Table 1.

6.4. Conscience

Early on in his career, Edwards explained conscience thus: "natural conscience is implanted in all mankind, there to be as it were in God's stead, and to be an internal judge or rule to all, whereby to distinguish right and wrong."[1388] Edwards described conscience as an instrument used by God to keep man in hand, functioning as a rule or judge.[1389] He believed that this moral sense did not function particularly well, because of sin,[1390] and that it could become dulled and weak.[1391] However, as noted earlier, by means of common grace, the Holy Spirit can assist it to function more effectively.[1392] When a new sense of the heart is given, conscience agrees perfectly with God's law.[1393] However, even for the unregenerate, it can still produce a sense of unease[1394] and fear.[1395] It works alongside reason;[1396] however, being a natural principle (rather than a divine one), it is "no more than a sentiment,"[1397] and even when functioning appropriately in the unregenerate, it cannot be considered "of the nature of true virtue."[1398] Functioning only at the level of the apprehension of "secondary beauty," wrong and right are not properly perceived.[1399] While the judgment of unregenerate conscience may agree with a divine or spiritual sense, its grounds and its approval or disapproval for the agreement are different.[1400]

Ramsey has documented how Edwards's thought on conscience developed over time. Although initially Edwards seemed to suggest that conscience was in some ways related to the divine—a kind of internal voice of God (cf. Calvin)—his more mature thought suggests a weaker, natural, more earth-bound function.[1401] Though implanted, it was less the voice of God, and more the means of restraining sin in the world,[1402] and a suggestive pointer to the existence of a supreme judge.[1403]

Having provided the above overview of reason and the light of nature, we can now proceed to consider Edwards's understanding of the Johannine prologue.

6.5. Edwards and the Johannine Prologue

For Edwards, the *Logos* is God's "internal" thought,[1404] and the "external" communication or revelation of God.[1405] Creation is peculiarly an activity and revelation of the Son.[1406] Strictly speaking, this communication, being spiritual, can only be received by a spiritually enlightened person and this is both theoretically and practically possible for humans, because they are created with a soul, and the Holy Spirit can quicken fallen humanity.[1407] For the unregenerate, Edwards allows for a kind of shadow of this revelation to be received, as seen in creation. Edwards believed God "communicates a sort of shadow or glimpse of his excellencies to bodies, which as we have seen, are but the shadows of being, and not real beings,"[1408] and "the beauties of nature are really emanations, or shadows, of the excellencies of the Son of God."[1409] These glimpses of the shadows of the *Logos*/eternal Son seen by humans appear to be the same as the light of nature in Edwards's thought, although I am not aware of him explicitly making this connection. It must be stressed, however, that this is not, for Edwards, true spiritual enlightenment—as has been established in the previous sections. Consistent with the argumentation above, I will demonstrate below, that Edwards did not seem to equate the light of nature with true spiritual *Logos* revelation (as documented in the Prologue), rather just the shadow of this truth.

Edwards made very few references to verses 4 and 5 of the Johannine Prologue. Indeed, a search of the *WJE* Online corpus indicates just three references[1410] in Edwards's writings.[1411] I reference two in what follows, and the third in later discussion. The first is: "Our food and life is hid in Christ; he is the life (*John 1:4*). He is 'the true God, and eternal life.'"[1412] The second is: "he is in the spiritual Θ [world] as the sun is in the natural which is full of light & dispels & scatters all darkness before it see 4 & 5 v. of the Context in him was life & the life was the light of men & the light shineth in darkness & the darkness Comprehended it not [break] First The Things He Here said were all true."[1413] The first reference is for Christians, and in the second he mentions the incarnation immediately after the key verses. The explicit reference to Christ, rather than the eternal Son should be noted. Keeping these interpretations in mind, I now turn to McDermott's interpretation of Edwards's exegesis of John 1:9.

McDermott provides some commentary on three references to John 1:9 in Edwards's works. Below, I label these A, B, and C for ease of reference.

(A) *John 1:9*. I.e. there is not, nor ever was, nor will be, any man in the world enlightened but by Jesus Christ. 'Every man that cometh into the world' that ever is enlightened is enlightened by him. Or hereby is meant that this light is not only to enlighten the Jews, but that it enlightens indifferently every man, let him be of what nation soever. It was fit that the True Light, when he came, should be a general light. Moses enlightened only the nation of the Jews, because he was not the True Light. See a very parallel expression, *Colossians 1:23*.[1414]

(B) Man by the fall extinguished that divine light that shone in this world in its first estate. . . . But God in infinite mercy has made glorious provision for the restoration of light to this fallen dark world; he has sent him, who is the brightness of his own glory, into the world, to be the light of the world. 'He is the true light, that lighteth every man that cometh into the world' [*John 1:9*], i.e. every man in the world that ever has any true light. But in his wisdom and mercy, he is pleased to convey his light to men by means and instruments; and has sent forth his messengers, and appointed ministers in his church to be subordinate lights, and to shine with the communications of his light, and to reflect the beams of his glory on the souls of men.[1415]

(C) The most universal expressions of any that are found in the Scripture, are sometimes used there in a limited sense, as *Colossians 1:23*, 'the gospel . . . which was preached to every creature which is under heaven'; and to the like purpose is that, *John 1:9*, 'This is the true Light, which lighteneth every man that cometh into the world.' In these places, the expressions are as if what was meant, was most universal with respect to individuals, when yet what is really intended is only universal with respect to kinds, and without limitation by any rule, or being limited or restrained from any one individual person by any rule given.[1416]

McDermott believes Edwards changed his mind on the meaning (from A to view B and C). He believes Quotation A to be a "universal enlightening" interpretation—a general light (in McDermott's view a religious light) to all, both Jews and Gentiles. McDermott reads Edwards to be saying that religious truth was given to all by Christ.[1417] McDermott argues that in his later years Edwards restricted the meaning, citing the "universal with respect to kinds" reference above in C.[1418] McDermott traces a possible impact from the Breck affair in effecting this change of interpretation.[1419]

In what follows, I provide my own interpretation. With regards to text A, I suggest that the enlightening of every man does not *necessarily* need to be understood as being universal here, namely that "everyone is enlightened." The two references to John 1:4–5 (referred to earlier) should be remembered here: neither referenced the eternal Son—the incarnation is very much in focus. Further, Edwards's language in text A can be understood to mean that it is possible *not* to be enlightened by Christ: "'Every man that cometh into the world' *that ever is enlightened* is enlightened by him [emphasis mine]." Edwards seems to be contrasting the more particular light of Moses to Israel (alone) with the light from Christ's ministry (to Jew and Gentile).

Turning to Quotation B, there is a clear statement that not everyone is enlightened, and the enlightening is linked to gospel preaching. Turning to Quotation C, "the respect to kinds" reference seems to be wholly consistent with my interpretation of the first two quotations: namely, not everyone is enlightened. The reference to the gospel in Col 1:23 in Quotation C indicates the enlightening to be a gospel light.

While it is possible that Edwards changed his mind, as McDermott suggests, the interpretation seems slightly tenuous. Taking into account the references to John 1:4–5 referenced earlier (which McDermott does not), it seems quite clear that when he wrote of the *Logos* in the prologue (whether verses 4–5 or verse 9), this was primarily understood to refer to the incarnate Christ, not the eternal discarnate Word. Turning to the third reference to John 1:4 (mentioned earlier), I believe this also supports this interpretation: "So is Christ in the spiritual world. *John 8:12*, "I am the light of the world." *John 1:4*, "The life was the light of men.""[1420] In connecting these two verses in this way, Edwards again seems to be equating *Logos* references at the very beginning of the Prologue to the incarnate Christ.

Theologically, the light of nature is not equated with true *Logos* light. Edwards does not seem to have a category for true spiritual discarnate *Logos* knowledge (cf. Justin and Augustine). We might term the light of nature the shadow of the light of the *Logos*. Human knowledge of such spiritual shadows helps humans in a limited way, though spiritually, not at all.

Conclusion

In this chapter I have documented Edwards's appeal to a "traditional" version of the *prisca theologia* tradition and interpreted it to be the cornerstone of his theology of religions. Edwards appealed to the tradition (especially in dealing with the deists) to argue that much of their right knowledge of God was from this. The tradition also explains why religions are as they are: what is good has been borrowed, and false religious practices mirror true practices which have been corrupted.

The devil is, in part, responsible for the corruption of this original revelation, which has led to the truth being mimicked in certain heathen practices. The devil, appearing as an angel of light, is not only responsible for perverting truth from the tradition, but is also behind the three main religious non-Christian groupings in Edwards's thought: Roman Catholicism, Islam, and Heathenism. Satan can manipulate people's imaginations as a first step to the creation of various forms of false religion.

Edwards carefully differentiated what was and was not known from the light of nature. He seemed reluctant to equate this with *Logos* enlightenment. Edwards believed that much was known from the light of nature (which he sharply differentiated from revelation); indeed, he argued that this light was bright enough to show those involved in non-Christian religions the falseness of their practices. False religion resulted from a departure from this light.[1421] However, it is also dull (from the human perspective), and quite unsatisfactory to help humans in our fallen condition. Edward contrasted the light of nature (a mere shadow of the eternal Son) with his understanding of the light of Christ as documented in the Johannine prologue,[1422] this more clearly related to sensible knowledge of God.

6

Daniel Strange

Background

DANIEL STRANGE'S THEOLOGY OF religions has been acclaimed by a number of Reformed theologians and also theologians of religions.[1423] While there have been other Evangelical and Reformed contributions to the field in the last thirty years, it would be fair to say that Strange's focused and ambitious work represents the current terminus of conservative Reformed thinking on the subject.[1424] Strange describes himself as a Reformed Evangelical, and terms the confessional outlook of his work "Protestant Reformed orthodoxy,"[1425] "conservative evangelical,"[1426] and also "Reformed evangelicalism."[1427] Strange documents his commitment to Scripture, primarily, followed by ecumenical creeds, the five *Solas* of the Reformation, and various Reformed creeds/confessions as well as a number of post '70s declarations.[1428]

In the introduction to his book outlining a theology of religions, Strange provides a brief biographical note in order to contextualize his work. He writes of his mixed ethnicity, and recalls some of his visits to Guyana and Canada, witnessing Indo-Guyan Hindu religious rites and celebrations as a boy.[1429] He became a Christian at sixteen,[1430] and given his varied religious background experiences and questions, chose to study Theology and Religious Studies at the University of Bristol.[1431] He singles out the positive contribution of Gavin D'Costa in his education, and the latter's encouragement to study a PhD, which Strange did and subsequently completed in 1999.[1432] Strange was the Co-ordinator for the Religions and Theological Studies Fellowship (with UCCF) from 2000–2005. He worked as a lecturer at Oak Hill Theological College from 2005 until 2018, when he was appointed Director. He then moved to Gateshead in 2021 where he is currently Director of the Crosslands Forum as well as a visiting Professor at Southeastern Baptist Theological Seminary, North Carolina.

Strange's PhD critically examined the inclusivism of Clark Pinnock, ultimately rejecting it on various grounds—including Pinnock's universality maxim, which Strange connects with Pinnock's views on trinitarian openness. Strange also documents what he considers to be unresolved tensions between universalism and particularity in Pinnock's thinking.[1433] Theology of religions occupies the focus of his two most substantial books,[1434] alongside a number of articles.[1435] His most recent contribution to the field is an introduction to a republication of J. H. Bavinck's *Church between Temple and Mosque*.[1436] While I will refer to most of his theology of religions writings throughout the chapter, it is his book, *For Their Rock Is Not as Our Rock*, (hereafter *Their Rock*)[1437] that is the primary focus in what follows. In it Strange presents his most developed Evangelical/Reformed theology of religions.[1438]

Unlike the other theologians studied in this thesis, Strange's *Their Rock* is an explicit and focused attempt to develop a theology of religions: Strange states the goal of the book is to "develop and deploy a biblically rich and nuanced theology of religions."[1439] His approach integrates a number of theological disciplines: "systematic theology, exegesis, biblical theology and missiology."[1440] Strange's goals are ambitious: he endeavors not only to provide a historical explanation for the origin and the makeup of religions, but also tries to understand and explain human religious psychology (this being the area of his work most clearly dependent on J. H. Bavinck). Given the scope of the project, he acknowledges the thin coverage in a number of areas.[1441] Several sub-disciplines are not discussed, and Strange has been criticized for having a weak anthropology, and for not more carefully considering the relationship between religion and culture.[1442] There are very few references to any particular religions within the book, and Strange notes that his more general dogmatic approach is responsible for this.[1443] He is very honest about the speculative nature of certain areas of his work—especially in the area of demons and his interpretation of the Babel event—which play a significant role in his argument on the origin of religions. Strange's style is not polemical; it is, rather, written to provoke further Reformed Evangelical engagement in the field,[1444] and to stimulate Christian mission.[1445]

Having provided the background above, I outline my approach in what follows. Firstly, I document and critique Strange's definition of non-Christian religions. In section 2, I consider the key influences on his work, also referencing his dependence/non-dependence on the four theologians whose thought has been discussed within this book. Following this, in section 3, I provide an overview of Strange's thought on the role of the demonic, *prisca theologia* and the *Logos*. In the fourth section, I critically examine three key ideas which are central to Strange's thinking about non-Christian religions—the antithesis, common grace, and his understanding of suppressed truth.

Throughout the chapter I consider Strange's dependency on and departure from C. Van Til, J. H. Bavinck and H. Kraemer. The reason for this particular approach is because I believe it is critical to "locate" Strange's work within Reformed thinking in the twentieth century and to examine which elements of thought from this era he has endorsed, and which he has left behind. While Strange acknowledges his dependency on the three theologians noted above, he does not state, explicitly, how this dependency takes shape. I seek to document this, also drawing on material from a written interview held with Strange in 2023 (available online) in doing so.

1. Overview of Daniel Strange's Theology of Religions

Strange states that two key Reformed doctrines impact his thinking on non-Christian religions—the antithesis and common grace.[1446] The former is fundamental, and the latter mitigates the consequence or impact of the antithesis.[1447] Strange notes that Romans 1:18–32 is the standard text appealed to by Reformed scholars in this field,[1448] and he strongly approves of Bavinck's exegesis of it.[1449] He believes idolatry to be the hermeneutical key to understanding non-Christian religion.[1450] In what follows, I document how Strange defines non-Christian religions:

> non-Christian religions are fashioned out of a suppression and distortion of . . . "natural" or "general" revelation.[1451]

> The relationship between Christianity and other religions is one of both principial discontinuity and practical continuity.[1452]

> [T]he Bible's presentation of the nature of non-Christian religions indicates that they must be understood as the impulse of opposition in fallen humanity towards the Creator God, who has made himself known in Christ Jesus.[1453]
>
> Phenomenologically religions are hermetically sealed interpretations of reality (worldviews) and as such are incommensurable, defying simple comparison.[1454]
>
> From the presupposition of an epistemologically authoritative biblical revelation, non-Christian religions are sovereignly directed, variegated and dynamic, collective human idolatrous responses to divine revelation behind which stand deceiving demonic forces. Being antithetically against yet parasitically dependent upon the truth of the Christian worldview, non-Christian religions are "subversively fulfilled" in the gospel of Jesus Christ.[1455]

I will focus primarily on the last definition in the analysis that follows as Strange repeats it five times throughout his book. I will, however, also make reference to the key elements in the other definitions in this and later sections.[1456]

The core of the most complete definition (the final one listed)—the idea of religion being a response to revelation—echoes numerous other Reformed definitions provided in the Introductory chapter. Strange's commitment to Scripture, and the Reformed emphasis on the sovereignty of God are evident in the definition. What divine revelation entails is not spelled out here, but Strange outlines his views on this elsewhere in the book, providing a four-fold revelation taxonomy (i.e., imaginal, remnantal, influential, and demonic revelation). To briefly introduce these revelations here, the first entails the *imago Dei* and general revelation,[1457] the second and third are covered by the *prisca theologia* tradition, and the last is wholly negative (a kind of demonic equivalence of inspiration). I make reference to this taxonomy throughout the chapter. Suffice to say here, the concept of revelation in Strange's definition is somewhat broader than in some other Reformed theologians' views, where general revelation *alone* has been in focus when discussing religions. The response to revelation in the definition is both overseen by God but also fashioned by humans—the key adjective being *idolatrous*. Religions are defined wholly negatively. The idea of subversive fulfilment is central to the definition, this standing in opposition to fulfilment theories.

Before proceeding, I will suggest that Strange's definition slightly misrepresents his own overall argument and emphases—in at least three ways. Firstly, while the antithesis (one of his key emphases) is specifically noted in the main definition, common grace is not.[1458] As a consequence the definition is weighted more towards the negative. The antithesis is not nuanced in any way in this definition—and yet Strange does nuance it.[1459] Having said this, Strange places the effects of common grace within the individual and inconsistent lived worldview, rather than in non-Christian religion, per se. Indeed, he explicitly rejects the idea of the Spirit working in religions.[1460] As such, the exclusion of common grace in the definition is understandable. At the same time, the relationship between religion and lived worldview (the *principial-practical* motif that pervades the book) is critical to Strange's thought, the antithesis and common grace being corollaries of the *principial-practical* distinction.[1461] This being so, the definition can be considered to be, in some ways, a purely theoretical construction—half of the full picture Strange presents.[1462] As will be noted in section 4, it is not always clear what "type" of religion Strange is speaking of: the principial or the practical variety. While Strange rejects the notion that his view of religions is more negative than that presented in the writings of Kraemer or Bavinck,[1463] I suggest that it is easy to see why some scholars have interpreted it to be so, if this definition has been the primary influence informing their judgment.[1464] At the same time, I will suggest that his overall *principial-practical* differentiation formalizes hints and ideas present in all of the theologians studied up to this point—the revelation of God *outside* religions—a subject I discuss further in the concluding chapter.

Secondly, the place of demons in the definition is a little unclear. While Strange describes this involvement as peripheral,[1465] at face value it appears more significant than this in the wording used. One of the main scholars whom Strange leans on in this area (Larry Poston) limits demonic involvement to *some* religions,[1466] and Poston is not alone in holding such a view.[1467] Strange's language in the definition, on the other hand, is more wide-ranging and not qualified.[1468] Strange recognizes that this aspect of his work is somewhat underdeveloped, but believes it be an essential part of theology of religions.[1469] Strange does not explore this ongoing demonic involvement in religions in the book.

Finally, I suggest that the idea of parasitic dependence is somewhat unclear. When he discusses the parasitic dimension in his book, Strange points to idolatry—the idea that a created thing is "turned into a god" in false religion.[1470] The parasitic idea is, therefore, that of counterfeiting of the True.[1471] One of the consequences of this is that there is "a thatness to our humanity."[1472] However, the idea that such dependence stems from "the Christian worldview" as documented in the definition, is not particularly apparent or clear in the book. The *thatness* element of parasitism points to religious consciousness (a necessary pre-cursor to idolatry), but Strange does not make a strong connection between this consciousness and the Christian worldview, per se. I discuss the concept of religious consciousness in more detail in section 2.1.2.

2. Influences on Strange's Work

As documented in the introductory chapter, Strange does not analyze or engage with the evangelical history of theology of religions, describing this as having been "ably done elsewhere."[1473] As stated previously, I believe this judgment to be somewhat questionable. He calls his own work "derived" going on to state, "In general I wish to demonstrate that there is a Reformed historical pedigree reaching back to the time of the Reformation regarding many of the conclusions I reach concerning the nature of the religious Other."[1474]

Strange does engage, to a greater or lesser extent, with the four theologians discussed in the previous chapters; however, with the possible exception of Edwards,[1475] none of these can be described as *major* influences on his own work. Given the quotation above concerning the derived nature of his work, it is important to note that Strange does not engage with post-Reformation creeds, confessions or councils (for example, there is no reference to "the Light of Nature" in the book).[1476] This is not a criticism, rather an observation concerning which areas of history Strange connects with, in developing his own thought.

2.1. Twentieth-Century Influence

Strange's main dependencies in developing his work are two missiologists and one philosopher theologian—all from the twentieth century. He states that his goal is to "republicize" their work.[1477] The scholars in question are J. H. Bavinck,[1478] H. Kraemer,[1479] and C. Van Til.[1480] In what follows I provide a brief overview of their contributions and Strange's use of their ideas. A consideration of how he brings together their different ideas in his own work is a significant motivation for the overview that follows.

2.1.1. Hendrik Kraemer

While Strange makes much of Kraemer's influence, it is not as strong as may be supposed.[1481] In what follows, I will explain the reasons for this evaluation.

The most obvious similarity between Strange and Kraemer is the opposition to fulfilment theologies. Kraemer's coinage of the term "subversive fulfilment"[1482] is taken up by Strange and made the cornerstone of his own theology.[1483] By his own admission, Strange re-tools the term and uses it more dogmatically than its creator did.[1484] What was no more than a tentative aside in Kraemer's thinking, a rather polemical response made against fulfilment theories of his era,[1485] is foundational to Strange's theology. Kraemer placed *dialectic,* not *subversive fulfilment* at the center of his own theology of religions.[1486] Indeed, he discounted the value and use of continuity and discontinuity models within the discipline.[1487] Strange, on the other hand, makes the concept (along with idolatry) central to his own work.[1488]

Strange documents two specific areas of disagreement with Kraemer: what he terms his neo-orthodox view of Scripture, together with his views concerning the status of the church and its relationship to Christianity and Christ.[1489] It is important to stress the significant difference on this latter point. While Strange compares non-Christian religions to Christianity (theologically and antithetically), Kraemer does not make this particular comparison central to his own work. Kraemer stated, "I propose to set the religions, including Christianity, in the light of the Person of Jesus Christ, who is *the* Revelation of God, and alone has the authority to criticize—I mean to judge discriminately and with complete understanding—every religion and everything that is in man or proceeds from him."[1490]

Strange rejects such an approach, arguing for a far closer identification between the church/Christianity and Christ than does Kraemer—who states, as noted above, that Christ judges Christianity, not just non-Christian religions.[1491] This is a significant difference in approach, and one I shall return to in section 4, where I consider the antithesis in Strange's thought. While Strange briefly justifies his position, he does not engage with this important methodological and theological difference in any detail, as noted by Statham.[1492]

There are other significant differences between Kraemer and Strange: for example the former's ambiguous view of what is going on in religions,[1493] his affinity to Barth,[1494] his rejection of the idea of general revelation,[1495] his emphasis on the role of the demonic against the church,[1496] the possibility of learning from non-Christian religions,[1497] and his understanding of *Logos* enlightenment.[1498] Having noted these differences, I do not mean to discount Kraemer's standing as an important and respected figure in Strange's thought. Historically, Kraemer was a hugely influential figure, and Strange recognizes this.[1499] While I believe Kraemer *is* an important reference point for Strange, I suggests he places Kraemer (respectfully) in Bavinck's shadow in the book, and I believe the differences noted above are responsible for this positioning.

2.1.2. J. H. Bavinck

J. H. Bavinck (hereafter Bavinck)[1500] is *the* key theology of religions influence on Strange: a point that Strange readily acknowledges for his work.[1501] Bavinck's influence is particularly strong in the areas of religious consciousness and the "magnetic points." In what follows I summarize these ideas.

Bavinck seemed to understand religious consciousness[1502] as the consequence of humankind's reception, suppression and substitution of God's revelation.[1503] He believed this consciousness to function around or to be governed by five ideas—what he termed magnetic points.[1504] These points are frames, though actual consciousness has a *whatness* to it: it is never empty. The revelation types which form the basis for this consciousness are listed by Bavinck[1505] as old religious traditions (i.e., a kind of remnantal revelation), general revelation (which he elsewhere unpacks as nature, human conscience and history)[1506] and "personal experience of God's guidance."[1507] He calls the seed of religion the "receptive organ"[1508] for the other revelations he mentions. He states that without the organ, one could not receive the revelation. How this seed relates to religious consciousness is not spelled out.[1509] Bavinck considers the relationship between the Gospel and revelation to be strong, but not the relationship between the gospel and religious consciousness, even though the latter is formed, in part, through revelation.[1510] I discuss this important relationship in more detail in section 3.3 below. For Bavinck, working religious consciousness is not a simple reception of revelation, more a confused, dreamlike apprehension, involving degrees of suppression and unsuccessful suppression of revelation, functioning around the five points.

Strange warmly embraces and endorses Bavinck's work on the magnetic points.[1511] There are, however, some differences. Strange more clearly differentiates and depends on the *thatness-whatness* distinction present in Bavinck's model, while recognizing that *thatness* is, in many ways, purely theoretical.[1512] Bavinck seems less interested in the concept of contentless frames,[1513] and I will suggest why in section 4. Strange appears to equate the *semen religionis* with the *imago Dei* and religious consciousness.[1514] In this he departs from Bavinck, who differentiates them, as noted above.[1515] Strange spends time discussing the *imago Dei*,[1516] and a primary argument in his work is that the *imago Dei* serves as a metaphysical check to the antithesis.[1517] He makes a connection between this check and the existence of the frames and the *thatness* of religions. How the *imago Dei* is a positive check to the antithesis, and also one of the four types of revelation that are suppressed in Strange's argumentation is not an area that Strange discusses in any detail.

I believe the most significant departure from Bavinck in Strange's work is in his thought on the *Logos* (see section 3.3). In addition to this, I will contend that in a number of areas Strange has not simply recycled Bavinck's work, but adapted it, the reason for the adaptation being appropriation of ideas from Cornelius Van Til. Strange's theology attempts, in certain areas, to bring together the thought of the apologetic-theologian Van Til[1518] and the missiologist Bavinck.[1519] Not surprisingly, the result of this "fusion" is a more dogmatic creation than is present in Bavinck's work. As I will seek to demonstrate in what follows, this eclectic approach is not always free of certain tensions.

2.1.3. Cornelius Van Til

Van Til's influence is evident in Strange's adherence to presuppositional apologetics, his view of the antithesis and common grace, and his "coherence" view of truth.[1520] Cornelius Van Til is a somewhat controversial figure in Reformed thought.[1521] Historical and contemporary disagreements over Van Til's work within Reformed thinking are not found in the context of understanding religions, per se: the focus is typically apologetics, epistemology and natural theology. Van Til's epistemology was developed in the context of the threat of liberal Christianity.[1522] He was not engaging with non-Christian religions in his writings—rather non-Christian thought (very generally), and in his book on common grace, specifically *Christian* differences over epistemology, the antithesis and common grace.[1523] Therefore, it is important to note, at the outset, that Strange's dependence on Van Til and the appropriation and subsequent use of some of his thought in the Christian theology of religions discipline, is not always straightforward. Given the importance of the influence of Van Til, I discuss the three areas of antithesis, common grace and truth in more detail in section 4.

2.2. Influence of Scholars Examined within this Book

Having given a brief background to the stated influences above, in what follows, I provide an overview of Strange's engagement with the theologians whose works are considered in chapters 2–5 of this book. As noted above, Strange makes only a mild claim to engage with the wider history of the field; nonetheless, it is helpful to provide this overview, because of the scope and focus of this book and my interest in tracing both areas of continuity and discontinuity in the understanding and use of the three key guiding parameters in focus in this study. Strange references all of the theologians discussed in previous chapters, but not in equal measure. I summarize this engagement below.[1524]

2.2.1. Justin Martyr

Strange believes that Justin Martyr's concept of the *Logos spermatikos* was taken up in the Roman Catholic documents *Lumen Gentium* and *Nostra Aetate*, and that it is a key element present in fulfilment views of non-Christian religions.[1525] He seems to support Bray's interpretation of Justin's view of the *Logos spermatikos*.[1526] He does not state what this was, but Bray argued that in Justin's thought a vague knowledge of Christ was known by some philosophers, due to the presence of the innate *Logos*. However, demonic darkness opposed this, the consequence being that truth was largely obscured.[1527] Strange believes Justin to have actually referenced the Johannine prologue.[1528] While, as noted previously, he supports the idea of the reality of imaginal revelation, he states that the appeal to the Johannine prologue is a "red herring" for the field.[1529] Turning to other aspects of Justin's thinking, Strange references Justin as a supporter of the idea of influental revelation (the idea that Judaeo-Christianity has influenced various religious traditions).[1530] While Strange, like Justin, appeals to the watcher angels and Jubilees and 1 Enoch in support of his view that the *běnê hā̆ĕlōhîm* are demons, he does not appeal to Justin as an authority in so doing.[1531]

2.2.2. Augustine

Strange makes little reference to Augustine other than noting his euhemerism argument.[1532]

2.2.3. Calvin

Strange quotes Calvin on a number of occasions. He documents Calvin's thought on the idea of imaginative gods,[1533] also referencing some of Bavinck's references to this.[1534] He notes Calvin's comments on the corruption of religion at the time of Abram,[1535] and to Melchizedek as a lone exemplar of faith.[1536] He believes Van Til and Calvin were both Christocentric in their Christianity—citing Calvin on the need for Christ's mediation to experience God's mercy.[1537] Strange, like many theologians, equates the *sensus divinitatis* and the *semen religionis*,[1538] and believes Calvin to have argued that these prove to be a restraint on sin.

Strange interprets Calvin's comments relating to *matter* and *sign* to support his view that "it is only the revelation of true religion that raises the forms and language of human culture from their 'natural state.'"[1539] He references Calvin's belief that demons are used by God to discipline believers,[1540] and that one of the roles of Islam is to be a "rod of correction" for the church.[1541] He cites Calvin's famous bleary-eyed spectacles analogy, and the fact that Scripture dispels the "confused" knowledge of God gained from nature and elsewhere.[1542] He documents what he considers to be Calvin's understanding of the interplay between Satan and humankind in the first sin—humans agreeing with Satan's slanders of God, along with the idea of human unfaithfulness.[1543]

2.2.4. Jonathan Edwards

Jonathan Edwards, in particular, is presented as providing Reformed support for Strange's remnantal revelation theory.[1544] While disagreeing with McDermott on a number of his interpretations of Jonathan Edwards,[1545] Strange supports McDermott's idea of there being planted types in religions,[1546] and he endorses the idea that a knowledge of God as creator and redeemer is gained from the *prisca theologia*.[1547]

While Strange adopts some of Edwards's ideas on the *prisca theologia*, he does so without reference to his thinking on the light of nature and reason and without consideration of how the *prisca theologia* fits into Edwards's wider thinking. I discuss this further in section 3.2. Strange refers to Edwards's comments on the new start with Abraham after religious corruption.[1548] He also documents Edwards's view concerning why false religion flourishes—namely God's own glory.[1549] He seems to support Edwards's argument that demonic perversion of true religion can be used by God: "Thus what Satan intends as a cruel and evil perversion is used by God towards the redemption of a people when the gospel reaches them."[1550]

2.3. Other Influences on Strange's Work

Regarding his wider eclectic approach, Strange appeals to various scholars in different areas of his work. For example, his thought on the demonic is largely dependent on Mody;[1551] and his original monotheism argument makes a number of references to Corduan.[1552] Strange documents his dependence on Kreitzer when connecting ethnicity to religion,[1553] and refers to a number of Reformed commentators on Genesis to support some of his interpretations.[1554]

In terms of the more immediate contextual historical background to his book, it is important to highlight that Strange came to it after his engagement with Clark Pinnock and "Evangelical inclusivism," as noted earlier. Strange has acknowledged that this critical engagement *may* have influenced his thought on the *Logos*—which I discuss further in section 3.[1555] Further, it is important to note that there is a clear shift in focus away from the importance of general revelation to the field as documented in his PhD,[1556] compared to his later work where remnantal and influental revelation play a far more significant role.

3. The Three Parameters in Strange's Thinking

Having covered this background, in what follows I provide an overview of Strange's thought on the three main parameters in focus in this book. As noted in chapter 1, of these only two are endorsed by Strange (the *prisca theologia* and the demonic). He rejects the concept of *Logos* enlightenment entirely, and as noted earlier makes imaginal revelation the third of his own four parameters. This being so, I make reference to imaginal revelation throughout the chapter, to ensure that all the key elements of religions in Strange's thought are discussed.

3.1. The Demonic

Strange notes that his own background has not helped him work through the subject of the demonic.[1557] At the same time, he argues for the necessity of including the typically "excluded middle" when considering non-Christian religions: for Strange, the demonic needs to be present in a theology of religions.[1558] Earlier on in his thinking, Strange seemed to highlight the role of *imagination* (rather than the demonic) as being foundational in some ways to false religion, but this idea seems to fall into the background in *Their Rock*—the role being substituted by demons.[1559] Strange calls his work on demons theologically and exegetically "speculative."[1560]

Strange believes it is right to see demonic involvement within the Genesis narrative, preferring not to see Satan moving off the earthly stage after the fall.[1561] Indeed, he seeks to keep the demonic present from Genesis 3 to Genesis 6:1–4, and considers a background of the demonic to be of fundamental importance in Genesis 11, in the light of his reading of Deuteronomy 4:19 and Deuteronomy 32.[1562] In the New Testament it is primarily Paul's discussion of idolatry (1 Corinthians 8 and 10) that he appeals to when considering demonic involvement with idols.[1563] Whilst he acknowledges that his own work is somewhat speculative, he refers to the biblical support for the relationship between idols and demons in the following way: "while biblical references to idols and demons are scarce, they are present, and moreover, thinking particularly of Deuteronomy 32:17 and 1 Corinthians 10:20, are presented in explicit fashion."[1564]

In forwarding his proposal, Strange references a pre-human fall of some of the angels.[1565] He believes that the involvement of Satan, while not primary in Adam and Eve's fall,[1566] nonetheless signals a kind of archetype of false religion.[1567] He believes the first sin of our parents to have been that of idolatry.[1568] Strange supports the view that the *bĕnê hāĕlōhîm* in Genesis 6 are demons.[1569] He appeals to various Reformed commentators in support of this position.[1570] Unlike Justin's emphasis, Strange's major focus (though framed hesitantly) is to tie the *bĕnê hāĕlōhîm* with what is going on at the Tower of Babel and Table of Nations.[1571] On this he states, "we may possibly be more specific that the objects of idolatrous worship at Babel, either directly or indirectly, through the worship of astral bodies, are 'fallen angels', that is to say that the *bĕnê hāĕlōhîm* are in reality demons. In Deuteronomy 32 this connection is certainly made (and also by Pss 96:4–5; 106:27, 37)."[1572]

Concerning the Babel incident, Strange writes, "My contention concerning the Babel incident in particular is that we have here both a historical and a theological account, not simply of the origin of 'religion', nor even the origin of 'false' religion, but rather the origin of the diversity of false 'religions.'"[1573]

While forwarding the above argument, Strange does not believe that too much weight rests on this viewpoint, or that his overall understanding of religions (primarily as being idolatrous, and subversively fulfilled in Christianity) would collapse if his arguments on this were undermined.[1574] Using Kraemer's term, though departing from his emphasis,[1575] Strange terms the demonic a "dark margin,"[1576] or "minor theme"[1577] compared to the *major* theme of idolatry in the Scriptures, which has a stronger human element to it.

Turning to demonic revelation (one of the four different types of revelation influencing religions in his view),[1578] Strange argues for a kind of demonic inspiration of ancient kings.[1579] Such "inspiration" produces a kind of counterfeit to true religion.[1580] Strange does suggest a kind of pedagogy in this counterfeiting,[1581] but explicitly rejects the idea of truths being present in religions, as will be noted later.[1582] While Strange is generally positive about John Frame (an acknowledged follower of Van Til) in his book, he nowhere endorses Frame's view that demons can speak truth.[1583]

Depending on Mody's work,[1584] Strange believes the idea of "co-option" to be helpful in explaining the relationship that exists between demons and idols.[1585] He documents Mody's co-optative view which, in his own words, "identifies demons and idols as distinct entities, the personal former standing behind and manipulating the lifeless latter."[1586] Strange states that there is no symmetry between God's power and Satan's, and he is keen to avoid a dualistic understanding of God and demons.[1587]

3.2. The *Prisca Theologia*

Strange's focus on the Babel event and remnantal revelation constitute a significant contribution to the field. Unlike other *prisca theologia* theories, in his understanding of borrowing the idea of plagiarism moves to the background, and oral tradition to the foreground.[1588]

Both *remnantal* and *influental* revelation are types of special revelation in Strange's thinking. While differentiating them, he notes their close relationship.[1589] Strange terms influental revelation the influence of the Judaeo-Christianity worldview on non-Christian religion/philosophy.[1590] He believes such a theory to have been present in some of the apologists' thinking in the early church.[1591] He spends very little time discussing influental revelation in his book. *Remnantal revelation*, on the other hand, is defined as revelation from creation up to Abrahamic revelation, this being passed down via tradition, and disseminated post-Babel.[1592] Strange focuses much more on the role of remnantal revelation (rather than influental revelation) in his theology, in part due to his goal of establishing a critical relationship between Babel and religions.[1593] In partial support of his position, he references work by Corduan on the idea of original monotheism being present in many religions around the world.[1594]

In an interview, Strange has stated that he holds to a position that he terms "dogmatic creationism,"[1595] entailing belief in a historical Adam, the Fall and the flood. He argues that belief in these makes the remnantal revelation argument more plausible than might initially appear.[1596] Strange states that when examining a religion (as opposed to engaging in a systematic consideration of revelations)[1597] it is difficult to untangle the influence of remnantal and influental revelation from general revelation as they merge.[1598]

Faircloth and D'Costa have suggested that the ongoing presence of special (remnantal or influental) revelation in non-Christian religions in Strange's theory opens the door for the Spirit to work salvation.[1599] However, Strange has explicitly rejected this possibility in his theory, by arguing that this revelation, and the truths contained within it are immediately distorted and suppressed by humans.[1600]

As documented earlier, Strange states that the *prisca theologia* tradition has been accepted within the Reformed tradition.[1601] He appeals primarily to Jonathan Edwards as a Reformed advocate of the remnantal revelation theory.[1602] He concurs with Edwards that there has been considerable deterioration of this over time.[1603] While appealing to Edwards, he recognizes that the sources used by Edwards to support that position may be suspect.[1604]

While Strange appeals to Edwards in support of remnantal revelation, he nowhere appeals to his work on the light of nature. I believe this is somewhat problematic, given the argument in chapter 5. To reiterate, it was noted there, that what was known from the light of nature was critically important to Edwards, both as a kind of non-spiritual foundation for "true" knowledge, and also because the *prisca theologia* could deteriorate. Edwards, on occasion, made an appeal to the light of nature over against the value of the *prisca theologia*: while the *prisca theologia* could deteriorate, the light of nature (while also subject to deterioration) seemed to have been appealed to as a last defense against false religion.

I suggest that Edwards came to hold this position as he seemed (albeit only vaguely) to foresee the danger of merging what was known from revelation and what was known from the light of nature in human experience.[1605] On at least two occasions Edwards appealed to the light of nature as enabling humans to differentiate true from false religion, even when these same humans were victims of such false religions.[1606] He stated that "pagan" American Indians (subjects of a deteriorated *prisca theologia*) are able to differentiate true from false religion, on the basis of this light. To allow merging between the light of nature and revelation within a religion did not seem to be an option for Edwards. Strange, on the other hand, seems not to focus on the possible outcomes of his merging theory, and does not consider possible tensions that might result between deteriorated special and still functioning general revelation. This may be because, in his thought, all such revelation is immediately suppressed.[1607] Having said this, Strange also speaks of incomplete suppression—a point I discuss further in section 4.[1608]

I suggest that Strange makes more of the positive role of common grace in relation to general revelation compared to remnantal revelation—see section 4.3.2. Having said this, unlike Calvin and Edwards, Strange plays down, rather than emphasizes what general revelation shows, arguing, for example, that what is known from general revelation does not provide an adequate basis for law in society.[1609]

Another difference (though not a major one) between Strange and Edwards on this subject is that Edwards spoke in slightly more positive terms of a kind of Gospel preparatory role of a demonically deteriorated *prisca theologia*. Strange largely limits the positive effects of such corrupted revelation to the preservation of "thatness" frames which make the missionary approach possible.[1610]

3.3. The *Logos*

In *Their Rock* Strange dismisses, rather cursorily, the relevance of the Johannine prologue and *Logos* enlightenment to the discipline of Christian Theology of Religions.[1611] Further, he rejects the idea of *Logos* enlightenment outside of religions as well,[1612] and seems to exclude any role the prologue may play in helping understand the meaning of the *imago Dei*.[1613] While Strange refers favorably to the idea of Calvin's *semen religionis* (equating it with the *sensus divinitatis*, as a gloss for what it means to be made in the image of God),[1614] he does not ground the *semen religionis* in the *Logos*/Eternal Word, or as a gift from his hand, as Calvin does, as documented in chapter 4 of this book. Like Jonathan Edwards, Strange has little room for the Prologue in informing his theology of religions.

Strange makes no reference to John 1:4, 5 (the key verses employed in this debate) in *Their Rock* or his PhD, referencing only the more contested John 1:9, supporting Ed Miller's exegesis of it.[1615] While recognizing that "a number of evangelicals" believe this latter verse to reference general revelation, the *imago Dei* and the idea of anthropological enlightening, he believes Miller's incarnational interpretation to be correct.

In his PhD Strange seemed to support, or at least comment fairly neutrally upon, non-inclusivist *Logos*-based theories of general revelation.[1616] He documents, inter alia, Ronald Nash's work. In Strange's words, Nash differentiates the cosmological *Logos*, "the agent through whom God brought the world into existence," from the epistemological *Logos*, "the ground of all human knowledge."[1617] Strange prefaces a quotation by A. A. Hodge by referring to a relationship between common grace and "Christ's cosmic and epistemological revelation."[1618] This idea is not discussed or developed in his later work. While Strange recognizes continuity of revelation in creation and redemption,[1619] he is largely silent on this theme in *Their Rock*.

In an interview Strange has suggested that his earlier work critical of inclusivism, and the appeal made to the *Logos* by some inclusivists, has possibly influenced him against considering this subject from other perspectives.[1620] At the same time he acknowledges a revelation *from* the eternal Son in General revelation, but not necessarily *of* the Son. In response to a question comparing Bavinck's christological view of general revelation (discussed below), and his own, Strange writes:

> If by "Christologically grounded" you mean that *ontologically*, the eternal Son is "behind" all revelation in terms of Col 1 (and all the other prepositions contained in that passage), then yes, natural revelation grounded in the Triune God, Father, Son and Spirit. However, if you mean *epistemologically* that Christ is revealed in natural revelation then I am far more cautious and would fall back on more traditional distinctions between natural revelation and special revelation, or in Calvin's terms "knowledge of God the Creator," and "knowledge of God the Redeemer."[1621]

In what follows, I consider Bavinck's thought in this area, and contrast it with Strange's. Strange recognizes that his "great hero" Bavinck appealed to *Logos* enlightenment as part of his theology of religions.[1622] He makes one reference to Bavinck's prologue argument—from *Church between Temple and Mosque*. In that book, in the context of discussing Romans 1:18–32, and in describing a missionary encounter, Bavinck stresses that the person who hears the words of the gospel has already had dealings with God. Christ is now presented to the man "in a new form." He then goes on to say:

> He [Christ] was, of course, already present in this man's seeking; and, because he did not leave Himself without a witness, Christ was wrestling to gain him, although he did not know it. John describes this in a most delicate way: The Logos "lighteth every man" and "the light shineth in the darkness and the darkness comprehended it not" (John 1:9,5). In the preaching of the gospel Christ appears once again to man, but much more concretely and in audible form.[1623]

In a book chapter on general revelation, Strange terms Bavinck's exegesis of Romans 1 brilliant; however, despite this accolade, he does not consider how Bavinck relates Romans 1 to the Johannine prologue,[1624] as Augustine, Calvin, and Kraemer had done before him.[1625] The quotation above is not the only time that Bavinck referenced *Logos* enlightenment. In what follows, I explore in more detail this aspect of Bavinck's thinking.

While Bavinck rejected certain *Logos* theologies (in particular what he understood to be the early church's understanding),[1626] *Logos* enlightenment still played an important role in his thinking. On the basis of my own analysis of the references (in English), I believe there to be four elements to Bavinck's appeal to a christological view of general revelation. I note these below, and provide one representative quotation, for each point.

1. General revelation (including that noted in Romans 1) is profoundly christological.[1627]

    > The darkness referred to here [in John 1:5] must then be the same darkness that Paul discusses. The shining of the Light of the Logos then refers to that general revelation or *manifestatio* that Paul treated. And that "overcome" ... must mean: "has not overcome it," or "could not extinguish it." This expression indicates, therefore, that general revelation is very directly related to the Logos or the Word that was from the beginning and that has become flesh in Jesus Christ.[1628]

2. Christological general revelation is not abstract, or related to reason, but personal and dynamic.[1629]

    Bavinck writes, "The point of departure for all of our considerations needs to be God's self-disclosure or the general revelation that nonetheless bears the nature of a very personal engagement of God with each person separately."[1630]

3. This christological general revelation is behind and responsible for religious consciousness (the magnetic points/*thatness* template).

    Bavinck states, "But people's religious consciousness—that product of illumination, repression and replacement—simply stands over against the gospel and is contradicted by the gospel."[1631]

4. There is a very close relationship between christological general revelation and the Gospel.[1632]

    Bavinck comments, "God's general and His special revelation are to be thought of as connected, and they continuously affect one another. Both of them are all about Jesus Christ. The Logos of John 1:14 who became flesh and dwelled among us is the same Logos who 'enlightens all people' (John 1:9)."[1633]

Whereas Bavinck's theology of revelation can be described as christologically robust, this emphasis or understanding is not present in Strange's work.[1634] As noted above, hints of such an idea are present in Strange's PhD, but nowhere developed in the later study. Strange focuses primarily on the idea of the subversive fulfilment of religions in Christ. His is very much a "forward looking" model: moving from religions to Christ (though not in the way of fulfilment). Bavinck, on the other hand, seemed to advocate both a backward and forward orientation of religions: both from Christ and to Christ (and like Strange, not in the way of fulfilment). I document the difference below:

Bavinck

Christ (in revelation) → Religion → Christ (in incarnational revelation and salvation)

Strange

Revelations (imaginal, remnantal, influental) (+demonic) → Religion → Christ (in incarnational revelation and salvation)

Bavinck argues that there is continuity between the Gospel and "what lies behind religious consciousness," indeed, he terms this an intimate relationship. It is important to highlight that the relationship is not between the Gospel and religious consciousness, but rather what lies behind religious consciousness—Christ himself.[1635] Bavinck seemed to argue that if "fulfilment" is in Christ, there must be continuity not only of who is revealing, but also who is revealed. Such an understanding provides a kind of continuity in human experience (though not straightforward) from unbelief to belief. From my reading, Bavinck did not seem to differentiate roles of the *Logos*/Christ (as Creator and Redeemer as is the case in Calvin's thinking). Strange, however, does refer to this distinction when discussing general revelation, and endorses it.[1636]

While Strange has spent considerable time considering the raw material from which religions are formed, these are not strongly grounded in Christ. In *Their Rock*, Strange does not mention the work or presence of the eternal Son in imaginal/general revelation (or other types of non-salvific revelation). Strange is cautious about what a revelatory presence of Christ in general revelation might mean.[1637] This difference in emphasis between his own work and Bavinck's is, I believe, quite significant.

4. Antithesis, Common Grace, and Truth

In this last section of the chapter, I focus on three areas where I believe Van Til's influence to be particularly evident in Strange's work. I will try to demonstrate how each of these specific influences leads to a subtle shift away from Bavinck. I document this, in part, to demonstrate how, in my understanding, the stated influences work out in practice—as Strange does not explicitly state how the influences of Kraemer, Bavinck, and Van Til actually impact his own work.

4.1. Introduction

Strange acknowledges that while common grace, the antithesis and the *imago Dei* constitute part of the grammar of the Reformed tradition, these doctrines are complicated and there are differences in views about how they function.[1638] In terms of his own positioning, he throws his lot in with presuppositionalism.[1639]

4.2. The Antithesis

The concept of antithesis is strongly associated with Abraham Kuyper.[1640] Van Til is both appreciative and critical of his and H. Bavinck's work in this area.[1641] In Frame's opinion, Van Til has re-worked Christian theology around the antithesis,[1642] terming Van Til "a kind of apostle of antithesis."[1643] Close alignment with Van Til's thinking in this area places Strange in a particular Reformed "camp."[1644] Suffice to say here, Reformed theologians who question Van Til's theological emphases in the areas of the antithesis and common grace may not agree with Strange's work in theology of religions, or aspects of it, because of this dependence.

Before proceeding further, it is important to make two key observations. Firstly, Strange's appropriation of Van Til's thought is not wholesale. While there is significant dependency on a few key statements, there are areas where Strange seems to depart from Van Til. Some of these would be Van Til's focus on the eschatological (rather than present) reality of the antithesis,[1645] the idea of true knowledge in the image of God,[1646] the questionable value of differentiating *thatness* and *whatness*,[1647] and the primacy of the image of God over against the antithesis.[1648] Secondly, and as noted earlier on, Van Til is not a theologian of religions, and he does not discuss these three key concepts as they relate to non-Christian religions. Accordingly, it is important to stress that Strange employs some of Van Til's ideas outside of their original context, transplanting them to theology of religions discussion.

As documented previously, Strange defines non-Christian religions antithetically to Christianity. He defines the antithesis in different ways: between religion rooted in Christ compared to that which is not,[1649] between the regenerated who say Jesus is Lord and those who do not,[1650] and between covenant keepers and covenant breakers.[1651] The antithesis is described as being current (rather than eschatological).[1652] The antithesis, in Strange's thought, is not just epistemological, it also covers intelligence and ethics as well.[1653] For Strange, the antithesis implies "radical discontinuity"[1654] which will "naturally influence one's perception of non-Christian religions."[1655] On Strange's appropriation of Van Til's thought in this area, Farnham states, "Daniel Strange is representative of exclusivists who see complete antithesis between Christianity and other belief systems. He seeks to carry a Van Tilian notion of absolute antithesis to its logical conclusion."[1656] I believe this is a fair judgment.

In what follows, I consider how Strange adopts and adapts the Van Tilian antithesis to theology of religions, and document how, as a result, Strange's approach seems to differ from J. H. Bavinck's. In order to help set out the key issues, I begin by considering the thought of the Reformed theologian Henry Stob.[1657] I choose to focus on Stob's contribution as he is one of the few Reformed theologians, of whom I am aware, who has given some detailed consideration to the subject of the antithesis in relation to non-Christian religions.

Stob notes that the term *antithesis* was popularized by Kuyper, and he provides the historical context as being a battle between Christianity and humanism.[1658] He argues for a scriptural grounding to the concept.[1659] In his discussion of Genesis 3:15, Stob notes that God does not initiate the antithesis, but rather God's action is a counter offensive—a splitting of the anti-God alliance between humans and Satan—ultimately seen in the incarnation.[1660] For Stob, the antithesis lies primarily between "God and Satan, between Christ and antichrist, between angelic and demonic forces, or more abstractly between grace and sin."[1661] Commenting on what he perceives to be the main argument in the work of Van Til and Hoeksema, Stob challenges the wisdom of centring the concept of the antithesis in the elect and reprobate (while not denying the truth of the grouping), stating that we do not know who exactly these are.[1662]

He also notes how the ongoing struggle with sin and the presence of the old Adam in the believer makes placing the antithesis between the regenerate and unregenerate questionable.[1663] While acknowledging some advantages in locating the antithesis between believer and unbeliever, he also discusses problems with such a placement.[1664]

In his book *Theological Reflections*, Stob considered the antithesis specifically in relation to non-Christian religions. He did not believe it to exist between historical instantiations of religions (as these can be, in his own words "more or less true to themselves")[1665] and also not between individuals (acknowledging that heathen lives can, at times, be better than Christian lives),[1666] nor between different theologies (which are in many parts human products).[1667] Rather, as noted earlier, he states the antithesis is, fundamentally, between grace and sin, and only in a qualified sense between Christianity and non-Christian religions, though it can be understood in this way.[1668]

Like Kraemer, Stob shifted the focus away from Christianity to Christ as the reference point for non-Christian religions; however, unlike Kraemer, Stob keeps Christianity in the picture too, because of its identification with Christ. Like Kraemer and Strange, Stob argues for a kind of subversive fulfilment in the religions: "Christianity is both the denial of the ethnic faiths and the fulfilment of them."[1669] At the same time, while holding these convictions, and being a firm believer in the antithesis, Stob was reluctant to locate the antithesis between non-Christian religions and Christianity:

> For though all religions, other than the religion of Christ, are false at the center, displeasing to God, and unable to save, there is yet in them an unwitting acknowledgement of God, there is power in some of them to raise the level of men's moral behaviour, and all of them keep alive in men's consciousness the reality of the Unseen. They are so far forth a protest against atheism, immorality and radical secularism.[1670]

Stob goes on to explain how, in his opinion, this less than completely antithetical state of affairs is possible. He does so by appealing to the inner knowledge of God (*sensus divinitatis*), general revelation, common grace and special revelation (both borrowing, and traditional memory). A key difference between Strange and Stob is that Stob sees a bestowal of grace in these revelations which somehow continues to exist in religions qua religions, despite humankind's depravity and rejection of God. While recognizing the fundamental falsehood of religions due to his view of the antithesis more generally, he believed that they are were not just evil. Religions contain grace, because of God's involvement in them.[1671]

In sum, Stob does not reject the concept of the antithesis, but rather challenges the wisdom of positioning non-Christian religions antithetically to Christianity in a Reformed theology of religions.

A key distinction should be made at this point concerning the locus of this non-saving grace in the thought of Stob and Strange. Strange, like Stob, makes grace (i.e., common grace) responsible for what is ethically good in non-Christian religions. However, this goodness is present only in the inconsistent version of religion in Strange's thought—not religions per se. This distinction, between the *principal* antithetical religion and *practical* common grace infused cultural version of religion, is of fundamental importance to Strange's thought. It is, however, not present in Stob's thought, because there is no such distinction between the principial and practical.[1672]

Having provided some necessary background, in what follows I compare Bavinck and Strange on this point. Like Strange, Bavinck believed there to be an important distinction between religion and culture: Bavinck argued that culture was the outworking of religion.[1673] However, at the same time, he insisted on a "hidden crack" being present between the two: the crack is a work of God, having its origin in his mercy.[1674]

Both Strange and Bavinck "decenter" non-Christian religion as the locus of the work of God outside the church. The belief that God works within humankind outside a religion, rather than within people within a "false" religion, is also present in the thought of Kraemer[1675] and Newbigin.[1676] This is an important viewpoint, and a somewhat neglected area of discussion in Christian theology of religions. Being so, it is a topic I will discuss further in the concluding chapter. Having established the importance of the religion-culture divide, and a seeming difference between Stob—who maintained the idea of grace *in* a religion—compared to Bavinck and Strange who emphasize the non-salvific work of God in humans (rather than in religions *qua* religions), I now consider another side of Bavinck's thought.

In his discussion on common grace and the antithesis, Klapwijk argues that J. H. Bavinck, in a similar way to his more famous uncle, did not hold such a strong view of the antithesis between Christianity and the religions as did Kuyper.[1677] While J. H. Bavinck makes clear antithesis-like statements about Christian and non-Christian religions, in the sense that he contrasts false religion with the true,[1678] and while he speaks of God working within individuals outside of their religions—as documented above—he also argues for grace being evident and present in religions. This is not just the hand of God in establishing the magnetic points of religious consciousness, and the *thatness* framework of religion. Neither is it an "add-on" common grace doctrine.[1679] For example, Bavinck states:

> This does not mean, however, that the idea of guilt is nowhere found in the non-Christian religions. There, too, we find penitential psalms, songs in which sin is confessed and grace is implored. These songs sometimes show traces of self-excuse. But it is not fair to say that they all ring untrue. We may say that by the grace of God, repression and substitution do not always succeed. Time and again we notice things in the history of religion which show that God has really concerned Himself with these people.[1680]

It is in religions *qua* religions that we find a locus of the grace of God in Bavinck's thinking in the quotation provided above. While Bavinck rejected neat classification theories of religions,[1681] he clearly differentiated some religions (*qua* religions, not lived-out worldviews under the influence of the Spirit in common grace) as being better than others—not just different, but better.[1682] Bavinck believed *religions* to vary greatly, and he attributed this to the grace of God.[1683] Bavinck seems much more interested in recognizing differences within religions than does Strange. This may be because of Strange's overall "dogmatic sketch" approach. Another possible explanation why Bavinck does this, and why he allows for grace to be present in a religion, is the fact that he stresses *both* the social and individual aspects of religion.[1684] The former is not a focus of Strange's work. While Bavinck differentiates religion and the religious adherent—and stresses the work of the Spirit outside religion in the individual (as noted earlier)—at the same time, he does not seem to prohibit such gracious workings informing religion: grace "spills over" back into a religion from the individual—a position that Strange seems to deny.[1685]

Bavinck's nuanced language concerning the work of God in other religions—especially his use of the word "mystery"—softens his view of the antithesis as existing *primarily* between non-Christian religions and Christianity.[1686] When Bavinck speaks of non-Christian religion, he describes it in strongly negative, yet at the same time ambiguous language.[1687] In contrast, Strange talks of two *versions* of religion: the principial and practical. His main focus in *Their Rock* is the principial, as noted above.

I would like to suggest that another possible reason for decentring the antithesis as existing between humans in Bavinck's thinking is his missionary motivation and orientation. While Bavinck could speak in language which is strongly antithetical,[1688] not only did he soften this when talking about religions (as noted above), he also insisted on balancing this by talking of the antithesis running through the heart of the Christian, the missionary and the church.[1689] No doubt Bavinck felt it necessary to make these comments as a result of his personal experience in Indonesia, and from attitudes he encountered within the church in the West. While a meeting in love must be based on a strong view of the antithesis, the grounds of meeting, for Bavinck, were common fallen humanity. In Bavinck's thought, standing next to was a necessary prerequisite to standing against in antithesis. If the former attitude were lost, the conversation could not begin. The antithesis could not be the only or the primary mover behind mission:[1690] it must always have a companion. Strange mentions the inconsistencies of the church,[1691] and the danger of Christian pride in his book.[1692] However, I suggest that these acknowledgements do not affect his theology of religions as much as they do Bavinck's. Perhaps the difference between Strange and Bavinck can be explained by Bavinck developing a theology of religions *alongside* a theology of mission, considering the relationship between the two, even when focusing on theology of religions.[1693]

In sum, I believe Bavinck has both a "softer" view of the antithesis existing between Christianity and non-Christian religions and a more self-conscious wider view of the antithesis operating within Christianity than does Strange. As such, the religions antithesis does not play such a central role in the Dutch missiologist's thinking of non-Christian religions. I believe making the principial antithetical position *primary* to his theology of religions is a key distinctive element in Strange's approach.

4.3. Common Grace

The idea of *common grace*, i.e., a non-salvific, undeserved kindness of God to all of humankind, is understood to be articulated in a number of Reformed confessions, although the term itself is not used.[1694] Within Reformed theology, this doctrine has typically been considered to be a necessary qualification or counterpoint to that of total depravity, needed in part to make sense of the "good" that exists in the world.[1695] Calvin has, rightly or wrongly,[1696] been touted as the "discoverer" of common grace.[1697] There are various understandings of this grace within the Reformed tradition, along with outright rejections of the concept.[1698]

Strange's working definition of common grace in *Their Rock*[1699] leans for support on Murray,[1700] Macleod,[1701] and Van Til,[1702] though primarily the latter. Strange's understanding of common grace counterbalances his view of the antithesis, alongside his view of the *imago Dei*, which, at times, he pairs with common grace.[1703] In his PhD, he provides some background to more recent discussion of the subject of common grace within the Reformed tradition.[1704]

4.3.1. Common Grace in Religions

In this section I will compare and contrast Strange's appeal to and handling of common grace with Bavinck's approach. While Bavinck only once spoke of common grace in the English translations of his theology of religions work, I will suggest that he had a strong belief in non-salvific grace, though a different emphasis to that seen in Strange's work.

As noted in the previous section, the antithesis between Christianity and non-Christian religions is foundational to Strange's theology of religions. However, this fact is, in Strange's words, "complicated" by two factors: "in practice there are a number of supplementary factors that 'complicate' this antithesis and provide commonality between believer and unbeliever. Van Til names these factors as the imago Dei and common grace."[1705] The idea that common grace "complicates" the antithesis is consistent with the idea that the antithesis is foundational to Strange's thought on religions. Below I quote Van Til's understanding of common grace, which is used by Strange throughout *Their Rock*:

> Their antithesis to God is therefore an ethical one. . . . Because of God's common grace, this ethical antithesis to God on the part of the sinner is restrained, and thereby the creative forces of man receive the opportunity of constructive effort. In this world the sinner does many "good" things. He is honest. He helps to alleviate the sufferings of his fellow men. He "keeps" the moral law. Therefore the "antithesis" besides being ethical rather than metaphysical, is limited in a second way. It is one of principle, not one of full expression.[1706]

Strange believes common grace to restrain humankind's hostility to God,[1707] it also being responsible for inconsistency in worldviews.[1708] He argues that common grace "limits" and "supplements" the antithesis.[1709] In the quotation above, it should be noted that common grace is spoken of in relation to the individual: it is not related to non-Christian religion, per se. Indeed, as noted in the previous section on the antithesis, Strange, at times, juxtaposes the non-working of the Spirit in religions with the Spirit's (non-salvific) work in individuals.[1710] For Strange, the *imago Dei* and common grace may operate "positively" within the sphere of the individual despite the religious root antithesis.[1711]

What are the impacts of common grace in religions *as* religions? In his treatise on common grace, on one occasion Van Til addresses this idea directly. He notes covenant breakers' contribution to the building of the temple at the time of Solomon, and how such were gifted by God to be skilled in crafting cedar trees, and how God both gave and used their skill for his own glory.[1712] Strange refers favorably to this example.[1713] While this is a biblical example, it can be argued that a focus on it skirts other texts which might be considered relevant to the idea of common grace operating *within* religions, particularly the idea of wisdom (rather than skilled labor) being present within them. In the section that follows, I consider this in more detail.

Both Bavinck[1714] and Kraemer[1715] believed there to be wisdom present in non-Christian religions. VanDrunen has recently referred to various Old Testament texts in support of his argument that wisdom was known to exist outside Israel, which Israel could learn from.[1716] He notes some similarities between Egyptian wisdom literature and Proverbs,[1717] and also references a number of OT verses which indicate the knowledge or presence of wisdom outside of Israel, including Proverbs 8:15–16, 1 Kings 4:30, Jeremiah 49:7, and Ezekiel 14. Concerning the tenor of a number of Proverbs, he comments, "Yet Proverbs makes clear that wisdom also exists among those who worship other gods. Proverbs, in fact, required Israel to recognize the universal dimension of wisdom and to learn from the wisdom of foreigners."[1718]

Does this wisdom constitute knowledge of God? VanDrunen makes careful distinctions in his comments.[1719] The relationship between (or indeed identification of) Wisdom and the *Logos* is a live issue in contemporary Johannine discussion.[1720] I will discuss this important subject in more detail in the concluding chapter.

While Strange typically places the work of the Spirit outside a religion—within culture and the individual (as noted above)—occasionally he seems to allow for a work within religions as religions. For example, Strange states, "there is a non-salvific work of the Spirit in other religions, restraining sin and exciting to a civic 'goodness.'"[1721] He also says, "How, and in whatever degree, non-Christian religions display God's common grace, they glorify him."[1722]

The first quotation seems to contradict the claim noted earlier in section 4.2. The question that must be asked at this point is what Strange means by "non-Christian religions" or "other religions" in the above quotations. Does he mean religions *qua* religions or the lived out inconsistent variety? The answer must be the second—not religions as he defines them in *Their Rock*—the type he presumably had in mind when arguing that God's Spirit does not work in religions.

Richard Mouw has perhaps been the most vocal critic of Strange's work in the area of common grace and religions. He argues that Strange's version of common grace, borrowed from Van Til, has no positives at all when considering religions: "Given that the standard interpretation of the doctrine of common grace is that it allows for a non-salvific attitude of divine favor toward the non-elect, it is difficult to find any element of the 'divine favor' element in Strange's depiction of non-Christian religions."[1723] Mouw's analysis is somewhat simplistic in that Strange does believe religions can be a tool of common grace (as noted) and in a later book Mouw seems to acknowledge this.[1724] Returning to Mouw's initial critique above, if describing *principial* religion in Strange's thought, the comments are relevant and accurate. What Mouw did not initially seem to appreciate is that Strange is, in fact, working with two versions of religion in his book.

4.3.2. The Relationship between Common Grace and General Revelation

Reformed scholars have interpreted the relationship between general revelation and common grace in rather different ways. Here I will consider three, namely: instrumental, enabling and embedded, and compare J. H. Bavinck and Strange's views on these, within the wider Reformed tradition. I will suggest that while there is overlap between the two theologians, there is also a significant difference.

Perhaps the most common understanding of the relationship between general revelation and common grace is instrumental. Macleod, for example, states that "the primary instrument of God's common grace is God's general revelation."[1725] Strange also argues for such a relationship, echoing the above comment.[1726] Turning to Bavinck, I do not believe that instrumentality is the *primary* focus in Bavinck's thinking, and the reason becomes clear when the third kind of relationship is noted.

Turning to the second relationship, Masselink stressed the work of the Holy Spirit in enabling the reception of general revelation *through* common grace. He argued that through creation and history the Spirit gives humankind both an awareness of God and of his moral law.[1727]

Such an idea is also present in Bavinck—though he also stresses the work of God against suppression of revelation.[1728] Strange mentions both the general enabling, plus the fact that grace works against suppression.[1729] I would suggest, however, that the anti-suppressive view of common grace in relation to revelation is the strongest relationship in Strange's thinking. As noted above, Strange argues that this restraint is partly responsible for an inconsistency within non-Christian worldviews,[1730] where common grace is responsible for the discrepancy between worldview and lived worldview.[1731]

Thirdly, a more direct "superimposition" understanding of the relationship between general revelation and common grace has also been argued by some Reformed theologians. Helm has posited that writers such as Herman Bavinck and Kuyper underestimated Calvin's positive view of natural law.[1732] This being so, he argues, they needed to look to common grace to explain the restraint of sin, gifting and blessings. Helm, on the other hand, suggests that a functioning natural law (not functioning perfectly, but functioning nonetheless) overrides the need for a full-blown "common grace" doctrine in Calvin's thought. Accordingly, he states that common grace and nature in Calvin be understood as being "complementary, or at worst overlapping, descriptions of the same phenomena; they are not at odds with each other, and so they are not to be set in opposition to each other."[1733] Given my observations in chapter 4, I would concur with this interpretation. I believe that a similar idea is present in J. H. Bavinck's thinking: general revelation actually *is* common grace. The only time that he used the expression *common grace*, Bavinck connects it directly with Romans 1:19, where he seems to view such revelation as common grace.[1734] This third way of considering the relationship between general revelation and common grace is also clearly found in Kraemer's thinking.¹⁷³⁵ I suggest that this particular understanding is less obviously present in Strange's work, for whom the positive role of common grace is seen rather to function *distinctly from* revelation (which is suppressed by humans in religions), mitigating the effects of the antithetically-grounded human response to it.

I do not believe Bavinck needed to appeal to common grace as a discrete doctrine as it seems that, for Bavinck, God's dealings with humankind are gracious, and not only so, this grace can, at times, overpower humankind's typically hostile rejection of such dealings—even in religions. The commitment of God to humankind in general revelation and the mystery of the power and grace of God in it were realities Bavinck did not really understand, but was, nonetheless, convinced of.¹⁷³⁶ Turning to Strange, his distinctive emphasis on common grace is a critically important part of his theology of religions—especially in supporting his *principial—practical* motif.

4.4. Truth in Non-Christian Religion

I turn now to the third and final subject of focus—truth. Unlike a number of historical figures and several Evangelical and Reformed theologians whom he cites favorably,¹⁷³⁷ Strange rejects the idea that any truth can be present in non-Christian religions, speaking only of "suppressed truth."¹⁷³⁸

> Given the comprehensive nature of idolatry and its truth supressing characteristics, and given that "every religion is an indivisible, and not to be divided, unity of existential apprehension", it is false to say that non-Christian religions are simpliciter "truthful" or even that they contain isolated sparks of verity mixed with error. Difficult as it is, we can talk only in terms of "supressed truth."¹⁷³⁹

In an interview, Strange provides the example of the doctrine of transcendence and immanence in Islam as suppressed truths.¹⁷⁴⁰ He describes himself as "a little allergic to a simplistic 'All truth is God's truth' statement,"¹⁷⁴¹ going on to say, "The systemic nature of an idolatrous worldview means that there is no 'truth' that has not been affected, and is not 'coated' by idolatry even where the restraint of sin in common grace is v. strong."¹⁷⁴²

Strange allows himself to be termed Van Tilian in his thought on this area.[1743] Rather simply, Van Til can be considered to have espoused a coherence-oriented theory of truth, grounded in the ontological Trinity.[1744] For Van Til, one cannot know anything truly without true knowledge of God.[1745] A coherence theory, as Farnham states, emphasizes a holistic notion of truth: "the center of a coherentist theory of truth and justification [is]—a proposition is true and justified to the extent that it coheres with the other beliefs in the system."[1746] A simple correspondence theory, on the other hand, accepts that a statement is true if it corresponds to fact, without consideration of the wider belief system, interpretational framework, or the subjective state of the one making the statement.[1747]

A huge amount has been written about Van Til in this area, and it is not my intention to discuss this here. Rather, I wish to consider similarities and differences between Strange and Bavinck on the issue of truth in non-Christian religion. Unlike Strange, I believe Bavinck makes statements supporting *both* coherence and simple correspondence positions, and in what follows I seek to document and understand this.

Bavinck was not impressed by superficial claims to similarities existing between Christianity and other religions.[1748] Visser summarizes Bavinck's thinking, which Strange quotes in full:

> The residues of revelation never lie hidden as petrified fossils in the soil of pseudo religion. False religion always presents itself as, and in actual fact invariably constitutes, a monolithic aggregate. Consequently, all ideas it absorbs become amalgamated with and deformed by the whole. In other words, it is not possible for isolated elements of verity, sparks of divine truth to exist in the midst of falsehood and error–in fact, if such sparks were present, they would lead to friction in and destruction of the very essence of pseudo religions.[1749]

On the basis of this statement, it seems that Bavinck, like Strange, supports the coherence view of truth, denying any possibility of truth existing in a false system. Of particular interest in the above quotation is the idea that truth cannot co-exist (peacefully) with falsehood—a position that Strange seems to endorse both in citing the above quotation approvingly, and in advocating the antithesis to be between Christianity and non-Christian religions.[1750]

However, I suggest that the above quotation does not represent the sum total of Bavinck's thinking. On a number of occasions, Bavinck seems to have expressed a rather different view.[1751] Like Calvin, he argued for the presence of sparks of truth in heathenism.[1752] In a statement that must be seen to balance the idea of truth being unable to exist alongside error, Bavinck suggests that truth and falsehood might exist side by side:

> Even the so-called elements of truth in [heathenism] it are a lie, because in the whole context of the totalitarian character of heathenism these elements of truth have a different sense and point in another direction. *Nevertheless, the admission of this fact does not imply that God's Word, which he is speaking to the individual Gentile is always thwarted and frustrated, or that it never stirs his heart or moves his mind. God can break the resistance: He is able to overcome the rebellious force* [emphasis mine]. He can prepare himself a point of contact in the sinful soul. Nor does the admission of this fact imply that the religious songs of the poets of India and the words of the woman-Saint Rabi'a of Basra are to be rejected as abominable deceit.[1753]

In the above quotation, while speaking of the individual heathen, Bavinck writes of religious artifacts too, thus suggesting that truth is not always thwarted in false religion. I would argue that Bavinck makes these comments about the presence of truth as he seeks to balance the idea of knowing and not knowing: of suppression and incomplete suppression and the role of non-Christian religions in this. Bavinck clearly argued both positions.[1754] While Strange also argues for both suppression and incomplete suppression,[1755] I suggest his view of incomplete suppression does not allow for anything to be known truly, whereas Bavinck does seem to allow this.[1756] Strange is more reluctant than Bavinck to speak of truth existing alongside falsehood: common grace is strong enough to overcome some sinful suppression for Strange, but not to totally overcome it.[1757]

I suggest that a consequence of Bavinck's position is that he spoke a great deal about tension within humankind's religious make-up.[1758] Logically, such tension cannot exist unless truth (rather than suppressed truth) is *actively* engaging with falsehood. The question whether truth can "survive" in an essentially idolatrous religion clearly divides theologians.[1759] Interestingly, Van Til explicitly rejected the idea that non-Christian thought could ever be internally coherent,[1760] and at times allowed for truth to co-exist alongside falsehood.[1761] John Frame, a follower of Van Til, argued similarly.[1762] I believe Strange would concur—though only when discussing inconsistent worldviews—rather than religions.

While Strange allows for some kind of truth-falsehood interface, this is in the area of *inconsistency* (rather than religious tension) between religion and lived worldview. The consequences of "knowing but not knowing" is *not* a major focus of Strange's work, or at least the tension that results from this reality is not stressed. This may be because of the *principial-practical* methodological approach to Strange's work: he does not focus on the interface between the two. Strange's psychological focus is on the frames, not the truth-falsehood interface.

As suggested above, I believe Bavinck allowed tension to exist *within* a religion, not just within individual religious consciousness. I suggest that a particular locus of this tension is living out "the good" in a religion. Bavinck believed that true things could be "known" and spoken within a religion, but that the heart could be far from these words. In commenting on some of the beautiful words of heathen literature, Bavinck wrote, "It is not the sound of the words that is decisive: it is the heart behind the words that is judged by God."[1763] Given this, and similar comments documented above, I do not believe Bavinck could hold a consistently coherentist "Van Tilian" view of truth in discussing either individuals or religions. Strange, I suggest, makes a more concerted effort to do so—although he seems, on occasion, to be inconsistent.[1764] In making a sharp distinction between *thatness* and *whatness*, between "structural continuity in systemic discontinuity" concerning the relationship between non-Christian religions and Christianity,[1765] Strange substitutes Calvin's and Bavinck's "sparks of truth" for contentless magnetic frames.[1766] Strange seems more insistent on excluding any truth from these frames, when compared to Bavinck, who did seem to allow some truth to survive in them.[1767]

Conclusion

In his book *For Their Rock Is Not as Our Rock*, Strange makes a significant contribution to theology of religions in the Reformed tradition. Combining biblical, theological and historical study, Strange has developed a thorough biblical theology of religions from a Reformed perspective. Its breadth and focus are without parallel within the tradition.

Concerning the three parameters in focus in this book, Strange's most original contribution, I suggest, is in the area of remnantal revelation (this sitting within the *prisca theologia* tradition). Strange has not simply duplicated Edwards's thought on the *prisca theologia*, but moved it away from "mere" borrowing theories, to explain the origin of religions from the biblical narrative in Genesis. Part of this argument connects religions with demons, and the latter's role in the Babel event. Strange's work on the make-up of religions (the four revelations informing them) has continued the Reformed shift away from an exclusive pre-occupation with general revelation when considering religions—a movement that was already clearly present in key thinkers of the twentieth century with whom Strange engages.

Concerning the rejection of the relevance of *Logos* enlightenment to the discipline, I submit that some of the positives occasionally associated with this, historically, have been transferred by Strange to his doctrine of common grace and general revelation—though neither has a particularly strong christological basis. Significantly, Strange explains the effects of common grace primarily with reference to the individual, rather than within religions, per se. Accordingly, Strange's differentiation of *principial* and *practical* (individual lived out) religion is, I believe, another significant contribution to the discipline. Strange echoes the work of all the theologians studied in the previous chapters in the view that God works outside religions: indeed, he makes it central to his thinking. He does not, however, consider tensions between revelations within religions (e.g., between deteriorated influential revelation and imaginal revelation) or between revelation embedded *within* religions and revelation from God *outside* religions.

In terms of his engagement with twentieth-century Reformed thinking, Strange has argued for a dogmatic subversive fulfilment model of religions, where the antithesis is located between Christianity and non-Christian religion, and in which the concept of idolatry is central. I have suggested that Strange's thinking is influenced by Van Til in the area of the antithesis, common grace and truth, and that this results in a subtle movement away from certain emphases present in the work of Bavinck. Strange does not simply recycle Bavinck's work: he develops his own distinctive theology of religions.

7

Conclusion

> *Just as there never will be one phenomenology of religions, but many . . . so there will never be one theology of religion and religions . . . but many, each stamped by the theological individuality of the writer, and diversified through the richness of possible approaches in Biblical thinking. This is a blessing because in the field of theological production also . . . the rule holds good that . . . from the clash of different opinions the truth springs forth.*[1768]
>
> —Hendrik Kraemer

Background

THE GOAL OF THIS study, as stated in the Introduction, has been to understand and document five church figures' theological thinking about non-Christian religions. In the preceding chapters, I have focused on the revelation-religion interface in the works of these theologians, paying particular attention to the *Logos*, the *prisca theologia* and the demonic. In addition, I have considered the relationships which have been drawn between these three parameters.

The rationale behind the approach I have adopted is based on the assumption that a theological understanding of religions needs to consider what revelations humans are encountering and how religions reject, reflect, modify or embody these divine initiatives. Borrowing Dhavamony's comment, though applying it to a rather different context than originally intended, the following belief underlies the study: "In order to have an intelligent understanding of a complex phenomenon, 'we have to know not only what it is, but also how it came into being."[1769] From a theological perspective, knowing what religions are, and by extension gaining a more careful understanding of the spiritual status of adherents of these religions, is of fundamental importance to the church as it considers its mission in the world and its engagement with the religious Other.

In this chapter I summarize and synthesize the different theories discussed in the preceding chapters, and using Kraemer's language quoted above, consider what truth might "spring forth" from documenting and comparing "the clash of different opinions" present within them.[1770] While there is a focus on differences, I also seek to highlight similar ideas and threads of continuity, where present.

The outline of the chapter is as follows. Firstly, I provide in tabulated form a brief synthesis of the different theologies discussed in the preceding chapters, through the lens of the threefold revelation methodology I have employed. After providing this synthesis, additional explanatory comment follows. In the second section, I advocate the value of employing a contextually reflective, reactive and fulfilling hermeneutic to help explain the different approaches adopted. I also consider the different emphases within each theologian's thinking. In the final section I consider possible avenues for future research.

1. A Comparative Analysis of the Different Theologies

The key findings are provided in Table 3, after which I proceed to provide some more detailed comments justifying the choices of symbols employed (given below). It should be noted that in referencing the demonic I do not just focus on a revelatory role but also consider anti-revelatory roles in religions as well.

Key

++ = of significant importance

+ = present

? = vague/unclear

– = absent

– – = rejection of relevance

CONCLUSION

Table 3—Synthesis of Theologies

Theologian	(a) The *Logos* of God	(b) The *Prisca Theologia*	(c) The Demonic	Notes
Justin Martyr	++ Contraposed to c Primarily ethical awareness of the eternal law embodied in Christ and his teaching	+? Not so significant What has been borrowed is not the heart of the Old Testament (prophecy of Christ's coming)	++ Contraposed to a Impasse results, with demons having the upper hand Demonic bondage conquered by life, death and resurrection of Christ	Clear *Logos* revelation *continuity* from non-Christian to Christian era (from part to whole) Important dispensational differentiation with coming of Christ
Augustine	++ Primarily Platonists in view Primary focus of illumination is metaphysical truths relating to God	? Minimal Ambivalent on Plato's borrowing, though one appeal made to a particular Sibyl	++ Significant counterfeiting parallel to the Christian faith Demons can be compelled to speak truth	Demonic is a counter-mediatorial system to the incarnate Christ, *not the Logos* The Eternal *Logos* does not mediate Clear differentiation of two roles of the *Logos* (creation and redemption) Philosophers turn from illumination to the demonic

Theologian	(a) The *Logos* of God	(b) The *Prisca Theologia*	(c) The Demonic	Notes
John Calvin	+ Seed of religion and natural law gifts *from* the Logos	– – Rejected Wary of authority conflict and negative impact of philosophy on the church	+? Not viewed as active agents, rather grateful recipients of false worship	Distinct *Logos* roles *Logos* gifting Gifting leads to idolatry Contrast between humankind's religious response and ongoing revelation (*semen religionis* versus *sensus divinitatis*)
Jonathan Edwards	– – Rejected, but light of nature mentioned often Light of nature is a non-spiritual shadow of the Logos	++ The most significant Dependent on reports of religions throughout the world	+ Some Working *against* the *prisca theologia* (rather than the light of nature) Responsible for false imaginations in people's minds	Writing to combat deism New awareness of religions in the world —containing truths Differentiates revelation from light of nature

CONCLUSION

Theologian	(a) The *Logos* of God	(b) The *Prisca Theologia*	(c) The Demonic	Notes
Daniel Strange	− − Explicitly rejected A significant emphasis on common grace The eternal Son *behind* general revelation	++ Significant emphasis on remnantal rather than influential revelation No truth resulting in religions (only suppressed)	+ Peripheral Of particular importance in discussing origins of religions	Appeal to remnantal revelation and Tower of Babel Distinct methodology (*principial* and *practical* distinction) Antithesis, Common Grace

An exclusive focus on the pluses and minuses in the table above, while informative, can lead to some unhelpful "flattening" of finer-grained differences in the different theologies. For example, while Justin Martyr and Augustine both have a significant role for *Logos* enlightenment, the relationship between this and the demonic is very different; while Jonathan Edwards and Daniel Strange have little room for the idea of *Logos* revelation, they can be considered to "replace" this in rather different ways.[1771] This being so, I provide a more fine-grained commentary below.

1.1. Justin Martyr

Overview

I believe all three parameters are present in Justin's thinking and that two are particularly significant within it. I believe the *Logos* of God is Justin's most important contribution—but must be understood in the light of his demonology. I argue that he viewed *Logos* enlightenment to be a vague awareness of the eternal law of Christ or even part of Christ himself. I suggest demonology is very significant to his thinking, but that the demonic mimesis element of this is of only limited pedagogical value. I posited that the borrowing theory is not as important as is often argued, because what is borrowed is not what Justin considered the heart of the Old Testament to be (i.e., prophecy of Christ's coming).

Discussion

In terms of the basic interactions and relationships, Justin Martyr contraposed the demons against both the eternal *Logos* and Christ. The antithesis for Justin is there—humans lie between the two, confused and troubled by the demons. Before the coming of Christ, humankind is vaguely aware of part of the *Logos*. My interpretation of this is that Justin believed the eternal *Logos* to communicate ethical truth. I have argued that this ethical understanding is fundamentally theological, in the sense that it arises from his view of God and right relationship with God.[1772] I believe that the primary interest Justin had in the Old Testament was its witness to the coming of Christ. This fact is far more important than his *prisca theologia* argument, which I believe to be largely tertiary to his thinking of religions. I have not argued for overlap in what is known from the *prisca theologia* tradition (some basic metaphysical facts about God and creation) and *Logos* revelation (knowledge of *Logos*-law). I have attempted to demonstrate that *Logos* revelation is fundamental to his apologetic.

Turning to the demonic, part of the weaponry of the demonic in Justin's thought is deception—demons sailing close to the wind in inspiring mimetically perverted truths which are then embedded in non-Christian thought. Demons speak truth deceitfully—to hide and to make obscure. My understanding of this aspect of his thinking is that this only confuses humans: it is not *positively* pedagogical, and does not help the pagan. At the same time, for the pagan background Christian, demonic counterfeiting strategies can be appealed to, at least temporarily, to give credence to the Christian viewpoint, for those tempted to return to paganism. For Justin, the coming of Christ signals the end of the impasse of history: Christ defeats the demons and their bondage of humanity. Christ's victory over Satan is profoundly important in Justin's understanding of the redemptive work of Christ, just as his view of Christ's teaching is profoundly important for his view of living and ethics. It is essential to keep both aspects of Justin's Christology together in order to understand his view of Christianity and its difference to non-Christian religions.

CONCLUSION

Justin does not really consider how it is possible that some people may have followed the truth (part of the *Logos*) and overcome demonic bondage before the coming of Christ. Was this argument purely polemical? I suggest not as the right ethics-right God relationship was, I believe, of profound importance in Justin's thought. He saw clear revelation continuity between the pre-Christ era and the post-Christ era. The *Logos* is this continuity. Christianity is not new. I have argued, implicitly at least, that Justin can in no way be considered an early pluralist or inclusivist, in that he believed Socrates knew and followed the same truth as did Abraham: he did not espouse or practice a *different* religion.[1773] While Abraham knew more than Socrates, their lived-out ethics were testimony to their rejection of the demons and of their clinging to the true God. Justin's understanding of Judaism, I suggest, was either not fully informed by the Apostle Paul's teaching, or departed from it. His view of sin would be considered, at best, "underdeveloped" by Reformed theologians today.

1.2. Augustine

Overview

Augustine was aware of the borrowing theory, and noted chronological problems with it. While he tried to rescue it from these, he was ambivalent concerning its importance. I argue that Augustine believed true philosophical insights to result from enlightenment from the eternal Word, but that these result in pride, ending in the practice of false religion. Unlike Justin, who emphasizes the eternal law aspect of *Logos* enlightenment, Augustine stressed the metaphysical awareness resulting from the Word's illumination. Demons play an important role in his theology of religions, actively engaged in certain pagan religious activities. Augustine made it clear that he believed religions could be more or less false.

Discussion

While both Augustine and Justin Martyr give demons a significant role in their theology of religions, there are, I believe, two significant differences in their ideas. The first is the relationship between the *Logos* and demons. Augustine sees the philosophers' response to *Logos* revelation as leading to pride, resulting in a subsequent alignment between humanity and demons. Humans are less the victims of demonic deception, and more the willing participants with demons in various kinds of false religions (some much worse than others). Human pride is behind this alignment. For Augustine, *Logos* illumination involves some kind of true (albeit transient) knowledge of God, seen from afar. However, this true knowledge is not lasting or ultimately positive. There is much less of an idea of this knowledge being ethical knowledge, which can result in moral living (when compared to Justin): it is metaphysical, and is quickly lost. Significantly, this *Logos* enlightenment is largely limited to philosophers, not extending to the common people. Augustine's understanding of the sinful human will did not permit him to consider it possible for a human to simply know and follow the *Logos*. The discarnate *Logos cannot* mediate in his thinking. Human sinfulness needs to be overcome, and the mediation of Christ and humble clinging to the cross of Christ achieves what philosophies and pale and confused demonic mediation schemes never could.

The second difference is that for Augustine the demons are not just involved in various types of evil (as in the case for Justin): they are viewed as part of a parallel kingdom to that of Christ's. There are two kingdoms existing in Augustine's thought, one headed by Christ, the other by Satan. The idolatrous religious systems are not so much *perversions* of truth, derived from the true, as they are independent counterfeit mini-kingdoms—all part of the greater kingdom of Satan who allows the demons under him to develop their own domains. While advocating an Euhemeristic view of the origin of religions, the demons are not just the recipients of false worship: they are active players in religious deception. A real, but ultimately false, mediatorial system operates in perverse mimicry of the true in Augustine's thinking. In his attempts to understand what was going on in pagan religions, and to explain some of the truths present within them, Augustine believed that demons could be compelled to speak truth. He states this in stronger and more unambiguous language than any of the other theologians studied in this book.

Augustine vacillated on the need to appeal to the borrowing theory. His reference to the Erythraean Sibyl makes him the only theologian studied to clearly support a kind of multilinear view of the *prisca theologia* tradition, though as noted this seemed somewhat half-hearted. Importantly, this is not an appeal to any one of the chain of sages in Ficino's thinking. Neither Augustine nor Justin seem to appeal to what Strange would later term *remnantal* revelation, the idea that oral tradition was disseminated through the ages. Both reference what Strange would later term *influental* revelation, though neither, I suggest, considered this as being particularly important in their thinking on religions.

1.3. John Calvin

Overview

Calvin relegated the role of the demonic in his theology of religions, substituting this, in large part, with his doctrine of sin. I argued that Calvin rejected both traditional and renaissance versions of the *prisca theologia* and suggest that he did so because of his concerns over the appeal to philosophers as a secondary source of Christian truth. I show that he developed a rather unique understanding of *Logos* enlightenment, arguing for gifting *from* the *Logos*—one of these gifts being the seed of religion—rather than revelation or enlightenment *of* the Logos to humankind.

Discussion

In contrast to Augustine, Calvin was less interested in considering where on the spectrum of false religion a particular religion lay: his binary view of religions is very stark. Concerning the demonic, I believe it is fair to say that Calvin was speculation-averse. He held a significantly reduced role for demons in his view of false religions, dismantling the rather elaborate demonic mediation structures present in Augustine's thinking. However, like Augustine, Calvin placed significant emphasis on the necessity of true mediation in his argumentation and thinking on non-Christian religion. While the devil ultimately received false worship in Calvin's thinking, it was the fallen human mind, rather than demons which was a key mover in the development of false religion. Calvin's historical interest in religions was, I suggest, governed by a desire to trace the continuing thread of human idolatry in history in its various forms, and little more than this. I have noted that much of this idolatry seems to have been perceived to occur at the level of mediator—not replacing God himself. In arguing this, I differentiated the deterioration of the *semen religionis* (resulting in the creation of false mediators and associated religions) from the *sensus divinitatis* (a fitful awareness of the true God) in Calvin's thought.

While for Augustine philosophers did not know the way to go after seeing the goal, for Calvin, humankind (though perhaps the Roman Catholic Church in particular) did not know how to correctly handle two gifts received from the *Logos*. Regarding his Christology, Calvin made a sharp distinction between what the *Logos* gives to all in the opening verses of the Johannine prologue and the giving of the *Logos* in incarnation in verse 14. Like Augustine, Calvin held to the idea of two very distinct roles of the *Logos*. There are, however, significant differences. The first is that Calvin in many ways sidestepped the more obvious reading of the idea of *Logos* enlightenment. His view of enlightenment from (rather than of) one role of the *Logos* in his theology of religions, is, I suggest quite exegetically speculative—when one considers what the text actually says. Equating the light of the *Logos* with human religiosity and conscience is a rather novel approach to the text (within its historical context). Calvin widened the scope of the reception of this *Logos* revelation (when compared to Augustine), with everyone knowing God's will—the light of nature—albeit confusedly. This included the need to worship God aright.

The second difference, related to the first point, is that Calvin does not really allow for true knowledge of the *Logos* in his theology of religions. Whereas for Augustine it was the *Logos* that the philosophers caught a transient glimpse of, for Calvin, this is not the case. There is some confused knowledge of God, but none of the Son. For both Augustine and Calvin, *Logos* illumination (while understood very differently) is the first step to false religion for fallen human beings (more specifically philosophers, in Augustine's thinking).

Turning to the *prisca theologia*, Calvin rejected the tradition, and was, I suggest, wary of the negative influence of philosophy on Christianity. His principled eclecticism allowed him to borrow from philosophers for support when this was needed, but he never allowed these borrowings to be considered in any way second-hand dependent on the Scriptures, which for him were the only authority to be appealed to.

CONCLUSION

1.4. Jonathan Edwards

Overview

Edwards's emphasis on the ancient theology tradition marks a significant shift away from Calvin's thinking. Unlike Justin and Augustine, who did not explicitly connect the tradition with the demonic,[1774] Edwards did: the devil was responsible for the deterioration of the tradition, and for leading a triumvirate of false religions in the world. Edwards considered the light of nature (which he differentiated from revelation) to be a shadow of the eternal Son, but not spiritual enlightenment of the *Logos*. In this he differed from Calvin, who equated the light of nature with Logos illumination. When Edwards speaks of *Logos* revelation he is primarily concerned with the revelation of the incarnation, this knowledge being necessary for salvation.

Discussion

I have suggested that for Edwards the *prisca theologia* plays a far more important role in his theology of religions than in either Justin's or Augustine's thinking. Edwards appealed to the tradition to explain the presence of various truths, philosophic insights and also religious frames in both historical and contemporary non-Christian religion. At the same time, and in opposition to this, he argued that demonic influence and corruption of the tradition (together with sin) led to false religious practices.

In Justin's thinking, demonic mimesis was an independent action of the devils: they listened to truths communicated in heaven, and instantiated them in myths. My understanding of Edwards's argument is that the devils *corrupt* true revelation on earth, this spreading among people in false religions. Edwards did not allow this strategy to be successful: he saw a divine hand behind it, one which had the ultimate victory. Edwards perceived the main demonic strategy in the world to be wily deception, with Satan appearing as an angel of light. He seemed to allow for a more active role of demons in non-Christian religion compared to Calvin. While Calvin discussed the mind as a factory of idols, Edwards considered the mind (particularly imagination) to be a key assaulting ground of demons: false religion resulted from deluded notions of what might be understood to be a kind of demonic inspiration. Edwards does not seem to tie together demons and idols as closely together as does

Strange. Edwards's eschatological views were profoundly impacted by his theology of religions (and perhaps vice versa), an influence I have not detected in the other theologians studied in this book.

Edwards makes much of the light of nature, but I suggest he restricts the spiritual meaning of this even more so than Calvin. Edwards does not really connect the light of nature with *Logos* enlightenment, which he understands to refer to spiritual enlightenment and the incarnation. One might term the light of nature a shadow of the *Logos*, but nothing more in Edwards's thinking.

In referencing considerable *light of nature* references in Edwards's thought, I highlighted certain unresolved tensions in his argument: while the *prisca theologia* argument seems to be the major weapon he employs against deism, at times he appealed to the light of nature as judging false religion (the product of the deteriorated *prisca theologia*). He never stated, however, that it judged deism. This, I believe, would have given too much weight to the light of nature, and to play into deist hands. While there was deterioration in both the *prisca theologia* and the light of nature, it was the light of nature that was his last bulwark of defense against false religion. While the demons attack original revelation, the light of nature enables humans (even those who are involved in false religions) to recognize false religion for what it is. While Edwards downplays the spiritual nature of this light, the shadow of the eternal Son enables humans to differentiate true from false religion. Common grace is appealed to in order to explain what is positive among unbelievers, and the external work of the Spirit is responsible for this.

1.5. Daniel Strange

Overview

Strange's theory of remnantal revelation is related to the traditional "borrowing" version of the *prisca theologia* tradition, though quite distinct from it—focusing on oral tradition. Like Justin, he appeals to the reality of demonic involvement in religions with a scripturally-based argument. For Strange, this appeal relates to the origin of religion—with little said about the ongoing role of demons in religions today. Strange dismisses the relevance of the Johannine prologue to the discipline. Common grace is foundational to his *principial-practical* differentiation of religions.

CONCLUSION

Discussion

Strange's goal is to develop a rigorous biblical theology of religions—seeking in a much more systematic way than any of the theologians discussed in this book to be guided by the Bible in developing an overarching dogmatic understanding of religions. As with Augustine and Calvin, though with some subtle differences, the concept of idolatry is fundamentally important to his attempts to understand non-Christian religions.

Strange has championed a rather specific version of the *prisca theologia* in his theology of religions. The somewhat questionable grounds for much of the data behind Edwards's thinking has been replaced by a biblical appeal—even though Strange recognizes its somewhat speculative basis. In contrast to the thought of Justin, Augustine, and also Edwards, philosophical borrowing falls into the background in Strange's thinking and oral tradition comes to the fore. This tradition is considered to be responsible for molding certain religions and practices, though not seen to be embedded as truth in religions. Rather than appealing to Euhemerism or to a chronological deterioration of the object of worship over time, Strange appeals to anthropological evidence regarding universal monotheism and the biblical accounts of the Tower of Babel, and the Table of Nations to support his argument concerning the genesis of false religions. Being that religions are at root demonic, Strange is very reluctant to allow for any positive impact of religions (*qua* religions) in the world.

Departing from certain emphases present in Bavinck, Kraemer, and also Calvin, Strange makes the demonic more central to his thinking on religions. However, unlike Justin who viewed the demons to be at war with the *Logos*, or Edwards who spoke of demons being responsible for deterioration of the *prisca theologia*, Strange focuses, primarily, on their role in the *origin* of historical false religions. He is vague concerning the dynamics of what this ongoing reality means (when compared with the ideas of Augustine, for example)—though endorsing a co-optative view on the relationship between idols and demons. In practice, the demons are indeed peripheral in his thinking—whereas in terms of his history of religions they are front and center.

Regarding the actual practice of religions today, Strange focuses far more on *idolatry* than demonology. In this, his focus is very similar to Calvin's. A significant difference is that Strange does not focus on idolatry operating at the level of mediator—which I believe to be the case for Calvin. While Strange and Edwards admit of a significant role for demons in their theologies, Edwards considers them to be active in the mind: for Strange they are primarily associated with idols. Strange does not discuss the role of demons apart from idolatry, other than in the tower of Babel event. Unlike Augustine, Strange seems to exclude the possibility of any "positive" impact of demonic revelation through divine compulsion. In part, this seems to be related to his holding to a particular theory of truth.

Unlike Justin, Augustine and Calvin, Strange does not consider John 1:4,5 as being relevant to the discipline.[1775] Strange argues that common grace leads to a basic inconsistency between demonically inspired religion, and the lives of adherents of such religions. Edwards hints, at the very least, that the light of nature can be in conflict with false religion, and condemn it. This is not an emphasis present in Strange's work. Strange develops two different theologies of religions—the one *principial* (with its historical roots in the demonic), and the other *practical* (at root inconsistent, because of the influence of common grace and the *imago Dei*). Strange does not focus on the interface between the two in his theology of religions.

2. Contextual Influences

As Klapwijk observes, there is a tension between antithesis and synthesis in theological attempts to explain religions.[1776] I believe this is evident in all of the theologies examined. As stated in the Introduction, the biblical texts which are appealed to in support of a Christian understanding of religions are somewhat limited, and not agreed upon. While Romans 1:18–32 arguably occupies the central position, there are significant differences in biblical focus in each of the different theologians' ideas discussed throughout this study. I will suggest below that a plausible way of explaining this variety is by appealing to context-specific challenges which needed to be addressed. As noted previously, Christian theologies of religions have typically been grounded in particular contexts: there is always a back and forward movement between the Bible and observed religion as theologians have tried to explain a particular religion. Attempts to do so have appealed to the Bible and also used the language and ideas of the time. I document

CONCLUSION

what I consider to be the key contextual influences below, in Table 4. I explain the contents in more detail, directly after the table.

Table 4—The Role of Contextual Influences

Theologian	Key contextual religious challenge	Response
Justin Martyr	Christianity not new	Appeal to OT prophecy for coming of Christ Appeal to *Logos* continuity
Augustine	Philosophical pride Demonic mediation	Incarnation conquers pride Christ the true mediator
Calvin	Idolatry	Emphasis on true spiritual mediation
Edwards	Reason and deism	Emphasis on revelation informing reason Spiritual enlightenment above reason
Strange	The excluded middle Evangelical inclusivism "Good" non-Christian people	Revival of role of the demonic Exclusion of *Logos* enlightenment—shift to common grace outside religions

In what follows, I provide a brief commentary on the above.

2.1. Justin

Christ was not new: this perhaps sums up Justin's major argument to a skeptical Roman audience, where tradition was valued and novelty repudiated. He could point to the OT to argue this, and to Socrates too—as well as to some stolen Christian treasures (due to borrowing). Christ as the continuation of existing revelation (rather than religion) was a powerful argument and the *Logos* concept buttressed and supported this position. Non-Christian religion was wholly against the *Logos*—although even demons came close to speaking the truth. Fulfilment was seen largely *outside* of what was happening in popular religion (the domain of the demonic) in revelation by the *Logos*, and in the Old Testament.

2.2. Augustine

Augustine needed to address different questions to those faced by Justin. These involved, *inter alia*, understanding the relationship of the state to its gods and the ebbs and flows of history. Augustine emphasizes the idea that two cities exist above the cities of the earth, and that these are the key realities in the world. He developed a quite sophisticated set of parallels between them. Existing popular pagan thought (including the hierarchy and activity of demons) were seen to be pale and inadequate reflections of what was going on in the kingdom of God, where Christ is the head of the true city and the true mediator between God and humankind. In relation to the philosophers, Christ was the solution to human pride, and the sinful will. The grace of God and the cross are humanity's salvation. Augustine believed enlightenment of the *Logos* to result only in demonic bondage of various types. His view of human nature would not allow the possibility of redemption without necessary humbling by way of adherence to the cross.

2.3. Calvin

Calvin's emphasis on true worship is central to his theology of religions. He traced and connected false worship from the OT and in pagan religion to the Roman Catholic Church. The turn to false mediators in his era (saints, relics, etc.) was anathema to him. For Calvin, true spiritual worship is antithetical to the use of elaborate physical paraphernalia in worship. Without Christ at the center of a religion, all human-made efforts of mediation are futile. Fallen humankind's responses to gifts from the *Logos* lead only to error. *Logos* light condemns fallen humanity. The Roman Catholic Church was, in his view, responsible for dethroning Christ as mediator, and placing alternative mediatory schemes before an already sinfully confused and wayward people. I have argued that the primary focus of Calvin's thinking is on what might be termed "mediation idolatry," rather than the replacing of the supreme God by idols, especially when it came to his thinking about the Roman Catholic Church.

2.4. Edwards

In his engagement with deists, Edwards dismissed their understanding of *Logos* of God enlightenment. I have argued that this was in all likelihood due to his concerns about the deist use of this idea to justify natural revelation/religion. What he perceived as the ascendancy of reason in discussion about religion was combatted by an attack on reason's competence in this field. The attacks were multi-pronged, and not always consistent: reason was sharply differentiated from revelation; reason was informed by revelation; reason was not the way to know God; reason could know many things about God; reason could be enhanced by the Spirit; those who reasoned well in some areas (e.g., science), were helplessly wrong in religion. Edwards was trying, as best he could, to respond to two new worlds: the world of new awareness of non-Christian religion and the world of the enlightenment. He sought to use different arguments to engage with both.

2.5. Strange

Strange has made a number of key decisions in his theology of religions. The increased interest in demons in missiology, associated with certain aspects of the charismatic movement, together with accounts from various mission fields, provide a background for greater interest in the demonic, and a correction to the Western church's recent historical neglect of the "excluded middle." Secondly, Strange openly acknowledges that his significant engagement against evangelical inclusivism may have led him to a rather too peremptory dismissal of discussion of *Logos* enlightenment. In Edwards's day the *Logos* appeal was in Deist "territory," and considered misused. One can argue that from a conservative Reformed perspective,[1777] it is similarly misused by some Roman Catholic and inclusivist theologians today. Thirdly, the appeal to common grace, a doctrine which became much more significant in Reformed thinking in the nineteenth and twentieth century, underpins Strange's attempt to differentiate principial religion and practical lived worldview. Indeed, this doctrine is central to facilitating this distinction.

2.6. Summary

Is the above analysis overly simplistic? In some ways yes: to reduce the key contextually significant issue/s to just one or two factors is admittedly open to such a charge. At the same time, as a way of explaining why particular Scriptures have been appealed to, why certain parameters have been handled as they have, and why certain relations between them have been drawn, it seems to be a quite valid interpretation. Each theology can be considered a biblically-informed reflective and reactive response to what has been observed—all of them focusing on how Christianity fulfils—even subversively fulfils—what is found in different religions.

While all five of these theologians have sought to appeal to Scripture to understand religions, I suggest that their individual contexts and observations have significantly influenced which parts of Scripture they have appealed to, and which they have not. I believe that treatment of the Johannine prologue, in particular, exemplifies this viewpoint.

3. Personal Influences

While not wishing to make too much of this point, as suggested by Kraemer in the quotation provided at the beginning of the chapter, it may also be appropriate to consider personal background experience as being an influence behind the development of the different theologies. To address this question with any degree of confidence a very different kind of research project would need to be developed than that presented here. Even so, I believe there are sufficient hints present in what has already been stated to make some brief comments on this.

Although there is significant debate about how Justin's account of his conversion is to be understood, what is clear is that right living—the good lives of Christians—played a profound role in his thinking. Living righteously was a critically important part of his view of what Christianity entailed. Christ taught Justin how to live right.

Turning to Augustine, there is no doubt that his pre-conversion engagement with philosophy and his battle against his own sinful will deeply impacted his theology of religions. The role of pride was a significant player in affecting his thinking. The mediation of the Incarnate Christ and his cross was his salvation.

Calvin reported how, as a young man, he was deeply disturbed at the devotion to and confusion about Roman Catholic icons in festivals.[1778] I suggest that this factor, plus his personal aversion to speculation, deeply affected his thinking about true religion.

Jonathan Edwards's intellectual gifts and his conversion stimulated him to think about the difference between true, spiritual religion and nominal Christianity. His voracious interest in the religions of the world, and his first-hand engagement with native Americans, undoubtedly influenced his thinking.

In the context of his own first-hand experience of religious pluralism in an academic environment, and within an era witnessing a significant shift to inclusivism within Evangelicalism, which he has decisively rejected, I suggest Strange has sought to ground Christian thinking far more rigorously and carefully in the Bible. His dogmatic sketch of religions, dogmatic view of creation and a more dogmatic position on the antithesis, and the absence of truth in non-Christian religions can be interpreted as responses to these movements.

In making the above, admittedly rather simple observations, I seek merely to recognize the legitimacy of Kraemer's observation.

4. Contribution to the Discipline

I began this study by stating that a revelation-oriented focus in historical theology of religions research is sorely needed. I argued that a focus on *Logos* illumination, the *prisca theologia* tradition and the revelatory and anti-revelatory activities of the demonic adequately covers the key bases for such a research project, when studying the Christian figures whose works have been considered. Furthermore, I noted that contemporary historical appeals within the discipline have not, generally speaking, been adequately methodologically grounded, and as a result mono-dimensional and incomplete understandings of historical contributions to the discipline have resulted.

The new pictures that have emerged in the preceding pages, developed through a multi-perspectival analysis are, I believe, valuable and helpful for the discipline. I have argued, inter alia, that one cannot understand Justin's *Logos* doctrine, unless one takes into account his demonology. Concerning Augustine, I have shown that one must take seriously the relationship that exists between illumination and the demonic in his thinking in order to understand why religion exists. Turning to Calvin, I pointed out that his use of the *sensus divinitatis* has, for too long, been considered outside his theology of religions, and his religious context. For Edwards, though relevant work has been published (especially by McDermott), I noted that the relationship between the *prisca theologia* and the light of nature has barely been touched upon in his thought. In addition to these findings, I have conducted the first comprehensive analysis of Daniel Strange's contemporary work, not only on its own merits, but also within the context of the Reformed tradition and the wider history of the Church.

Each theology is rather different, and each should be understood as having been developed within its own context. As I have demonstrated in Tables 3 and 4, understandings vary, and the connections made between the revelations (and the demonic) also vary. Rather than being reductionistic, I suggest that the methodology employed facilitates a nuanced understanding, not only of a particular understanding of a parameter, but also of the varied relationships drawn between each parameter. Does an examination of these parameters in some sense constitute the discipline? If revelation is the primary focus, and the Bible is the key source text to be used, I would suggest "yes," though it is clear that much more work on the revelation-religion interface remains to be done—indicative of the infancy of Reformed thinking in this field of study. In particular, the question surrounding what *Logos* illumination entails, and the relationship of this to the *imago dei* and general revelation, requires further consideration. While I would argue that a focus on the revelation of God and the demonic constitutes the heart of the discipline, I would be the first to acknowledge that this is just one major focus, other legitimate foci being anthropological, missiological, soteriological and eschatological. Cognisant of these additional important considerations, the somewhat limited scope of the current study must be recognized.

5. Future Directions

In this closing section, I will suggest areas for future research, based on what I believe to be some of the critical issues arising from this study.

5.1. Demonology and Idolatry

Should Evangelical missiologists and theologians invest more effort in trying to understand the demonic in relation to non-Christian religion?

Probably. It is clear that much of the thought on the demonic in this book is contextually reflective and/or speculative. This being so, one might question its current value. As Strange has noted, more work needs to be done in this area. At the same time, such a focus may need to run in parallel with research focusing on the demonic and the church—a point which Kraemer highlighted, as noted in chapter 6.

5.2. Influential Religion and Secular Society

Strange has not focused very much on the influence of Christianity on the world in the last two thousand years in his theology of religions: early remnantal influence and the role of Babel, rather than influence post-Pentecost has been far more significant in his thinking. This, I believe, is due to his focus on the origin of religions. But what about religions now? Research taking into account the spread of Christianity over the last 2000 years and its impact on the religions is worth more consideration. Has the influence of Christianity had positive impacts in multi-religious communities? Has impact, whether positive or negative, influenced (even subconsciously) the development of hermeneutical approaches to non-Christian texts? Perhaps it is time for twenty-first century Gales, Cudworths and Stillingfleets to embark on much more carefully conducted research to shed light on this subject.

5.3. The *Logos* as Wisdom

Is there wisdom in religions? How is this different to wisdom in the Bible?[1779] What is the relationship between true wisdom (Christ the wisdom and the power of God) and wisdom as present in non-Christian religious texts and traditions? Wisdom literature has not played a significant role in any of the five theologians' attempts to understand religions. Should it be more central? Calvin, I suggest, battled with this issue more than others. He was insistent on the need to learn from non-Christian thinkers, and yet drew a very sharp line between religious and non-religious learning. The relationship between Hebrew wisdom and the *Logos* in the Johannine prologue is a serious and lively subject of enquiry for New Testament theologians.[1780] Theologians of religions, should, I suggest, pay careful attention to this research and consider its outcomes and relevance to the discipline.

5.4. Grace and Religions

Are non-Christian religions an evidence of God's common grace?[1781] Is it "better" for a person to be brought up in a non-Christian religion, compared to living in an atheistic secular society? One might answer that it all depends. J. H. Bavinck's thought on this question is that the modern western world has lost a lot in its flight from religion, to its serious spiritual detriment.[1782] If grace does "infiltrate" religions is this solely in relation to texts (if present) or practices too? What do we mean by grace in this context? Is it a synonym for truth, or is it primarily undeserved kindness? How is kindness embedded in religions which do not honor Christ? I suggest that it is very hard to allow for common grace to be at work in individuals, and not to allow this to impact religious ideas and practices. I would recommend that more serious engagement with various common grace theologies, and research investigating the religions-common grace interface be undertaken to help address this complex subject.

5.5. The Christological Grounding of General Revelation

Does the eternal *Logos* or Christ reveal himself in general revelation? Justin, Augustine and more recently J. H. Bavinck clearly believed this to be the case. For Justin, this revelation could be positive: for Augustine this non-mediatory revelation led only to idolatry. For Bavinck, such revelation is a pre-cursor to a fuller revealing in the Gospel, it being behind religious consciousness, though differentiated from it. Significantly, none of the above theologians fell into inclusivist theologies—not even Justin, who is quite often considered an early advocate of this view. Wary of this possibility, I suggest Calvin shifted the focus of *Logos* light to gifts from the *Logos*, rather than enlightenment of the *Logos*. For Edwards, the light of nature did not reveal the Logos, and Strange is likewise sceptical of how general revelation reveals Christ.[1783] I suggest that very serious concerns surrounding inclusivism should in no way discourage Reformed Evangelical scholars considering this subject in more depth. Subversive fulfilment, I would tentatively suggest, needs a christological starting point.

CONCLUSION

5.6. Other Historical Figures

I noted at the beginning of this work that Evangelical Reformed Christians and theologians need to be more aware of our tradition in the theology of religions field. This study has only scratched the surface in addressing this lack. Many more key figures and their contributions, if considered from the same methodological approach, or an adapted one, if necessary, will, I believe, give Evangelical Reformed theologians a much stronger base from which to work through key issues.[1784] Future research might cover Ulrich Zwingli, Gilbert Voetius, Geerhardus Vos, Hermann Bavinck, and Carl Henry from the post-Reformation era. I would also suggest that the thought of missiological figures such as Samuel Zwemer and lesser known nineteenth-century figures who lived in the midst of different religion be studied in more depth. The experience of converts to Christianity from different religions could also play a more significant role, moving forward.

5.7. Theology of Religions or Theology of Revelations?

This book has focused on revelation and the revelation-religion interface. As noted at the beginning of this chapter, it has been assumed that an adequate understanding of this "interface" can help theologians of religions understand religions better. However, on the basis of one of the findings of this study, the full picture is arguably more complex than this. The idea that God reveals himself *outside* the revelation-religion interface is a common position held by all of the theologians: Justin believed *Logos* revelation to come to Socrates outside of the popular religions; Augustine believed some (the philosophers) to experience something of the *Logos* outside the religions; Calvin believed the true sense of the divine to continue to operate alongside false religion; Jonathan Edwards believed native American Indians to know, deep down, due to the light of nature, what religion was true and false; Daniel Strange draws a sharp line between religions, and inconsistent world views: God's common grace being responsible for the latter. Bavinck,[1785] Newbigin,[1786] and Kraemer[1787] also made clear and important statements on this matter.

These observations raise the rather paradoxically awkward question whether Christian theology of religions is ultimately a rather unsatisfactorily incomplete discipline, missing a major part of what God is doing in the world today. While Clooney[1788] has supported the idea of a shift to comparative theology away from theology of religions, on the grounds that more real engagement with the religious Other is needed, a different way of ensuring this, while keeping theology to the fore of the discipline, is to expand the focus of investigation. Why should Christians limit the focus to the revelation-religion interface? Does the "default" activity of comparing Christianity with other religions fail to take into account God's revelation *outside* religions (as well as within them)? Is it time to shift the focus to a *Christian Theology of Revelation/s*, where religion is just one part of the discussion? Given the common argument regarding the reality of the work of God outside religions across the theologians studied, I suggest that this is a subject worth considering further.

Conclusion

Part of the motivation for this study has been to address the lack of Reformed theological engagement with its own history in the theology of religions field. I believe, as suggested above, that the varied theologies examined were developed, in large part, to address specific contextual challenges. Biblical reflection on these challenges has led to quite distinct theologies being developed, though clear lines of continuity in argumentation between the theologians are also evident to see. Contemporary critical reflection on these engagements can, I believe, help Reformed theologians develop theological models for today.

Kraemer, towards the end of his important book *Religion and the Christian Faith*, notes the church's indebtedness to the Reformers and the value of their contribution to theology of religions—speaking in glowing terms of Calvin's work, in particular. While noting this indebtedness, he encourages fresh engagement with the issues, and not a simple "parroting" of the Reformers' ideas. He goes on to provide the following advice, which I believe serves as a suitable conclusion to this study: "the Bible urges us to lead our thinking into the captivity of Christ, here and now, and not into the captivity of the Fathers, the *magisterium* of the Church, Tradition, Confessions, Augustine, Calvin, Luther or whoever else but simply to test how far *they* have thought in the captivity of Christ."[1789]

Endnotes

1. McGrath in chapter 2 of *Evangelicalism and the Future of Christianity*, 53–79, considers there to be six central beliefs or emphases which help define an Evangelical. He believes these center around: the authority of Scripture, Jesus Christ's majesty, the lordship of the Holy Spirit, conversion, evangelism, and Christian community. I suggest that this is a helpful working definition. See also McDermott and Netland, *Trinitarian Theology of Religions*, 4–5, who discuss alternative definitions. Bebbington famously identified four tenets in *Evangelicalism in Modern Britain*, 3: a "quadrilateral of priorities," these being conversion, activism, Biblicism, and crucicentrism.

2. For representative comments, see Strange, *Their Rock*, 32; Netland, *Encountering Religious Pluralism*, 308; Netland, "Theology of Religions," 142.

3. See Strange, *Their Rock*, 32. Braaten in *No Other Gospel!*, 92, suggests a negative influence from Barth, (though not specifically on Evangelicals): "Barth's negative judgment on religion gave no compelling reason to wrestle theologically with the religions."

4. Tidball differentiates contemporary Reformed Evangelicals from other forms of Evangelical spirituality on the basis of their historical indebtedness to the Puritans in *Who Are the Evangelicals?*, 22. Strange points to several texts which he believes exemplify contemporary Reformed theology, these written by William Edgar, John Frame and Michael Horton (see *Their Rock*, 33n22).

5. The two early church figures are Justin Martyr and Augustine. Goudriaan, "Reformed Theology," 9–23, notes the sometimes-uncomfortable relationship between the Reformers and the Church Fathers. Both appropriation and repudiation of ideas are evident to see. Justin is commended in Voetius's disputations (see Goudriaan, "Reformed Theology," 16). Calvin attributes *Monarchia* to Justin in *Institutes* 1.10.3, although today this would be considered Pseudo-Justin. Backus "Calvin and the Greek Fathers," 266, notes that in his disputes with Servetus on the Trinity, Calvin terms Justin an "illustrious patron" of the orthodox position. Note also Van Houten's comment: "Justin escaped Calvin's censure as one of those who compromised his beliefs in favour of philosophy," in "Earthly Wisdom and Heavenly Wisdom," 253. Contemporary Reformed theologians have also embraced Justin's theology of religions (See, e.g., Bray, "Explaining Christianity to Pagans," 9–25; Sparks, "Was Justin Martyr a Proto-Inclusivist?" 495–510). As Goudriaan, "Reformed Theology," 15–16, notes, Augustine's dominant role as a patristic authority figure for a host of Reformed scholars from the

early modern period onwards, is plainly evident.

6. In stating this I am conscious of the key role presuppositions play in theological discussion as noted by Braaten, *No Other Gospel!*, 94: "A Christian theology of religions calls for a candid approach that should acknowledge its presuppositions clearly rather than obscurely." See also Kraemer, *Religion and the Christian Faith*, 143: "On scientific and philosophical grounds, theology is fully entitled to formulate the case and to say its personal word on the problem of religion and religions, on the basis of its peculiar presuppositions." I recognize the difficulty in defining, in any detail, what "Reformed" means, aware of contemporary debate over varied understandings of the term, and who is considered "in" or "out" according to the criteria one applies. I do not wish to try to set out or discuss these varied criteria here, in part because the debate becomes even more complicated when considering theologians from different eras—as this study does. Suffice to say, I believe that if one considers oneself to be "Reformed" or even "somewhat Reformed," one would be interested to know about and learn from these theologians, in large part due to their known association with and respect within the tradition.

7. On the importance of the idea of *Sola Scriptura* within the tradition, see Strange, *Possibility of Salvation*, 140–42; Strange, "Perilous Exchange," 100–102. See also Bavinck, *Impact of Christianity*, 98, on the importance of Scripture guiding the theology of religions enquiry. Balancing these comments, concerning the role of tradition in Reformed theology, see D'Costa, "Gavin D'Costa Re-responds," 187–88.

8. On historical appropriation, note the comment of Goudriaan, "Reformed Theology," 14:

> Identifying the agreement with patristic doctrine was essential in order to show that the Reformation remained within the boundaries of Christian orthodoxy and thus was a part of the one catholic church in terms of a succession of doctrine (rather than a succession of bishops). Without patristic endorsement, Reformed theology would seem to be not ancient but a late innovation and, therefore, sectarian rather than catholic. Therefore, numerous works were published with the purpose of demonstrating the genuine catholicity of the Reformed faith.

Two recent books focusing on the importance of Evangelical historical connectedness would include Ortlund, *Theological Retrieval for Evangelicals*; Litfin, *Getting to Know the Church Fathers*.

9. Strange, *Their Rock*, 34. He references, *inter alia*, works by Kärkkäinen and Netland in making this claim. I suggest that the overviews by these authors are valuable, but rather brief, and not clearly methodologically grounded.

10. Bavinck, *Church between Temple and Mosque*, 122, 201. See also his comments in "Religious Consciousness in History," 259–64.

11. Pinnock prefers to follow these rather than Augustine, Luther, and Calvin (in the same order), as documented in *A Wideness in God's Mercy*, 182–83.

12. Strange, *Their Rock*, 108.

13. Netland, after defining the discipline, goes on to document what he believes to be two essential conditions which need to be met to develop an appropriate evangelical theology of religions. The first of these is that it must be biblically grounded and also "faithful to the central confession of the Church throughout the centuries," in *Encountering Religious Pluralism*, 313.

14. Irving Hexham in the first chapter of *Understanding World Religions* provides a helpful overview of different definitions and understandings of religion. I recognize that the term *religion* is a highly contested one, particularly in current thinking, where some critical religion theorists may challenge the existence or value of the category of religion, and where post-liberals may understand religion purely pragmatically. It must also be acknowledged that some theologians who are considered Reformed seem to have no place for theology of religions—non-Christian religions being considered a purely human product—as I will note below. Four of the theologians studied in this book provide definitions of religion, which I comment on in the relevant chapters. (I have not encountered a definition by Justin Martyr.) Like the biblical definition of religion (Jas 1:27), it is "true religion" which is in focus in the explanations of Augustine, Calvin, and Edwards. What is not true is termed by these scholars, "superstition," "false religion," and "hypocrisy and a vain show," respectively, as I will document. Such comments constitute the theologians' interpretations and understandings of the beliefs, practices and behaviors of the religious Other around them—whether Pagan, Roman Catholic or traditional native American—as they considered these with reference to the Bible. In contrast to Augustine, Calvin and Edwards, Daniel Strange explicitly defines non-Christian religion and his definition is, arguably, wide enough to cover secular atheism, although he does not focus on secularism in *For Their Rock is Not as Our Rock*. While I recognize the need for definition, I do not believe that any of the formal sentence definitions of Christian or non-Christian religion considered throughout the pages that follow adequately capture the full range of understandings present in the thought of any of these theologians—as I will demonstrate. However, for the sake of orientation, I can be understood to be following Corduan's understanding of the term, while recognizing that within each chapter of this study *religion* is always a contextually and historically specific phenomenon. Winfried Corduan writes: "A religion is a system of beliefs and practices that by means of its cultus directs a person toward transcendence and, thus, provides meaning and coherence to a person's life," in Corduan, *Neighbouring Faiths*, 28. Kraemer in *Religion and the Christian Faith*, 37, notes the difficulties surrounding definition.

15. In stating this, I do not mean that this is the *only* false religion in Calvin's thinking.

16. On the dating of the discipline to the late twentieth century, see Dupuis, *Toward a Christian Theology*, 2–3; Netland, "Theology of Religions," 142. Morali, "Catholic Theology," 81, believes that the term "theology of religions" was first used by H. R. Schlette in 1959. As Johnson notes, newness of discipline should not be confused with newness of thought or engagement with religions, for which there is a long history. See Johnson, *Rethinking the Trinity*, 32n31. Paul Visser makes the strong claim that engagement with non-Christian religion has, in some ways, been central in the history of the church: "The relationship between Christianity and the extra-biblical religions has been the life-and-death problem with which the church has dealt in all the centuries of its existence," in Visser, "Religion in Biblical and Reformed Perspective," 30.

17. McDermott and Netland state, "While there continue to be debates over its proper subject matter and methodology, something of a consensus concerning the new discipline has emerged," in *A Trinitarian Theology of Religions*, 9.

18. Focusing just on content at this point, I believe my judgment is justified even if one limits the scope of enquiry to definitions written by Evangelical figures. For example, Johnson, "Christian Theology of Religions," 366, believes four areas are included in the field, namely "theological interpretation of human religiosity . . . truth

and goodness in non-Christian religions . . . salvation in non-Christian religions . . . and . . . contextualization in Christian mission." Netland, in *Encountering Religious Pluralism*, 310, states that theology of religions has to address three issues: the destiny of the un-evangelized; a theological explanation for the phenomena of human religiosity; and missiological issues relating to adaptation and context. In a later work ("Theology of Religions," 145) he stated it should address two questions: the theological explanation of human religiosity and its varieties. Kärkkäinen, *Introduction*, 20, defines the field as "that discipline of theological studies which attempts to account theologically for the meaning and value of other religions. Christian theology of religions attempts to think theologically about what it means for Christians to live with people of other faiths and about the relationship of Christianity to other religions." Kärkkäinen's definition focuses much less on explanation (cf. Netland) and much more on Christian living in a multi-religious environments. Turning to a Roman Catholic definition, Dupuis focuses on the issue of identification, i.e., what non-Christian religions are. In particular, he considers the universality of religious experience and how faith is related to revelation, religion and salvation. In his view all of this is to be considered "in the light of the Christian faith," (*Toward a Christian Theology*, 7). Carl Braaten (a Lutheran scholar) in *No Other Gospel!*, 93, believes the discipline "aims to think about the world religions in light of the Christian faith,"—a rather general view. The above sample, I suggest, does not signal consensus, while it is acknowledged that overlaps of focus are readily apparent. I address methodological differences in approach in more detail in what follows.

19. This key difference is discussed in more detail in section 3.1.

20. Whitehead, "Pauline Approach to the Theology of Religions," 18, reviews methodological differences in the approaches of Kraemer, Panikkar, and Schlette, especially regarding the place of Christianity in method. I discuss this in more detail in chapter 6.

21. Kraemer in *Religion and the Christian Faith*, 6, argues that the religious consciousness present and demonstrated in religions, rather than religions per se, should be a key starting point.

22. I preemptively, and somewhat incidentally, introduce what I believe to be the key parameters which can help guide theology of religions enquiry here, and provide a brief summary of these in section 3.2.

23. O'Collins, *Second Vatican Council*, 16.

24. See chapter 2 for more comments on this.

25. O'Collins, *Salvation for All God's Other Peoples*, 215.

26. Dupuis, *Toward a Christian Theology*, 57–60, 71.

27. Dupuis, *Toward a Christian Theology*, 60.

28. Dupuis, *Toward a Christian Theology*, 71.

29. Bray, "Explaining Christianity to Pagans," 9–25. Bray's interpretation is supported by Strange in *Their Rock*, 224n29.

30. Bray, "Explaining Christianity to Pagans," 24. See also Sparks, "Was Justin Martyr a Proto-Inclusivist?," 495–510, who refers positively to Bray's interpretation.

31. In chapter 2, I explain why I do not follow Bray's understanding of Justin's Christianisation of Socrates. At this point I simply wish to recognize his more robust methodological approach compared to O'Collins and Dupuis.

32. Kärkkäinen, "Calvin and Religions," 270. There is some evidence that Kärkkäinen changed his view on Calvin. In his earlier *Introduction*, 75–77, he interprets

ENDNOTES

Calvin's thought about non-Christian religion as only negative.

33. Bouwsma, *John Calvin*, 102, states, "Respect for the religious insights of the natural man, even after the Fall, is . . . implicit in Calvin's belief in the superiority of Greek religion to other expressions of ancient paganism."

34. Eire, "John Calvin," 149.

35. Eire, "John Calvin," 150.

36. He bases the conclusion on Calvin's comments in *Institutes* 1.11.1. He neglects to quote what follows (italics mine in quotation below): "There was almost no animal that for the Egyptians was not the figure of a god. Indeed, the Greeks seemed to be wise above the rest, because they worshiped God in human form. *But God does not compare these images with one another, as if one were more suitable, another less so; but without exception he repudiates all likenesses, pictures, and other signs by which the superstitious have thought he will be near them.*"

37. Morali, "Catholic Theology," 87, states, "By introducing the term, 'theology of religions' (plural form), a bond is in fact established between Sacred Theology, the object of which is normally the content of revelation, and other religious traditions which do not contain that same revelation."

38. I provide some representative Reformed definitions here: "For what we call religion is just the reaction of the human soul to what it perceives God to be," as stated by Warfield, *Calvin and Calvinism*, 37. "Every religion is a reaction to divine revelation," according to Berkouwer, *General Revelation*, 162. I provide a number of relevant statements from Herman Bavinck in *The Philosophy of Revelation* in what follows: "religion has its foundation in revelation and derives from it its origin," 160; "The investigation of the essence of religion has . . . made as clear as the day that religion and revelation are bound together very intimately, and that they cannot be separated," 163; "all religions, in harmony with their own idea, rest upon conscious and spontaneous revelation of God," 163; "Revelation is the foundation of all religion, the presupposition of all its conceptions, emotions, and actions," 165; "religion is, not only with reference to its origin and essence but also with reference to its truth and validity, founded in revelation," 169. Kraemer, *Religion and the Christian Faith*, 350, states, "All religions are huge systems of manifold, partly more or less positive, partly more or less negative, responses to God." Bavinck comments, "The history of religion is a very remarkable thing; its main theme is that holy work of God in his general revelation to which humans are always reacting," in "Human Religion in God's Eyes," 52. Elsewhere, Bavinck writes, "Religion is by its very nature a communion, in which man answers and reacts to God's revelation . . . at the bottom of it lies a relationship, an encounter," in *Church between Temple and Mosque*, 19. In the same book he states, "Religion is the way in which man experiences the deepest existential relations and gives expression to this experience," 112. Bavinck also says, "God speaks and all human stammering about God is to be understood as nothing other than an answer and a response," in "Religious Consciousness in History," 235. Brunner, *Revelation and Reason*, 262, writes, "Apart from real revelation the phenomenon of religion cannot be understood." Tiessen, *Who Can Be Saved?*, 358, says, "Formalized religions are ambiguous responses to divine revelation." He also states, "Religions develop as inherently religious people respond to God's revelation in the forms that are accessible to them. Consequently, religions are ambiguous constructions, incorporating both the appropriation of divine truth and its suppression, due to human fallenness and demonic deception," 297. Braaten writes in *No Other Gospel!*, 99 "We find in the religions an echo of God's activity in all expressions of life because God has not left himself without a witness among the nations (Acts 14:16–17), which

means that the reality of God and his revelation lie behind the religions of humanity as anonymous mystery and hidden power," 67–68. He also comments, "God is behind the quest for God," 68, and "The God revealed in Jesus Christ is the same God hiddenly at work throughout the world in all the religions of humankind."

39. Karl Barth famously stated that religion is in no way related to revelation in Church Dogmatics: "We start by stating that religion is unbelief. It is a concern, indeed, we must say it is the one great concern of godless man," Barth, *CD* 1/2:299. In the same volume he also wrote, "From the standpoint of revelation religion is clearly seen to be a human attempt to anticipate what God in his revelation wills to do and does do. . . . It is the attempted replacement of the divine work by a human manufacture," 302. He goes on to argue that religion "contradicts" revelation and that "in religion man bolts and bars himself against revelation by providing a substitute, by taking away in advance what has to be given by God," 303. Indeed, he sees something of an antithesis between the two: "Revelation does not link up with a human religion which is already present and practised. It contradicts it, just as religion previously contradicted revelation," 303. Having noted this, Barth does not deny the presence of good in religions (*CD* 1/2:300). I do not engage with Barth's view of religions in this thesis. There are different interpretations of it, as discussed by Chandler, "Contribution of Karl Barth," 14–15. Ensminger, *Karl Barth's Theology*, 46, believes that the surface reading of section 17 of *Church Dogmatics* 1/2 does not represent Barth's true position on religions. He argues that Barth's main focus was on Christian religious activity, and that Barth was actually engaging with Schleiermacher in the quotations provided above. However, he concedes that the more common reading and understanding has some justification in terms of textual support: "Nonetheless, the mention of different religions makes the taking up of this paragraph into the interpretative staple of readings on the subject understandable," 79. See also Knitter's comments on Barth in *No Other Name?*, 80–87, and Braaten's in *No Other Gospel!*, 53–59. Braaten detects a softening from the earlier reference in *Church Dogmatics* compared to his later thought, and believes Barth to state that there is revelation outside the church and the Bible and within non-Christian religions, what Barth termed "Parables of the Kingdom" in *Church Dogmatics*, 4/3:114.

40. See Thomas "Introduction," in *Attitudes Toward Other Religions*, 20. He notes the rarity of the idea that non-Christian religions are totally false in the history of the church. Bavinck, after discussing Buddha and Mohammed in *Church between Temple and Mosque*, goes on to state that "every religion contains, somehow, the silent work of God," 200.

41. As noted, for example by Corduan, *Tapestry of Faiths*, 9; Netland, *Encountering Religious Pluralism*, 310, documents the typical Evangelical focus to be on soteriology and mission, rather than "a theological explanation for the phenomena of human religiosity," as does McDermott, *Can Evangelicals Learn from World Religions?*, 39.

42. Race, *Christians and Religious Pluralism* presented three broad class theologies which he termed: exclusivism, inclusivism and pluralism. Paul Hedges in "Reflection on Typologies," 17–33, provides an overview of the responses to the uptake of and challenges to the typology. D'Costa comments on some of the problems he believes to be inherent in Race's typology in *Christianity and World Religions*, 34–37. Johnson voices similar concerns to those of D'Costa in *Rethinking the Trinity*, 34–35. There seems to be something of a consensus within the field that these broad class terms are not as helpful as once thought.

43. The title of an article by a Reformed theologian in which an inclusivist theology of salvation is tacitly assumed valid, and the means of achieving this are then

sought, neatly highlights this issue of presupposed directionality: Mangum, "Is There a Reformed Way?," 121–36. One of Mangum's goals is to "'rescue' some of the best inclusivist insights that have, up to now, been "trapped" within an inherently un-Reformed soteriological model, so that they may be safely incorporated into a classically Reformed soteriology," 125.

44. A similar position has been argued by other theologians of religions. For example, Kraemer, *Religion and the Christian Faith*, 145, argues for this, as does D'Costa, "Revelation and Revelations," 166: "I will contend that the theology of religions properly and principally lies with the question of revelation." As Braaten, *No Other Gospel!*, 8, notes, "Not all revelation is saving revelation; nonsalvific revelation of God gives rise to the unending quest for salvation in the religions." See also page 71 of the same book: "Revelation and salvation are not coterminous."

45. Hick, *Christian Theology of Religions*, 16, states:

> If we define salvation as being forgiven and accepted by God because of the atoning death of Jesus, then it is a tautology that Christianity alone knows and teaches the saving truth that we must take Jesus as our lord and saviour, plead his atoning death, and enter into the church as the community of the redeemed, in which the fruits [sic] of the Spirit abound. *But we've seen that this circle of ideas contradicts our observation that the fruits [sic] of the Spirit seem to be as much (and as little) evident outside the church as within it* [emphasis mine].

Hick's suggestion that the fruit of this same Spirit is evident in those who do not have saving faith would, I suggest, make little sense to the Apostle Paul. See also Netland, *Encountering Religious Pluralism*, 312, who critiques Hick's approach.

46. On the validity and need for a theological starting point see Kraemer, chapter 6, "The Validity of the Theological Starting-Point in Religion and the Christian Faith," in *Religion and the Christian Faith* and also Netland, "Theology of Religions," 144:

> But if indeed God has spoken we are to submit to his revelation as truth and to allow it to control our beliefs, even where this truth may not be particularly palatable to contemporary tastes. Evangelicals, in line with the witness of Scripture, insist that God has indeed revealed himself in an authoritative manner to us in the written Scriptures and preeminently in the Incarnation. Thus neither theology of religions nor missiology can be reduced to comparative religion. Both must acknowledge the inspired Scriptures as the authoritative framework from within which issues of religious diversity are to be addressed.

See also Bavinck, "Debating Religious Consciousness," 232, on the need for a theological approach.

47. On the important place of Scripture within the Evangelical tradition see McGrath, *Evangelicalism and the Future of Christianity*, 54–60. Richie, "Hints from Heaven," 48, comments, "An Evangelical theology of religions is consistent with Scripture, continuous with its tradition, and confirmed in its community testimony. Evangelicals tend to start with Scripture. Whatever else we do, our theology must agree with and conform to Holy Scripture." On the importance of the Bible for a Reformed theology of religions, see Visser, "Religion in Biblical and Reformed Perspective," 11; Allert, "What Are We Trying to Conserve?," 327–48. See also Carson, *Enduring Authority of the Christian Scriptures*; Bavinck, *Impact of Christianity*, 102: "All human speculations are useless; we should only listen to what God reveals to us about His work among the Gentiles."

ENDNOTES

48. For treatments of non-Christian religions in their Biblical contexts see Gill, "Behind the Classical Façade"; Block, "Other Religions in Old Testament Theology." See also Beale, "Other Religions in New Testament Theology."

49. Strange, *Their Rock*, 211, suggests that a "hermeneutical bridge" exists between contemporary religions and those mentioned in the Bible. He believes "anthropological universals" connect them, namely the *imago Dei* and "false faith." He also argues that there may be connections between the religions of today with their Old Testament forebears.

50. There are at least two reasons why this would be questionable practice: the first is that they are different. The second is that the biblical treatment of other religions is highly context specific within the drama of redemption. See Netland, *Encountering Religious Pluralism*, 313–15, on the role of Scripture for an evangelical theology of religions. He notes that Scripture does not answer all the questions we may have, but points to biblical principles that can help.

51. See Visser, *Heart for the Gospel*, 151.

52. Of the five theologians studied in this book, only the last (Daniel Strange) develops what might be considered a more abstract theology of religions. In *Their Rock*, 307, he states, "As has been emphasized throughout this study, rather than focusing on one non-Christian religion I have primarily been concerned with providing a dogmatic sketch of non-Christian religions in general." All the other theologians directly address the religions of the day with which they are engaged. On the need for such engagement, note the second part of Netland's definition concerning what a theology of religions should address, namely: "how do we account theologically for the particularities of religious expression, the many diverse beliefs and practices we find among the religious traditions?," in "Theology of Religions," 145. Knitter, *No Other Name?*, 18, makes a similar statement, in the second part of his comment concerning the basis of a sound theology of religions: "A theology of other religions will have to be worked out primarily on the basis of Christian tradition—that is, in light of what the gospel reveals concerning the nature and value of other religions. *But it will also require that the theologian have some knowledge of the other religions* [emphasis mine]."

53. Here I make a brief comparison of Kraemer, Bavinck and Strange on this subject. For Kraemer, *Religion and the Christian Faith*, 240, the directly relevant texts when considering religion and religions are: Rom 1:19–32; 2:1–16; 3:29, 30, and *to a lesser extent* Acts 14:15–17; 17:6, 22–37. For J. H. Bavinck, the key references when considering revelation are Job 33:14–18; John 1: 4, 5, 9; Acts 14:15–17; 17:26,27; and *especially* Romans 1:19–32: see Visser, *Heart for the Gospel*, 120–21. Strange, *Their Rock*, 155, documents the significance of both Romans 1:18–32, and also Acts 17: 16–34 (see also page 286) as the key texts in his theology. However, he discounts the relevance of John 1:1–9, and pays little attention to Romans 2 (page 89n111) or Job 33 (page 136). I suggest the different choice of texts evident in this snapshot of theologians is an early contributory indicator of the different conclusions to be drawn by them, as considered in this study. I will reflect on the role of Scripture in Theology of Religions discussion in more detail in the concluding chapter.

54. The very real possibility of not adequately interpreting the phenomenon must be acknowledged at the outset.

55. I differentiate Daniel Strange's writings here from the other four theologians, as there is much less in the way of observation present in his work—a fact he readily acknowledges.

56. D'Costa, "Revelation and Revelations," 165, is rightly wary of some theological approaches which he describes as having "provided overarching theological structures that have answered all the questions prior to any real meeting with other religions and therefore prejudge the question." At the same time, it must be recognized that even "real meetings" will be influenced by presuppositions, prejudice, convictions and belief.

57. It should be noted here that while I occasionally refer to the theologians' views of Judaism, this book is not oriented to cover this focus.

58. This is a strong, but I believe, justified claim, which I will endeavor to demonstrate throughout this study.

59. See chapter 2.

60. See Levitin, *Ancient Wisdom*, 22.

61. Walker, *Ancient Theology*, 20.

62. I discuss the idea of truth in a *correspondence* theory as compared to a *coherence* theory in chapter 6.

63. For Daniel Strange it is not so much truth but rather frameworks—see chapter 6.

64. I borrow this term from Idel, "Prisca Theologia in Marsilio Ficino," 137–39.

65. More pejorative references present in the literature include *theft* or *stealing*.

66. I do not discuss the relationship between the true and false here, but discuss this in more detail in chapter 6.

67. Walker, *Ancient Theology*, 20.

68. He also notes that one may adopt a position which has space for both of the two main theories: "a Gentile revelation may be supposed to be reinforced or completed by a Jewish one," Walker, *Ancient Theology*, 20. As will be discussed throughout the book there are variations within this other tradition, with directionality of borrowing questioned, and different views expressed concerning the role of reason, alongside various views on inspiration.

69. Idel, "Prisca Theologia in Marsilio Ficino," 137, 141–42.

70. Such an idea is countenanced by Augustine and possibly suggested by Justin, and also Jonathan Edwards.

71. This is seen most clearly in Augustine, though it is also suggested in Justin and Jonathan Edwards.

72. See chapter 4.

73. This is the viewpoint of Strange, "Response to Question 3," in McGee, "Interview with Daniel Strange."

74. If God reveals *himself*, this might be considered a redundant issue: but if God reveals aspects of his character—for example beauty, or reveals his wrath, the idea of differentiation of what is revealed becomes more meaningful.

75. See, for example, McDermott, *Can Evangelicals Learn from World Religions?*, 77–78.

76. See Strange, *Their Rock*, 261, who notes there is scarcity of biblical material on the demonic. One might add that there is even greater scarcity on the demons-religions interface.

ENDNOTES

77. I discuss the relationship between general revelation and *Logos* enlightenment in section 4.2, below.

78. Beyerhaus, "My Pilgrimage in Mission," 174.

79. Netland, *Encountering Religious Pluralism*, 331.

80. It should be stressed that the demonic is *wholly* negative in his thinking; cf. my earlier comments on the devil being a mouthpiece of God, in addition to playing a negative role.

81. See next section.

82. Some representative quotations are provided here. Bavinck states, "The history of religion is a very remarkable thing; its main theme is that holy work of God in his general revelation to which humans are always reacting," in "Human Religion in God's Eyes," 52; Visser comments, "The variegated religiosity of today shows that many do not succeed in radically suppressing God's revelation," in "Religion in Biblical and Reformed Perspective," 22. Demarest, *General Revelation*, 259, writes, "On the basis of God's universal general revelation and common enabling grace, undisputed truths about God, man and sin lie embedded to varying degrees in the non-Christian religions.... The world's non-Christian religions ... are essentially false, but with glimpses of truth afforded by general revelation."

83. This is, admittedly, a simplified distinction, and one that has been criticized. I do not mean here that there is a common understanding of what each revelation entails or the relationship between them. For some Reformed discussion of this point see Demarest, *General Revelation*; Berkouwer, *General Revelation*; and Anderson, *Reason and Worldviews*. See also Smith, "Religions and the Bible: An Agenda for Evangelicals," and Visser, "Religion in Biblical and Reformed Perspective," 13. A helpful summary of different views and understandings among Evangelicals can be found in Ash, *A Critical Evaluation of the Doctrine of Revelation in Evangelical Theology*, 79–97. See also Tennent, "Evangelical Theology of Religions," 249–50; Netland, *Encountering Religious Pluralism*, 317; Corduan, *Tapestry of Faiths*, 31–78. McDermott and Netland discuss the distinction between and identification of the Bible and revelation in *A Trinitarian Theology of Religions*, 100–102.

84. A representative comment regarding this relationship would be: "A theology of religions seeks, in a coherent and consistent manner, to answer questions concerning the relationships among world religions, special revelation, general revelation, and salvation," according to Miles, *A God of Many Understandings?*, 7. "The history of religion is a very remarkable thing; its main theme is that holy work of God in his general revelation to which humans are always reacting," according to Bavinck, "Human Religion in God's Eyes," 52.

85. Braaten, *No Other Gospel!*, 97, writes, "The classical way of constructing the relationship between special revelation in the gospel and general revelation in other religions hinged on the distinction between the concrete Logos in the flesh (*ensarkos*) and the universal Logos outside the flesh (*asarkos*)."

86. Some more modern twentieth century theologians have also given general revelation a strong christological basis (e.g., Bruce Demarest, Carl Henry, and Ronald Nash). I refer to their work in chapter 6.

87. In this interpretation I differ from Kärkkäinen, *Introduction*, 75, who states, "The starting point for Calvin's theology of religions is his view concerning general revelation."

ENDNOTES

88. See chapter 6, and also Strange, "General Revelation," 74.

89. Different collocations are used by different theologians.

90. Hypothetically, one might assume that a comparable Roman Catholic trajectory may have chosen the same first two (Justin and Augustine), and then turned to Aquinas, possibly followed by conciliar documents, followed by Dupuis, Rahner, or D'Costa. A Pentecostal trajectory analysis, on the other hand, might choose a different figure from the Reformation, and end with the work of Amos Yong.

91. See, for example, Dulles, *History of Apologetics*, 33; Wilken, *Spirit of Early Christian Thought*, 4.

92. Van Houten, "Earthly Wisdom and Heavenly Wisdom," 253, comments, "Justin escaped Calvin's censure as one of those who compromised his beliefs in favour of philosophy."

93. Teselle believes that Luther, Zwingli and Calvin all attributed their conversions to reading Augustine. See "Augustine and Augustinianism," 17.

94. A comparison of Reformation era treatments would prove to be of considerable interest. I make some comments on other Reformers in chapter 4, but not in detail.

95. See, for example, Strange, *Their Rock*, 34.

96. Strange, *Possibility of Salvation*; Strange, *Their Rock*.

97. See, for example, his contributions in *Only One Way?* Strange has also published a chapter in a multi-viewpoint book on religions, entitled "Exclusivisms."

98. Terrance Tiessen describes himself as belonging to the Reformed tradition in "God's Work of Grace," 166. His significant volume *Who Can Be Saved?* can be considered a more inclusivist oriented theology of religions when compared to Strange's work. Strange's thought, I suggest, has been more readily embraced by the conservative Reformed tradition.

99. Exceptions to this would be D'Costa's and Knitter's arguments in *Only One Way?* Criticisms of the idea that Strange follows Kraemer are forwarded by Djung in *Revelation and Grace*. See also Faircloth, "Daniel Strange on the Theological Question of the Unevangelized."

100. With the exception of Daniel Strange—and this is a very short biography. I provide this as he is a less well-known figure.

101. For a single figure study, see Thomas, *Christ and the World of Religions*. For comparative studies involving two theologians, see Capetz, "Seed of Religion," and Little, "Significance of Theology."

102. McDermott, *God's Rivals*. He examines the ideas of Justin Martyr, Irenaeus, Clement of Alexandria, and Origen.

103. Saldanha, *Divine Pedagogy*.

104. In passing, it needs to be said that a study focusing on Reformed theologians from the same era is long overdue. For research comparing Zwingli and Calvin, see Preus, "Zwingli, Calvin, and the Origin of Religion." See also Williams, "Erasmus and the Reformers."

105. More specifically I am considering key theologians' ideas.

106. I use the term lightly here, given the treatments of Justin and Augustine.

ENDNOTES

107. It should be noted that I make very few comparative comments within the main chapters, where my focus is almost exclusively on the theologian within his context.

108. I do, occasionally, note apparent inconsistencies.

109. See Dulles, *History of Apologetics*, 33. See also Dupuis, *Toward a Christian Theology*, 56; Troxel, "All Things to All People"; Ulrich, "Justin Martyr"; Wilken, *Spirit of Early Christian Thought*, 4; Thorsteinsson, "Justin and Stoic Cosmo-theology"; Richardson, *Early Christian Fathers*, 228.

110. See Grant, *Greek Apologists*, 59; Daley, *God Visible*, 62; Hayes, *Justin against Marcion*, xiii; Osborn, "Justin Martyr and the Logos Spermatikos."

111. For example, D'Costa, *Christianity and World Religions*, 22–23; Kärkkäinen, *Introduction*, 56–57; McDermott and Netland, *Trinitarian Theology of Religions*, 14–15; Dupuis, *Toward a Christian Theology*, 70–77; Drummond, *Toward a New Age in Christian Theology*, 28–29; Netland, *Encountering Religious Pluralism*, 251–52; McDermott, *God's Rivals*, 85–97; Bavinck, *Church between Temple and Mosque*, 126–27; Kraemer, *Religion and the Christian Faith*, 147–51.

112. He did, however, have Jewish precedent, and the influence of Philo on his thinking has been discussed extensively. Goodenough, *Theology of Justin Martyr*, is the most well-known proponent of this influence. Runia, "Philo and the Early Christian Fathers," 214, summarizes more recent thought. Droge, "Justin Martyr and the Restoration of Philosophy," 314n40, challenges the idea that Justin knew Philo's writings. For possible Stoic influence on Philo see Jackson-McCabe, *Logos and Law*, 89.

113. There is significant disagreement among scholars about how much of the NT Justin was aware. See Ulrich, "Justin Martyr," 62; Dunn, *Christianity in the Making*, 3:79; Saldanha, *Divine Pedagogy*, 58–62; Davey, "Justin Martyr and the Fourth Gospel," 117–22.

114. See Osborn, *Beginning of Christian Philosophy*, 19; Ulrich, "Justin Martyr," 30–31; Malherbe, "Towards Understanding the Apologists," 799; Barnard, "Logos Theology of St. Justin Martyr," 140; Holte, "Logos Spermatikos Christianity," 128; Chadwick, "Justin Martyr's Defence," 297.

115. Minns and Parvis, *Justin, Philosopher, and Martyr*, 70; Litfin, *Getting to Know the Church Fathers*, 50; Purves, *Testimony of Justin Martyr*, 50; Chadwick, *Early Christian Thought*, 10; Corey, *Light from Light*, 77–78; Bray, "Explaining Christianity to Pagans," 10; Hayes, *Justin against Marcion*, xiii; Ulrich, "Justin Martyr," 65; Richardson, *Early Christian Fathers*, 237; Kärkkäinen, *Introduction*, 56. Osborn, "Justin Martyr and the Logos Spermatikos," 155.

116. Tatian and Tertullian might be considered obvious and notable exceptions to the idea of 'following', but scholars are divided on this. See Ulrich, "Justin Martyr," 65; Dariusz Karlowicz, *Socrates and Other Saints*, 67; Holte, "Logos Spermatikos Christianity," 109–10. Those who see a significant departure from Justin in the works of Tatian include Osborn, "Justin Martyr and the Logos Spermatikos," 157, and Charles Nahm, "Debate on the 'Platonism' of Justin Martyr," 130, who also adds Tertullian to Tatian as a non-follower.

117. This is noted by Norris, "Apologists," 38.

118. As documented by Nilson, "To Whom Is Justin's Dialogue with Trypho addressed?," 539. A lost text (*Against Heresies*) is alluded to in 1 *Apology* 26: "We have a treatise written against all the heresies that have arisen, which, if you wish to read, we

will give to you," translated by Thomas B. Falls in *Writings of Saint Justin Martyr*. All references to Justin's writings in what follows are from the Thomas Falls translation.

119. These can be grouped into three (church, those outside the church and a mixture).

120. As Farrar, "Intimate and Ultimate Adversary," 544, notes, whereas "Satan" occurs over forty times in the *Dialogue*, he only appears once in the *Apologies* (*1 Apol.* 28). On page 544, he explains the varied usage by suggesting a specific readership: "Justin tailors his Apologies to a Greco-Roman audience familiar with demons but not Satan." A key motif appearing (with variation) in Justin's writings is LXX Ps. 95:5 "All the gods of the gentiles are idols of demons," occurring seven times in total: *1 Apol.* 41, *Dial.* 55, *Dial.* 73 (x2), *Dial.* 79, *Dial.* 83 (x2).

121. Sheather, "Apology" summarizes the variety of views.

122. Sheather, "Apology," 118–22, provides arguments for and against, and documents the problematic issues.

123. Minns and Parvis, *Justin, Philosopher, and Martyr*, 34, mention the issue concerning the names and titles given: "There are a number of variations between the Paris manuscript and Eusebius respecting their names, titles, and relationships."

124. Ulrich, "Apologists," 29, states, "Naturally Justin Martyr's first apology is primarily addressed to the Emperor, with the aim of moving him to change the unjust and absurd legal position the Christians are confronted with." See *1 Apol.* 2.

125. See Norris, "Apologists," 39.

126. See *1 Apol.* 68. Saldanha, *Divine Pedagogy*, 41, writes, "What Justin sought through his first apology was not principally a conversion of his readers to Christianity—if that were to take place so much the better—but a fair judgment that he knew would acquit Christians of all the charges brought against them and afford them legal protection."

127. *1 Apol.* 3.

128. A number of different structures have been proposed. See Ulrich, "Justin Martyr," 53–54; Goodenough, *Theology of Justin Martyr*, 82–84; Richardson, *Early Christian Fathers*, 236; Barnard, *Justin Martyr*, 14–17; Minns and Parvis, *Justin, Philosopher, and Martyr*, 49–54; Pretila, "Re-appropriating Marvelous Fables," 2.

129. Buck, "Justin Martyr's *Apologies*," 53.

130. "There are three venerable theories. There are those who think there are indeed two apologies-two separate works; there are those who think there is only one, continuous text, unfortunately and inappropriately divided the manuscript tradition; and there are those who split the difference and argue for one-and-a-half," according to Minns and Parvis, *Justin, Philosopher, and Martyr*, 19. See also Ehrhardt, "Justin Martyr's Two Apologies"; Williams, *Defending and Defining the Faith*, 101–3, gives an overview of the theories concerning the relationship between the two Apologies.

131. See Thorsteinsson, "Literary Genre."

132. Ulrich, "Justin Martyr," 54.

133. Rajak, "Talking at Trypho," 75–80, provides a helpful summary of views.

134. Allert, "Revelation," 124.

135. Allert, "Revelation," 162.

ENDNOTES

136. Allert, "Revelation," 160.

137. Allert, "Revelation," 91.

138. Scholars holding the threefold view include Holte, "Logos Spermatikos Christianity"; Wright, "Christian Faith." Droge, "Justin Martyr and the Restoration of Philosophy," 307, argues for two—not mentioning the demonic—as is the case also for Bavinck, *Impact of Christianity*, 83. Latourelle, *Theology of Revelation*, 91, argues that Justin believed the *same* truths could be known from the two different sources (i.e., the *Logos* and borrowing).

139. I will seek to justify this definition in what follows. Note that I limit the focus to a specific role of the *Logos*, rather than Justin's view of the *Logos* within the Trinity—arguably relevant to the current discussion, but a much bigger area of research.

140. See section 4 for an overview.

141. "The names of the so-called gods are really the names of demons (1 Apol. 5; 9) who enslave humans to them by means of magic and dream visions (1 Apol. 14) and cause wickedness on the earth (1 Apol. 10)," according to Reed, "Trickery of the Fallen Angels," 161. Giving more detail, Reed states on 148n13 of the same article:

> Justin's innovation upon the early Jewish exegesis of Gen 6.1–4 is not the association of the Watchers' sons with demons, as some scholars have suggested. . . . Rather, it is his equation of pagan gods with the fallen angels of Gen 6.1–4. This equation combines the Book of the Watchers' notion that demons are the spirits of the Giants with the identification of the "gods of the nations" as daimones in LXX Ps 95.5, but it transforms these traditions significantly by positing three distinct levels: the corrupted humans who worship idols, the demons who pretend to be gods, and the fallen angels who are ultimately responsible for orchestrating this farce.

See also Davids, "Justin Martyr on Monotheism and Heresy," 233. Skarsaune, "Conversion of Justin Martyr," 65, notes the role of Jewish apocalyptic literature in Justin's thought on demons. In a book chapter, Skarsaune, "Judaism and Hellenism," 593, writes that Rabbinic thought did not equate evil spirits with pagan gods.

142. *2 Apol.* 13.

143. See McDermott, *God's Rivals*, 91. Note also the comments by Goodenough, *Theology of Justin Martyr*, 106, and Saldanha, *Divine Pedagogy*, 64, on the idea that Justin borrowed the loan theory from Jewish apologists. See also Droge, "Justin Martyr and the Restoration of Philosophy," 307, on the use of the loan theory, and the precedent of borrowing on pages 310–12. See also Lohr, "Theft of the Greeks," for useful background. On Justin's contribution see especially pages 406–9. See also Nyström, *Apology of Justin Martyr*, 78–82, for his comments on the theft theory in Justin.

144. Walker, "Prisca Theologia in France," 204. See also Idel, "Prisca Theologia in Marsilio Ficino"; Roth, "Theft of Philosophy."

145. Roth, "Theft of Philosophy," 63.

146. Roth, "Theft of Philosophy," 64, notes that Philo's version of the theft theory was less direct in that Moses first learned from Egypt and Greece, before exceeding them in knowledge. He goes on to comment that Clement of Alexandria roughly followed Philo's version on page 65.

147. Edwards, "Justin's Logos."

148. Nyström, *Apology of Justin Martyr*, 82, states, "Exerting a great influence on

the Christological developments of later church fathers, the Logos doctrine is often counted as one of, if not the most important contribution Justin made to the formulation of Christian orthodoxy."

149. For example, Pretila, "Re-appropriating Marvelous Fables," on pages 134 and 150 has argued that the richest revelation is from the demonic and the vaguest from the *Logos*. Nyström, *Apology of Justin Martyr*, 95, argues that the theft and *Logos* "theories" are actually two different strategies. Specifically, he thinks theft is used to refute the newness of Christianity, and the *Logos* to provide accountability. For Nyström, the two ideas "are simply used to solve two very different ideas," 96. Holte, "Logos Spermatikos Christianity," on the other hand, suggests that the loan theory and Logos spermatikos theory "belong together quite naturally," 162, and that "The loan theory is introduced in order to explain the truths which do not fall under the above-mentioned categories [*Logos spermatikos* truths]," 163. Osborn, "Justin Martyr and the Logos Spermatikos," 143, believes the "logos spermatikos was central to his argument," stating elsewhere in Osborn, *Justin Martyr*, 200–201, that "the Greek challenge to Christian maturity cannot be answered by both the spermatic logos and the charge of Greek plagiarism. Either God has given seeds of truth or the Greeks have stolen them. Both accounts cannot be true." Daniélou, *Gospel Message*, 46–47, on the other hand, argues for a certain amount of duplication of content between the loan and seed theory: "Nevertheless it must be admitted that the forms of words used are extremely general, and could equally well be interpreted in the sense of a double source for the same truths."

150. Nyström, *Apology of Justin Martyr*, 90n68, calls Holte's efforts to differentiate the moral (seed) and the doctrinal (loan) "rather forced and difficult to substantiate." However, he provides little evidence to support this assertion.

151. Daniélou, *Gospel Message*, 47, states, "It will be clear at once that this interpretation [demonic mimesis] is a secondary form of the theory of borrowings from revelation."

152. See Ferguson, *Demonology*, 59, who writes, "The Greco-Roman world was very conscious of demons. Their presence was part of the disturbing world view of the time."

153. On referring to a passage from Plutarch, Ferguson, *Demonology*, 35, notes various referents: gods, souls of the dead, and "intermediary spiritual beings which may become either good or bad." He also notes a fourth meaning in Plutarch, "a personal guardian spirit." On page 36, he goes on to state: "The word demon in classical Greek meant a divine or superhuman power or activity. It possessed for the ancient Greeks none of the negative or evil associations which it has for us."

154. Skarsaune, "Judaism and Hellenism," 594, states, "Justin's demonology is biblical and Jewish, not Greek and philosophical." Osborn, *Justin Martyr*, 57, argued that Justin relied on apocryphal materials (specifically Enoch and Jubilees) for the *Apologies*, and OT material for the *Dialogue*. Williams, *Defending and Defining the Faith*, 104–5, also notes the significant influence of Jewish literature on Justin's demonology.

155. As Williams, *Defending and Defining the Faith*, 105, notes, demons are literally everywhere in Justin's thinking in *Apology* 1.

156. "The eternals (i.e., gods of Mt. Olympus) would have been the fallen angels for Justin while the immortals or sons of Zeus would have been understood by the apologist as their demonic offspring," in Pretila, "Re-appropriating Marvelous Fables," 89. Reed, "Trickery of the Fallen Angels," 144, states, "Justin's association of the fallen angels and their demonic progeny with the pagan pantheon initiates a new stage in the history of exegesis of Gen 6.1–4." See also *1 Apol.* 5.

ENDNOTES

157. *1 Apol.* 58.
158. *1 Apol.* 5.
159. *1 Apol.* 5.
160. *1 Apol.* 5.
161. *1 Apol.* 5.
162. *1 Apol.* 5; *2 Apol.* 7.
163. *1 Apol.* 12.
164. *1 Apol.* 14.
165. *1 Apol.* 26; 56.
166. *1 Apol.* 44.
167. *2 Apol.* 9.
168. *1 Apol.* 23.
169. *2 Apol.* 5.
170. *1 Apol.* 54.
171. *1 Apol.* 54.
172. *1 Apol.* 21.
173. *2 Apol.* 13.
174. *1 Apol.* 62.
175. *1 Apol.* 66.
176. *1 Apol.* 64.
177. *1 Apol.* 55.
178. *1 Apol.* 57.

179. Reed, "Trickery of the Fallen Angels," 161, states, "According to Justin, "Christ was made man" for two interconnected reasons: "for the sake of believing people and for the destruction of the demons" (*2 Apol.* 6)."

180. *2 Apol.* 6; *Dial.* 30.

181. *Dial.* 69,

182. Reed, "Trickery of the Fallen Angels," 143, comments, "For him [Justin], the teachings of the fallen angels serve to explain the origins and continued practice of Greco-Roman religions."

183. *1 Apol.* 57.

184. *Dial.* 131.

185. *1 Apol.* 1. Reed, "Trickery of the Fallen Angels," 154n28, states, "Justin's heresiology is, of course, tightly tied to his demonology as well; esp. *1 Apol.* 26, 56; 66.1; 63.1; *Dial.* 7, 82.3." "Heresiarchs are put forward by Satan as his final protest against an alternative to the Christian doctrine which after Christ has reached the whole world," according to Davids, "Justin Martyr on Monotheism and Heresy," 234.

186. Saldanha, *Divine Pedagogy*, 45–46, believes that Justin's strong opposition to idolatry can be traced directly to OT Scripture.

187. Reed, "Trickery of the Fallen Angels," 167.

188. Advocates of this position would include Skarsaune, "Judaism and Hellenism," 594–5, and Saldanha, *Divine Pedagogy*, 51. Bray, "Explaining Christianity to Pagans," 23, states, "None of them [the apologists] had a good word to say about pagan religion, which they regarded as both illogical and immoral." Wright, "Christian Faith," 80, comments, "It will be obvious, therefore, that Justin differentiated sharply between polytheism and philosophy. The Greek pantheon and all their works are consistently condemned by Justin. Any echoes of Christianity must be identified as demonic suggestions." Keith, "Justin Martyr and Religious Exclusivism," 70, writes, "Justin has produced the curious, but convenient framework whereby he could dismiss pagan religious parallels to Christianity as demonic counterfeits, whereas he welcomed parallels to the truth in every other sphere of Greek culture." Pretila, "Re-appropriating Marvelous Fables," 57, traces the antagonism noted above to the work of Andresen, *Logos und Nomos*. He states, "Andresen has developed a popular narrative that has informed not only Chadwick but a whole host of contemporary scholars who all argue that although Justin could be somewhat accepting of Greek philosophy, the same of which could not be said regarding his approach towards Greek mythology." Pretila challenges the distinction as does Reed, "Trickery of the Fallen Angels," 145.

189. As noted by Nyström, *Apology of Justin Martyr*, 91n74. They are noted here: *1 Apol.* 20; 44 ; *2 Apol.* 13.

190. *1 Apol.* 20. Menander was a third to fourth century BC Greek dramatist.

191. Pretila, "Re-appropriating Marvelous Fables," 151.

192. E.g., *2 Apol.* 12.

193. Contreras, "Christian Views of Paganism," as cited in Pretila, "Re-appropriating Marvelous Fables," 5.

194. Widdicombe, "Justin Martyr, Allegorical Interpretation, and the Greek Myths," 234, states, "Justin has an ambivalent attitude to the myths. He uses the phenomenon of the myths both negatively and positively to bolster his argument for the uniqueness and the superiority of the Christian faith."

195. For example, as evident in the work of Daniélou, *Gospel Message*, 75.

196. "Unlike previous scholarly assessments of Justin Martyr's use of Greco-Roman mythology, I will contend that his varied use of myth as seen in 1 Apology reveals a form of pedagogy in which the apologist intentionally incorporated certain aspects of these popular religious narratives and yet was able to declare Christianity's separation from the ancient tradition," according to Pretila, "Re-appropriating Marvelous Fables," 1.

197. Pretila, "Re-appropriating Marvelous Fables," 157, 164.

198. Pretila, "Re-appropriating Marvelous Fables," 25, states:

> If Justin were writing 1 Apology with the intent of strengthening the "belief of believers" . . . why would the apologist constantly allude to the symbols of an ancient religion his audience was tempted to revert back to? While Justin's ultimate goal was that his readers decisively abandon their ancestral religion, he also perceived a resource of images from this same tradition which could be utilized to reinforce belief in the Christian faith.

199. Pretila, "Re-appropriating Marvelous Fables," 11, writes, "It helps our thesis to see how Justin shared a similar outlook to the pagan world regarding the inherent "doubleness" of truth and falsehood contained within the writing of the poets."

200. Pretila, "Re-appropriating Marvelous Fables," 17.

201. "Despite their primary function to rival the person of Christ through imitation they were paradoxically the most fecund in revelation compared to that of "loan theory" and Logos Spermatikos," according to Pretila, "Re-appropriating Marvelous Fables," 134. He continues on footnote 6 of the same page:

> This should not be a surprise that "demon theory" possesses the fullest revelation amongst the three avenues mentioned. . . . Justin held that pre-Christian pagans did not anticipate Christ's coming—hence aspects of his person foreshadowed in Moses and the Prophets would have not appeared in pagan texts based upon their own initiative (i.e., without demonic influence). That is why demon-theory myth is so ironic; while its purpose is to undermine Christian belief—it is the only one amongst the three that provides any sort of sketch of the person of Christ in pre-Christian pagan literature.

202. Pretila, "Re-appropriating Marvelous Fables," 149–50.

203. See Pretila, "Re-appropriating Marvelous Fables," 135.

204. Pretila, "Re-appropriating Marvelous Fables," 46, states, "Justin initially employed a typological framework between myth and the emerging New Testament narrative, not because he believed in the historicity of the myths but rather because his audience did."

205. "So while Justin worked with his audience inherent simultaneous suspicion and reverence to myth early on in 1 Apology, by the time one gets towards the end of the work the apologist has shattered this tension altogether placing his full energies in further bolstering his reader's suspicion towards these pagan religious narratives," according to Pretila, "Re-appropriating Marvelous Fables," 42.

206. Saldanha, *Divine Pedagogy*, 50. Regarding Justin's comments in 1 *Apol.* 58, Saldanha writes, "there could not possibly be any divine educative activity here, leading people to Christ, but only the power of evil, holding them in the bonds of slavery."

207. This being a kind of borrowing from the angels, and events in history.

208. See for example, Nyström, *Apology of Justin Martyr*, 86, and Carl Francis Baechle, "Reappraisal," 69, concerning various possible translations of *Logos*.

209. See also Saldanha, *Divine Pedagogy*, 52–54, on these references.

210. 1 *Apol.* 5: "And not only among the Greeks were these things through Socrates condemned by reason, but also among the non-Hellenic peoples by the Logos Himself, who assumed a human form and became man, and was called Jesus Christ."

> 211. We have been taught that Christ was First-begotten of God [the Father] and we have indicated above that He is the Word of whom all mankind partakes. Those who lived by reason are Christians, even though they have been considered atheists: such as, among the Greeks, Socrates, Heraclitus, and others like them; and among the foreigners, Abraham, Elias, Ananias, Azarias, Misael and many others whose deeds or names we now forbear to enumerate, for we think it would be too long.

> 212. We know that the followers of the Stoic teaching, because they were praiseworthy at least in their ethics, as were also the poets in some respects, because of the seed of reason implanted in all mankind, were hated and killed. As examples, we could mention Heraclitus as we already stated, and Musonius of

our own times, and others. For, as we pointed out, the demons always brought it about that everyone, who strives in any way to live according to right reason and to avoid evil, be an object of hatred. Nor is it surprising that the demons are proved to be the cause why they are much more hated who do not live according to only a part of the seminal word, but by the knowledge and consideration of the whole Word, which is Christ.

213. Beyond doubt, therefore, our teachings are more noble than all human teaching, because Christ, who appeared on earth for our sakes, became the whole Logos, namely, Logos and body and soul. Everything that the philosophers and legislators discovered and expressed well, they accomplished through their discovery and contemplation of some part of the Logos. But, since they did not have a full knowledge of the Logos, which is Christ, they often contradicted themselves.... There was no one who believed so much in Socrates as to die for his teaching, but not only philosophers and scholars believed in Christ, of whom even Socrates had a vague knowledge (for He was and is the Logos who is in every person, and who predicted things to come first through the prophets and then in person when He assumed our human nature and feelings, and taught us these doctrines), but also workmen and men wholly uneducated, who all scorned glory, and fear, and death. Indeed, this is brought about by the power of the ineffable Father, and not through the instrumentality of human reason.

214. When I learned of the evil camouflage which the wicked demons had thrown around the divine doctrines of the Christians to deter others from following them, I had to laugh at the authors of these lies, at the camouflage itself, and at the popular reaction. I am proud to say that I strove with all my might to be known as a Christian, not because the teachings of Plato are different from those of Christ, but because they are not in every way similar neither are those of other writers, the Stoics, the poets, and the historians. For each one of them, seeing, through his participation of the seminal Divine Word, what was related to it, spoke very well. But, they who contradict themselves in important matters evidently did not acquire the unseen [that is, heavenly] wisdom and the indisputable knowledge. The truths which men in all lands have rightly spoken belong to us Christians. For we worship and love, after God the Father, the Word who is from the Unbegotten and Ineffable God, since He even became Man for us, so that by sharing in our sufferings He also might heal us. Indeed, all writers, by means of the engrafted seed of the Word which was implanted in them, had a dim glimpse of the truth. For the seed of something and its imitation, given in proportion to one's capacity, is one thing, but the thing itself, which is shared and imitated according to His grace, is quite another.

215. Saldanha, *Divine Pedagogy*, 54–58, provides a helpful summary of the different schools of interpretation of the *Logos* theology, before adding his own support for the Johannine hypothesis on pages 58–62. Holte, "Logos Spermatikos Christianity," 135–48, provides a close textual analysis of the key material, engaging with different background interpretations as he does so. Grillmeier, *Christ in Christian Tradition*, 108, believes: "There are two sources for the Logos doctrine of the Apologists: Christian tradition (the prologue of the Gospel of John) and Hellenistic philosophy (of the Middle Platonic and Stoic types); a Judaistic exegesis is sometimes combined with both of these. Philo is significant here, above all else, different though the verdicts on his influence may be." Grillmeier argues for strong Stoic influence on his *Logos Spermatikos* thought on page 91.

216. Nahm, "Debate on the 'Platonism' of Justin Martyr."

217. Jackson-McCabe, *Logos and Law*, 127, states:

> Justin, in a manner analogous to Cicero and the author of the *Apostolic Constitutions*, conceives of the initial endowment of the logos given to humanity as an "implanted seed." It is likely that Justin was himself aware that the roots of this terminology lie in the Stoic doctrine of implanted preconceptions; his use of such expressions is in any case clearly to be understood in light of this doctrine. Nonetheless, . . . Justin adapted the Stoic theory of natural law to accommodate a set of religious and historical convictions alien to Stoicism.

A key departure was in Justin's rejection of the non-specific content to this law. Jackson-McCabe, *Logos and Law*, 88, writes, "The very notion, first of all, that the "right reason" which comprises natural law can find definitive verbal expression in some set of ethical directives seems to have been quite alien to the original Stoic idea."

218. Holte, "Logos Spermatikos Christianity," 164.

219. Holte, "Logos Spermatikos Christianity," 163.

220. Holte, "Logos Spermatikos Christianity," 128.

221. Holte, "Logos Spermatikos Christianity," 128, comments:

> In Stoicism, Logos was thought of as the principle for both physical and spiritual life, but it was understood materially, and the epithet spermatikos gave an immediate association with an organic physical development. . . . Philo . . . has dared to use the term symbolically on a spiritual plane. But only with Justin is it used as a principle for natural revelation, i.e., for the ethical and religious knowledge implanted in creation, on account of which Man can be held responsible to God.

222. Hillar, *From Logos to Trinity*, 146, argues for a dispositional understanding, identifying the seed of truth with "the moral and intellectual striving of men, which is the moral disposition implanted in the soul of men as a part of the whole, the divine Logos, Christ." Williams, *Divine Sense*, 30–31, states, "The Christological principle is reflected in an anthropological one. Later theology would forge a link between the two by asserting the imago Dei. Justin does not. His equivalent, both substantively and systematically, is the notion of the Logos spermatikos." Skarsaune, "Judaism and Hellenism," 606, writes, "I think the basically biblical idea of mediatorship at creation by the Wisdom / Logos is what Justin is trying to express with the Logos spermatikos term." Saldanha, *Divine Pedagogy*, 63, defines the seed of the Logos primarily as truth: "The result of that presence and activity of the logos, namely man's knowledge of the truth, no matter how fragmentary or imperfect." Nyström, *Apology of Justin Martyr*, 63, argues similarly to Saldanha. Lilla, *Clement of Alexandria*, 25n1, disagrees that only a few ideas are sown: "I do not think that the activity of Justin's Logos Spermatikos is limited to the sowing of a few general conceptions, such as the idea of God," arguing that many doctrines are known from it. He extends the "coverage" to include various doctrines and laws. Goodenough, *Theology of Justin Martyr*, 215 and 288, equated the seed of the word with "the higher mind of man" or "the highest power in each man." On page 271, he states, "The eternal moral law of which all men have had inklings is to Justin practically complete in the sermon on the mount. He can imagine no higher ethical standard."

223. Edwards, "Justin's Logos," 262.

ENDNOTES

224. Edwards, "Justin's Logos," 265.

225. Edwards, "Justin's Logos," 272.

226. Edwards, "Justin's Logos," 272, states, "Holte, in attributing to Justin a belief that makes the knowledge of God ubiquitous by nature, does little to reconcile this with the more famous and influential claim advanced in the First Apology: namely, that the knowledge of divine things in pagan circles, and especially in Plato, was entirely derived from casual acquaintance with the Scriptures."

227. Edwards, "Justin's Logos," 273.

228. Edwards, "Justin's Logos," 273.

229. Edwards, "Justin's Logos," 273, writes, "This question is determined, on the other hand, by the Dialogue with Trypho, where the old man, who is the mouthpiece of paternal revelation, forces Justin to renounce his Platonism and confess that the mind has no innate communion with God (Dial. 4.2)."

230. Edwards, "Justin's Logos," 276. Admittedly, he goes on to soften this somewhat, in referring to natural human chastity, but the statement is nevertheless made.

231. Edwards, "Justin's Logos," 276.

232. Edwards, "Justin's Logos," 275.

233. Others that seem to support Edwards's views are Lohr, "Theft of the Greeks," 408n19, and Smith. "Was Justin Martyr an Inclusivist?," 209.

234. Edwards, "Justin's Logos," 275.

235. Edwards, *Image, Word, and God*, 85.

236. Edwards, "Socrates in the Early Church," 128.

237. Holte, "Logos Spermatikos Christianity," 142.

238. See 2 *Apol.* 6 and *Dial.* 69.

239. 1 *Apol.* 28; 2 *Apol.* 7.

240. 2 *Apol.* 2. Edwards, "Justin's Logos," 276, notes the chastity reference but argues that the knowledge of what is right and wrong comes from Scripture:

> Justin states elsewhere that both the motion of the heavens and human chastity are in the course of nature (2 *Apol.* 2.4, 4.2), and that human beings have an innate capacity to choose between good and evil (2 *Apol.* 14.2), but without presuming anywhere that knowledge of divine truths is inborn. His references to partaking or methexis of the logos, though they are often thought to bespeak his pagan schooling, are amply covered by our thesis. Propositional truth "partakes" of Scripture, since the Scripture itself contains all revelation

241. 2 *Apol.* 7.

242. See Kelly, *Early Christian Doctrines*, 167.

243. Edwards, "Justin's Logos," 276.

244. Holte, "Logos Spermatikos Christianity," 128, states, "In Justin, the natural revelation is sometimes described as an active enlightenment of man by Logos, at the same time as the contrary activity of demonic powers in blinding Man is strongly emphasised." Reed, "Trickery of the Fallen Angels," 167, writes, "In a precise inversion of the activity of the Logos in human history demons promulgate irrational beliefs and

behavior." Skarsaune, "Judaism and Hellenism," 591, contrasts reason and the demonic as "antagonistic entities." He further comments (page 591), "Demons extinguish reason, [sic] reason unmasks and expells [sic] demons." Adolf Harnack, *History of Dogma*, 185, writes, "The dominion of demons and revelation are the two correlated ideas."

245. 1 *Apol.*; 2 *Apol.* 7.

246. Allert, "Revelation," 103.

247. Contra Edwards, "Justin's Logos," 279. "Our conclusion, therefore, is that in the two Apologies, no less than in the Dialogue with Trypho, Christ is the Logos who personifies the Torah. In Jewish thought the Word was the source of being, the origin of Law, the written Torah and a Person next to God."

248. As will be noted later, Justin had reservations about parts of the decalogue—in particular the sabbath.

249. Sheather, "Apology," 128, notes that approximately one third of the apology relates to Jesus as fulfilling the Old Testament prophecies. Richardson, *Early Christian Fathers*, places sections 30–53 under the proof from prophecy material. Ulrich, "Justin Martyr," extends this (30–60), and Minns and Parvis, *Justin, Philosopher, and Martyr* extend it even further to sections 23–60.

250. Concerning civil obedience see 1 *Apol.* 17. For exemplary morality see: 1 *Apol.* 12, 15, 16, 29.

251. 2 *Apol.* 12.

252. See Williams, *Divine Sense*, 29.

253. 1 *Apol.* 5, 14, 58.

254. 1 *Apol.* 3, 68.

255. Chadwick, "Justin Martyr's Defence," 295.

256. 2 *Apol.* 7.

257. 2 *Apol.* 10.

258. See Dulles, *History of Apologetics*, 29.

259. 1 *Apol.* 44.

260. Minns and Parvis, *Justin, Philosopher, and Martyr*, 305n3, state, "Justin believed that philosophers and poets derived knowledge of punishments after death from the prophets (1 A 44.9), and that Christians were taught the same thing by Christ (2 A 7[8].5), which Justin may have specifically in mind here). He would also have assumed that the existence of divine sanctions was made known through participation in reason. The word 'Logos' covers all three cases."

261. 2 *Apol.* 9.

262. 1 *Apol.* 4, 27.

263. *Dial.* 2.

264. As noted in 2 *Apol.* 9.

265. 2 *Apol.* 9.

266. 2 *Apol.* 10. Thorsteinsson, "Justin's Debate," 472, states, "It is indeed true, says Justin, that there are different laws and different opinions of good and bad among human beings. But the laws of the Christians are the only truly good laws. While some aspects of other teachings are good, the Christian teaching is the greatest. The rest of chapters 9–13 basically functions as a support for this claim."

267. See 2 *Apol.* 10. Grillmeier, *Christ in Christian Tradition*, 1:81.

268. This is especially evident in his exposition of the sermon on the mount—See 1 *Apol.* 15 and 16.

269. Williams, *Divine Sense*, 27, writes: "Indeed, it is not in Clement of Alexandria, but in Justin, that we find the first extended reflection on the theme of Christ the Teacher." Hayes, "Justin's Christian Philosophy," 24–25, says, "Indeed, Justin's primary description of Christ is that of a teacher (didaskalos)." Ulrich, "Justin Martyr," 57, comments, "In the beginning of the second main section of First Apology Justin argues for the truth and rationality of Christianity primarily by referring to Christ's teachings, which he exhorts the emperors to test (1 *Apol.* 14.4)." Purves, *Testimony of Justin Martyr*, 161, observes, "the object of Christ's coming was, in Justin's thought, primarily to teach." Purves goes on to note numerous other reasons (including conquering death and saving through cleansing) but believes that Justin viewed Christ primarily as a teacher.

270. As noted in section 4.2.1.

271. Edwards, "Justin's Logos," 276.

272. Edwards, "Justin's Logos," 276.

273. In Holte's view the knowledge gained from the seed is "imperfect, obscure and difficult to attain" due to limited human capacity, this resulting in contradictions between different ideas and the mixture of error and truth: see Holte, "Logos Spermatikos Christianity," 151. Allert, "Revelation," 104, comments, "Since the demons had led astray humanity we have only a dim understanding until the incarnation of the Logos." See also 2 *Apol.* 10. Admittedly, Justin referred to the powerlessness of the Mosaic law to save in his discussion with Trypho in Dialogue 122: "'No,' I replied, looking straight at Trypho, 'for, if the Law had the power to enlighten the Gentiles and all those who possess it, what need would there be for a new testament?'" In context, Justin is arguing for the obsolescence of the mosaic law—proved by the coming of Christ. Accordingly, I would question the legitimacy of allowing this exchange to influence the interpretation I am arguing for here.

274. 2 *Apol.* 13.

275. 2 *Apol.* 2.

276. Jackson-McCabe, *Logos and Law*, 126, comments:

> The phrases "teaching of Christ" . . . "right reason," and "the law of nature" are essentially interchangeable here. Thus can we understand Justin's repeated description of Christ as "the lawgiver," or even of Christ himself as the "new law" . . . given Justin's knowledge of the common Stoic definition of law in terms of "right reason" in its function of commanding and prohibiting, it is not surprising that he identifies Christ's teaching further with natural law.

277. Edwards, "Justin's Logos," 276, states, "Justin states elsewhere that both the motion of the heavens and human chastity are in the course of nature (2 *Apol.* 2.4; 4.2), and that human beings have an innate capacity to choose between good and evil (2 *Apol.* 14.2), but without presuming anywhere that knowledge of divine truths is inborn."

278. Holte, "Logos Spermatikos Christianity," 156.

279. *Dial.* 18, 19, 21, 44, 45, 46, 67.

280. Bates, "Justin Martyr's Logocentric Hermeneutical Transformation," 546, writes, "The writings of Moses are understood by Justin as bipartite, containing a narrowly Jewish ritual code (which nonetheless anticipates the Christian dispensation) and universal laws. In fact, the ritual code was always intended for the Jews alone, and its primary function was to curb idolatry and mark out the Jews for their distinctively pernicious obduracy."

281. *Dial.* 44. See the discussion in Rokeah, *Justin Martyr and the Jews*, 45–46, for a summary of the bi- and tripartite interpretations.

282. On this section Keith, "Justin Martyr and Religious Exclusivism," 63, comments, "Justin believed that every nation (not simply the Jews) has a knowledge of universal and immutable standards of righteousness."

283. Note the inclusion of fornication. On *Dial.* 93, Harakas, "Eastern Orthodox Perspectives," 105, writes, "It is true that Justin does not identify the natural moral law with the Decalogue in so many words. Yet as the above reference indicates, he does identify it with what are concrete injunctions of the Decalogue." I would suggest that Justin was more reticent to make this equation than Harakas suggests.

284. *Dial.* 93.

285. *Dial.* 28, 93.

286. *Dial.* 45.

287. *Dial.* 23.

288. Goodenough, *Theology of Justin Martyr*, 89.

289. Rokeah, *Justin Martyr and the Jews*, 47, states, "those who observed the Mosaic commandments before the advent of Jesus will be saved, not because of their observance of the temporary ritual commandments, but because of their adherence to eternal, universal principles found in the torah (45:4)."

290. *Dial.* 12, 14, 18.

291. *Dial.* 12, 14, 24, 34.

292. Moses is also termed a lawgiver in the dialogue: *Dial.* 1, 127.

293. *Dial.* 43, 122.

294. Goodenough, *Theology of Justin Martyr*, 119.

295. See Martens, *One God, One Law*, 96; Chesnut, "Ruler and the Logos," 1312n3.

296. Jackson-McCabe, *Logos and Law*, 88. See also Copeland, "Nomos as a Medium of Revelation," 58.

297. For example, *Dial.* 46.

298. Wendel, *Scriptural Interpretation and Community*, 141.

299. *Dial.* 67.

300. Koskenniemi, "Forgetting an Epic Battle," 158, believes that "the dialogue does not have anything negative to say about Moses or the law but strictly criticizes Jews and their use of the law." I suggest it is more realistic to argue that Justin would have endorsed the rightness of the temporal aspects of the Mosaic law, while not believing these necessarily embodied anything of God's eternal law: in this sense (only) he was negative. Note the dismissive tone concerning aspects of the Torah and the boasting of Christian obedience to the law of the new lawgiver in *Dial.* 18.

301. Moll, *Arch-Heretic Marcion*, 150, stresses the idea of replacement.

302. *Dial.* 11.

303. *Dial.* 11.

304. Perhaps the clearest of these is *Dial.* 46.

305. See Holmes, "Biblical Canon," 411.

306. See Allert, "Revelation," 96.

307. Skarsaune, "Conversion of Justin Martyr," 62–63.

308. See also Purves, *Testimony of Justin Martyr*, 100, for Justin's rather negative view of the mosaic law.

309. The undisputed, clear borrowing references are 1 *Apol.* 44, 1 *Apol.* 59, and 1 *Apol.* 60. What is borrowed are the ideas of there being "no guilt in God," and right ideas about "immortality of the soul, or retribution after death, or speculation on celestial matters." 1 *Apol.* 59 covers the Creation account, and 1 *Apol.* 60 touches on the "nature of the son of God" and the role of the Spirit in creation.

310. Heraclitus is mentioned in 1 *Apol.* 46, and also mentioned in 2 *Apol.* 8. Although I focus primarily on Socrates in what follows, I also make some references to Heraclitus.

311. Edwards, "Socrates in the Early Church," 128; Sigountos, "Did Early Christians," interprets the claim similarly. Smith, "Was Justin Martyr an Inclusivist?," 210, makes essentially the same point.

312. Socrates is mentioned in passing as a teacher in 1 *Apol.* 18, but without reference to the content of that teaching.

313. Nyström, *Apology of Justin Martyr*, 90, divides the various names and classes of people noted by Justin into writers (Plato, Pythagoras, Stoics, and Poets) and non-writers (Socrates, Heraclitus and named Hebrews). He terms the latter "idealised humans who lived rationally." The former, it can be argued, constitute the borrowers in Justin's thought. If this is, so, Socrates is not a borrower in Justin's thinking. "In large, Socrates is portrayed quite differently from Plato and he plays an inverse role to that of the poets and mythmakers in Justin's rhetoric. Socrates did not 'steal' his doctrines from the prophets, but through reason he was able to draw ethical conclusions, and order his life in conformity with the very moral teaching of Christ himself," according to Nyström, *Apology of Justin Martyr*, 93. Daniélou, *Gospel Message*, 46, comments, "It is interesting that Socrates is the figure mentioned in connection with participation in the Logos, Plato the one associated with the borrowings." Droge, "Justin Martyr and the Restoration of Philosophy," 308, states, "Justin carries out his literary proof of the priority of Moses chiefly with respect to Plato." If Plato had been named in 1 *Apol.* 46, Edwards's argument would have been supported somewhat. The fact he was not opens up different possibilities of interpretation.

314. Edwards, "Justin's Logos," 278–79.

315. See Baechle, "Reappraisal," 70, esp. nn117–18.

316. Baechle, "Reappraisal," 71.

317. Baechle, "Reappraisal," 71. Note also Holte, "Logos Spermatikos Christianity," 159, on the same issue: "The interpretation of *meta logou* as alluding to reason seems therefore to contain a discrepancy which disappears if we understand it to mean the divine Logos or Christ."

318. Hacker, "Religions of the Gentiles," 257, writes, "what Socrates, as seen by Justin, criticised as pernicious was religion precisely practised in his society. What guided Socrates was not the customs of his environment but something like a private revelation, not a perfect but a dim and reflected or refracted light, yet nevertheless a light."

319. Wolfson, *Philosophy of the Church Fathers*, 21.

320. Holte, "Logos Spermatikos Christianity," 165.

321. Droge, "Justin Martyr and the Restoration of Philosophy," 316.

322. Nyström, *Apology of Justin Martyr*, 98.

323. Daniélou, *Gospel Message*, 48.

324. Horbury, *Jews and Christians in Contact and Controversy*, 152–53, explains the grouping thus: "he [Justin] evidently takes the prophets of Israel to have the downfall of Rome as a main subject, in the manner of Hystaspes and the Sibyl."

325. Saldanha, *Divine Pedagogy*, 69n271.

326. See Abdelnour, *Comparative History*, 24; O'Collins, *Second Vatican Council*, 18; Dupuis, *Toward a Christian Theology*, 60.

327. Pinnock, *Wideness in God's Mercy*, 36.

328. Sanders, *No Other Name*, 239: "Logos Christology is, in many ways, the forerunner of inclusivism."

329. McDermott, *Can Evangelicals Learn from World Religions?*, 41.

330. Smith, "Was Justin Martyr an Inclusivist?," 194, on Justin's naming of some philosophers Christians comments, "he [Justin] did not mean the word literally," and on page 205: "Perhaps 'Christians' is more like a literary technique or metaphor related to common experience and actions than a declarative statement about the salvation of Greek philosophers."

331. For example, Adam Sparks, "Was Justin Martyr a Proto-Inclusivist?," 500, who argues that Socrates was appealed to as a Christian as he opposed idolatry. Skarsaune, "Conversion of Justin Martyr," 65, states, "they all denounced idolatry." See also Skarsaune, "Judaism and Hellenism," 597 and 601. Bray, "Explaining Christianity to Pagans," 19, believes Socrates and Heraclitus were awarded honorary Christian status because "they were persecuted for their lack of belief in the pagan theological system." For the idea that Justin may have imported the honorary status idea from Judaism (which had a place for honorary Jews) see Skarsaune, "Judaism and Hellenism," 591. Price, "Are there Holy Pagans in Justin Martyr?," 169, believes, "Justin's concern [in the labelling] is . . . with those who could be represented as Christian fellow travellers and as fellow victims of demonic malice." Sigountos, "Did Early Christians," 233, writes, "He merely affirms that some throughout human history have exposed the demonic deception of pagan religion." Droge, "Justin Martyr and the Restoration of Philosophy," 314n41, believes, "Common to all these men [Greek and Hebrew] is their 'atheism,' that is, their refusal to worship the demons." Chadwick, "Gospel a Reduplication," 237n1, believes Heraclitus was appealed to because of his "reservations about popular cults."

332. See Skarsaune, "Judaism and Hellenism," 602, referring to Jubilees 11:14—12:31.

333. Droge, "Justin Martyr and the Restoration of Philosophy," 314n41, writes, "Abraham rejected polytheism; Ananias, Azarias, and Misael refused to worship Nebuchadnezzar; and Elijah rejected the worship of Baal. Plato's name is missing from this list, no doubt, because he participated in the pagan cults of his day."

ENDNOTES

334. Nyström, *Apology of Justin Martyr*, 88–89, is one of the very few Justin scholars, of whom I am aware, who acknowledges the importance of the accountability context background to 1 *Apol.* 46.

335. Daniélou, *Gospel Message*, 161.

336. Justin is very strong on his denunciation of Hebrew persecution of the true Israel. For example, he states in *Dial.* 93: "But, as for you Jews, you have never evidenced any friendship or love either toward God, or toward the Prophets, or toward one another, but you have shown yourselves always to be idolaters and murderers of the just; in fact, you even did violence to Christ Himself."

337. Holte, "Logos Spermatikos Christianity," 129, notes that for Justin, like Paul, natural theology is opposed to idolatry.

338. On *Apol.* 5.4, Nyström, *Apology of Justin Martyr*, 92, comments, "the nature of Socrates' wisdom is practical and related to ethics. In this, Justin is following a tradition which saw Socrates primarily as a moral philosopher." On the same page he continues, "He [Socrates] is portrayed by Justin, not mainly as a preacher of sound doctrine, but as an ethical example." He also states, on page 93, "Justin primarily frames the teachings of Jesus as an ethical message, and one with which Socrates easily could have concurred."

339. Holte, "Logos Spermatikos Christianity," 156, also de-emphasizes the focus on Socrates as teacher: "Justin is not primarily interested in recommending Socrates' philosophical method as in itself worth following. The point lies in the fact that the *result* which Socrates attained by his method i.e. to disclose idolatry, tallies with the content of Paul's doctrine on natural revelation." It should be noted that in 1 *Apol.* 18 Socrates being a teacher is noted.

340. While Justin made no secret of his approval of Stoic ethics, he made it clear that he had no time for other aspects of their teaching, e.g., 2 *Apol.* 7 "The Stoic philosophers also, in their moral teaching, always respect the same principles [as legislators and philosophers who have correctly stated what is right and wrong], so it is easily seen how wrong they are in their teaching on principles and incorporeal beings." See also 2 *Apol.* 8 "We know that the followers of the Stoic teaching, because they were praiseworthy at least in their ethics, as were also the poets in some respects, because of the seed of reason implanted in all mankind, were hated and killed." *Dial.* 2 is also relevant to the point: "When I first desired to contact one of these philosophers, I placed myself under the tutelage of a certain Stoic. After spending some time with him and learning nothing new about God (for my instructor had no knowledge of God, nor did he consider such knowledge necessary)."

341. Thorsteinsson, "Justin's Debate," 469, notes two problems with Justin's appeal: "Justin is badly informed here: Heraclitus . . . was not a Stoic and, as far as we know, neither he nor Musonius (first century C.E.) were 'put to death,'" For possible reasons why Heraclitus was appealed to see Thorsteinsson, "Justin and Stoic Cosmo-Theology," 541 and 562. Helleman, "Justin Martyr and the Logos," 143, notes a possible influence of Heraclitus on later Stoic thought.

342. Chadwick, *Early Christian Thought*, 17.

343. Goodenough, *Theology of Justin Martyr*, 262, states, "It is true that he makes room for the salvation of such men as Socrates and Abraham, but in both cases it was because of their faith which believed in the truth of the utterances of God."

344. Bouquet, "Revelation and the Divine Logos," 194, also notes this focus on *following* in this part of Justin's writings.

ENDNOTES

345. *2 Apol.* 6:

> But His Son, who alone is properly called Son, the Word, who was with Him [God, the Father] and was begotten before all things, when in the beginning He [God, the Father] created and arranged all things through Him [the Son], is called Christ, because He was anointed and because God the Father arranged all the things of creation through Him. This name also has an unknown meaning, just as the term "God," which is not a real name, but the expression of man's innate opinion of a thing that can scarcely be defined.

346. *Dial.* 1:

> Moreover, they try to convince us that God takes care of the universe with its genera and species, but not of me and you and of each individual, for otherwise there would be no need of our praying to Him night and day. It is not difficult to see where such reasoning leads them. It imparts a certain immunity and freedom of speech to those who hold these opinions, permitting them to do and to say whatever they please, without any fear of punishment or hope of reward from God.

347. E.g., 1 *Apol.* 16 refers to Matt. 7:15, 17, 19, and 1 *Apol.* 40 refers to Ps. 1:1–6.

348. *2 Apol.* 12.

349. Copeland, "Nomos as a Medium of Revelation," 55, writes, "It may be said, then, that Nomos was viewed as the ethical expression of Logos [in Cicero's thought]."

350. Jackson McCabe, *Logos and Law*, 69.

351. Jackson-McCabe, *Logos and Law*, 88:

> The very notion, first of all, that the "right reason" which comprises natural law can find definitive verbal expression in some set of ethical directives seems to have been quite alien to the original Stoic idea. Second, and perhaps more important, is the fact that the origin of this law was no longer associated with the immanent deity of the Stoics. The author of this law was now the transcendent god whose past interaction with humanity, and with the descendants of Abraham in particular, is recorded in the Jewish scriptures, and whose future activity, at least in much of the Christian literature, would include an eschatological judgment.

352. 1 *Apol.* 13: "We shall prove that we worship Him with reason, since we have learned that He is the Son of the living God Himself, and believe Him to be in the second place, and the Prophetic Spirit in the third."

353. 1 *Apol.* 6.

354. For example, *Dial.* 44: "No one can by any means participate in any of these gifts, except those who have the same ardent faith as Abraham, and who approve of all the mysteries." See also *Dial.* 92: "Abraham, indeed, was considered just, not by reason of his circumcision, but because of his faith. For, before his circumcision it was said of him: 'Abraham believed God, and it was reputed to him unto justice.'"

355. *Dial.* 19: "Furthermore, all these men were just and pleasing in the sight of God, yet they kept no sabbaths. The same can be said of Abraham and his descendants down to the time of Moses." *Dial.* 27: "And why did He not instruct those persons who lived before the time of Moses and Abraham to observe these same precepts; men, who are called just and were pleasing to God, even though they were not circumcised in the flesh, and did not keep the sabbaths?"

ENDNOTES

356. As noted in *Dial.* 46, plus the false prophet reference in *Dial.* 69.

357. *Dial.* 87: "Solomon had the spirit of wisdom, Daniel that of understanding and counsel, Moses that of strength and piety, Elias that of fear, Isaias that of knowledge."

358. "And Daniel the righteous was thrown to the lions, and Hananiah, Azariah, and Mishael were hurled into the fiery furnace and endured it for the sake of God" (4 Macc 16:21 RSV).

359. *Dial.* 19: "Furthermore, all these men were just and pleasing in the sight of God, yet they kept no sabbaths. The same can be said of Abraham and his descendants down to the time of Moses."

360. Harnack, *History of Dogma*, 1:179, writes, "But Justin conceived the Decalogue as the natural law of reason, and therefore definitely distinguished it from the ceremonial law."

361. *Dial.* 12: "The New Law demands that you observe a perpetual Sabbath, whereas you consider yourselves pious when you refrain from work on one day out of the week, and in doing so you don't understand the real meaning of that precept." *Dial.* 21: "As I stated before, it was by reason of your sins and the sins of your fathers that, among other precepts, God imposed upon you the observance of the Sabbath as a mark." In *Dial.* 27 after discussing the sabbath (singular) and circumcision, Justin states, "And why did He not instruct those persons who lived before the time of Moses and Abraham to observe these same precepts; men, who are called just and were pleasing to God, even though they were not circumcised in the flesh, and did not keep the sabbaths?"

362. This may sound odd, as Jesus summarized the Mosaic Law in the sermon on the mount. However, as noted earlier, for Justin, Jesus sifted it and focused on the universal elements within it in his exposition. Accordingly, there is a difference.

363. See, for example, Romans 3:1–2. I am suggesting a significant non-alignment between Justin and the Apostle Paul here. Dunn, *Christianity in the Making*, 3:701, suggests several possible reasons why Paul may not have played a bigger role in Justin's thinking, noting the rather dismissive perception of the Jews in Justin's view:

> Why is Paul not paraded by Justin as a Jew whose arguments with respect to the gospel and Jews could surely be drawn on? One possible answer is that he ranked Paul's letters less highly than the OT and the Jesus tradition/Gospels, though that would be somewhat surprising if the attitude expressed in 2 Pet. 3.16 was more widespread. Alternatively, perhaps he was conscious that while Paul had been arguing that uncircumcised Gentile believers could nevertheless be included in the seed of Abraham (Rom. 4; Gal. 3), Justin was rather more dismissive of Jewish status before God (§46.6g). Paul's relative positiveness towards his own people was perhaps something of an embarrassment for Justin. Another possibility is that Justin was all too aware that Paul was being made use of by Marcion and gnosticizing groups (§47.5) and regarded Paul as a lost cause. Consequently, although Justin cannot be regarded as a strong witness to second-century reverence for Paul and to the influence of his writings, at the same time he cannot be regarded as a negative testimony on the same point, far less as a witness that Paul was regarded as a dangerous precedent in Christian tradition.

364. See Purves, *Testimony of Justin Martyr*, 97. Note also Keith, "Justin Martyr and Religious Exclusivism," 63, who makes a similar point: 'With his stress on a revelation of God to all nations, Justin tended to undermine the special nature of God's revelation to the Jews."

365. "The presupposition of the first Apology is that divine revelation is not confined to a small elite, but is addressed to the whole of humanity," according to Chadwick, "Gospel a Reduplication," 245.

366. Thyssen, "Philosophical Christology," 158, writes:

> Because men in this way are created as rational beings or endowed with reason . . . they are morally responsible . . . to God (2 Apol. 14.1). For participation in Logos means knowledge of ethical principles (2 Apol. 8.1), which are innate in every human being (2 Apol. 14.2). Whoever has been living according to these principles or according to reason . . . is a Christian (1 Apol. 46.3). Justin illustrates this by mentioning Socrates and Heraclitus (and Musonius 2 Apol. 8.1) and the friends of Daniel, as examples of reasonable pre-Christian Greeks and pre-Christian Jews respectively. The purpose is to say that salvation is possible for men of the pre-Christian era also because of the universal presence of the Logos.

367. See, for example, *Dial.* 55: "Hence, we readily understand why, on account of your iniquity, God has hidden from you the power of discerning the wisdom of His words, with the exception of those few to whom, in His infinite mercy, He has left a seed for salvation." *Dial.* 29: "For we believe and obey them [the Scriptures], whereas you, though you read them, do not grasp their spirit." Wendel, *Scriptural Interpretation and Community*, 252, comments:

> Whereas Trypho and other Jews purport to bring light to their proselytes through their interpretation of the Mosaic law, Justin concludes that they could not possibly provide illumination for non-Jews because they fail to comprehend the true intent of the law (Dial. 123.2-3; cf. Isa 29:14). They neither teach nor embody covenant faithfulness because they do not recognize how Christ fulfilled the Jewish scriptures (Dial. 122.1-6; cf. Dial. 11.4-5; 12.1-3).

368. *Dial.* 130:

> For, when He exclaims, "Rejoice, ye Gentiles, with His people," He gives them a share in a similar legacy and attributes to them a similar name; but by calling them "Gentiles," and stating that they rejoice with His people, He does so as a reproach to your nation. For, just as you angered Him by your acts of idolatry, so has He deemed them, though they are likewise idolaters, worthy to know His will and to share in His inheritance.

369. Reed, "Trickery of the Fallen Angels," 159, writes, "Jews may need redemption from their propensity to repeat the disobedience of Adam and Eve, but the experience of pagans is characterized by another type of enslavement whose origins also lie in primordial history but somewhat later: the enslavement of humankind by the angels who descended before the flood and by the demonic progeny born of their impure union with human women." Saldanha, *Divine Pedagogy*, 50, argued similarly: "He [Justin] attributed all their [i.e., pagan] errors and aberrations not to themselves, but to demons. The pagans were "misled," "intimidated," "seduced," but they were not the real culprits."

370. Reed, "Trickery of the Fallen Angels," 145, states, "whereas Justin uses the sins of the primeval couple to explicate the nature of Jewish wickedness as willful disobedience, his retelling of the angelic descent myth functions to account for pagan error as the product of unwitting deception by the demonic mimesis of the divine."

371. Allert, "Revelation," 97.

372. Reed, "Trickery of the Fallen Angels," 168, states, "just as Eve "brought forth disobedience" by succumbing to the Serpent (*Dial.* 100), so Jews now turn away from God and towards the demons through their own free will. By contrast, the pagan condition is characterized by enslavement to the angels who fell before the flood."

373. Allert, "Revelation," 103, writes, "man is a sinner because he allows the demons to lead him into rebellion against the Law of God which every man has within him as a part of the divine equipment in life."

374. 1 *Apol.* 33: "I think that even you will concede that the Prophets are inspired by none other than the Divine Word." *Dial.* 8:

> When he had said these and many other things which it is not now the fitting time to tell, he went his way, after admonishing me to meditate on what he had told me, and I never saw him again. But my spirit was immediately set on fire, and an affection for the prophets, and for those who are friends of Christ, took hold of me; while pondering on his words, I discovered that his was the only sure and useful philosophy.

375. Holte, "Logos Spermatikos Christianity," 132.

376. Holte, "Logos Spermatikos Christianity," 166: "It is the same Logos who was active among both the Greeks and the Jews. . . . But in the former case he appeared enveloped in human thoughts only. . . . And even in the latter case he appeared by the medium of something foreign to himself."

377. Holte, "Logos Spermatikos Christianity," 158–59, writes, "in Justin's opinion, the Old Testament revelation revealed *far more of the truth* than is accessible to the capacities of human reason. The activity of Logos has not been of the same kind among Jews and heathen. The patriarchs had never been referred to the "seed" through which the Greeks were illuminated, but were led by the prophetic revelation of Logos [emphasis mine]." Horner, "Problem with Abraham," 245n18 makes essentially the same point, without providing any specific support for it: "Justin's explication of the Logos as it related to the patriarchs differs significantly from the Logos as it was experienced by the 'heathen' philosophers. In this way, Justin saw the patriarchs as special and intimate 'knowers' of the Logos and thus Christ."

378. Dupuis, *Toward a Christian Theology*, 59.

379. 2 *Apol.* 10.

380. Grillmeier, *Christ in Christian Tradition*, 92, writes, "So when Justin assumes of the ancient philosophers, like Heraclitus or Socrates, that they lived in accordance with the Logos, he understands by this Logos not reason (ratio), but the divine Logos. But these philosophers knew this Logos only obscurely and partially."

381. "Though Socrates and Heraclitus may in a way be called Christians, they cannot be so designated in any real sense. Reason is clogged with unreasonableness, and the certainty of truth is doubtful wherever the whole Logos has not been acting; for man's natural endowment with reason is too weak to oppose the powers of evil and of sense that work in the world, namely, the demons," according to Adolf Harnack, *History of Dogma*, 2:184. Holte, "Logos Spermatikos Christianity," 161, states, "Justin shows a very deep pessimism concerning the capacity of natural reason . . . man's normal state is characterized by his being imprisoned by demons."

382. A good example would be O'Collins in *Second Vatican Council on Other Religions*. While making numerous references to Justin's thought on the Logos (e.g., 16–18), he makes no reference to his demonology. As already observed, Mark Edwards also fails to engage with this area of Justin's thought.

383. In 1 *Apol.* 26 Justin suggests that the accusations of immorality thrown at Christians be investigated among Christian *heretics*—especially Marcionites: "We do not know whether they are guilty of those disgraceful and fabulous deeds, the upsetting of the lamp, promiscuous intercourse, and anthropopagy, but we do know, that you neither molest nor execute them, at least not for their beliefs." Hayes, *Justin against Marcion*, 206, writes:

> Somewhat like the demons hearing what was said of Christ by the prophets (*1 Apol.* 54.4) and imitating them without understanding, so these imposters [heretics] may speak some of Christ's words *but show by their actions that they do not understand them, that they are not "Christians."* Any who appear to be followers of Christ but whose actions betray them are, in the words of Jesus, workers of wickedness. Following this, Justin has Jesus introduce the imposters in his name as not only false candidates for "Christians" but as scheming and dangerous tricksters. *Those who are not truly "Christian" are therefore wicked and duplicitous.* Here in particular we find an obvious allusion to Marcion, who is described as a wolf and his followers like lambs led away from the truth: "Many, believing him [Marcion] as if he alone knew the truth, laugh at us, though they have no demonstration for the things they say, but, being irrational, *they are snatched away, like lambs by a wolf, and become fodder for godless doctrines and demons"* (*1 Apol.* 58.2) [emphases mine].

Goodenough, *Theology of Justin Martyr*, 270, comments, "Justin quotes most of the moral maxims of the Sermon on the Mount, and demands that anyone not living according to these teachings be punished, for such can be a Christian only in name." In support of this claim, Goodenough references 1 *Apol.* 16: "And we ask that you also punish all those who call themselves Christians, but are not living according to His teachings.'"

384. *Sifre Deut* 28 cited in Skarsaune, "Judaism and Hellenism," 602. Skarsaune provides additional, similar examples.

385. See Skarsaune, "Judaism and Hellenism," 587–88, concerning the debate on Justin's knowledge and interaction with rabbinic traditions, and also Edwards, "Justin's Logos," 266.

386. Allert, "Revelation," 128: "In Dial 1.4 he states that philosophers neglected God, and thus their ethical conduct was contaminated."

387. Justin consistently asserts and stresses Jewish idolatry, e.g., *Dial.* 22, 46, and 130.

388. On *Apol.* 5.4, Nyström, *Apology of Justin Martyr*, 92, comments, "the nature of Socrates' wisdom is practical and related to ethics. In this, Justin is following a tradition which saw Socrates primarily as a moral philosopher." Nyström, on the same page, goes on to say, "He [Socrates] is portrayed by Justin, not mainly as a preacher of sound doctrine, but as an ethical example." See also his observations on page 93: "Justin primarily frames the teachings of Jesus as an ethical message, and one with which Socrates easily could have concurred."

389. Sigountos, "Did Early Christians," 233.

390. Grant, *Greek Apologists*, 105.

391. Holte, "Logos Spermatikos Christianity," 147. See also his comments on the distinction of the seed and the Logos (on pages 142 and 153). Holte, "Logos

ENDNOTES

Spermatikos Christianity," 146, states, "The term *to sperma tou logou* does not mean that the Logos or some part of him is sown in man. The meaning is on the contrary that a seed is sown in man by the personal Logos, a seed that is clearly distinguished from him but is nevertheless an imitation of Logos, a knowledge in which he is reflected."

392. Barnard, "Justin Martyr," 159-60.

393. Daniélou, *Gospel Message*, 44.

394. Lilla, *Clement of Alexandria*, 22.

395. See Jackson-McCabe, *Logos and Law*, 34. Referring to the work of Horsley, Jackson-McCabe, *Logos and Law*, 84, notes, "'Cicero clearly distinguish[es] God from the law,' whereas 'Stoic doctrine had identified God with law as well as with reason.'"

396. Daniélou, *Gospel Message*, 44.

397. As Goodenough, *Theology of Justin Martyr*, 120, noted, for Justin "Christ is the Right in the ethical realm, the principle of Truth in the metaphysical realm."

398. *Dial.* 34.

399. *Dial.* 100.

400. Horner, "Problem with Abraham," 239, fn.13.

401. Concerning Justin's belief that Jewish obedience to the Law is no longer efficacious post-incarnation, Goodenough, *Theology of Justin Martyr*, 122, comments, "The faithful of old . . . are saved in so far as they conformed to the Eternal Law. But now since that Eternal Law has been revealed in Christ salvation is hereafter possible only by becoming His disciples. All Jews who remain Jews are cut off from the good time coming. There is one door open for them as for all mankind, through Christ, the Eternal Logos-Law." Sparks, "Was Justin Martyr a Proto-Inclusivist?," 504, writes, "Justin nowhere suggested that anyone living 'according to the Logos' in his own day (and by extension in the current age) could be saved on this basis."

402. *Institutes*, 4.14.26.

403. Brown, Doody, and Paffenroth, *Augustine and World Religions*. Note that I do not engage with Augustine's thought on the Jews and Judaism in this chapter. For treatment on this see Fredriksen, *Augustine and the Jews*.

404. Completed in 427. The dates provided in the three footnotes that follow are taken from *Augustine Through the Ages*, xliii-il except when indicated otherwise.

405. Dated December 406 by Allen D. Fitzgerald in Augustine, *Homilies on the Gospel of John 1-40*, 18.

406. This has been dated new year's day 404 by Edmund Hill in "Sermon against the Pagans," in *The Works of Saint Augustine*, 180.

407. In the order in which they appear throughout the chapter these texts and the dates when they are believed to have been written are: *Retractions* (426/427); *True Religion* (390/391); *De Doctrina Christiana* (396; 426/427); *Psalm 96* (dated 405 in *A Select Library of the Nicene and Post Nicene Fathers of the Christian Church: Volume 8, Saint Augustin*, edited by Philip Schaff, 470n5); *On Free Will* (387-88/395); *Genesis against the Manichees* (388/389); *The Literal Interpretation of Genesis* (401/415); *Confessions* (397/401); *On the Trinity* (399-422/426); *Demonic Divination* (406); *Commentary on Romans* (394/395); *Contra Faustus* (397/399); *Harmony of the Gospels* (399/400?); *Letter 258* (A letter to an old friend—Martianus—who was a pagan, but had become a Christian, dated after 395 by Ramsey in *The Works of Saint Augustine*,

11); *Sermon 341* (Entitled, "On the Three Ways of Understanding Christ in Scripture: Against the Arians" dated 417 by Hill in *The Works of Saint Augustine*, 283); *Letter 137* (a letter to Lord Volusianus, discussing the incarnation and the Doctrine of God dated 412 by Schaff in *A Select Library of the Nicene and Post Nicene Fathers of the Christian Church: Volume 1*, 473).

408. See, e.g., Brown, *Augustine of Hippo*.

409. Wilken, "Religious Pluralism," 380. See also Jones on the difference between current understanding of the term and that of the ancient world: "*Religio* and *Res Publica*," 8. On the importance of practices and tradition in ancient religion see Strand, "Gods of the Nations," 30.

410. Wilken, "Religious Pluralism," 380.

411. See Strand, "Gods of the Nations," 30.

412. Strand, "Gods of the Nations," 62.

413. Augustine, *City of God*, section 10.1. He also connects it to *relegere* (choose again) in *City of God* 10.3. Further references to this translation of the *City of God* use the abbreviation *CoG*.

414. In *Saint Augustine: The Retractions*, section 1.12.9. Augustine stated that he is aware of other understandings of the etymology of the word but that the "binding" etymology is his preferred understanding.

415. See Jones, "*Religio* and *Res Publica*," 108–9.

416. Jones, "*Religio* and *Res Publica*," 109–20.

417. Including *latreia, servitus, thrêskeia, theosebeia* noting the usage and possible difficulties with each one. See *CoG* 10.1.

418. *CoG* 10.3.

419. Augustine, *On Christian Belief*, 55.111, 113.

420. Jones, "*Religio* and *Res Publica*," 111, writes "Augustine's doctrine of the elevative power of grace, sometimes missed by his modern commenters, is at the heart of his discussion of true *religio*."

421. Jones, "*Religio* and *Res Publica*," 58.

422. On this see Kahlos, *Debate and Dialogue*, 93.

423. Augustine *De Doctrina Christiana*, edited and translated by Green, 2.74: "Something instituted by humans is superstitious if it concerns the making and worshipping of idols, or the worshipping of the created order or part of it as if it were God, or if it involves certain kinds of consultations or contracts about meaning arranged and ratified with demons, such as the enterprises involved in the art of magic, which poets tend to mention rather than to teach."

424. Jones, "*Religio* and *Res Publica*," 73, comments, "in the mind of Augustine, all false *religio* is not created equal. The citizens of the city of man may be more or less wrong, and so more or less worthy of condemnation."

425. *CoG* 7.27.

426. *CoG* 7.27. Kahlos, *Debate and Dialogue*, 145, notes how Augustine considered Varro's worship, because directed to the true God, to be less reprehensible than contemporary practice which was not so directed.

427. The World Soul was considered a kind of living cosmos, created by the Demiurge in Platonic thought.

428. Augustine, *True Religion* 38.68–69.

429. Augustine, *Sermon* 198.35.

430. *CoG* 7.26. The Great Mother, also termed "Cybele," embodied ideas of fertility and motherhood.

431. Augustine, *Sermon against the Pagans*, s.33.

432. *CoG* 7.27.

433. See Jones, "*Religio* and *Res Publica*," 159 and 222. Jones speaks of "grades of truth" in Augustine's view of pagan religion on page 28.

434. See Jones, "*Religio* and *Res Publica*," 165.

435. Wiebe, "Demons," 5, writes, "demons emerge as a highly integrated component of his broader theology, rooted in his conception of angels as the ministers of all creation under God, and informed by the doctrine of evil as privation and his understanding of the fall, his thoughts on human embodiment, desire, visions, and the limits of human knowledge, as well as his theology of religious incorporation and sacraments."

436. Ivanovska, "Demonology of Saint Augustine," 400:

> The demonology of Augustine of Hippo is essentially an ancillary system of thought, driven more by rhetoric and polemical need than by a systematic interest in demons as a distinct topic. Unlike the schools of Middle-Platonism and Neo-Platonism, that developed elaborate demonologies, Augustine does not seem to develop his ideas concerning the devil and demons as an independent topic of interest. Rather, he discusses issues of demonology to buttress and to elucidate other topics of theological interest, most notably the topics of cosmology, soteriology and anthropology.

437. Wiebe, "Demons," 9.

438. Otto and Stausberg, "Augustine of Hippo," 33.

439. See Wiebe, "Demons," 176. See also Ivanovska, "Demonology of Saint Augustine," and Burns, "Augustine on the Origin."

440. As noted by Klein, *Augustine's Theology of Angels*, 57.

441. Ivanovska, "Demonology of Saint Augustine," 350 and 398. Note also Kahlos, *Debate and Dialogue*, 45, who says, "Christian apologetic and polemic gives us a remarkably biased and unidimensional picture of polytheistic cults and practices."

442. Ivanovska, "Demonology of Saint Augustine," 6–7.

443. See Wiebe, "Demons," 200; see also Bradnick, *Evil, Spirits, and Possession*, 41.

444. Wiebe, "Demons," 5. See Augustine's comments on Ps. 96. 5 and 6 for the equation of the gods with devils in *Expositions on the Book of Psalms*, 472. See also Kahlos, *Debate and Dialogue*, 169.

445. Wiebe, "Demons," 8.

446. On this departure see Bradnick, *Evil, Spirits, and Possession*, 42–43.

447. *CoG* 3.3–4.

448. *CoG* 15.23.

449. As noted by Gassman, "Ancient Account of Pagan Origins," 86n14.

450. Bradnick, *Evil, Spirits, and Possession*, 31.

ENDNOTES

451. See Klein, *Augustine's Theology of Angels*, 179.

452. See Ivanovska, "Demonology of Saint Augustine," 295–322.

453. Bradnick, *Evil, Spirits, and Possession*, 43.

454. *CoG* 6.7, also mentioned in *CoG* 7.27.

455. Kahlos, *Debate and Dialogue*, 155.

456. *CoG* 8.26.

457. *CoG* 8.26.

458. *CoG* 7.18. See also *De Doctrina Christiana*, 2:21.80

459. Wiebe, "Demons," 202, calls it the "historic kernel" from which false religion flows in Augustine's theory.

460. See Kahlos, *Debate and Dialogue*, 155

461. *CoG* 7.18.

462. Salih, "Idol Theory," 19, calls an idol "an artifactual shell that contains an invisible spirit."

463. See Salih "Idol Theory," 18.

464. *CoG* 7.18.

465. *CoG* 4.27.

466. *CoG* 7.35. See Wiebe, "Demons," 202, for a summary of the process.

467. See Ivanovska, "Demonology of Saint Augustine," 274–75. See also Klein, *Augustine's Theology of Angels*, 59–60, on the self-absorbed behavior of demons in Augustine's thinking.

468. *CoG* 3.2. See also Ivanovska, "Demonology of Saint Augustine," 277.

469. See Ivanovska "The Demonology of Saint Augustine," 277.

470. King, *On the Free Choice of the Will*, 3.10.29–30.

471. See Wiebe, "Demons," 204.

472. See Wiebe, "Demons," 204, 224.

473. Bradnick, *Evil, Spirits and Possession*, 42.

474. See Ivanovska, "Demonology of Saint Augustine," 14–15; Teske, "Homo Spiritualis," 67, questions the mileage that Augustine made of such references, suggesting that Paul's words were misinterpreted by him. Ivanovska, "Demonology of Saint Augustine," 283, on the other hand, prefers to see concord between biblical references and pagan thought on demons.

475. Apuleius was a second century Platonist philosopher, the author of what Augustine referred to as *The Golden Ass*.

476. See, e.g., Wiebe, "Demons," 238; Ivanovska, "Demonology of Saint Augustine," 183.

477. *CoG* 9.19. Salminen, "City of God," 107–8, notes the Christian understanding to be totally negative. This is compared with Plutarch and Porphyry who spoke of some negative examples, in contrast to Plato, whose demons were always good. See also Wiebe, "Demons," 240.

478. *CoG* 9.19.

479. *CoG* 9.19: "In the demons, then, there is knowledge without charity."

480. *CoG* 9.3; 9.8. However, as Ivanovska, "Demonology of Saint Augustine," 363, notes, Apuleius did actually speak of demon virtues in other parts of his writings.

481. *CoG* 9.1: "They [the Platonists] believe also that, because no god has dealings with mankind, these same demons are appointed as mediators between men and the gods, to carry our prayers to them and to bring their answers back."

482. *CoG* 9.18. See Wiebe, "Demons," 243–44.

483. *CoG* 9:23:

> On the other hand, those beings who do occupy an intermediate position, having immortality in common with those above, and misery in common with those below, and deserving their misery because of their malice: these cannot confer upon us a blessedness which they do not have themselves, but can only envy us for it. The friends of the demons, then, do not bring forward any worthy reason why we should worship the demons as our helpers rather than shunning them as deceivers Alternatively, if anyone says that the demons can have contact and dealings with men without thereby becoming contaminated, then clearly the demons must be better than the gods; for if the gods were to mingle with men, they would be contaminated. For it is said to be a special virtue of the gods that they are set apart on high, where contact with human beings cannot contaminate them.

484. *CoG* 8.20: "What a wonderful thing the holiness of a god is, then . . . if he has no dealings with a man seeking forgiveness, yet allies himself to the demon who persuaded him to commit wickedness."

485. *CoG* 9.3.

486. *CoG* 9.15. "It was, therefore, fitting for the Mediator between us and God to have both transient mortality and everlasting blessedness, so that, in His transient condition, He might resemble those destined to die, and might translate them from their mortality into His everlasting condition."

487. *CoG* 9.15.

488. *CoG* 9.17.

489. Wiebe, "Demons," 244; Ivanovska, "Demonology of Saint Augustine," 187.

490. Ivanovska, "Demonology of Saint Augustine," 358n778.

491. Wiebe, "Demons," 111.

492. Ivanovska, "Demonology of Saint Augustine," 194–95; *CoG* 8.22: "Rather, they are spirits whose sole desire is to harm us: who are entirely alien to justice, swollen with pride, livid with envy, and subtle in deceit. They do indeed dwell in the air; but they do so only because they were cast out from the sublimity of the higher heaven, and justly condemned for their irreparable transgression to dwell in this region as in a prison appropriate to them." See also Augustine, *Gen. litt.* III.10.15:

> But if those transgressors wore celestial bodies before they transgressed, it is also hardly surprising if these were turned as a punishment into something like air, so that they could now be acted upon and suffer pain from fire, that is, from the element higher up in the natural scale. In any case they were not allowed to occupy the loftier and purer regions of the air, but only these murky parts, which serve as a kind of prison for them until the time of judgment.

493. Bradnick, *Evil, Spirits, and Possession*, 40.

494. Wiebe, "Demons," 8.

495. Salminen, "City of God," 115; Bradnick, *Evil, Spirits, and Possession*, 41; Ivanovska, "Demonology of Saint Augustine," 400. Note also the comment of Evans, *Augustine on Evil*, 110: "The demons are all in God's hand. The evil in the world is 'contained' already, although it is still abroad among us." On the idea of demons having delegated power, see the same author and volume, page 106.

496. Ivanovska, "Demonology of Saint Augustine," 293; Kahlos, *Debate and Dialogue*, 167; Wiebe, "Demons," 160–61; Bradnick, *Evil, Spirits and Possession*, 42.; *CoG* 2.23.

497. Ivanovska, "Demonology of Saint Augustine," 292; Brown, *Augustine of Hippo*, 240–41, makes a similar point.

498. On Augustine's opposition to Manichaestic views of evil see Burns, "Augustine on the Origin."

499. Ivanovska, "Demonology of Saint Augustine," 200, 299, 323; Wiebe, "Demons," 57.

500. Burns, "Augustine on the Origin," 20, documents the shift over time from Satanic instrumentality to spontaneous sin—noting the mature thought present in *The Literal Commentary on Genesis* and the *City of God*.

501. Babcock, "Human and the Angelic Fall," 135, states, "When Augustine turns to the becoming-evil of the will, however, there also takes place a sharp change in the cast of characters and the setting of the scene in his discussion. For one thing, the devil no longer has a role to play. However, the opening toward the evil, realized in the hidden places of the will, is to be explained, it is not by appeal to an intervention from outside." Ivanovska, "Demonology of Saint Augustine," 399, comments, "Augustine's sensitivity to the issues raised by Pelagian controversy had brought him to conclude that the diabolical temptation in the Paradise was in fact posterior to and revelatory of the prior sin of pride that must have already plagued the wills of the first human couple."

502. Ivanovska, "Demonology of Saint Augustine," 288.

503. See Burns, "Augustine on the Origin," 9; Ivanovska, "Demonology of Saint Augustine," 83, 221, 323, 331; Wiebe, "Demons," 57, 69.

504. Edwards, *Freedom of the Will*, 3.25.76. Square brackets in the original.

505. Wiebe, "Demons," 69. Ivanovska, "Demonology of Saint Augustine," 331, writes, "It remains but to conclude that Augustine can no longer make a substantial distinction between the sin of the devil and the sin of the first humans. The devil freely apostatized from God in the first act of his will, while the freely humans apostatized from God maybe in their one hundred and first act of their will. But both wills were entirely free, uncaused, and beyond all explanation."

506. See Wiebe, "Demons," 187, 210.

507. Brown, *Augustine of Hippo*, 310: "With Augustine . . . the nexus between men and demons was purely psychological. Like was drawn to like. Men got the demons they deserved." See also Wiebe, "Demons," 257. See also *On Christian Doctrine* 2.92: "For those spirits which are bent upon deceiving, take care to provide for each person the same sort of omens as they see his own conjectures and preconceptions have already entangled him in."

508. Augustine, *Confessions*, 10.42.67.

509. *CoG* 14.15: "Rather, he was divided against himself, and now, instead of enjoying the freedom for which he so longed, he lived in harsh and miserable bondage to the devil: a bondage to which he consented when he sinned."

510. See Hanson, *Rethinking Augustine's Early Theology*, 167–97, on the fall and human sinfulness.

511. See Klein, *Augustine's Theology of Angels*, 178; Graf, "Augustine and Magic," 102. Ivanovska, "Demonology of Saint Augustine," 372, notes that the varied forms of magic were all grouped together in his thinking.

512. *CoG* 21.6. See also Dufault, "Augustine and the Invention of Magical Dissent," 11; Wiebe, "Demons," 197.

513. Otto and Stausberg, "Augustine of Hippo," 34; Ivanovska, "Demonology of Saint Augustine," 346–47.

514. Wiebe, "Demons," 193; Klein, *Augustine's Theology of Angels*, 64.

515. Graf, "Augustine and Magic," 102.

516. *CoG* 10.10; 18.18; Ivanovska, "Demonology of Saint Augustine," 343n742; Wiebe, "Demons," 150.

517. *CoG* 18:54; Ivanovska, "Demonology of Saint Augustine," 396, believes that in *De Doctrina Christiana* Augustine sets out this understanding clearly. See also Wiebe, "Demons," iv and 7; Klein, *Augustine's Theology of Angels*, 184.

518. *CoG* 2.5–6.

519. Augustine, *Demonic Divination* (written circa 406–410) was written, in large part, to explain the mechanics of such divination. See Zarotiadis, "Religious Conflict."

520. On Augustine's acceptance of the reality of demonic foretelling see *On Christian Doctrine* 2.87 and *Demonic Divination (De divinatione daemonum)* in *On Christian Belief*.

521. Augustine, *Demonic Divination* 1.2 and Ivanovska, "Demonology of Saint Augustine," 288–89.

522. See Fiedrowicz's introductory notes to *Demonic Divination* in *On Christian Belief*, 202; Wiebe, "Demons," 118; Ivanovska, "Demonology of Saint Augustine," 284–85.

523. Augustine, *Demonic Divination* 3.7. See also Otto and Stausberg "Augustine of Hippo," 33 on acute senses.

524. Augustine, *Demonic Divination* 3.7. See also Klein, *Augustine's Theology of Angels*, 71, and Augustine, *On the Trinity* 4.17.22—23.

525. Wiebe, "Demons," 165.

526. Augustine, *Demonic Divination* 6.10.

527. Dupont, "Relation," 99.

528. I do not focus on the others (e.g., Orpheus, Pythagoras), simply because less attention is given to these figures in Augustine's writing.

529. I adopt the *unilinear* term here from Idel, "Prisca Theologia in Marsilio Ficino," 137.

530. The possible exclusion to this is one of the Sibyls—as I note in section 3.4.

531. *CoG* 18.37.

532. *CoG* 18.39. Salaman, "Echoes of Egypt," 116, believes Augustine to have thought there were two Hermes. The younger was the grandson of the contemporary of Moses. While the older authored the texts, the younger translated them.

533. See Augustine, *Augustine on Romans*. See also Bolt et al., "Legacy of Paul's Epistle," 465: "referring to Romans 1:3b, Augustine qualifies the scope and implications of his 'Empire theology' when he observes that Paul's crucial addition of the phrase, 'in the Holy Scriptures' (Rom 1:3b), was intended 'to show that the writings of the Gentiles, so very full of superstitious idolatry, ought not be considered holy just because they say something about Christ.'"

534. *CoG* 18.41.

535. *CoG* 18.41.

536. See Hooker, "Use of Sibyls," 358.

537. It is generally recognized that Plato was not read first hand by Augustine. Strand suggests in "The Gods of The Nations," 61, that it is Plotinus's *Enneads*, rather than Plato's works which influenced Augustine and mediated Plato to him. Howlett, *Marsilio Ficino and His World*, 36, also notes the mediating works of Plotinus and Porphyry for Augustine's knowledge of Plato.

538. In *On Christian Doctrine* 2.108, Augustine outlines (favorably) Ambrose's position that Jeremiah was a contemporary of Plato, and that the latter became acquainted with the writings of Jeremiah on a visit to Egypt. He retracted this view in *Retractions* 30.2. On the dependency on Ambrose, see Pelikan, *Emergence of the Catholic Tradition*, 33.

539. Specifically, the argument is that Plato was born around 100 years after Jeremiah's prophecies, together with the non-availability of Scriptures in Greek at the time of Jeremiah's death.

540. Haines, *Natural Theology*.

541. O'Daly *Augustine's City of God*, 137.

542. Van Oort writes of the Manichean veneration of Hermes as a prophet who foretold the coming of Christ. See his article "Augustine and Hermes Trismegistus." He also believes Augustine would have been well aware of Hermes's teaching during his Manichean wilderness years.

543. Augustine, *Contra Faustus* 13.15.

544. Hooker, "Use of Sibyls," 357. Van Oort, "Augustine and Hermes Trismegistus," argues similarly, as does Hadas, "Christians, Sibyls and Eclogue 4," 117.

545. Fowden, *Egyptian Hermes*, 210, notes that, for Augustine, Hermes was "a perilously ambiguous figure," and documents his motivation to highlight these errors, as compared to Lactantius. It should also be noted here that Hermes may have been particularly confusing to understand because of an unintentional translation/language mistake Augustine made regarding both his praising and criticizing of god-making. See Hanegraaff, "Hermetism," 1135–39. Orpheus is mentioned in *CoG* 18:14 and not endorsed because he was "not able to abstain from disgraceful fables concerning the gods."

546. Augustine, *Contra Faustus* 13.15: "For while they [poets, theologians, sages, philosophers, including Hermes] spoke, because they could not help it."

547. *CoG* 8.26.

548. *CoG* 8.24.

549. *CoG* 8.26. Note also the equating of such spirits with the demons on earth at the time of Christ in *CoG* 8.23.

550. This idea of compulsion among demons is found elsewhere. In Augustine, *Harmony of the Gospels* 20.28, Augustine writes, "For I stop not to state that those things which we can read in their books repeat a testimony on behalf of our religion, that is, the Christian religion, which they might have heard from the holy angels and from our prophets themselves; just as the very devils were compelled to confess Christ when He was present in the flesh." Ivanovska, "Demonology of Saint Augustine," 258, speaks of the inability of the demons to conceal truth in Augustine's thought. She goes on to note, however, that, lacking charity, the demons are in no better position for their acknowledgement of truth, 268n607.

551. Hooker, "Use of Sibyls," 355.

552. *CoG* 8.23.

553. *CoG* 8.24: "Consider if it is not by divine power on the one hand that he is compelled to reveal the past error of his forefathers, and by diabolic power on the other that he is led to mourn the future punishment of the demons."

554. *CoG* 8.23.

555. Augustine, *On the Trinity*, 4,17.23.

556. Hadas, "Christians Sibyls and Eclogue 4," 55.

557. Hadas, "Christians Sibyls and Eclogue 4," 57. Walker, *Ancient Theology*, 1, dates the Sibylline prophecies (along with the *Hermetica* and other supposedly ancient texts) to the first four centuries AD.

558. This occurred with the destruction of the temple of Jupiter.

559. Further background information is available in Hanson, "Christian Attitude," 944.

560. Hadas, "Christians Sibyls and Eclogue 4," 117n339.

561. *CoG* 18.23.

562. See also Augustine, *De Doctrina Christiana* 2.146, where Lactantius is named, favorably, among others who have engaged in the Christian plundering of pagan material. See Roberts and Donaldson, *Divine Institutes*, book 1 of *Lactantius*, 16. Garnsey, "Augustine and Lactantius," 160, comments, "Lactantius was the first to read the words of the Sibyl in Virgil's fourth Eclogue as foretelling the coming of Christ and the Salvation of the Golden Age that he would bring. Lactantius's positive appraisal of the Sibyl appears to have been unique among Christian apologists of the second and third centuries." See also *CoG* 18:23, and Pelikan, *Emergence of the Catholic Tradition*, 65.

563. In *Against Faustus* 8.15, the Sibyls are linked with Hermes as being of value in refuting Pagan error, but no more. In Augustine's commentary on Romans 1:2, the Sibyl is considered a prophet that did not come from God, though there is a favorable allusion to it in Vergil's eclogue, in Augustine, *Augustine on Romans: Propositions from the Epistle to the Romans and Unfinished Commentary on the Epistles to the Romans*. In *Letter 258*, Augustine states that he believes Virgil to have copied some true comments from the Cumaean Sibyl, expressing the opinion that the Sibyl had been compelled to speak this truth from what she had heard. Hooker, "Use of Sibyls," 357, 363, notes the dating of the Roman Commentary and the letter as being roughly contemporaneous—i.e., around 395 AD.

564. Hooker, "Use of Sibyls," 394.

565. *CoG* 18.23.

566. In *CoG* 10.28, Augustine speaks of Virgil (not by name) stating that he spoke truth about Christ, though not realizing it, and seems to support dependency on the Cumaean Sibyl.

567. Hadas, "Christians Sibyls and Eclogue 4," 119.

568. Hooker, "Use of Sibyls," 347.

569. *CoG* 18.46 and 18.47. Hooker, "Use of Sibyls," 369, notes that these suspicions did not surround Hermes and Orpheus.

570. *CoG* 18.47.

571. Hadas, "Christians Sibyls and Eclogue 4," 119–20.

572. Garnsey, "Augustine and Lactantius," 180n10 is inclined to see the influence of Lactantius behind Augustine's understanding of this Sibyl.

573. The importance of the Apostle Paul in Augustine's thinking is noted by Norris, "Theological Structure," 34. On page 162, he also writes of the general appeal to Paul to clarify meaning in the tractates, alongside appeals to the Psalms.

574. Gioia, *Theological Epistemology*, 196, notes, "generations of generations of scholars have tried to systematize [his thought] in vain."

575. Nash believes there to be three theories, to which he adds his own fourth: see "Illumination Divine," 438–40 and *The Light of the Mind*. I summarize these very briefly in what follows. The first is the active intellect theory (God giving the ability to know); the second is the view that enlightenment refers to the impression of the forms in the mind; the third is the formal theory, in which light enables judgment of certitude. The fourth interpretation (Nash's own) is a modified ontological view. Nash argues that Augustine rejects the idea that the forms can be known through teaching, the senses, or Platonic remembrance, and he argues for a kind of innatism. He writes, "Every human knows the forms because God endows him or her with this knowledge and continually sustains the intellect in the knowing process," 91. Nash understands the human mind to be both passive (receiving the forms as a stamp) and active in relating the things sensed to the forms. He believes that Augustine argued that the forms are present in three places: in the mind of God; in created particulars (of the forms), and finally in the human mind. Nash, *Light of the Mind*, 109, comments, "The forms or eternal ideas in the human mind are a priori, virtual preconditions of knowledge."

576. See Schumacher, *Divine Illumination*, 7–8, for a summary.

577. Some scholars, e.g., Norris, "Theological Structure," 97, and Fitzgerald, "Introduction," 23, have suggested a significant Donatist polemic backdrop to the series. Dermer, "Magna Gratiae," 109, argues against taking the Arian and philosopher references present in the text too literally, believing these to refer more to attitudes than particular opponents. Non-polemic external influences have also been forwarded as significant, e.g., the ascent psalms (Dermer, "Magna Gratiae," 79); and "catechetical effectiveness," as argued by Heintz in "Immateriality and Eternity of Word," 395. Dermer "Magna Gratiae," 56, Miller, "Conceiving Knowledge," 43–44, and Cruess, "Augustine's Biblical Christology," 60, have all argued that the series is relatively free from polemically influenced external agenda. Aucoin, "Augustine and John Chrysostom," 126, believes the instruction of the faithful to be the primary concern.

578. Dermer, "Magna Gratiae," 100, calls the prologue "a theological reference

point for his interpretation of the entire Gospel of John." On the importance of the prologue in Augustine's approach to John see also Norris, "Theological Structure," 265. Cruess, "Augustine's Biblical Christology," 62, calls the human and divine in the prologue "a guiding principle for Augustine's understanding of the complexity of the Gospel narrative concerning the Incarnate Word." He also terms it "something of an internal hermeneutic," 67.

579. Schumacher, *Divine Illumination*, 59. Fitzgerald in Augustine, *Homilies on the Gospel of John*, 16, calls the prologue "a mainstay" in Augustine's experience, and also his understanding of Paul. Studer, *Grace of Christ*, 40, notes the proliferation of references to verses 1–3 and 14 in the Augustine corpus.

580. Augustine, *Homily* 1.12. See also Cruess, "Augustine's Biblical Christology," 107.

581. Augustine, *Homily* 1.11, 12. Dermer, "Magna Gratiae," 106, comments, "For Augustine, the incorrect belief that the Word is a creature jeopardizes the very possibility of moral purification, which is necessary for the ascent to understanding."

582. Augustine, *Homily* 2.8. Concerning the early reference to 1 Cor. 2:14, Dermer, "Magna Gratiae," 102, believes the initial reference to Paul "sets the agenda for the entire discourse on John 1:1–5." See also *Homily* 1.19: "He was here by his divinity; he came here by his flesh because when he came here by his divinity, he could not be seen by the stupid and the blind and the unjust."

583. Augustine, *Homily* 3.5.

584. Augustine, *Homily* 3.5.

585. Augustine, *Homily* 1.18.

586. Augustine, *Homily* 1.18.

587. Augustine, *Homily* 3.4.

588. Augustine, *Homily* 2.4.

589. Augustine, *Homily* 2.4: "Certain philosophers in this world have sought the creator through the creature—because he can indeed be found through the creature, as the apostle clearly tells us." *Homily* 2.4: "he did not say, 'Because they have not come to know God,' but because they had come to know God."

590. Augustine, *Homily* 2.4.

591. Augustine, *Homily* 2.4. In *Confessions* 7.ix 13–14, Augustine documents what he did not find in the philosophers' books. What was missing from the Platonist works was the account of the incarnation noted in John, the account of Christ's coming in the form of man (Phil 2. 6–11), the atonement and charity.

592. In contrast to those who do not see the goal.

593. Augustine, *Homily* 2.2. On the inability to remain, see Gilson, *Christian Philosophy*, 121.

594. Augustine, *Homily* 2.2. As Hardy, "Incarnation and Revelation," 207, notes, revelation is "most perfectly accomplished" in the incarnation, because, in his words, "by it the sense (material) barrier is overcome since in it the Word becomes accessible sensibly as well as spiritually to man."

595. Augustine, *Homily* 2.4. See also Cruess, "Augustine's Biblical Christology," 33, on Christ as the way and the homeland. A similar idea is present in *Teaching Christianity* 1.11.11: "Of this we would be quite incapable, unless Wisdom herself had seen fit to adapt herself even to such infirmity as ours, and had given us an example of how to

live, in no other mode than the human one, because we too are human. . . . So since she herself is our home, she also made herself for us into the way home." On Augustine's identification of Wisdom and the *Logos* here, see the concluding chapter.

596. Augustine, *Homily* 1.1.

597. Augustine, *Homily* 2.3: "Therefore, it is better to fail to see what is with the mind and even so not draw back from the cross of Christ, than to see what is with the mind and scorn the cross of Christ." Later on in the same *homily*, he writes, "Those little ones, however, who cannot understand this, by not backing away from Christ's cross and passion and resurrection, are ferried in this boat to what they do not see; those who do see arrive in the very same boat."

598. *CoG* 9.17.

599. Miller, "Conceiving Knowledge," 47.

600. Miller, "Conceiving Knowledge," 48–49.

601. Cushman, "Faith and Reason," 290, in discussing Augustine in relation to Plato and the cave dwellers, notes that as far as Augustine was concerned, there would never be a will to move away from the shadows: humans are quite happy to remain in the cave. He states, "As Augustine conceived the matter, men are in the Cave and willingly committed to Cave-knowledge. The will is the problem. The solution was the divine Visitant and the divine Emancipator. The Word made flesh, the Mediator, so moves the will that man is enabled to love the good of which he has been aware without acknowledgement, without caritas [original capitalization retained]."

602. Gioia, *Theological Epistemology*, 45 and 221. Gioia recognizes that understanding philosopher knowledge in Augustine's thought is very hard, 55.

603. Schumacher, *Divine Illumination*. See esp. 51 and 62–63.

604. Demarest, *General Revelation*, 27.

605. Nash, *Light of the Mind*, 37. Nash is more careful to limit this illumination to Platonists, and not to universalize it, something which Demarest, *General Revelation*, 29, does not do.

606. Haines, *Natural Theology*, 113, 118, 131–32.

607. Aucoin, "Augustine and John Chrysostom," 127.

608. Gioia, *Theological Epistemology*, 301.

609. Schumacher, *Divine Illumination*, 60.

610. Demarest, *General Revelation*, 27: "A general illumination from God overcomes man's depravity in relation to eternal things. Through the benefits of God's common grace, the powers of the intellect and will are partially restored." Similar comments are made on pages 28–29. Demarest acknowledges that Augustine does not use or appeal to the idea. Nash, *Light of the Mind*, 30, also appeals to common grace. See also Cavadini, *Visioning Augustine*, 250–51, for an appeal to grace to explain knowledge.

611. See Gilson, *Christian Philosophy*, 219; and Haines, *Natural Theology*, 118.

612. See Edwards, *Image, Word, and God*, 178; and Cushman, "Faith and Reason," 280. The basic argument is that if humans did not have some true knowledge (a kind of memory), they would not know there was a place to return to.

613. Augustine, *Confessions* 7.20.26. See also, Cushman, "Faith and Reason," 273.

614. See also *CoG* 8.6. A clear statement that God revealed himself to Platonists is also present in *Sermon against the Pagans*, section 29:

> Now let the same apostle tell us how we may uncover their pride. And first let us just note that some of them too had attained to a knowledge of God, and yet he still wished them to be saved through Christ. You see, they had attained to a knowledge of God, but had not attained to salvation. I mean, it's one thing to attain to a knowledge of God, another to attain to salvation, when knowledge itself reaches its fullness, when the knower clings to the one known.

See also *On The Trinity* 4.15.20: "some of them have been able to penetrate with the eye of the mind beyond the whole creature, and to touch, though it be in ever so small a part, the light of the unchangeable truth."

615. Cavadini, *Visioning Augustine*, 242. He notes this especially in relation to the *City of God*.

616. Edwards, "Books 8–10," 122.

617. Ando, "Pagan Apologetics," 194.

618. Cushman, "Faith and Reason," 276.

619. Cushman, "Faith and Reason," 279: "Great, then, are the powers of the natural reason as illuminated by the discarnate Son, the eternal Word of God."

620. Miller, "Conceiving Knowledge," 92, writes, "According to Augustine, the Logos gives light both in creation and in the healing work of salvation, and grants us proper understanding of the word, and proper vision of sin's wickedness." See also his comment on page 84: "As it is the one Logos who gives life in both creation and salvation, it is the same Logos who gives light in both creation and salvation."

621. See Austine, *Sermons*, 5 vols.

622. Augustine, *Sermon* 341.2.

623. Cruess, "Augustine's Biblical Christology," 82.

624. Augustine, *Confessions* 10.43.68. A similar point is made in *CoG* 9.15: "He is not, however, the Mediator because He is the Word; for, as the Word, supremely immortal and supremely blessed, He is far removed from miserable mortals."

625. See Augustine, *Letter* 137.2.4. Augustine writes, "I wish you to understand that the Christian doctrine does not hold that the Godhead was so blended with the human nature in which He was born of the virgin that He either relinquished or lost the administration of the universe, or transferred it to that body as a small and limited material substance."

626. Augustine, *Letter* 137.2.7: "Understand the nature of the Word of God, by whom all things were made, to be such that you cannot think of any part of the Word as passing, and, from being future, becoming past. He remains as He is, and He is everywhere in His entirety." See also Augustine, *Homily* 2.8.1: "So what then? If he came here, where was he? He was in this world (Jn 1:10). He was here and he also came here; he was here in his divinity, he came here in the flesh, because though he was here in his divinity, he could not be seen by fools and by the blind and by the wicked."

627. Brachtendorf, "Augustine on the Glory," 6, states, "In these tractates, he explicates the relationship of philosophy and Christian faith by assuming, modifying and augmenting Plato's image of ascent. According to Augustine, we do not have to rise up from a cave into the light of day as Plato imagines; rather, we have to scale a mountain from the plains. Just as Plato's cave person beholds the sun from the earth's surface."

628. Brachtendorf, "Augustine on the Glory," 6. On page 11, he writes, "the achievement of perfect understanding does not suffice to set right the will."

629. Brachtendorf, "Augustine on the Glory," 11.

630. Augustine, *Confessions* 7.20.26.

631. Augustine, *Confessions* 7.20.26.

632. LaChance, "Christian *Aeneid*," 81. See also Brachtendorf, "Augustine on the Glory," 11: "Augustine maintains that philosophical insight is incapable of resolving this dilemma of the will. Reason alone cannot make us virtuous."

633. Brachtendorf, "Augustine on the Glory," 7.

634. LaChance, "Christian *Aeneid*," 86.

635. Gilson, *Christian Philosophy*, 235.

636. LaChance, "Christian *Aeneid*," 85.

637. Norris, "Theological Structure," 263, believes it to be incarnation. Stefano, "Lordship over Weakness," 3, believes the focus to be "the kenotic character of the humility of the Word." Aucoin, "Augustine and John Chrysostom," refers to the purpose of the incarnation (on page 126) and grace (on page 130) as key governing ideas.

638. Russell, "Role of Neoplatonism," 163, argues for two key points of attack—the first the meaning of beatitude and the second the issue of mediatorship. See also Clooney, "Augustine, Apuleius, and Hermes Trismegistus," 143. See also Von Bredow, "Superbia of the Platonists," 74.

639. Cameron, "Augustine and John's Gospel," 269–70.

640. Brachtendorf, "Augustine on the Glory," 8; Wiebe, "Demons," 258.

641. Augustine, *Confessions* 7.21.27: "None of this is in the Platonist books. Those pages do not contain the face of this devotion, tears of confession, your sacrifice, a troubled spirit, a contrite and humble spirit (Ps. 50: 19), *the salvation of your people*, the espoused city (Rev. 21:5), the guarantee of your Holy Spirit (2 Cor. 5: 5), the cup of our redemption [emphasis mine]." See also Marenbon, *Pagans*, 31, on the elitist charge.

642. See, for example, *CoG* 10.32.

643. Fiedrowicz, introductory notes in *On True Religion*, 24.

644. Augustine, *Homily* 2.3–4. See *Sermon* 198.61 for a kind of expanded commentary on this point.

645. See especially Augustine, *Homily* 2.3.

646. Brachtendorf, "Augustine on the Glory," 7.

647. Augustine, *Homily* 2.3. See also *Sermon against the Pagans* 198.59, which contains pastoral comfort for the little ones.

648. See Brachtendorf, "Augustine on the Glory," 7, and Edwards, "Books 8–10," 124, on this knowledge.

649. See Brachtendorf, "Augustine on the Glory," 9, on the problem of history for Platonists.

650. In *Confessions* 7.ix.13–14, Augustine documents what he did not find in the philosophers' books. What was missing from the Platonist works was the account of the incarnation noted in John, the account of Christ's coming in the form of man (Phil 2:6–11), the atonement and charity.

651. Augustine, *On the Trinity* 4.15.20: "But what does it profit one who is proud and is, therefore, ashamed to ascend the wood to perceive from afar his native land across the sea?"

652. Augustine, *Homily* 2.4.

653. Augustine, *Tractate* 2 in *Tractates on the Gospel of John*.

654. See also Jones, "*Religio* and *Res Publica*," 111.

655. Marenbon, *Pagans*, 28–29.

656. The subject is not specified, but refers to "those who have tried to return to you." Because of the reference to pride, it is difficult not to conclude that the subjects are the Neoplatonists.

657. Jones, "*Religio* and *Res Publica*," 166, writes, "Augustine draws a dichotomy between love of God and worship of the demons, and does not admit of a third term."

658. Wilken, "Religious Pluralism," 389.

659. Marenbon, *Pagans*, 27.

660. Marenbon, *Pagans*, 30.

661. Augustine, *On True Religion* 3.2; Augustine, *Against Faustus* 13.15; Augustine, *Sermon against the Pagans*. Also to be mentioned are the Porphyry engagement texts in *City of God*, esp. 10.1 and 10.3.

662. Gioia, *Theological Epistemology*, 43–44, commenting on *The Trinity* 4.20–24, states, "After the section on demons, broadly organized around the idea of pagan worship and its inability to purify, a new section is devoted to philosophers, i.e. those who think that they can purify themselves and that they do not need any mediator at all." See also Dupont's comments on the *Sermon against the Pagans* in "The Position of Gentiles and Pagans," 182. He writes, "Pagan pride comes in two forms: (1) Philosophers trusting their own capacities, as if they do not need a mediator. Augustine however explained that nobody can be liberated without *confiteri* their own sins and without Christ the *mediator*. (2) The use of magic to attain God."

663. Wiebe, "Demons," 257.

664. Marenbon, *Pagans*, 27. On page 30, he states, "Sometimes, in The City of God, a reminiscence of Paul's words is linked to a qualification, which makes it clear that some of the philosophers, although not open opponents of polytheism, did not themselves worship more than one God." This claim seems to differ from comments of Augustine, such as *CoG* 8.12, which has the heading: "That even the Platonists, though they did well in believing that there is one true God, nonetheless held that sacred rites are to be performed for many gods."

665. Marenbon, *Pagans*, 30.

666. Marenbon, *Pagans*, 31.

667. Marenbon, *Pagans*, 32. There is no issue with this view as Augustine names Porphyry as doing this: *CoG* 10.24 specifically refers to Porphyry's rejection of Christ incarnate.

668. Marenbon, *Pagans*, 28–30.

669. Hill, in his comments on this sermon in Augustine, *Sermons*, 229, believes it to be his longest (approximately three hours)—delivered to keep his congregants in church and to keep them from engaging in new year pagan festivities.

670. Augustine, *Sermon against the Pagans*, section 36.

671. Marenbon, *Pagans*, 27, 30.

672. Augustine, *Sermon against the Pagans*, section 36. In section 32, Augustine also suggests this—though notes the requirement for humility for it to be the case:

> They should not, you see, have arrogated to themselves what he had granted them, nor have preened themselves on what they had got from him, not from themselves. This, of course, should have been credited to him, so that in order to hold on to what they had been able to see, they might be healed by the one who had enabled them to see. Because if they had done this, they would have preserved humility, and been able to be purified and so continue to cling to that most blissful contemplation. It is to such people as that, after all, that the true and truthful physician would have revealed himself, the mediator, the overthrower of pride, the exalter of humility.

673. Augustine, *Sermon against the Pagans*, section 36.

674. Augustine, *Sermon against the Pagans*, section 37: "But there are others who have seen and believed that there is a God with whom they must be reconciled, and have not relied presumptuously on their own powers, and so they have wanted to be purified by sacred rites."

675. Salzman, "Christian Sermons against Pagans," 350.

676. Augustine, *Sermon against the Pagans*, section 58.

677. Augustine, *Sermon against the Pagans*, section 36.

678. *CoG* 8.9.

679. Marenbon, *Pagans*, 29.

680. Marenbon, *Pagans*, 29. The idea of Porphyry vacillating is clearly present in *CoG* 10.9.

681. In *CoG* 10.30.

682. In *CoG* 10.23.

683. In *CoG* 10.32.

684. *CoG* 10.9 and 10.26.

685. *CoG* 10.10; 10.27: "It is not, then, from Plato, but from Chaldean masters that you have learned to elevate human failings up to the ethereal and empyrean heights of the universe, so that theurgists might be able to obtain divine revelations from your gods."

686. Note the reference to the religion of Plato in *CoG* 8.21.

687. *CoG* 10.10: the immediate context is the Athenians. Note also the link Augustine made between Athenians and Platonists in *Confessions* 7.9.15.

688. *CoG* 8.12.

689. See Augustine, *On the Trinity*, 13.19.24.

690. See Cavadini, *Visioning Augustine*, 247.

691. Plotinus receives complimentary comments in *CoG* 9.10 and *CoG* 10.2 (concerning his ideas and the Johannine Prologue). Augustine approves of his ideas about providence in 10.15. However, in 10.28, he disagrees with his view on reincarnation.

692. Indeed, at one point he makes Porphyry to be worse than Apuleius: *CoG*

10.27: "Of the impiety of Porphyry, which transcends even the error of Apuleius." On the idea of a clear division in Augustine's thinking concerning older and newer Platonism see Jones, "*Religio* and *Res Publica*," 97–98, and Clooney, "Augustine, Apuleius, and Hermes Trismegistus," 144.

693. *CoG* 10.10; 10.27.

694. Marenbon, *Pagans*, 30, terms Plato (in Augustine's view) "a strict and unhesitant believer in the one God." There are clear references to Plato's monotheism in the *City of God*—for example 8.10. The issue is whether this was consistent. Kahlos, *Debate and Dialogue*, 140, acknowledges the monotheistic doctrine, but states that it exists alongside polytheistic practices.

695. *CoG* 8.13.

696. *CoG* 9.16.

697. *CoG* 8.13.

698. He notes this four times: *CoG* 8:18; 8.20; 9.1; 9.16.

699. *CoG* 9.23.

700. *CoG* 10.1.

701. *CoG* 10.3.

702. Good angels would never seek this: *CoG* 10.16.

703. *CoG* 12.27.

704. *CoG* 12.25.

705. *CoG* 12.25.

706. *CoG* 12.25.

707. Augustine, *Sermon against the Pagans*, section 46.

708. *CoG* 7.27: (Heading) "Of the inventions of the natural philosophers, who neither worship the true Divinity nor cultivate that worship by which the true God should be served."

709. *CoG* 12.27. It should be noted here that not all follow this conclusion. Jones, "*Religio* and *Res Publica*," believes Augustine to argue that it was good angels that Plato worshipped. However, given ambiguous references to good or evil, and the previous discussion concerning the involvement of demons where pride is present, I believe this supports an overall more negative conclusion.

710. Madec, "Augustin et le Neoplatonisme," 47, cited in Jones, "*Religio*," 13.

711. See Jones, "*Religio* and *Res Publica*," 98, on the idea of the wrong religion of Plato becoming worse with his later followers in Augustine's thinking.

712. See Wiebe, "Demons," 235–36.

713. Gioia, *Theological Epistemology*, 45.

714. Varro (116–27 BC) was considered one of Rome's greatest intellectuals and writers.

715. In *CoG* 6.5–9, Augustine outlines and critiques Varro's mythical, civil and natural theology distinction. He supports the validity of the natural (see also *CoG* 8.5) and scorns both the civil and mythical. See also *CoG* 6.12.

716. *CoG* 8.10.

717. While I would agree with Haines in his book *Natural Theology*, on the existence

of a kind of natural theology in Augustine's thinking, to stop there is to stop short of the conclusions he drew concerning the consequences of this theology.

718. Jones, "*Religio* and *Res Publica*," 22: "The culpability of the Roman and Greek masses' ignorance and superstition may be difficult to establish, but Augustine is confident that the philosophers should have known better."

719. Augustine, *Confessions* 10.6.10:

> Surely this beauty should be self-evident to all who are of sound mind. Then why does it not speak to everyone in the same way? Animals both small and large see it, but they cannot put a question about it. In them reason does not sit in judgement upon the deliverances of the senses. But human beings can put a question so that "the invisible things of God are understood and seen through the things which are made" (Rom. 1: 20). Yet by love of created things they are subdued by them, and being thus made subject become incapable of exercising judgement.

720. "However good a case can be made out for the metaphysical monotheism of the philosophers, the fact remains that they were practising polytheists, and that the Neoplatonists, who could have accepted Christianity, did not," as stated by Walker, *Ancient Theology*, 7.

721. See Jones, "*Religio* and *Res Publica*," 21–22 and 120; See also Edwards, "Books 8–10," 122; Ando, "Pagan Apologetics," 195.

722. Corey, *Light from Light*, 99. See also Hanson, *Rethinking Augustine's Early Theology*, 178.

723. Cushman, "Faith and Reason," 286.

724. Westerholm, "Work of the Trinity," 11.

725. Augustine, *On the Trinity* 13.19.24.

726. Jones, "*Religio* and *Res Publica*," 104.

727. Some of the material in this chapter has been previously published in McGee, "Reconsidering the *Sensus Divinitatis*" and re-used here by permission. Some of the material in this chapter has been previously published in McGee, "John Calvin," and used in accordance with the CC-BY-4.0 licence.

728. See Kärkkäinen, "Calvin and Religions"; Du Preez, "John Calvin's Contribution to a Theologia Religionum," 69–78; Potgieter, "Calvin and Other Religions"; Preus, "Zwingli, Calvin, and the Origin of Religion"; Williams, "Erasmus and the Reformers"; Eire, "John Calvin."

729. Regarding the lack of interest claim, see Capetz, "Seed of Religion," 162; Potgieter, "Calvin and Other Religions," 150; Bonnington, "Calvin and Islam," 78; Preus, "Zwingli, Calvin, and the Origin of Religion," 187. Calvin was rather behind Bullinger and Bibliander in his interest in Islam, according to Campi, "Early Reformed Attitudes towards Islam."

730. Muller, *Unaccommodated Calvin*, 42.

731. Bouwsma, *John Calvin*, 111–27, and Breen, *John Calvin*.

732. Muller, *Unaccommodated Calvin*, 45, 57.

733. Lane, *John Calvin*.

734. Muller, *Unaccommodated Calvin*, 16: "If the *Institutes* is a theological system,

it is not a theological system that was ever intended to have a function independent of the work of exegesis. Nor was it ever intended to take the place of the commentaries as a synopsis of all theological points made by Calvin in the course of his exegesis." Pitkin, *What Pure Eyes Could See*, 7, writes, "as it was Calvin's explicit view that the commentaries and the Institutes be read together, his thought cannot be abstracted from one without consideration of the other."

735. Muller, *Post-Reformation Reformed Dogmatics*, 1:113.

736. Calvin, *Institutes* 1.2.2.

737. On the Reformed definition, see Capetz, "Seed of Religion," 97, 316. On the affective element see Capetz, "Seed of Religion," 332. On the knowledge of self, see Venema, "Twofold Knowledge of God," 159.

738. Comm. Hosea 2:4–5.

739. See Eire, *War against the Idols*, 198. On page 199, Eire states, "Commenting further on the dispute over worship that divided Christendom, Calvin asserts that it is not an insignificant struggle at all, but rather a life-and Death combat over what is most essential to the Christian life: "For it is not true that we dispute about a worthless shadow. The whole substance of the Christian religion is brought into question.""

740. Balserak, *John Calvin as Sixteenth-Century Prophet*, 82.

741. Eire, *War against the Idols*, 196: "As the corruption of man's proper relationship with God, the problem of idolatry assumes a key position in the thought of Calvin. In fact, Calvin's attack on idolatry is an attack on the corruption of all religion, it is an involved defense of the truth of the Gospel against its antithesis. The significance of this defense cannot be underestimated, since it lays bare many of the central points of Calvin's theology."

742. See, for example, his *Comm. Ps.* 9:11; *Zeph.* 1:5; *Zech.* 14:9.

743. See Calvin, *Treatise on Relics*, 281.

744. Calvin, *Comm. Hosea* 2:8:

> It is the same with the Papists of the present day; they have their Baalim; not that they regard their patrons in the place of God: but as they dread every access to God, and understand not that Christ is a mediator, they retake themselves here and there to various Baalim, that they may procure favour to themselves; and at the same time, whatever honour they show to stones, or wood, or bones of dead men, or to any of their own inventions, they call it the worship of God.

Calvin, *Institutes* 1.11.10:

> We do not call them "our gods," they [Roman Catholic Church] say. Neither did Jews nor pagans of old so speak of them, and yet the prophets did not hesitate repeatedly to accuse them of fornications with wood and stone [Jer. 2:27; Ezek. 6:4 ff.; cf. Isa. 40:19–20; Hab. 2:18–19; Deut. 32:37] only for doing the very things that are daily done by those who wish to be counted Christians, namely, that they carnally venerated God in wood and stone.

See also *Institutes* 1.12.2 for his critique of the differentiation between *latria* and *dulia*.

745. Calvin, *Institutes* 1.11.9: "All idolaters, were whether Jews or pagans, motivated just as has been said. Not content with spiritual understanding, they thought that through the images a surer and closer understanding would be impressed upon them."

746. Calvin, *Comm. Acts* 14:15:

> They [the Gentiles of Lystra] turned, indeed, the name of an idol sometimes into the name of God, but under that color they did nevertheless cherish the old errors, which they should have endeavored to redress. So the priests of France begat the single life of great Cybele. Nuns came in place of the vestal virgins. The church of All Saints succeeded Pantheon, (or the church of All Gods;) against ceremonies were set ceremonies not much unlike. At length came in the multitude of gods, who they thought would be lawful and tolerable if they had once decked [masked] them with the titles of saints. Corruptions are not by this means purged, neither are the stables, both profane and full of filth, turned into the temple of God; but the name of God is mixed with profane pollutions, and God himself is brought into a filthy stall. Wherefore, let us remember that the apostles did not only employ themselves to overthrow idolatry which had long time reigned in former ages, but did also take great heed that pure religion might reign afterward, having put all corruptions to flight.

See also Eire, *War against the Idols*, 38, and his reference to Erasmus's comments that the Virgin Mary had replaced the duties of Venus in protecting sailors over time.

747. Eire, *War against the Idols*, 13.

748. Calvin, *Comm. Ps.* 115:8.

749. Calvin, *Institutes* 1.11.8.

750. Calvin, *Comm. Mic.* 7:18.

751. Calvin, *Comm. Deut.* 12:29.

752. Calvin, *Institutes* 1.11.5.

753. Calvin, *Comm. Isa.* 41:24.

754. Calvin, *Comm. Exod.* 20:6; Calvin, *Institutes* 1.11.9.

755. Eire, *War against the Idols*, 216.

756. As argued by Eire, *War Against the Idols*, 308. See also Leith, "John Calvin's Polemic against Idolatry," 111.

757. Calvin, *Institutes* 1.11.8.

758. Calvin, *Institutes* 1.12.3.

759. Calvin, *Comm. Isa.* 19:1.

760. Calvin, *Comm. Ezek.* 8:7–11.

761. See Bouwsma, *John Calvin*, 102.

762. See my comments on this in the introductory chapter. See also *Institutes* 1.11.1.

763. See Eire, "John Calvin," 147, and Muller, *Post-Reformation Reformed Dogmatics*, 1:113. Muller, *Unaccommodated Calvin*, 24, documents research suggesting an influence of Zwingli on Calvin in developing his true and false religion distinction.

764. See Capetz, "Seed of Religion," 318.

765. Calvin, *Institutes* 1.4.3.

766. Calvin, *Institutes* 1.5.13.

767. Calvin, *Institutes* 3.14.3.

768. See Potgieter, "Calvin and Other Religions," 156. On the seeking of illicit knowledge see *Comm. Deut.* 12:29; 18:9 and 10. The idea of seeking after illicit knowledge being humankind's first sin in Calvin's thought is argued by Vorster, "Calvin on the Created Structure of Human Nature," 180. If correct, humankind's religious history is similar to the error of our first parents in Calvin's thought.

769. Capetz, "Seed of Religion," 144.

770. An example of a *superstitions* reference is in Calvin, *Comm. Ps.* 97:7. For the *false religion* label see *Comm. Deut.* 5:32; *Ps.* 19:9; *Isa.* 37:18–19.

771. Calvin, *Comm. Ps.* 32:1.

772. Wilhelm Niesel, *Theology of Calvin*, 241, summarizes Calvin's thought in the following way: "Rulers are threatened by the temptation "of supposing that they can stand in their own strength and of evading the command of God, as though there were no Judge in heaven.""

773. Calvin, *Comm. Dan.* 3:6-7: "The different kinds of gods are well known as divided into three—the Philosophical, the Political, and the Poetical."

774. Calvin, *Comm. Dan.* 3:6-7.

775. Calvin, *Comm. Deut.* 18:19; *Lev.* 23:10.

776. Calvin, *Comm. Dan.* 11:38–39.

777. Calvin, *Comm. Jer.* 2:10–11; 18:13.

778. Calvin, *Comm. Isa.* 40:19; 41:6, 7.

779. Calvin, *Institutes* 1.5.4.

780. Calvin, *Comm. Jer.* 2:10–11.

781. Calvin, *Comm. Acts* 14:12.

782. Calvin, *Comm. Mic.* 7:18; *Deut.* 32:16.

783. Calvin, *Comm. Acts* 17:25; *Ps.* 32:1.

784. Calvin, *Comm. Zeph.* 1:5.

785. Calvin, *Comm. Eph.* 2:12; *Ps.* 96:4; 115:4; *Isa.* 37:18–19.

786. Calvin, *Comm. 1 Cor.* 8:4.

787. E.g., Calvin, *Comm. Gal.* 4:8.

788. Calvin, *Comm. Hos.* 2:13.

789. Calvin, *Comm. Acts* 17:24; *Gen.* 31:19; *Isa.* 57:6; *Institutes* 1.4.1.

790. Calvin, *Institutes* 1.11.8.

791. Calvin, *Institutes* 1.11.9.

792. Calvin, *Institutes* 1.11.8.

793. Calvin, *Comm. Jer.* 16:20.

794. Sermon on Gal 4:8–11, cited in Potgieter, "Calvin and Other Religions," 156.

795. Calvin, *Comm. 1 Pet.* 1:3.

796. See Partee, *Theology of John Calvin*, 72–73.

797. Calvin, *Institutes* 1.14.16.

798. Calvin, *Institutes* 1.14.15.

799. Calvin, *Institutes* 1.14.16.

800. Calvin, *Institutes* 1.14.18.

801. Calvin, *Institutes* 1.14.17.

802. Calvin, *Institutes* 1.14.17.

803. Calvin, *Institutes* 1.14.4.

804. Calvin, *Comm. Gen.* 6:2.

805. Calvin, *Comm. Hab.* 2:19.

806. Calvin, *Comm. Isa.* 19:3; 42:8.

807. Calvin, *Comm. Deut.* 18:9. On the earlier reference to illicit knowledge, see section 1.3.

808. Calvin, *Comm. Deut.* 18:11.

809. Calvin, *Comm. Ps.* 73:25.

810. Calvin, *Comm. Exod.* 12:12.

811. Calvin, *Comm. Isa.* 19:1.

812. Calvin, *Comm. Jer.* 43:13.

813. Calvin, *Comm. Ezek.* 20:8; *Exod.* 3:18

814. Calvin, *Comm. Exod.* 5:1.

815. Calvin, *Comm. Num.* 33:4.

816. Calvin, *Comm. Jer.* 10:6; *Deut.* 32:16; *2 Cor.* 4:4.

817. Calvin, *Comm. Deut.* 32:17.

818. Calvin, *Comm. Jer.* 10:6.

819. Calvin, *Comm. Ps.* 96:5.

820. Calvin, *Comm. Mark* 1:21.

821. Calvin, *Comm. Titus* 1:12.

822. Calvin, *Comm. Titus* 1:12.

823. Eire, "John Calvin," 159

824. Eire, "John Calvin," 162.

825. Eire, "John Calvin," 150n18.

826. Rubiés, "Theology, Ethnography, and the Historicization of Idolatry," 583, comments, "By contrast with Aquinas, Calvin made all human religious impulses idolatrous as a result of the fall." See also Vandici, "Reading the Rules of Knowledge in the Story of the Fall," 183.

827. Calvin, *Institutes* 2.2.22; *Comm. 1 Cor.* 1:21. See also Van Houten, "Earthly Wisdom and Heavenly Wisdom," 230.

828. Eire, "John Calvin," 162.

829. Partee, *Theology of John Calvin*, 74, and also *Institutes* 1.14.17.

830. Calvin, *Comm. Exod.* 4:22. See also Prefatory address *Institutes* 1:17.

831. See Walker, "Prisca Theologia in France," 210–11, for the traditional view of Champier.

832. Walker, "Prisca Theologia in France," 204. See also Malusa, "Renaissance Antecedents," 4–5.

833. These being Hebrew primacy of revelation, the revelatory basis of religious knowledge, and a unilinear view of revelation dissemination.

834. For example, Giordano Bruno (1548–1600) believed Pythagorean wisdom to predate and to be a source for Christianity. See Nongbri, *Before Religion*, 89.

835. See De Jonge, "Sibyls in the Fifteenth and Sixteenth Centuries," 12.

836. See Idel, "Prisca Theologia in Marsilio Ficino," 141.

837. Malusa, "Renaissance Antecedents," 52.

838. On the relationship of Steuco to Ficino and Pico, see Schmitt, "Perennial Philosophy," 524.

839. See Malusa, "Renaissance Antecedents," 39.

840. On the use of Augustine's earlier work by Ficino see Levi, "Ficino, Augustine, and the Pagans," 103.

841. Kristeller, *Eight Philosophers*, 40, dates the translation of Plato into Latin by Ficino to before 1469. See also Nongbri, *Before Religion*, 87.

842. Nongbri, *Before Religion*, 88, dates the beginning of this project from soon after 1463—though only published in 1471.

843. See Kristeller, *Eight Philosophers*, 38, on the view that writings wrongly attributed to Hermes, Zoroaster, Orpheus, and Pythagoras were considered by Ficino to pre-date and to have influenced Plato. As Stengel, "Reformation, Renaissance, and Hermeticism," 106, notes, despite Casaubon's work (dated 1614), the *Corpus Hermeticum* continued to be considered of great historicity, preceding Moses or Greek philosophy for many years thereafter. See also Salaman, "Echoes of Egypt," 117.

844. See Howlett, *Marsilio Ficino and His World*, 54, on Ficino's attempts to find harmony among the different works he was examining. Malusa, "Renaissance Antecedents," 15, terms Ficino's focus, "the need to trace a unified, organic history of the emergence and diffusion of philosophical-theological truths among the peoples of antiquity."

845. See De Jonge, "Sibyls in the Fifteenth and Sixteenth Centuries," 11–12.

846. Edelheit, *Ficino, Pico, and Savonarola*, 208.

847. For the idea that the earlier sages were, in some senses, preparatory for Plato in Ficino's thought, see Edelheit, *Ficino, Pico, and Savonarola*, 233.

848. As Levi, "Ficino, Augustine, and the Pagans," 111, writes, Hermes was originally the first in the list, but Zoroaster went on to usurp him by 1469. Salaman, "Echoes of Egypt," 116–17, documents some vacillation in the scheme. See also Nongbri, *Before Religion*, 88, on the placement of Zoroaster in first place.

849. As Edelheit, *Ficino, Pico, and Savonarola*, 231, notes, the chain of sages, placed in historical order to support the ancient theology tradition, was a unique contribution of Ficino.

850. George Gemistos Plethon (1355–1453) was a Greek philosopher and scholar.

851. Idel, "Prisca Theologia in Marsilio Ficino," 141.

852. As noted, for example, by Screech, *Laughter at the Foot of the Cross*, 14.

853. See Van Gelder, *Two Reformations*, 56; Malusa, "Renaissance Antecedents," 16.

854. Kristeller, *Eight Philosophers*, 49–50.

855. On the idea of complementation see Edelheit, *Ficino, Pico, and Savonarola*, 205, 234n68. See also Kristeller, *Eight Philosophers*, 49, on the same point.

856. See Edelheit, *Ficino, Pico, and Savonarola*, 207.

857. See Edelheit, *Ficino, Pico, and Savonarola*, 211; Nongbri, *Before Religion*, 88.

858. Edelheit, *Ficino, Pico, and Savonarola*, 229.

859. See Nongbri, *Before Religion*, 88; Kristeller, *Eight Philosophers*, 49.

860. Edelheit, *Ficino, Pico, and Savonarola*, 209.

861. Edelheit *Ficino, Pico, and Savonarola*, 223: "Even the pagan religious innovators enjoyed some divine inspiration; so much more so Moses and the Hebrew prophets, who were exposed to a proper—although as yet imperfect—divine revelation."

862. Howlett, *Marsilio Ficino and His World*, 48.

863. Cited in Idel, "Prisca Theologia in Marsilio Ficino," 151.

864. Kristeller, *Eight Philosophers*, 49.

865. Idel, "Prisca Theologia in Marsilio Ficino," 145.

866. Idel, "Prisca Theologia in Marsilio Ficino," 145–47.

867. Idel, "Prisca Theologia in Marsilio Ficino," 145–46.

868. Idel, "Prisca Theologia in Marsilio Ficino," 147.

869. Howlett, *Marsilio Ficino and His World*, 50.

870. See Schmitt, "Perennial Philosophy," 511–13; Malusa, "Renaissance Antecedents," 26; Kristeller, *Eight Philosophers*, 55, 59–60, for a summary of this.

871. Stengel, "Reformation, Renaissance, and Hermeticism," 106, describes the aim of these to show agreement between "all theologians and philosophical schools of thought under a unified, monotheistic understanding of God."

872. See Garin, "Gian Francesco Pico Della Mirandola," 529.

873. See Kristeller, *Eight Philosophers*, 60.

874. Sudduth, "Pico della Mirandola's Philosophy of Religion," 61–80, argues that the motivation to seek truth behind diverse systems was the Christan faith, and he believes the methodology to have been Christo-centric.

875. Sudduth, "Pico della Mirandola's Philosophy of Religion," 64.

876. See Malusa, "Renaissance Antecedents," 30–31.

877. See Schmitt, "Perennial Philosophy," 522; Malusa, "Renaissance Antecedents," 20.

878. See Williams, "Erasmus and the Reformers," 330, on the influence of Italian humanism. On the rejection view see Walker, "Prisca Theologia in France," 255; Boyle, *Christening Pagan Mysteries*, 11; Wallace, *Shapers of English Calvinism*, 280.

879. See Van Herwaarden, "Erasmus and the Non-Christian World," 73, concerning the salvation of the heathen. See also Williams, "Erasmus and the Reformers," 334 and 336 on the same subject. Pitkin, "Spiritual Gospel?," 194, noted the idea of revelation to all. On the making of connections, see Van Herwaarden, "Erasmus and the Non-Christian World," 69; Williams, "Erasmus and the Reformers," 328.

880. See Stengel, "Reformation, Renaissance, and Hermeticism," 118.

881. See Williams, "Erasmus and the Reformers," 338.

882. Williams, "Erasmus and the Reformers," 338, states, "Luther observed that among all peoples there survives, from the primordial revelation in Paradise, a vague 'light and reason' with regard to the existence of God."

883. Boyle, *Christening Pagan Mysteries*, 82.

884. Ziegler, "Natural Knowledge of God and the Trinity," 153–54.

885. See Williams, "Erasmus and the Reformers," 355, Kok, "Influence of Martin Bucer," 79.

886. Kok, "Influence of Martin Bucer," 78–79.

887. Kok, "Influence of Martin Bucer," 84.

888. Muller, "Was It Really Viral?," 512–13. Also the reference to "men of letters" with "platonic ideas in their heads" is suggestive: See Van Gelder, *Two Reformations*, 269.

889. On Lefèvre's exposure see Bedouelle, "Attacks on the Biblical Humanism of Jacques Lefèvre d'Etaples." See also Walker, "Prisca Theologia in France," 206, concerning Italian humanist influence in France. For Champier's understanding of the *prisca theologia* see Walker, "Prisca Theologia in France," 214–15. On the influence of Florentine Platonism on French humanism see Partee, "Soul in Plato," 286.

890. Calvin, *Institutes* 1.3.3.

891. See Stengel, "Reformation, Renaissance, and Hermeticism," 106, on the Cabbala; Walker, "Prisca Theologia in France," 221, 223–24, on etymological issues surrounding the *prisca theologia*, and Wallace, *Shapers of English Calvinism*, 116.

892. Walker, "Prisca Theologia in France," 248.

893. On the traditional view see Walker, "Prisca Theologia in France," 249. On the pantheistic influence, see Walker, "Prisca Theologia in France," 250. Walker states (on page 256) that Cavin did not specifically single out the Hermetic or Platonist tendencies in Servetus.

894. Calvin, *Institutes* 4.16.19.

895. Calvin, *Comm. Gen.*, "Author's Epistle Dedicatory," 1:xlix.

896. See earlier, plus Sudduth, "Pico della Mirandola's Philosophy of Religion," 64, on Pico's view, and also Van Gelder, *Two Reformations*, 20, on how philosophy could help with Christian piety. For Calvin's rejection of such an idea, see McLelland, "Calvin and Philosophy," 52.

897. For an overview of Ficino's view—noted above—see Nongbri, *Before Religion*, 89. See earlier comments in section 1.1 on Calvin.

898. See De Jonge, "Sibyls in the Fifteenth and Sixteenth Centuries," 19–20, on the idea of three channels of revelation in the Neoplatonic tradition, made with reference to Ficino and Pico: The channels are the Hebrew, Sibyls and the ancient theology sages.

899. On the more positive analysis of human anthropology in Ficino see Stengel, "Reformation, Renaissance, and Hermeticism," 108. On page 114, Stengel goes on to contrast Luther's view of the corruption of human nature (which Calvin would have shared) with the more positive view of Pico and Ficino.

ENDNOTES

900. On the peripheral positioning of the cross in the Florentine school see Stengel, "Reformation, Renaissance, and Hermeticism," 115–16.

901. See Garin, "Gian Francesco Pico Della Mirandola," 529, on the contradictions between various philosophical schools. See Malusa, "Renaissance Antecedents," 44–45, on Gianfrancesco Pico's criticism of the variety present within and disagreement among various philosophical schools.

902. Regarding certainty, see Calvin, *Institutes* 3.2.7, 15 and 16, and *Comm. Acts* 17:22. On absurdities see *Comm. 1 Cor.* 1:21.

903. Wallace, *Shapers of English Calvinism*, 116.

904. Wallace, *Shapers of English Calvinism*, 116.

905. Nuovo, "Calvin's Theology," 1. See also McLelland, "Calvin and Philosophy."

906. See Partee, "Soul in Plato," 294. See Calvin's comments in *Comm. John* 1:3 concerning the negative influence of Plato on Augustine.

907. See Partee, "Soul in Plato," 290, on Calvin's rejection of being labelled a Platonist. See also Kok, "Influence of Martin Bucer," 77; Calvin, *Institutes* 1.5.11.

908. For Calvin's open appreciation of Plato and other philosophers, see *Institutes* 1.8.1. On the turn to Plato see McLelland, "Calvin and Philosophy," 45.

909. Representatives of this position would include Nuovo, "Calvin's Theology," and Partee, "Soul in Plato," as well as Partee, *Calvin and Classical Philosophy*. Backus, "Calvin and the Greek Fathers," 276, notes Calvin's keenness on citing ancient sources, while at the same time terming him "allergic" to philosophy, rejecting attempts at synthesis or integration.

910. Calvin, *Institutes* 1.8.1; 2.2.13; 2.2.15; 2.2.16; *Comm. Gen.* 4:2; *Comm. 1 Cor.* 15:33.

911. Calvin, *Institutes* 2.2.15.

912. Calvin, *Institutes* 2.2.18.

913. Calvin, *Comm. John* 4:36: "I acknowledge, indeed, that some grains of piety were always scattered throughout the whole world, and there can be no doubt that—if we may be allowed the expression—God sowed, by the hand of philosophers and profane writers, the excellent sentiments which are to be found in their writings."

914. Calvin, *Institutes* 2.2.15n58.

915. Calvin, *Institutes* 2.2.18.

916. Note also a similar observation and emphasis by Herman Bavinck, *Reformed Dogmatics, Prolegomena*, 1:319: "All the elements and forms that are essential to religion (a concept of God, a sense of guilt, a desire for redemption, sacrifice, priesthood, temple, cult, prayer, etc.), though corrupted, nevertheless do also occur in pagan religions. *Here and there even unconscious predictions and striking expectations of a better and purer religion are voiced* [emphasis mine]."

917. E.g., Calvin, *Comm. Ps.* 104:9 and strong approval of a religious insight of Plato:

> We continue to live, so long as he sustains us by his power; but no sooner does he withdraw his life-giving spirit than we die. Even Plato knew this, who so often teaches that, properly speaking, there is but one God, and that all things subsist, or have their being only in him. Nor do I doubt,

that it was the will of God, by means of that heathen writer, to awaken all men to the knowledge, that they derive their life from another source than from themselves.

918. Calvin, *Institutes* 3.25.2: "The ancient philosophers anxiously discussed the sovereign good, and even contended among themselves over it. Yet none but Plato recognized man's highest good as union with God, and he could not even dimly sense its nature. And no wonder, for he had learned nothing of the sacred bond of that union."

919. Bouwsma, *John Calvin*, 155–56, writes:

> He [Calvin] most opposed it [philosophy] when it 'contaminated' religion; he thought philosophers peculiarly tempted to attempt "to penetrate heaven."... But he reserved his full scorn for speculative philosophy, of which Athens was his symbol as it had been for Tertullian. "There is no doubt," he asserted, "that God allowed the Athenians to fall into extreme folly so that they might demonstrate to every age that all the acuteness of the human mind, aided by learning and teaching, is only foolishness in relation to the Kingdom of God." Philosophers were his "most potent example" of human weakness: "not one of them can be found who has not fallen away from solid knowledge into pointless and erroneous speculations. Most of them are sillier than old women."

920. Calvin, *Institutes* 3.25.2; *Comm. Acts* 17:18.

921. See Niesel, *Theology of Calvin*, 51–52.

922. Kok, "Influence of Martin Bucer," 83, states, "Calvin and Melanchthon appreciate pagan literature, but they do not grant it the status of revelation, even to an inferior degree."

923. Calvin, *Comm. Ezek.* 20:18.

924. On Calvin's aversion to speculation, see *Comm. 1 Cor.* 15:33; *1 John* 2:22–23; *Institutes* 1.4.1

925. See Van Gelder, *Two Reformations*, 268.

926. Stengel, "Reformation, Renaissance, and Hermeticism," 108.

927. Malusa, "Renaissance Antecedents," 53.

928. See Malusa, "Renaissance Antecedents," 40–41.

929. For general comments on the development of religion, see Calvin, *Institutes* 1.11.8; 1.12.3. On accountability, see the first 5 chapters of the *Institutes*, Book 1.

930. Preus, "Zwingli, Calvin, and the Origin of Religion."

931. Preus, "Zwingli, Calvin, and the Origin of Religion," 196.

932. Walker, *Ancient Theology*, 3, suggests another reason for the Reformers' rejection of the ancient theologians—their association with magic.

933. Backus, "Calvin and the Greek Fathers," 261. Larsson, *God in the Fourth Gospel*, 64, observed that Calvin translated his Latin version of the Gospel of John commentary into French in 1553.

934. For this dating, see Larsson, *God in the Fourth Gospel*, 63.

935. Larsson, *God in the Fourth Gospel*, 96.

936. Larsson, *God in the Fourth Gospel*, 66.

ENDNOTES

937. Larsson, *God in the Fourth Gospel*, 66-67.

938. Larsson, *God in the Fourth Gospel*, 69.

939. Larsson, *God in the Fourth Gospel*, 97.

940. Pitkin, "Spiritual Gospel?," 190.

941. Pitkin, "Spiritual Gospel?," 188-89; 204.

942. Pitkin, "Spiritual Gospel?," 181.

943. Pitkin, "Spiritual Gospel?," 203.

944. Calvin, *Comm. John* 1:5.

945. Calvin, *Comm. John* 1:5.

946. Calvin, *Comm. John* 1:5.

947. Calvin, *Comm. John* 1:5.

948. Calvin, *Comm. John* 1:5.

949. Calvin, *Comm. John* 1:5.

950. This is because it is *only* responsible for the cultivation of science and the liberal arts.

951. Pitkin, "Spiritual Gospel?," 192.

952. Pitkin, "Spiritual Gospel?," 194.

953. Pitkin, "Spiritual Gospel?," 194.

954. Pitkin, "Spiritual Gospel?," 194.

955. St. John Chrysostom: *Commentary on Saint John the Evangelist*, 81, interprets enlightening to be the gospel on verse 9 in Homily 8. On Chrysostom's status as Calvin's preferred patristic Bible commentator, see Holder, "Calvin as Commentator on the Pauline Epistles," 252.

956. See Canlis, *Calvin's Ladder*; Willis, *Calvin's Catholic Christology*; Wyatt, *Jesus Christ and Creation*; Edmondson, *Calvin's Christology*; Cumin, *Christ at the Crux*.

957. For additional references to the idea of the two-fold mediation of Christ, see Calvin, *Comm. Hos.* 12:4; *Gal.* 3:19; *Institutes* 2.13.4. See also Pitkin, *What Pure Eyes Could See*, 151; Edmondson, *Calvin's Christology*, 29-30, citing extracts from Calvin's letters (the *Stancaro* Affair).

958. Backus, "Calvin and the Greek Fathers," 274.

959. Cyril of Alexandria, *Ancient Christian Texts*. See especially pages 4, 33, 35-39, on the idea of participation.

960. Calvin, *Comm. Gen.* 2:9. See also Vorster, "Calvin on the Created Structure of Human Nature," 165. On Calvin's rejection of the soul as being of God's essence, see *Institutes* 1.15.5. See also Larsson, *God in the Fourth Gospel*, 77, on Calvin's stress on human dependence.

961. On the pre-fall participation in God idea see Calvin, *Institutes* 2.2.1. See *Institutes* 2.10.7, on Adam, Abel, Noah, Abraham and other patriarchs and their participation in God: "For theirs was a real participation in God, which cannot be without the blessing of eternal life."

962. On the Stoic *logos spermatikos*, see Horowitz, "Stoic Synthesis," 10. On Calvin's wariness of pantheism, see Capetz, "Seed of Religion," 91.

ENDNOTES

963. There are a number of references to the *seed of religion* in the *Institutes* and commentaries. Agreeing with Cicero, Calvin (*Institutes* 1.3.1) argues that the seed of religion is universal, resulting in religious practice worldwide. In *Institutes* 1.5.1, he describes how the seed enables people to come to know God; this seed is coupled with daily revelations of God through creation. In *Institutes* 1.14.1, he states how the seed does not ripen or produce fruit. In *Institutes* 1.15.6, when discussing the soul, he writes how the idea of shame and honor remains among humankind, despite the presence of vices. The expression "seed of religion" occurs four times in the commentaries (outside John 1). On Numbers 22:5, Calvin explains that the desire for peace and pardon is due to the implanting of the seed of religion. In commenting on Isaiah 14:14, he makes a causal link between the presence of the seed of religion and "the belief of some superior being." In Isaiah 46:8, Calvin refers to Jewish corruption of the seed, and in passing to its universal corruption. On Daniel 11:38 and 39, he states that true piety or humility is the seed of religion, which leads to the acknowledgement of "some deity."

964. Horowitz, "Stoic Synthesis," 3.

965. Horowitz, "Stoic Synthesis," 16. See also Bouwsma, *Usable Past*, 25. See Horowitz, "Stoic Synthesis," 3, for the connection.

966. Eire, "John Calvin," 156. See also Preus, "Zwingli, Calvin, and the Origin of Religion," 195, on the same point.

967. Horowitz, "Stoic Synthesis," 4.

968. See Horowitz, "Stoic Synthesis," 11 and 16, on potential and page 3 on education.

969. On the role of training see Horowitz, "Stoic Synthesis," 13.

970. Calvin, *Institutes* 1.15.6.

971. See Horowitz, "Stoic Synthesis," 13, on the idea of man retaining divinity within himself in Stoic thought.

972. Williams, "John Calvin," 73.

973. Wolterstorff, "Reformed Tradition," 204.

974. Calvin, *Comm. 1 Cor.* 1:21.

975. Calvin, *Comm. 1 Cor.* 2:11.

976. See Muller, *Unaccommodated Calvin*, 199.

977. See, for example, Oliphint, *Reasons for Fait*; Oliphint, "Historical and Theological Studies"; Plantinga, *Warranted Christian Belief*; Jeffreys, "How Reformed is Reformed Epistemology?"; Jones, *Calvin and the Rhetoric of Piety*, 161.

978. In passing, it should be noted that Oliphint, *Reasons for Faith*, 36, rejects the idea that internal and external revelation can be clearly distinguished in Calvin's thought.

979. Calvin, *Institutes* 1.6.1.

980. If Calvin was influenced by Stoic thought on innateness, it may be that the innateness idea he had in mind differs somewhat from the version famously critiqued by Locke. Horowitz, "Stoic Synthesis," 8, comments: "The ancient Stoics held what we might call the moderate theory of innate ideas. They believed that the mind is born predisposed to certain ideas which are not yet consciously held. These ideas are evoked and developed through the stimulus of sense impressions and the development of reason."

981. Calvin, *Institutes* 1.3.1.

982. Calvin, *Institutes* 1.3.1.

983. Calvin, *Institutes* 1.3.1.

984. Calvin, *Institutes* 1.3.1.

985. Calvin, *Institutes* 1.3.1.

986. Calvin, *Institutes* 1.3.1.

987. Calvin, *Institutes* 1.3.3.

988. Calvin, *Institutes* 1.4.4.

989. Calvin, *Institutes* 1.3.3.

990. Calvin, *Institutes* 1.3.3.

991. Calvin, *Institutes* 1.4.2.

992. Calvin, *Institutes* 1.4.1.

993. Calvin, *Institutes* 1.5.12.

994. Calvin, *Comm. Acts* 17:23.

995. Calvin, *Comm. Ps.* 97:7.

996. See my summary of the discussion in McGee, "Reconsidering the Sensus Divinitatis."

997. Dowey, *Knowledge of God*, 51–52.

998. Parker, *Calvin*, 17–18; McNeill in Calvin, *Institutes*, 1.3.1n2; Bavinck, *Prolegomena*, 278; Jones, *Calvin and the Rhetoric of Piety*, 388; Hoitenga, "Faith and Reason in Calvin's Doctrine," 26; Eire, "John Calvin," 149; Potgieter, "Calvin and Other Religions," 153.

999. See Calvin, *Institutes* 1.3.1; 1.4.1.

1000. Capetz, "Seed of Religion," 329.

1001. Woolford, "Natural Theology," 89.

1002. Gootjes, "Sense of Divinity," 342.

1003. Gootjes, "Sense of Divinity," 342.

1004. Preus, "Zwingli, Calvin, and the Origin of Religion," 197n47.

1005. Calvin seems to support this distinction in *Institutes* 1.12.3 and in *Comm. Zech.* 14:9; *Dan.* 2:11; 4:9; 6:20; *Ps.* 115:8; *Isa.* 45:18.

1006. It should be noted that the *seed* reference in Acts 17:28 is not termed the *seed of religion*. However, I interpret this to be Calvin's meaning here, in part because the description agrees with the comments on the *seed of religion* in the prologue of John's Gospel.

1007. Calvin, *Comm. Acts.* 17:28.

1008. Calvin, *Comm. Jer.* 10:7.

1009. Calvin, *Institutes* 1.11.9: "In these images, nevertheless, the Jews were convinced that they were worshiping the eternal God, the one true Lord of heaven and earth; the pagans, that they were worshiping their gods whom, though false, they imagined as dwelling in heaven."

1010. Bavinck, "Religious Consciousness and Christian Faith," 288, makes a comment concerning Tertullian, which I suggest is similar to Calvin's thinking on this point. He states, "I have the impression that Tertullian puts his finger on one of the most remarkable phenomena in religious studies when he points out that pagans, in their rare moments of existential fear, forget all their own gods and scuttle their cheap myths as they call out to God. In this respect, Tertullian seems to me to be one of the most modern of all the early church fathers."

1011. Calvin, *Institutes* 2.6.4.

1012. Note also Calvin, *Institutes* 1.12.1: "Here we must more carefully attend to those subtleties with which superstition disports itself. Indeed, it does not so decline to other gods as seemingly to desert the highest God, or to reduce him to the level of the rest. But while it concedes to him the supreme place, it surrounds him with a throng of lesser gods, among whom it parcels out his functions." See also *Institutes* 1.12.2 on the non-exclusive nature of the worship of the true God: "For it is obvious that the honor the papists give to the saints really does not differ from the honoring of God. Indeed, they worship both God and the saints indiscriminately, except that, when they are pressed, they wriggle out with the excuse that they keep unimpaired for God what is due him because they leave latria to him."

1013. Calvin, *Comm. Deut.* 4:35.

1014. For example, as argued by Jones, *Calvin and the Rhetoric of Piety*, 163.

1015. See, e.g., Calvin, *Comm. Isa.* 10:11.

1016. Capetz, "Seed of Religion," 68.

1017. Calvin, *Comm. John* 1:5.

1018. See Lee, "Spark That Still Shines," 636. Dowey, *Knowledge of God*, 58, refers to conscience as "the ability to know and actual knowledge, as well as the ability to judge and a criterion of judgment."

1019. See, Calvin, *Institutes* 1.15.8; 2.2.22.

1020. The standard to which conscience refers is variously termed: "the light of reason" (*Institutes* 1.15.8), "law righteousness" (*Institutes* 2.2.22), "natural law" (*Institutes* 2.2.23), and "natural light of righteousness" (*Comm. Rom.* 2:14).

1021. Calvin, *Institutes* 3.19.16: "Therefore, as works have regard to men, so conscience refers to God."

1022. See, e.g., Calvin, *Comm. Rom.* 2:3.

1023. See Calvin, *Comm. Gen.* 4:7: "The declarations even of heathens testify that they were not ignorant of this truth; for it is not to be doubted that, when they say 'Conscience is like a thousand witnesses,' they compare it to a most cruel executioner."

1024. See Calvin, *Institutes* 4.20.16; 2.8.1; 2.2.24; 2.2.13; *Comm. Rom.* 2:15.

1025. See esp. Calvin, *Comm. Rom.* 2:15

1026. Calvin, *Institutes* 4.20.9.

1027. Calvin, *Comm. Matt.* 12:8. See also *Institutes* 2.7.2; 2.7.8, *Comm. Ps.* 19:8; *Rom.* 4:15. For comment see Moon, "Lex Dei Regula," 106; Horton, "Calvin and the Law-Gospel Hermeneutic," 31.

1028. On natural law in the reformed tradition, Muller, *Post-Reformation Reformed Dogmatics*, 1:191, comments, "this form of natural theology carries with it only the elenctical or condemnatory function of the Law, not the full usus paedagogicus."

Moon, "Lex Dei Regula," 255, states, "We should bear in mind that when Calvin deals with the threefold use of the law, he refers to the whole law (lex tota) which is spiritual and clothed with the grace of God by Christ's mediation of the law." See also Hesselink, "Law and Gospel or Gospel and Law?," 74.

1029. See Calvin, *Institutes* 2.8.7. Hesselink, "Christ, the Law, and the Christian," 189, comments, "For Calvin there is no inconsistency in referring sometimes to the law and other times to Christ as the norm or rule of godly living and as the expression of the will of God."

1030. Calvin, *Institutes*, 2.9.4; 2.10.2. See also Hesselink, *Calvin's Concept of the Law*, 52; Partee, *Theology of John Calvin*, 142.

1031. See Moon, "Lex Dei Regula," 221; Partee, *Theology of John Calvin*, 142.

1032. Hesselink, "Law and Gospel or Gospel and Law?," 71.

1033. See Calvin, *Institutes* 2.8.7; Moon, "Lex Dei Regula," 9.

1034. Calvin, *Institutes* 2.7.12. Moon, "Lex Dei Regula," 12, comments, "Calvin gives no full definition of the law, though he mentions it in two ways, directly yet epistemologically that the law is the expression of God's will, and indirectly yet ontologically that Christ is the truth, substance, soul, and end of the law."

1035. Calvin, *Comm. John* 1:5: "It ought to be understood that the Evangelist speaks of natural gifts only and does not as yet say anything about the grace of regeneration." See also *Comm. John* 1:9: "Those persons, therefore, reason absurdly and inconclusively, who refer this light, which the Evangelist mentions, to the gospel and the doctrine of salvation."

1036. See Backus, "Calvin's Concept," 8–10. See also Leithart, "Stoic Elements in Calvin's Doctrine of the Christian life," 43; Leithart, "That Eminent Pagan," 9. An additional key comment on natural law in Calvin's thought is found in *Comm. Rom.* 2:14.

1037. See McNeill, "Natural Law in the Teaching of the Reformers," 180. On Stoic thought, see Horowitz, "Stoic Synthesis," 5.

1038. See Horowitz, "Stoic Synthesis," 16.

1039. See Backus, "Calvin's Concept," 13, 25.

1040. See, e.g., Pelkonen, "Teaching of John Calvin on the Nature and Function of the Conscience," 77, 84; Thomas, "Place of Natural Theology in the Thought of John Calvin," 127; Van der Kooi, *As in a Mirror*, 40; Lee, "Spark That Still Shines," 616.

1041. On the functioning conscience in Calvin, see *Institutes* 1.3.3; 2.8.1; 1.15.2; 2.2.22; *Comm. Gen.* 4:7, 9; *Rom.* 3:21; *Isa.* 57:20.

1042. While Gibson connects both the *sensus divinitatis* and the *semen religionis* to conscience, I believe that a stronger case can be made that it is the former which fits better in this context. See Gibson, "Development of the *Sensus Divinitatis*," 94.

1043. Calvin, *Comm. Mic.* 7:18. See also *Comm. Acts* 17:25; *Ps.* 32:1.

1044. Calvin, *Comm. Dan.* 2:11; *Jer.* 10:7; *Jon.* 1:5; *Isa.* 10:11; 45:18; *Institutes* 1.12.3.

1045. Eire, "John Calvin," 149.

1046. Eire, "John Calvin," 150.

1047. Preus, "Zwingli, Calvin, and the Origin of Religion," 197.

1048. Nuovo, "Calvin's Theology," 61.

ENDNOTES

1049. Concerning sin, note the comment of Pitkin, "Erasmus, Calvin, and the Faces of Stoicism," 152: "Calvin's anthropology differed from Erasmus's in his deeper sense of the noetic and volitional effects of human sinfulness." See also *Comm. John* 4:36.

1050. Eire, "John Calvin," 157.

1051. Kraemer, *Religion and the Christian Faith*, 194.

1052. As Partee, *Calvin and Classical Philosophy*, 46, noted, "Calvin does not discuss the philosophers in terms of the two-nature Christological doctrine." Calvin did, however, speak of some benefits to society from Plato: see *Comm. Ps.* 109: 4.

1053. See Niesel, *Theology of Calvin*, 51.

1054. Some of the material in this chapter has been previously published in McGee, "Revelation and Religions," and reproduced here by the kind permission of the editor of *Themelios*.

1055. Kimnach et al., "Editors' Introduction," ix.

1056. See Nichols, "Absolute Sort of Certainty," 14–15, for the classification and examples of scholars who have considered Edwards from different presuppositions and perspectives. Nichols uses the fourth of these, *apologetic*, as a lens for his own work.

1057. *Works of Jonathan Edwards Online* (hereafter *WJE*), 1, 157. See also *WJE* 1, 131. See also Minkema, "If Thou Reckon Right," 406.

1058. On this reading of Crisp and Strobel, *Jonathan Edwards*, 5, write, "he was attempting to reconfigure classical theology in light of early Enlightenment thought." See also Elwood, *Philosophical Theology*, 6: "his [Edwards's] great overarching concern was to reconstruct the framework of historic Calvinism along Neoplatonic lines."

1059. See Schweitzer, "Rage against the Machine," 64; *WJE* 21, 1.

1060. *WJE* 9, 391.

1061. *WJE* 2, 64. Ramsey discusses the relative scarcity of quotations and considers possible reasons for this.

1062. See *WJE* 26, 53, on the use of Augustine. Thuesen comments, "Among patristic sources, Augustine—the most 'Calvinistic' of the Fathers—fares somewhat better in Edwards' corpus, though actual mentions of him are rare . . . in Original Sin, Edwards attacked latter-day 'Pelagians' for their belief in the self-determining power of the will, but he did not enlist Augustine directly in his polemic."

1063. See, e.g., Crisp and Strobel, *Jonathan Edwards*, 155.

1064. In *WJE* 8, 742, Ramsey comments, "In theology Edwards was demonstrably dependent upon the writings of Francis Turretin (1623–87) and Peter van Mastricht (1630–1706), two of the greatest seventeenth-century theologians in the Reformed tradition." Interestingly, Edwards did not follow Turretin when it came to the latter's argument for the importance of general revelation over against the *prisca theologia* tradition (see chapter 6, section 3.2. for Turretin's repudiation of the tradition).

1065. *WJE* 8, 742.

1066. Marsden, *Jonathan Edwards*, 73.

1067. Marsden, *Jonathan Edwards*, 17.

1068. Thuesen, "Edwards' Intellectual Background," 22.

1069. Noll, *America's God*, 23.

1070. Concerning the influence of Henry More in areas of science, see Marsden, *Jonathan Edwards*, 72.

1071. Smith, "Jonathan Edwards as Philosophical Theologian," 316.

1072. Zakai, "Theological Origins of Jonathan Edwards's Philosophy of Nature," 719. These would include Boyle.

1073. For Locke's influence on Edwards, see Helm, *Human Nature*, 222. Helm comments:

> Edwards did not offer a blanket endorsement of Locke's philosophy, however. While appropriating significant elements of it, there are equally features that Edwards was silent on. For example, Locke is known as a skeptic over innate ideas. His Essay commences with an attack on them. But Edwards is silent on this matter, and what he elsewhere writes about mankind's creation in the image of God or about conscience, for example, strongly suggests that he retained innateness in some form.

1074. Crisp and Strobel, *Jonathan Edwards*, 22.

1075. Morris, *Young Jonathan Edwards*, 219–20.

1076. See Elwood, *Philosophical Theology*, 6.

1077. Sholl, "Excellency of Minds," 34: "Edwards's published and unpublished works are polemical, apologetic, and speculative, but never methodologically systematic."

1078. See, e.g., Bombaro, "Beautiful Beings," 22; Bombaro, "Dispositional Peculiarity," 123; Waddington, "Unified Operations," 49; McDermott, "Jonathan Edwards, John Henry Newman, and Non-Christian Religions," 130.

1079. Crisp and Strobel, *Jonathan Edwards*, 94: "He was no Reimarus, teaching in public doctrines that he secretly despised or rejected."

1080. For example, Holmes, *God of Grace and God of Glory*, 35. Similar reservations are expressed by Strange, "Secret Diaries of Jonathan Edwards," 42.

1081. Chamberlain in *WJE* 18, 8–9.

1082. Marsden specifically includes the miscellanies when referring to the materials which would have made up Edwards's magnum opus. See Marsden, *Jonathan Edwards*, 472.

1083. As Chamberlain notes in *WJE* 18, 9–10.

1084. Waddington, "Unified Operations," 49.

1085. *WJE* 1, 133.

1086. *WJE* 1, 133.

1087. *WJE* 2, 102–3.

1088. *WJE* 2, 95.

1089. *WJE* 21, 171–72.

1090. Nichols, "Absolute Sort of Certainty," 89.

1091. Erdt, "Calvinist Psychology of the Heart," 167.

1092. *WJE* 2, 101.

1093. Discussed in more detail in sections 6.2 and 6.3.

1094. See McDermott, *Jonathan Edwards Confronts*, 65; Schweitzer, "Rage against the Machine," 73; Ricketts, "Primacy of Revelation," 288.

1095. *WJE* 2, 207; *WJE* 21, 192; Sholl, "Excellency of Minds," 121; Strobel, *Jonathan Edwards's Theology*, 163.

1096. *WJE* 18, 459.

1097. Holifield, *Theology in America*, 103, writes, "A 'speculative knowledge' was of 'infinite importance' for without it there could be no 'practical knowledge.'"

1098. *WJE* 17, 409.

1099. *WJE* 2, 272.

1100. Elwood, "Philosophical Theology," 134.

1101. Ricketts, "Primacy of Revelation," 212.

1102. Sholl, "Excellency of Minds," 122.

1103. Sholl, "Excellency of Minds," 123.

1104. *WJE* 18, 156.

1105. *WJE* 21, 179.

1106. *WJE* 18, 155. See also Elwood, *Philosophical Theology*, 146.

1107. *WJE* 2, 316.

1108. *WJE* 2, 315–16. It should be noted that Edwards refers to Augustine (Austin) concerning the pride of philosophers here.

1109. *WJE* 31. See also *WJE* 5, 359. On the appreciation of philosopher attainments in reason in affairs of the world, Conrad Cherry believes Edwards's thought to have been similar to Calvin's. See Cherry, *Theology of Jonathan Edwards*, 60.

1110. *WJE* 25, 611.

1111. *WJE* 8, 176.

1112. *WJE* 21, 169.

1113. Ramsey in *WJE* 1, 70.

1114. For example in the writing and publication of *Freedom of the Will*.

1115. Zakai, "Age of Enlightenment," 83; McDermott, *Jonathan Edwards Confronts*, 39; Zhu, *America's Theologian beyond America*, 137.

1116. Harrison, *"Religion" and the Religions*, 62; Byrne, *Religion and the Enlightenment*, 100. See also McDermott, *Jonathan Edwards Confronts*, 19–21.

1117. Barnett, *Enlightenment and Religion*, 2.

1118. Barnett, *Enlightenment and Religion*, 17, 26.

1119. Harrison, *"Religion" and the Religions*, 164.

1120. Harrison, *"Religion" and the Religions*, 164, cites and comments on the following extract from Toland, *Christianity Not Mysterious*, 146: "'Reason', John Toland insisted, in tones redolent of the Cambridge Platonists, 'Reason is not less from God than revelation . . . tis the Candle, the Guide, the Judg he has lodg'd within every Man that cometh into this World.'"

1121. Smith, "Jonathan Edwards and 'the Way of Ideas,'" 155, states, "He [Locke] affirmed reason as 'natural revelation.'"

1122. Hudson, *English Deists*, 30.

1123. See Zakai, "Age of Enlightenment," 82; Brown, *Jonathan Edwards and the Bible*, 134.

1124. Manuel, *Eighteenth Century Confronts the Gods*, 59, writes, "What Calvin in the Institutes recognized as a glimmer of truth in the darkness of paganism became the Deist natural religion embodied in different forms and shapes."

1125. See Harrison, *"Religion" and the Religions*, 137–38.

1126. Mori, "Natural Theology and Ancient Theology," 189, 200. See also Zhu, *America's Theologian beyond America*, 128

1127. Byrne, *Natural Religion and the Nature of Religion*, 83; Brown, *Jonathan Edwards and the Bible*, 158.

1128. See Sakamoto, *Julius Caesar Scaliger*, 29; McDermott, *Jonathan Edwards Confronts*, 211.

1129. See McDermott, *Jonathan Edwards Confronts*, 12.

1130. Schweitzer, "Interpreting the Harmony," 46, writes, "Thomas Chubb has the dubious honour of being the most quoted Deist overall in Edwards' notebooks, but on the subject of natural theology, Edwards was responding to Tindal directly and to Chubb only indirectly."

1131. Schweitzer, "Interpreting the Harmony," 46, believes, "Matthew Tindal (1657–1733) was the most influential Deist thinker of Edwards' time, and Edwards was primarily responding to him on the issue of natural theology." See also Zhu, *America's Theologian beyond America*, 133, on Edwards's familiarity with Deist writers.

1132. *WJE* 19, 719.

1133. *WJE* 9, 432.

1134. Edwards stated, "But we, having always lived in the enjoyment of gospel light and being accustomed to it, are hardly sensible how dependent we are upon it, and how much we should be in the blind and dark about things that now seem plain to us, if we never had had our reason assisted by revelation," in *WJE* 17, 74. Edwards also wrote, "We hardly can have a conception how it would be, if there never had been any revelation, for we are bred up in the light of revelation from our very infancy," in *WJE* 13, 425.

1135. See Brown, *Jonathan Edwards and the Bible*, 140.

1136. *WJE* 23, 459.

1137. Edwards, "Man's Natural Blindness in the Things of Religion," 253–54.

1138. Brown, *Jonathan Edwards and the Bible*, 161.

1139. Gale, *Court of the Gentiles*, 2. Original language and punctuation maintained.

1140. *WJE* 23, 453.

1141. *WJE* 20, 245

1142. See also *WJE* 15, 418.

1143. *WJE* 13, 424.

1144. *WJE* 15, 370.

1145. *WJE* 13, 424.

1146. *WJE* 20, 222–23. See also Miscellany 970 and comments there on the Trinity.

1147. *WJE* 23, 575.

1148. *WJE* 20, 13–14. See also *WJE* 13, 136.

1149. Levitin, *Ancient Wisdom*, 150.

ENDNOTES

1150. McDermott, *Jonathan Edwards Confronts*, 189.

1151. Levitin, *Ancient Wisdom*, 152.

1152. Brown, *Jonathan Edwards and the Bible*, 159.

1153. Brown, *Jonathan Edwards and the Bible*, 159.

1154. Bombaro, "Beautiful Beings," 289; McDermott, *Jonathan Edwards Confronts*, 108; Jenson, *America's Theologian*, 129–30; Zhu, *America's Theologian beyond America*, 158.

1155. See Brown, *Jonathan Edwards and the Bible*, 159; Schmitt, "Perennial Philosophy," 524, for more details.

1156. See Schmitt, "Perennial Philosophy," 527; Levitin, *Ancient Wisdom*, 153; McDermott, *Jonathan Edwards Confronts*, 187; Sakamoto, *Julius Caesar Scaliger*, 22.

1157. McDermott, *Jonathan Edwards Confronts*, 25

1158. *WJE* 15, 369–70.

1159. This particular point has become quite contentious. Gilbert, "Nations will Worship," 60, comments, "The deists would have been overjoyed if Edwards had truly believed that the *Prisca theologia* provided enough truth to lead to salvation." On page 62, he argues it never did. Bombaro, "Beautiful Beings," 266, concurs that the Prisca theologia "was never intended to redeem." However, cases such as Job and Melchizedek seem to fit well with the argument that it was understood by Edwards to have been a redemptive tool (as noted by McDermott, "Response," 79). At what point it became too corrupt to serve such a purpose is not clear, but that it did in Edwards's thought is apparent. Sweeney recognizes the time-dependent element in his comment that "it seems to me . . . that neither the prisca theologia nor extrabiblical inspiration provide a knowledge of God sufficient for salvation-*at least not now* [emphasis mine]," in Sweeney, "Jonathan Edwards and the World Religions," 4.

1160. *WJE* 27.

1161. *WJE* 20, 310.

1162. *WJE* 23, 452.

1163. *WJE* 23, 190–91.

1164. For the agnostic claim see *WJE* 52, 443, and *WJE* 9, 179. For the idea of rapid descent see *WJE* 3, 171–73.

1165. *WJE* 43.

1166. *WJE* 15, 370.

1167. *WJE* 52.

1168. *WJE* 23, 543.

1169. For strong condemnation of the actual religious attainments of Plato, Aristotle, and Cicero see Miscellanies 977 and 979.

1170. *WJE* 31. Original language and punctuation maintained.

1171. *WJE* 23, 443. See also *WJE* 2, 316.

1172. *WJE* 23, 444.

1173. *WJE* 23, 442–43.

1174. *WJE* 23, 446. See also *WJE* 52.

1175. *WJE* 11, 193.

1176. *WJE* 11, 193.

1177. *WJE* 20, 13.

1178. *WJE* 20, 245.

1179. The others being by his word, visions and miracles. See *WJE* 19, 710.

1180. *WJE* 24, 1190.

1181. *WJE* 19, 710.

1182. *WJE* 23, 84. Original language and punctuation maintained.

1183. As an aside on this last reference, in Edwards's thinking the devil mixes truth with deceit, and could even use biblical texts in an attempt to deceive (see *WJE* 2, 144). The idea that the devil speaks truth in false religion is, however, not one which Edwards develops. The devil's wiles and deceit are a significant element of Edwards's theology of non-Christian religions, as will be discussed in section 5.2.

1184. Of what these consisted has been argued over by Gilbert, "Nations Will Worship"; McDermott, "Response"; Sweeney, "Jonathan Edwards and the World's Religions"; Jenson, *America's Theologian*, 129.

1185. *WJE* 20, 225. See also *WJE* 11, 193.

1186. Pauw in *WJE* 20, 13.

1187. Brown, *Jonathan Edwards and the Bible*, 157, believes Edwards needed to appeal to inspiration to account for doctrines not "readily connected with the transmission of Noahic or even Israelite tradition, which preceded Jesus' lifetime." While I believe this is probably sound, I am not convinced that Edwards can be described as readily embracing this idea of inspiration, as Brown goes on to argue. I believe it to be more likely that the hypothesis was polemically necessary, even desperate.

1188. Pauw notes this inconsistency in Edwards's approach to dealing with heathen insights: "What linked these persistent but not always consistent apologetic strategies was Edwards' heavy investment in refuting deist claims," in *WJE* 20, 15.

1189. For more detailed discussion on this see McGee, "Revelation and Religions."

1190. McClymond and McDermott, *Theology of Jonathan Edwards*, 274, suggest a number of reasons for this, the most important, in their opinion, being only relatively recent availability of the miscellanies. Pauw, "'Where Theologians Fear to Tread,'" 45, provides a brief overview.

1191. McClymond and McDermott, *Theology of Jonathan Edwards*, 293, note that demons occur more in public communication, whereas angels make more appearances in the miscellanies.

1192. Reaske, "Devil and Jonathan Edwards," 124.

1193. Juchno, "Beyond Salem and Secularism," 93, 83, and 80, respectively.

1194. Minkema, "If Thou Reckon Right," 402–3.

1195. Seay, "Satan and His Maleficium," 276.

1196. Minkema, "If Thou Reckon Right," 400.

1197. See Marsden, *Jonathan Edwards*, 167.

1198. *WJE* 18, 306.

ENDNOTES

1199. Jonathan Edwards, *Works of President Edwards*, 8:13–15. As noted below, native Americans were considered to be peculiarly under the reign of devils. It is possible, therefore, that the sermon points may be especially directed to the audience. However, as will be observed, Edwards also considered European and European immigrants to America to be in a comparable situation—if not worse.

1200. Juchno, "Beyond Salem and Secularism," 83.

1201. *WJE* 13, 306.

1202. *WJE* 13, 366–67:

> By means of Christ the Redeemer, God renders all Satan's incessant labors and endeavors for the overthrow of mankind, and for defeating God's design of glorifying himself in them, a means of his own confusion and vexation, and of abundantly more brightly manifesting the glory of God and advancing the happiness of the elect. He is a means of one of mankind being his judge. And so the event of his own great endeavors will prove every way [an] exceeding contradiction and mortification of his own restless, proud, malicious and revengeful spirit.

1203. Minkema, "If Thou Reckon Right," 406; McClymond and McDermott, *Theology of Jonathan Edwards*, 275.

1204. Seay, "Satan and His Maleficium," 278n22, refers to appeals made to Charles Owen and John Glas in Miscellany 1057, and to Girolami Zanchi and Francisco de Suarez in Miscellany 1261.

1205. *WJE* 5, 108.

1206. *WJE* 13, 401–2. See also *WJE* 18, 306.

1207. *WJE* 13, 304.

1208. *WJE* 13, 382–83.

1209. *WJE* 18, 70. On the casting out of Satan, and the influence of Milton, see Minkema, "If Thou Reckon Right," 404–5.

1210. Minkema, "If Thou Reckon Right," 405.

1211. *WJE* 20, 191.

1212. Seay, "Satan and His Maleficium," 280n68.

1213. Reaske, "Devil and Jonathan Edwards," 131, believes that "The element of disguise is the most frequently mentioned specific characteristic of Satan."

1214. References would include *WJE* 2, 290 and *WJE* 19, 122.

1215. *WJE* 2, 286–87.

1216. *WJE* 2, 286.

1217. *WJE* 2, 288–89.

1218. *WJE* 20, 297.

1219. *WJE* 13, 403.

1220. *WJE* 2, 86.

1221. *WJE* 19, 127: "God hath sent his Son, the Great Prophet, into the world. The devil, to ape God in this, has raised up a false prophet Mahomet, and drawn away a great part of the world to trust in him."

ENDNOTES

1222. *WJE* 13, 227.

1223. *WJE* 20, 299. I consider typology in more detail in section 5.4.1 below.

1224. *WJE* 5, 139.

1225. *WJE* 13, 186.

1226. *WJE* 9, 409–11.

1227. *WJE* 5, 176.

1228. *WJE* 5, 173–74.

1229. *WJE* 9, 463.

1230. *WJE* 9, 410, 415.

1231. See *WJE* 9, 415–16, for a brief overview of Edwards's thoughts on Mohammed and for comments on Islamic history and also *WJE* 23, 332–33.

1232. *WJE* 9, 399. He also writes of borrowing here.

1233. *WJE* 23, 326–27.

1234. *WJE* 23, 328.

1235. *WJE* 23, 328; See also *WJE* 23, 249–50.

1236. See McDermott, "Jonathan Edwards and Islam," 93.

1237. *WJE* 8, 310–11.

1238. *WJE* 9, 433–34.

1239. *WJE* 13, 424.

1240. *WJE* 23, 454: "The doctrine of St. Paul concerning the blindness into which the Gentiles fell, is so confirmed by the state of religion in Africa, America, and even China, where, to this day, no advances towards the true religion have been made, that we can no longer be at a loss to judge . . . of the insufficiency of unassisted reason to dissipate the prejudices of the heathen world, and open their eyes to religious truths." See also Zhu, *America's Theologian beyond America*, 132, on Edwards's engagement with Chinese religion.

1241. See Zakai, *Jonathan Edwards's Philosophy of History*, 263. See also *WJE* 9, 434, for a representative statement on this issue.

1242. See McDermott, *Jonathan Edwards Confronts*, 203; Marsden, *Jonathan Edwards*, 385.

1243. See, e.g., McDermott, *Jonathan Edwards Confronts*, 201, 203.

1244. McClymond and McDermott, *Theology of Jonathan Edwards*, 189.

1245. *WJE* 11, 146.

1246. I have coined this term based on the collocation "vertical typology" used by Kimnach in *WJE* 10, 229.

1247. See Knight, "Typology."

1248. One expansion was in the direction of plenitude, that is the number of redemptive types seen to be present in the Old Testament. According to Stein, "Edwards' typological hermeneutic provided a means to connect virtually any text with Christ and his work of redemption," (see *WJE* 15, 26). The second expansion was in breadth—to see types which were not strictly speaking christological or redemptive. This also pushed existing boundaries, in the sense that Christ was for some, exclusively the antitype. In Wilson's words: "In rigorous versions of typology, types referred only to Christ," in *WJE* 9, 58. For example, Edwards saw the Adam and rib reference in Genesis as a type of husband-wife relation: see *WJE* 11, 196–97. A third expansion was one of Testament blurring—to see types in the New Testament not just the Old. For example, the dove is interpreted as a type of the Holy Spirit by Edwards in *WJE* 11, 151. Accordingly, it can be said that Edwards's expansive biblical typological hermeneutic was multi-dimensional—pushing at every existing boundary.

1249. *WJE* 10, 230. See also comments of the editors in *WJE* 11, 31.

1250. See Cherry, "Symbols of Spiritual Truth," 265.

1251. Butler, "God's Visible Glory," 15, writes, "When Calvin's views are properly understood, it is clear that Edwards substantially borrowed from Calvin's theological thought on nature." See also Fabiney, "Edwards and Biblical Typology," 97, for some historical background on the use of types in the church.

1252. See Bonaventure, *Soul's Journey into God*, 75–76; Studebaker and Caldwell, *Trinitarian Theology of Jonathan Edwards*, 207.

1253. See editor comments in *WJE* 10, 223–24.

1254. *WJE* 10, 235. See also Cherry, *Theology of Jonathan Edwards*, 46.

1255. Studebaker, "Jonathan Edwards' Pneumatological Concept of Grace," 338.

1256. See *WJE* 11, 100: "The silkworm is a remarkable type of Christ. Its greatest work is weaving something for our beautiful clothing, and it dies in this work." Note also "The rising and setting of the sun is a type of the death and resurrection of Christ," in *WJE* 11, 64. Winslow, "Great And Remarkable Analogy," 130 and 221, has classified the 241 images (in 212 entries) into two categories—those which recur and those which are mentioned only once. She notes that the latter seem to be more specifically scientific in nature (e.g., crocodiles, telescopes and watches), while the former deal with more familiar objects (e.g., moon, trees, water). In terms of the specific images Edwards provided, Winslow classes the majority as doctrine of God (75), followed by spiritual formation (49) with the same number of Christology (44) and evil/temptation (44) references, and finally, the church / eschatology (29). This categorization clearly indicates the presence of redemptive types in nature in Edwards's thinking.

1257. See editor comments in *WJE* 9, 49.

1258. See editor comments in *WJE* 11, 167.

1259. *WJE* 11, 82.

1260. *WJE* 10, 230.

1261. *WJE* 10, 229.

1262. Sweeney, "Jonathan Edwards and the World's Religions," 5.

1263. Butler, "God's Visible Glory," 24; Winslow, "Great and Remarkable Analogy," 195–96; Knight, "Typology," 205; Anderson, Lowance and Watters in *WJE* 11, 164; Ramsey in *WJE* 8, 758; Schweitzer, "Interpreting the Harmony," 38; Sweeney, "Jonathan Edwards and the World's Religions," 4; Waddington, "Unified Operations," 147.

1264. In his earlier analysis McDermott, *Jonathan Edwards Confronts*, 112, comments, "God's character and humanity's future could be read in the creation, if only by those with a new sense of the heart and the Bible in their hands," and on page 117: "Obviously, if types are divine pedagogy, human beings must be able to comprehend them. If the typological system is 'a certain sort of language, as it were, in which God is wont to speak to us,' we must be able to understand that language Edwards was convinced that we are—if we possess a (regenerate) sense of the heart." On page 118, he states, "His point seems to be that a person with the sense of the heart is to use the biblical precedents and his or her own sense of what is harmonious with the work of redemption to discover and then interpret a type," and on page 122, he writes, "the Scriptures also remained the hermeneutical standard against which all the other types in nature and history were to be measured." Later, in McDermott, "Was Jonathan Edwards an Evangelical?," 238–39, he states, "Edwards believed that the creation is full of types pointing to the Trinitarian God. There is proportion or analogy between things in the world and their Creator. Ordinary unregenerate reason can discern many of these types and proceed from them to God. That is, unregenerate minds can see something from the world that can give them truth about the true God."

1265. *WJE* 11, 98: "The very wiser heathens seemed to be sensible that the divine Being, in the formation of the natural world, designed to teach us moral lessons: so Ovid, concerning the erect posture of man."

1266. See McGee, "Revelation and Religions," 620–40.

1267. In Sweeney's words: "We should remember that Edwards did not teach that types themselves provide a knowledge of God sufficient for salvation," in "Jonathan Edwards and the World Religions," 4.

1268. McDermott, *Jonathan Edwards Confronts*, 9.

1269. McDermott, *Jonathan Edwards Confronts*, 125.

1270. *WJE* 13, 391–92.

1271. McDermott, *Jonathan Edwards Confronts*, 125.

1272. McDermott, *Jonathan Edwards Confronts*, 126.

1273. McClymond and McDermott, *Theology of Jonathan Edwards*, 586, write, "Edwards used his typology to argue that God was constantly communicating truths wherever the eye could see and the ear could hear. God spoke in the history of religions to point persons of all faith traditions to the true religion, Christianity."

1274. McDermott, "What If Paul Had Been from China?," 32.

1275. McDermott, "What If Paul Had Been from China?," 29, states, "So if the types in non-Christian religions are only broken and partially distorted access to divine realities, they are similar to Old Testament types—which point to truth but sometimes obscurely." Sparks, in *One of a Kind*, challenges this understanding.

1276. As noted earlier.

1277. See McDermott, *Can Evangelicals Learn from World Religions?*, and "What If Paul Had Been from China?"

1278. Elsewhere McDermott actually argues this (with McClymond) in *The Theology of Jonathan Edwards*, 129: "Even the ghastly practice of human sacrifice, inspired by the devil, was used by God to prepare peoples for the sacrifice made by the God-man." Note that in this quotation the inspiration is from the Devil, not from God.

1279. McDermott, *Jonathan Edwards Confronts*, 145: "For him [Edwards] there was no inconsistency whatsoever between the possibility of reconciliation for the heathen (because of the *prisca theologia*, God's types in the religions, and a dispositional soteriology) and the probability that only a precious few of the heathen had ever been saved." Note that I do not discuss the dispositional soteriology point in this chapter. For recent critical treatments of that, see Bombaro, "Beautiful Beings," and "Dispositional Peculiarity," and also Waddington, "Unified Operations," together with Waddington, "Must We Believe?"

1280. *WJE* 9, 134 and 137.

1281. McDermott, "Possibility of Reconciliation," 181. See also McClymond and McDermott, *Theology of Jonathan Edwards*, 133, and 584.

1282. McDermott, "What If Paul Had Been from China?," 28.

1283. While I have come to this conclusion from the argument noted above, both Corduan and Tiessen concur with this judgment, though arriving at it by different routes. Corduan, *Tapestry of Faiths*, 42n25, rejects McDermott's argument regarding an independent planting of types in Edwards's thinking. He states, "by the time we have accumulated general revelation along with the persistence of original revelation, we do not need to resort to this further form of revelation." Tiessen, "God's Work of Grace," 185, writes, "when McDermott speaks of this [the providential work of God within religions] as indication that 'God sometimes plants within the religions types of His fuller Christian realities,' he discerns a divine intentionality in the situation which I do not think is necessitated by his own description of Edwards' concept."

1284. See chapter 6 where I discuss the idea of frames in Daniel Strange's work.

1285. On the idea of Satanic counterfeiting see *WJE* 2, 146, and 158–59.

1286. *WJE* 3, 381–82.

1287. *WJE* 46, 225.

1288. *WJE* 3, 50.

1289. *WJE* 8, 236; *WJE* 17, 333–34.

1290. "The Son endued men with understanding and Reason. The Holy Ghost endued him with a holy will and inclination with original righteousness," in *WJE* 24, 126.

1291. Nichols, "Absolute Sort of Certainty," 59.

1292. See Waddington, "Unified Operations," 78.

1293. This doubly disadvantaged status is captured well by Elwood, *Philosophical Theology*, 71: "One of the tragic consequences of man's regression to a primitive state of existence is the decline of the power of reason so that it functions inconsistently with itself and out of harmony with 'the end for which God created the world.'"

1294. *WJE* 23, 359.

1295. For example, Helm, *Human Nature*, 234: "to a large extent Edwards agrees with Locke on reason and revelation, even though their particular judgments about what is reasonable or unreasonable in religion may differ." Smith, "Jonathan Edwards and 'the Way of Ideas,'" 153, states, "A reading of Edwards' writings reveals him to be in fundamental agreement with at least two basic principles of Locke's epistemology, i.e., knowledge is concerned with ideas and is to be defined in terms of the relation between ideas, and intuition is the most certain 'degree' of knowledge."

1296. Smith, "Jonathan Edwards and 'the Way of Ideas,'" 157, goes on to write that "Edwards explicitly disagrees with Locke's view that the only way in which man can know God is by using the instrument of reason to analyze God's works." Helm, *Human Nature*, 222 also notes differences over innatism. Wainwright, *Reason and the Heart*,

52, comments, "Edwards's view ... differs from Locke's. Fully rational judgments are not only determined by one's evidence and evidential standards; they are also determined by feelings and attitudes that express theological virtues."

1297. See McDermott, *Jonathan Edwards Confronts*, 75.

1298. *WJE* 3, 116; *WJE* 25, 664.

1299. *WJE* 23, 442–45; *WJE* 20, 142.

1300. *WJE* 20, 142; *WJE* 2, 275.

1301. *WJE* 46, 232. See also Holbrook, *Ethics of Jonathan Edwards*, 63–64.

1302. *WJE* 23, 457.

1303. *WJE* 19, 713.

1304. *WJE* 20, 143.

1305. *WJE* 23, 458.

1306. Toland, *Christianity Not Mysterious*, 146.

1307. *WJE* 17, 422. Wainwright, "Jonathan Edwards and the Hiddenness of God," 108, comments:

> While natural reason at its best can discern many truths about God, it can't discern the beauty of holiness, and hence can't appreciate the great truths of Christianity. A perception of the beauty of holiness is a function of the operation of a truly benevolent heart and the hearts of most of us are *not* truly benevolent. God's hiddenness is thus more accurately described as human blindness—a blindness that is ultimately our fault.

1308. *WJE* 17, 422. See also Wainwright, *Reason and the Heart*, 28: "Reason does not have an affective dimension and is not the source of new simple ideas. The cognition of true beauty, on the other hand, has an affective dimension since it involves relish or delight. Furthermore, its object is a new simple idea. Spiritual cognition must therefore be some kind of sensation or perception."

1309. *WJE* 17, 410.

1310. In relation to these different engagements Simonson, *Jonathan Edwards*, 27, comments, "The former [intuitive knowledge] enables a person to experience the illuminating power of divine excellence; the latter [rational or speculative knowledge] confines him to the natural world of substance and logic."

1311. Cherry, *Theology of Jonathan Edwards*, 60.

1312. *WJE* 13, 470.

1313. Ricketts, "Primacy of Revelation," 288–89.

1314. McDermott, *Jonathan Edwards Confronts*, 66, suggests this foundation is Christ in Edwards's thought: "For Edwards, then, reason can show many religious truths, but they are not known properly unless they are seen in relation to Christ and his redemption."

1315. Lee, *Philosophical Theology of Jonathan Edwards*, 131.

1316. Elwood, *Philosophical Theology*, 115, states, "Edwards acknowledges, with Locke, that much of our so-called 'knowledge' is bare 'cogitation' in which we substitute external signs or arbitrary names for actual ideas." He continues on page 117: "The idea of God in our minds may be far removed from a living experience of God. Yet we may deceive ourselves into thinking that it is God that we experience directly, when in fact it is only an external sign that interposes itself between our minds and God."

1317. *WJE* 18, 455–56.

1318. *WJE* 17, 421.

1319. *WJE* 21, 157.

1320. *WJE* 17, 421.

1321. *WJE* 23, 453.

1322. *WJE* 23, 457.

1323. *WJE* 13, 423. See also *WJE* 9, 278; *WJE* 20, 293.

1324. *WJE* 52.

1325. Gerstner, *Rational Biblical Theology*, 1:101, classifies the rational limitations as follows: "*First*, it cannot make the knowledge of God 'real' to unregenerate man. *Second*, it cannot yield a supernatural, salvific revelation or even a 'sense' of it. *Third*, if it recognizes a revelation, it cannot thereafter determine what that revelation may and may not contain. *Fourth*, reason cannot 'comprehend' divine revelation."

1326. Wainwright, "Jonathan Edwards and the Hiddenness of God," 103, argues thus: "Ultimately, our failure to discern God is due to (1) our inattention to the ideas we have of Him and signs of His presence, and to (2) the absence of the simple idea of true beauty. Both are consequences of a lack of true benevolence and hence of sin (for sin just is the lack of true benevolence, a voluntary fixation of the will on 'private systems' rather than being in general)."

1327. *WJE* 23, 259; *WJE* 25, 131.

1328. *WJE* 19, 710.

1329. "The will of God, as manifested either by the light of reason or by his Word, is the proper rule of men's actions," *WJE* 19, 520. Note that I consider *light of reason* to be synonymous with *light of nature* in this quotation.

1330. *WJE* 20, 52–53.

1331. *WJE* 20, 52–53.

1332. Wainwright, "Jonathan Edwards and the Hiddenness of God," 105.

1333. The corpus search method used is a *light of nature* collocation search in the *WJE* corpus.

1334. *WJE* 13, 200.

1335. *WJE* 52, 441.

1336. *WJE* 14, 169.

1337. *WJE* 13, 226.

1338. *WJE* 10, 360.

1339. *WJE* 18, 77.

1340. *WJE* 14, 232.

1341. *WJE* 54, 507.

1342. *WJE* 23, 344; *WJE* 23, 457.

1343. *WJE* 14, 513–14.

1344. *WJE* 23, 451.

1345. *WJE* 17, 49.

1346. *WJE* 20, 52–53.

1347. *WJE* 23, 175; *WJE* 23, 259.

1348. *WJE* 23, 449.

1349. *WJE* 21, 432.

1350. *WJE* 9, 134.

1351. *WJE* 25, 131.

1352. *WJE* 18, 324.

1353. *WJE* 15, 64.

1354. *WJE* 14, 413.

1355. *WJE* 23, 215.

1356. *WJE* 23, 534–35.

1357. I provide the full quotations here, as I refer to these references in more detail later on, and also in chapter 6, section 3.2: "The light of nature shows that the religion of heathens, consisting in the worship of idols, and sacrificing their children to them, and obscene and abominable rites and ceremonies, is wickedness. And the superstitions and idolatries and usurpations of the church of Rome, are no less contrary to the light of nature," *WJE* 9, 445. "And we have also this advantage, that our religion would recommend itself more to their reason and to the light of nature in 'em than the religion of the French," in *WJE* 16, 442.

1358. *WJE* 21, 432.

1359. Edwards says of the Stoic philosophers that "in their doctrine and practice [they] came the nearest to Christianity of any of their sects. . . . [T]he light of nature and reason in the wisest and best of the heathen, harmonized with, and confirms the gospel of Jesus Christ," in *WJE* 1, 372. "Socrates, that great gentile philosopher, who worshipped the true God, as he was led by the light of nature, might pray to God, and he attended his duty when he did so; although he knew not the revelation, which God had made of himself in his Word," in *WJE* 12, 300.

1360. *WJE* 2, 491 revised and corrected by Hickman.

1361. Owen famously wrote, "Though men know God by the light of nature, yet they cannot come to God by that knowledge," in *Selected Works of John Owen*, 3:134.

1362. *WJE* 20, 287–88.

1363. *WJE* 17, 49.

1364. *WJE* 23, 534–35.

1365. For example: "The very light of nature, or tradition from ancient revelation, led the heathen to conceive of death as in a peculiar manner an evidence of divine vengeance," *WJE* 3, 208; "That the Deity maintains a moral government over the world, and is the supreme head and fountain of laws and judgment, seems to be a notion that the heathen generally entertained by the light of nature together with ancient tradition, as they did the being of a God, the immortality of the soul, etc.," in *WJE* 20, 226. On various insights of Cicero, Edwards comments, "This universal apprehension——— whether we suppose it to be from the Clearness of the Light of nature———or from universal Tradition. or from both together. it equally serves our purpose———," in *WJE* 61, 706.

1366. In the following extract, Edwards seems to equate the two: "The will of God, as manifested either by the light of reason or by his Word, is the proper rule of men's actions. This will of God, as manifested in the works of God and by the light of nature, is called the rule of right reason; and the other is the rule of God's Word," in *WJE* 19, 520. A more specific example is when he connected the knowledge of the sabbath to both light of nature (see Table 1) and the light of reason: "I need nothing to convince me that 'tis evident to the light of reason, that there ought to be a time set apart to be spent wholly in the service and worship of God and the more immediate duties of religion amongst all nations, yea, in gospel times," in *WJE* 13, 310.

1367. *WJE* 13, 262.

1368. Pauw, "Trinity," 46.

1369. Pauw, "Trinity," 46.

1370. *WJE* 19, 710.

1371. *WJE* 1, 181.

1372. *WJE* 3, 229.

1373. *WJE* 8, 690; *WJE* 10, 357; *WJE* 21, 318–19.

1374. *WJE* 3, 381–82.

1375. *WJE* 2, 275; *WJE* 8, 93.

1376. *WJE* 2, 123.

1377. *WJE* 21, 316–17.

1378. *WJE* 10, 359.

1379. *WJE* 25, 64.

1380. *WJE* 8, 605.

1381. *WJE* 10, 357.

1382. *WJE* 10, 227.

1383. *WJE* 8, 607.

1384. *WJE* 8, 613.

1385. *WJE* 8, 584.

1386. *WJE* 8, 411.

1387. *WJE* 8, 601.

1388. *WJE* 8, 613.

1389. *WJE* 2, 156.

1390. Holbrook, "Jonathan Edwards Addresses," 222.

1391. *WJE* 8, 614.

1392. *WJE* 17, 410–11. Ramsey comments, "God's common grace often assists conscience to do its office more fully in the unregenerate," in *WJE* 8, 49.

1393. *WJE* 8, 594.

1394. *WJE* 8, 589.

1395. *WJE* 10, 357.

1396. *WJE* 48.

1397. *WJE* 8, 623.

1398. *WJE* 8, 595 and 616.

1399. *WJE* 13, 55.

1400. *WJE* 8, 263 and 595–96.

1401. *WJE* 8, 699.

1402. *WJE* 8, 616.

1403. *WJE* 18, 77.

1404. *WJE* 13, 393.

1405. *WJE* 13, 409.

1406. *WJE* 13, 272.

1407. Studebaker, "Jonathan Edwards' Pneumatological Concept of Grace," 339: "The human soul is the apex of the ad extra communication in creation and . . . is created for the purpose of receiving the ad extra communication in redemption."

1408. *WJE* 13, 279.

1409. *WJE* 13, 279.

1410. I exclude *WJE* 23, 415, where he lists John 1:1–4 alongside some other texts.

1411. References from David Brainerd's diary are naturally excluded.

1412. *WJE* 15, 209.

1413. *WJE* 45. Original language and punctuation are not edited.

1414. *WJE* 24, 923.

1415. *WJE* 25, 89.

1416. *WJE* 27.

1417. McDermott, *Jonathan Edwards Confronts*, 144.

1418. For McDermott's interpretation, see *Jonathan Edwards Confronts*, 144.

1419. McDermott, *Jonathan Edwards Confronts*, 144, suggests an influence from one element of the Breck affair. Specifically: "Robert Breck had concluded that since there can be salvation without profession of Christ, it was not absolutely necessary for people to believe that Christ died for sinners."

1420. *WJE* 22, 53.

1421. *WJE* 23, 453.

1422. "He [Christ] brought to Light a further degree of Truth. . . . Beyond what could be known by the Light of nature," *WJE* 45, 163.

1423. As is evident from endorsements of his work in *For Their Rock Is Not as Our Rock*.

1424. Other Reformed contributions would include Miles, *God of Many Understandings?*; Sparks, *One of a Kind*; Whitehead, "Pauline Approach to the Theology of Religions." Reformed inclusivist contributions would include Tiessen's *Who can be Saved?* Evangelical contributions would include Corduan, *Tapestry of Faiths*, Netland, *Encountering Religious Pluralism* and McDermott's *Can Evangelicals Learn from World Religions?*

1425. Strange, "Perilous Exchange," 92.

1426. Strange, "Perilous Exchange," 92.

1427. Strange, *Their Rock*, 41.

1428. Strange, "Perilous Exchange," 92–93; Strange, *Their Rock*, 41–42. The declarations include The Frankfurt Declaration (1970), the Lausanne Covenant (1974), and The Manila Manifesto (1989).

1429. Strange, *Their Rock*, 18–19.

1430. Strange, *Their Rock*, 18–19.

1431. In *Their Rock*, 21, Strange terms the department at Bristol "extremely 'pluralistic'" in outlook, documenting the challenges of being an Evangelical in that context.

1432. The title of the PhD is the same as the name of the book: *The Possibility of Salvation among the Unevangelised: An Analysis of Inclusivism in Recent Evangelical Theology*.

1433. Strange, *Possibility of Salvation*, 286. I make a number of references to the book version of the PhD in what follows.

1434. Strange, *Their Rock*; Strange, *Possibility of Salvation*.

1435. Strange also publishes as a contributing editor to *Themelios* and has produced two popular works on culture: *Plugged In* and *Making Faith Magnetic*. He has co-edited with Duce: *Getting Your Bearings: Engaging with Contemporary Theologians*; and also co-edited a book on Barth (with David Gibson): *Engaging with Barth*. He has also co-written a book on the Bible's trustworthiness with Michael Ovey: *Confident: Why We Can Trust the Bible*.

1436. Bavinck, *Church between Temple and Mosque*. This is republished by Westminster Seminary Press. In what follows and has preceded, references to this particular text are from the earlier 1981 version, published by Eerdmans.

1437. Also published as *Their Rock Is Not Like Our Rock: A Theology of Religions* by Zondervan.

1438. He states that the book is "for Reformed Christians, written by a Reformed Christian"; Strange, *Their Rock*, 33.

1439. Strange, *Their Rock*, 28.

1440. Strange, *Their Rock*, 35.

1441. For example, Strange, *Their Rock*, 35: "I hope those scholars who come from those backgrounds [Old Testament, New Testament, Biblical Theology, Missiology] will charitably recognize the integration I am trying to achieve and offer more rigorous contributions in the future, all with the aim of edifying God's church worldwide."

1442. Mark Pickett in his review of *Their Rock*, in "Hard Rock Theology," 91, states, "All religions and cultures . . . are the products of human agency (Geertz's 'webs of significance') interacting with a multitude of influences thrown up by our spiritual, ecological, social, political and economic environments. . . . Strange's argument . . . suffers from an ethnographically poorly informed and resultantly insufficiently robust method." Bavinck, *Impact of Christianity*, 55, seems to acknowledge that culture is not *just* outlived religion: "The culture of a people is that complex of spiritual, moral, technical and agricultural forces wherein a tribe or a people tries to express its basic feelings towards God, towards nature, and towards itself. The culture of a people is its common attitude of life, its style of living and thinking, rooted in its apprehension of reality."

1443. Strange, *Their Rock*, 36: "As has been emphasized throughout this study, rather than focusing on one non-Christian religion I have primarily been concerned with providing a dogmatic sketch of non-Christian religions in general." See also the same book, page 307.

1444. Strange, *Their Rock*, 336.

1445. Strange, *Their Rock*, 338.

1446. Strange, *Their Rock*, 79.

1447. Strange terms this an "ethical 'check' on the antithesis" (Strange, *Their Rock*, 94, 319).

1448. Strange, *Their Rock*, 239.

1449. Strange, "Perilous Exchange," 112. I pick up on this endorsement in section 3.3.

1450. Strange, *Their Rock*, 273.

1451. Strange, *Their Rock*, 103.

1452. Strange, "Perilous Exchange," 114.

1453. Strange, *Their Rock*, 310.

1454. Strange, "Perilous Exchange," 117. See also Kraemer, *Christian Message*, 135.

1455. Strange, *Their Rock*, 42, 98, 156, 239, 335.

1456. It should be noted that Strange has withdrawn support for his "incommensurable" claim in the fourth definition (see Response to Q.4).

1457. For clarification that general revelation is included in this, see Strange, "Interview with Strange," Response to Q.7. Available online.

1458. As noted in the introduction to section 4, Strange stresses the importance of considering the antithesis alongside common grace.

1459. See section 4.3 and the discussion on common grace.

1460. Strange, "Perilous Exchange," 121: "God through his Spirit does not strive with religious traditions and systems but with individuals made in his image."

1461. Strange, "Interview with Strange," Response to Q.3: "I think I distinguish at various places the distinction between the 'principial' and the 'practical' which is also a comment on the relationship between 'antithesis' and 'common grace.'"

1462. More accurately, I would state more than half, as the focus of the book is on the principial version of religion.

1463. Strange, "Interview with Strange," Response to Q.1.

1464. Philip Djung in his review of *Their Rock*, 421, states:

> Strange is right to point out that there are divine, human, and demonic elements in human religions. However, he overemphasizes the human and demonic parts and fails to give priority to the divine work. As a result, non-Christian religions are perceived as neither positive nor dialectic but wholly negative. Such an assessment certainly fails to capture the thoughts of H. Bavinck, J. H. Bavinck, and Hendrik Kraemer, on which Strange has attempted to build his theology.

See also the comments of the same author in his book *Revelation and Grace*, 56. Pickett, "Hard Rock Theology," 90, states, "Strange's emphasis is entirely negative, which is understandable if we consider that 'non-Christian religions' are the outworking of deceiving demonic forces." See also Mouw, "Discerning the Spirit in World Religions," 203.

1465. Strange, *Their Rock*, 239: "However, one more ingredient must be mentioned, for shadowing this major theme of idolatry, and 'behind' it, is the presence of the demonic. This is a minor theme but deserves some mention and analysis."

1466. Poston, "Bible and the Religions," cited by Strange, *Their Rock*, 148.

1467. Johnson is similarly careful not to overgeneralize demonic involvement. See Johnson, *Rethinking the Trinity*, 191. Netland, *Encountering Religious Pluralism*, 335, is also cautious. He states, "It would be too simplistic to hold that *all* non-Christian religious phenomena are merely satanic in origin. But it would be equally naive to suggest that *none* of them are [emphases in original]."

1468. Note also the differentiation which Calvin makes—see chapter 4.

1469. Strange, "Interview with Strange," Response to Q.5: "However, in *TR* [*Their Rock*] I know that I needed to tackle the issue however blunt my analysis was." In the same response, concerning the demonic he states, "So I think there is 'something to it' but I am not as certain about it as other areas of my theological argumentation and construction."

1470. Strange, *Their Rock*, 207.

1471. Strange, *Their Rock*, 246–47.

1472. Strange, *Their Rock*, 270: "Because idols are parasites and counterfeits of *the* God, Yahweh, there is a *thatness* to our humanity."

1473. Strange, *Their Rock*, 34. Strange provides his own very brief overview in "Exclusivisms," 37–44.

1474. Strange, *Their Rock*, 34.

1475. I say "possible" here, as the focus of Strange's *prisca theologia* argument is not the same as Edwards's.

1476. This term is present in both the Westminster Confession (1.1,6; 10.4; 20.4; 21.1) and the Canons of Dort (3.4,5 and 6).

1477. Strange, *Their Rock*, 34: "If my work does nothing more than republicize and champion Kraemer and even more particularly J. H. Bavinck to a new generation of Christians, then I shall have achieved much." "I am not embarrassed to admit my indebtedness to certain neglected Reformed missiologists on whose shoulders I sit and whom I wish to steer back into the limelight." See also Strange, "For Their Rock Is Not as Our Rock," 394.

1478. For background and Information see especially Visser, *Heart for the Gospel*.

1479. For background information see Perry, *Radical Difference*.

1480. For background information see Frame, *Cornelius Van Til*.

1481. See Strange's claim of dependence in *Their Rock*, 34

1482. Kraemer uses the term in a chapter entitled "Continuity or Discontinuity," in *Authority of the Faith*, 4. I provide some context in what follows. Before introducing it, he notes that there is no natural path from nature, reason or history to Christ, but that there are human longings which Christ "may be termed *in a certain sense* the fulfilment," (p. 2) but that this is never a perfecting—rather the "crisis of all religions," (p. 3). Kraemer rejects the idea of natural theology, while not denying that "God has been working in the minds of men outside the sphere of the Christian revelation," (p. 4) stating that there are "men of faith," (p. 4) outside the church, and in other religions within whom the Spirit has worked. Kraemer rejects the idea that religions are, in any way, a schoolmaster, leading to Christ. He then makes a key statement: "Only an attentive study of the Bible can open the eyes to the fact that Christ 'the power of God' and 'the wisdom of God' stands in contradiction to the power and the wisdom of man. Perhaps in some respects it were proper to speak of contradictive or subversive fulfilment," (p. 4). In context, Kraemer is saying that Christ is not as human wisdom perceives him to be. When he goes on to speak of the idea of God working in non-Christian thought, which he terms "a baffling and awful problem," (p. 13) he states that continuity advocates appeal to fulfilment and general revelation, while others within this camp go so far as to develop a natural theology upon which revelation builds. Turning to the discontinuity model, he notes that it rejects a natural theology, and also the idea of general revelation alongside any idea of fulfilment. He goes on to argue that Clement represents the first, continuity position, and Barth the second, discontinuity position. He strongly aligns himself with Barth, as he sees Clement as failing to recognize the discontinuity between wisdom (see earlier) and Christ: "Yet, the reason that Barth's position is more compelling is not a matter of better and simpler logic, but of deeper and more consistent religious and theological thinking. Clement's handicap is that to him revelation and philosophy are essentially wisdom, knowledge," (p. 20). He believes that the crux of the issue is starting point and whether that be "the essence of religion" or "the revelation of Christ" (p. 21).

1483. It is included in major heading for chapters 7 "'For Their Rock Is Not as Our Rock': The Gospel as the 'Subversive Fulfilment' of the Religious Other'" and 8 "'A Light for the Gentiles': Missiological Implications of 'Subversive Fulfilment.'" It also seems fairly central in the main definition, discussed above. He also foregrounds the idea in the chapter "Perilous Exchange," and in "For Their Rock Is Not as Our Rock: The Gospel as the 'Subversive Fulfillment' of the Religious Other." In *Their Rock*, 273, Strange states:

> In conclusion, it is my contention that subversive fulfilment, or alternatively "fulfilling subversion," captures better than any model I have come across the relationship between the gospel of Jesus Christ and the religious Other. Such a model demonstrates both continuity and discontinuity and coheres well with both the complex theological anthropology of human beings and the fundamental analysis and anatomy of idolatry, that pervasive biblical concept that has been offered as the hermeneutical lens through which we are to view the religious Other.

In "Perilous Exchange," 128, Strange terms subversive fulfilment "the only description that does justice to a fully orbed biblical interpretation of others religions." Strange believes that the idea was present in Hermann Bavinck, before Kraemer (Strange, *Their Rock*, 267).

1484. See Strange, "Interview with Strange," Response to Q.4.

1485. Perry, *Radical Difference*, 117, notes how Kraemer often overstated for rhetorical purposes, especially in his earlier work.

1486. Kraemer, *Religion and the Christian Faith*, 6: "In what sense (positive or negative, or both combined) are they [religions and philosophies] responses and places of encounter? And how far are they so? The answer given in this book is dialectical, as a parallel to the dialectical character of Religious Truth, manifest in Biblical Revelation." On page 8 of the same book, Kraemer speaks of "the religious consciousness as the place of dialectic encounter with God," contrasting this emphasis with his previous work: "I take now a far more dialectical view of this thesis [human achievement in religion] than in my previous book."

1487. Kraemer, *Religion and the Christian Faith*, 351, states, "The two dialectics, the divine and human, which I have repeatedly explained as manifesting their interplay in countless ways in the religions, make the whole controversy of "continuity" or "discontinuity" superfluous." On page 352, he continues:

> In the last resort, if we really take our direction from revelation, in the dynamic and concrete sense we have tried to explain, all those controversies about "*praeparatio evangelica*" or not, "fulfilment" or not, "continuity" or "discontinuity," appear as secondary, so that one finds oneself often in the factual situation of discovering (to take only one example) "continuity" and "discontinuity" at the same time in regard to the same complex of spiritual reality. This is paradoxical, but true! However, this can never be made into a theory or into a system, because everything depends on the amount of obedient openness to the revelation without which this liberty in Christ can neither grow nor exist.

1488. Concerning idolatry, Strange, *Their Rock*, 156, writes, "Although much maligned as a tool for theological analysis, it will be argued that idolatry is perhaps the hermeneutical master key with which to unlock the nature of non-Christian religion and religions." See also "Perilous Exchange," 111: "Far from being an anachronistic and 'blunt' concept, idolatry is a sophisticated analytical tool with which we can understand non-Christian religions."

1489. Specifically, Kraemer argued that Christianity (with all its imperfections) is similar to non-Christian religions, being "a form of religion" like others (See Strange, *Their Rock*, 39n39). Kraemer's doctrine of Scripture which Strange describes as having a "neo-orthodox feel," is documented in *Their Rock*, 48n68. See also page 239n4.

1490. Kraemer, *Why Christianity?*, 15. See also pages 89 and 110 of the same book. On page 102, he writes, "He [Christ] breaks through every such 'system,' Christian and non-Christian alike, whatever its origin may be." While Kraemer argues that there is no true religion (*Why Christianity?*, 110), Strange's theology relates non-Christian religions to "the truth of the Christian worldview" (as per his definition) not Christ, per se. More recently, Tiessen adopts a similar position to Kraemer: "Inevitably, we must face the question of Christianity's place among the religions and it should now be apparent that I see institutional Christianity as no different from any other religion in its character as a humanly constructed institution," in "God's Work of Grace," 172. However, Tiessen immediately goes on to say (on the same page), "Nevertheless, Christianity is intrinsically superior because of its being the institutional response to the *ultimate* revelation of God in Christ, even though it is also ambiguous as a sinful human response to that revelation." Interestingly, Visser positions J. H. Bavinck closer to Kraemer than does Strange in his interpretation of this issue. Visser writes as follows concerning Bavinck's position, with a quotation from Bavinck embedded in the observation: "Moreover, it is not only something of the past [the idea that Christians suppress truth]: 'In the Christian the pagan continues to live and breathe.' This makes it impossible to speak of the absolute truth of Christian faith; it never constitutes an adequate reflection of the content of the gospel. Absolute truth holds only for God's revelation in the gospel of Christ," in Visser, "Religion in Biblical and Reformed Perspective," 31.

1491. Strange, *Their Rock*, 39 "Therefore, there is an inextricable link between

Christ himself, Christ's gospel and Christ's bride (the church), consisting of Christ's people (Christians) and given sacred historical, social and institutional expression in what we call the 'Christian faith' and 'Christianity.'" See also n39 of the same page.

1492. See Statham, Review of *Their Rock Is Not Like Our Rock*, 83.

1493. Kraemer, "Continuity," 14: "The problem whether and, if so where, and in how far, God, i.e. the God and Father of Jesus Christ, the only God we Christians know—has been and is working in the religious history of the world and in man in his quest for goodness, truth and beauty, is a baffling and awful problem." Kraemer, *Christian Message*, 127, writes, "To indicate systematically and concretely where God revealed Himself and wrestled and wrestles with man in the non-Christian religions is not feasible. Every effort to do so is hazardous." In *Religion*, 257, he calls religions, "conscious or unconscious responses to God, wrong, partly right, sometimes really right."

1494. See, e.g., "Continuity," 20. The Pro-Barth position is clearly stated in *Christian Message*, 116, and also *Religion*, 188–96. This should not be taken to imply that Kraemer is not critical of Barth at times. See Strange's comments in *Their Rock*, 39n39. Strange distances himself from Barth's theology in the "Interview with Strange"—Response to Q.4.

1495. Kraemer, *Religion and the Christian Faith*, 342, suggests that the term "general revelation" should be abolished. He goes on to state, on page 354, that God does not reveal himself in nature or history.

1496. Kraemer arguably stresses the role of Satan in Christianity more than in non-Christian religions. See *Religion*, 335–38.

1497. Kraemer, *Why Christianity?*, 123–24: "We can learn a lot from them; and we must be ready and eager to do so." Strange rejects a similar argument made by McDermott in *Their Rock*, 306.

1498. While Strange rejects the relevance of the Johannine prologue for the discipline (see section 3.3, below), Kraemer, like J. H. Bavinck, did understand there to be a role—though rejecting what he considered the church fathers to argue. See *Religion*, 149–55, 263–80.

1499. See Perry, *Radical Difference*, 9–10, on the significance. Strange recognizes this in his brief historical overview in "Exclusivisms," 43.

1500. When referring to *Herman* Bavinck this will be signalled. All later references to Bavinck are to J. H.

1501. In Strange, "Perilous Exchange," 93, and *Their Rock*, prefatory material: "In the Spirit and on the shoulders of J. H. Bavinck."

1502. This is discussed in Bavinck, *Church between Temple and Mosque*, 35–114, and also 145–302 in *The J. H. Bavinck Reader*.

1503. The idea that religious consciousness is the *product* of the human response to revelation is clear in "Religious Consciousness and Christian Faith," 297: "The outcome of this entire process (understanding and seeing clearly as well as repressing and replacing) is the religious consciousness that from the very beginning is unique to human beings. . . . [I]t should only be understood as the response or reaction to the voiceless speech of God's self-revelation."

1504. Bavinck, "Debating Religious Consciousness," 226:

> There seems to be a kind of framework within which human religions need to operate. There appear to be definite points of contact around which

all kinds of ideas crystallize. There seem to be quite vague feelings—one might better call them direction signals—that have been actively brooding everywhere.... [T]here seem to be definite magnetic points that time and again irresistibly compel human religious thought.

These points are the sense of cosmic relationship, the idea of religious norm, the human as an active or passive player in their destinies, redemption, and who God is. See Bavinck, *Church between Temple and Mosque*, 37–106, for more detail on these points.

1505. In *The Impact of Christianity*, 103–5, Bavinck lists these as 1. Old traditions, 2. Divine revelation, 3. Personal guidance, 4. The seed of religion, and 5. Christianity.

1506. Visser, *Heart for the Gospel*, 124–26, believes Bavinck included nature, human conscience and history in his idea of general revelation—what might be considered a fairly standard Reformed view. Bavinck believed the Holy Spirit was constantly working inside humans, though as Visser notes, on page 126, this is not stressed in his work.

1507. Bavinck, *Impact of Christianity*, 104.

1508. Bavinck, *Impact of Christianity*, 104.

1509. In "Religious Consciousness and Christian Faith," 281–82, Bavinck downplays a focus on the *principium internum* but still insists on its reality.

1510. Bavinck, "Religious Consciousness and Christian Faith," 297: "No continuity exists between the gospel and human religious consciousness, although definite continuity does exist between the gospel and what lies behind human religious consciousness, namely God's general revelation."

1511. Not only in *Their Rock*, but also in the popular work he has written: *Making Faith Magnetic*.

1512. Strange, *Their Rock*, 281.

1513. For example, in "General Revelation and the Non-Christian Religions (2013)," 107. Bavinck argues that there has been a kind of positive influence of general revelation—particularly in conscience: i.e., there is content within the frames.

1514. Strange, *Their Rock*, 319–20: "First, the imago Dei variously described and unpacked throughout this study in terms of Calvin's sensus divinitatis, semen religionis or J. H. Bavinck's thatness (together with his 'magnetic points') can function as a divine restraint on sin and its effects, thus preserving the order of creation. Just as God graciously preserves in animals a fear of humankind (Gen 9:2)." See also "Exclusivisms," 54, where he equates the *imago Dei* to religious consciousness, the five magnetic points and thatness. Note also *Their Rock*, 71: "human beings are created in the *imago Dei*, and 'sons of God' are created as 'religious' beings, revealing God, representing him, and built for relationship with him, with each other and with the rest of creation. This 'religious' nature, *sensus divinitatis* or *semen religionis*."

1515. Specifically, the seed of religion is part of the make-up of religious consciousness—the organ of reception of revelation for Bavinck.

1516. Strange, *Their Rock*, 61–72.

1517. E.g., Strange, *Their Rock*, 319.

1518. In *Jerusalem and Athens*, a book composed of essays dedicated to Van Til, the editor—E. R. Geehan—terms Van Til both a philosopher and theologian, recognizing his significant contribution to apologetics (inside cover).

1519. Visser, "Religion, Mission, and Kingdom," 117, comments, "JHB [J. H.

Bavinck] was a passionate thinker who developed an existential (psychological) approach to theology and missions."

1520. I explain this in section 4.4.

1521. See, for example, the exchanges in Geehan, *Jerusalem and Athens*, vii; Cowen, *Five Views on Apologetics*; Sproul et al., *Classical Apologetics*. On Van Til's version of common grace, Douma, *Common Grace in Kuyper, Schilder, and Calvin*, 374, states, "I believe that Van Til is too schematic and fails to provide proof from Scripture."

1522. See Wallace, "Antithesis Revisited."

1523. In Van Til, *Common Grace and the Gospel*, 103, the author makes clear that his interest is in Christian views of common grace, not the impact of common grace in religions.

1524. This analysis is based solely on material from the book, Strange, *Their Rock*.

1525. Strange, *Their Rock*, 224.

1526. Strange, *Their Rock*, 224n29.

1527. See my comments on Bray's thought in the introductory chapter to this book, plus observations in chapter 2. See Bray, "Explaining Christianity to Pagans," 20–21.

1528. Strange, *Their Rock*, 224.

1529. Strange, *Their Rock*, 224.

1530. Strange, *Their Rock*, 255.

1531. Strange, *Their Rock*, 148–49.

1532. Strange, *Their Rock*, 112–13.

1533. Strange, *Their Rock*, 240.

1534. Strange, *Their Rock*, 155.

1535. Strange, *Their Rock*, 196.

1536. Strange, *Their Rock*, 201.

1537. Strange, *Their Rock*, 245–46.

1538. Strange, *Their Rock*, 319.

1539. Strange, *Their Rock*, 325.

1540. Strange, *Their Rock*, 331.

1541. Strange, *Their Rock*, 331.

1542. Strange, *Their Rock*, 46n63.

1543. Strange, *Their Rock*, 74.

1544. Strange, *Their Rock*, 108. Strange acknowledges his engagement with Edwards is primarily via McDermott.

1545. Strange, *Their Rock*, 324.

1546. Strange, *Their Rock*, 324. See chapter 5 where I challenge this reading.

1547. Strange, *Their Rock*, 324.

1548. Strange, *Their Rock*, 185n94.

1549. Strange, *Their Rock*, 308.

1550. Strange, *Their Rock*, 324.

1551. Strange, *Their Rock*, 263. See Mody, "Relationship between Powers of Evil and Idols"; Mody, *Evil and Empty*.

1552. Strange, *Their Rock*, 115. See Corduan, *In the Beginning God*.

1553. Strange, *Their Rock*, 122–27. See Kreitzer, *Concept of Ethnicity in the Bible*.

1554. See section 3.1.

1555. See Strange, "Interview with Strange"—Response to Q.9.

1556. General revelation is flagged as a useful research focus in Strange, *Possibility of Salvation*, 288 (along with common grace).

1557. Strange, "Interview with Strange"—Response to Q.5: "I come from a church background and theological tradition which does not place demonic activity or a certain view of spiritual warfare front and centre. As such my thinking is not as developed and so I have to somewhat 'force' myself to remember it's there and needs to be mentioned. However, in TR [*Their Rock*] I know that I needed to tackle the issue however blunt my analysis was."

1558. Strange, *Their Rock*, 330.

1559. Strange, "Exclusivisms," 49: "In a variety of ways, Christian Scripture describes there to be principially a fundamental discontinuity between the truth of the Christian faith, built on the foundation of God's revelation, and the falsity of all other worldviews/philosophies/pseudo-gospels, *built on the foundation of human imagination* [emphasis mine]." In "Perilous Exchange," 113, he references, "human nature as a 'perpetual factory of idols.'" In an interview Strange has clarified that because of his interlocutors and audience he did not discuss the demonic in these texts. See Strange, "Interview with Strange"—Response to Q.5.

1560. Strange, *Their Rock*, 35–36, 122, 141.

1561. On the basis of a favorable citation of Boice, *Their Rock*, 139. See Boice, *Genesis*, 1:248.

1562. See Strange, *Their Rock*, 170, 260, 141–49.

1563. Strange, *Their Rock*, 260.

1564. Strange, *Their Rock*, 262.

1565. Strange, *Their Rock*, 78.

1566. Strange, *Their Rock*, 77n78.

1567. Strange, *Their Rock*, 77: "The decision of Adam and Eve to side with the serpent's interpretation of reality created a deep division between God on one side and Satan and the fallen human race on the other." Strange cites John Murray with approval concerning the role of Satan not being primary.

1568. Strange, *Their Rock*, 77.

1569. Strange, *Their Rock*, 148–49.

1570. See chapter 4 of *Their Rock*, referencing Franz Delitzsch, Karl Auberlen, James Candlish, H. Bavinck, Meredith Kline, James Jordan, and J. M. Boice.

1571. Strange, *Their Rock*, 125.

1572. Strange, *Their Rock*, 147. It should be noted that Strange suggests that fallen angel-human offspring continued after the flood on page 148.

1573. Strange, *Their Rock*, 127.

1574. Strange, *Their Rock*, 35–36. See also Strange, "Interview with Strange"—Response to Q.5

1575. Kraemer's actual reference to the "dark margin" (*Religion*, 379) is to hardening of hearts (and implicitly Satan's role in this) rather than the demonic, per se. This emphasis does not come out in Strange's own treatment. Note also that in *Religion*, 380, after mentioning hardening of hearts and Judas, Kraemer comments, "Without minimizing in the least the Biblical teaching that the gospel, the *glad* tidings of God's invitation, is meant for the whole world, we should not lose sight of the important *marginal flashes* the Bible throws on the mystery that man can get by his own acts into an irretrievable situation, and that God puts the seal upon it by *making* it irretrievable [emphasis mine]." Here Kraemer hints at the combined demonic and the human role in hardening, but nothing more.

1576. Strange, *Their Rock*, 141.

1577. Strange, *Their Rock*, 239.

1578. Strange, *Their Rock*, 259.

1579. Strange, *Their Rock*, 259.

1580. Strange, *Their Rock*, 259.

1581. Strange, *Their Rock*, 326n73: "What I am suggesting here is that in his sovereignty God providentially uses these 'satanic' elements in non-Christian religions to drive his elect to Christ."

1582. Strange, *Their Rock*, 306.

1583. Frame, "Presuppositional Apologetics," 211–12, stated: "Even the demons sometimes face up to reality. In Mark 1:24 an evil spirit says truly that Jesus is the 'Holy One of God.'"

1584. See n129.

1585. Strange, *Their Rock*, 263–66.

1586. Strange, *Their Rock*, 264.

1587. Strange, *Their Rock*, 78.

1588. Influential revelation receives only passing references in Strange, *Their Rock*, while remnantal revelation receives a whole chapter (chapter 3). Corduan's work on remnantal revelation preceded and seems to have influenced Strange's thought—as he acknowledges (e.g., *Their Rock*, 115). While Corduan's monograph on original monotheism came out just before *Their Rock* (in 2013), the basic idea and argument is clearly present in *A Tapestry of Faiths* (2002), chapter 2, which Strange references.

1589. Strange, *Their Rock*, 255 "Closely related to the concept of remnantal revelation is that of influental revelation, by which I am referring to the impact or 'influent' of the Judeo-Christian worldview on living religious traditions, both historically and presently."

1590. Strange, *Their Rock*, 255.

1591. Strange, *Their Rock*, 255.

1592. See Strange, *Their Rock*, 201 and 296.

1593. See Strange, "Interview with Strange"—Response to Q.6.

1594. E.g., Strange, *Their Rock*, 115.

1595. See Strange, "Interview with Strange"—Response to Q.6.

1596. See Strange, "Interview with Strange"—Response to Q.6.

1597. See Strange, "Interview with Strange"—Response to Q.7: "In dogmatic terms, the distinction between 'general' revelation and 'special' revelation holds and is important particularly when discussing soteriological questions which of course was the subject of doctoral thesis."

1598. E.g., Strange, "General Revelation," 74: "The "messiness" in the history of revelation and the revelation of history means that it is difficult, if not impossible, to excavate the history of a religious tradition and separate out the influence of general revelation and special revelation." See also in the same chapter, 72: "Our theological categorization of revelation, general and special, as hermetically sealed compartments can be shown to be rather inadequate." The mixture of revelations is documented in Strange, "Perilous Exchange," 121: "An even deeper complexity is manifested as we view this anthropological picture from a historical or phenomenological perspective, for here the 'categories' of general revelation and special revelation break down somewhat. Homo adorans is a complex historical mix." In *Their Rock*, 104, Strange comments, "Given a monogenetic understanding of human origins, what is being posited here is a 'single-source' theory of revelation and knowledge, when the whole of humanity was in proximity of redemptive-historical events and which therefore defies a simplistic categorization as either natural 'general' revelation or supernatural 'special revelation.'" In "This Rock Unmoved," 72–73, he states,

> The revelatory "stuff" which sinful humanity suppresses and substitutes, and which becomes part of a tradition and memory in idolatrous religion, is an admixture of different types of revelation. It contains not only natural, general revelation but also special revelation in terms of God's words and his redemptive acts in history that have been witnessed not only by God's chosen covenant people, but by those outside as well.

1599. In discussing Strange's comments about special revelation inflowing religions, D'Costa, "Gavin D'Costa Responds," 149–50, states, "while other religions are ultimately false in so much as they do not teach the truth of God's triune self-revelation, they are capable of mediating 'special revelation', which means that there is the possibility of knowing the one true God within that religion." Faircloth, "Daniel Strange on the Theological Question of the Unevangelized," 68, comments, "The problem for Strange is that in claiming there is a vestige of special revelation among the unevangelized, the logical structure of his argument requires that he allow for the Spirit's work of special grace as well; otherwise there remains an internal dissonance in his theory."

1600. Strange, *Their Rock*, 104: "Such revelatory material [i.e., remnantal] is always sinfully corrupted, distorted and degenerates to the point of being salvifically useless." Strange, in "This Rock Unmoved," 73, states, "The point that I stress in various places in the book, which Kyle picks up on, and which I reiterate again here, is that because of the idolatrous impulse, such revelatory material is immediately corrupted and distorted in sin and so is not salvific." Later on in the same page he writes, "I do not agree with Kyle that the establishment of remnantal revelation 'opens the door wide for speculation on its salvific possibilities', because we are dealing with suppressed truth which is counterfeit and not genuine." See also Strange, "Perilous Exchange," 127–28: "With regard to proto-word revelation, oral tradition and the inflow of special revelation into other traditions, I have already indicated the sinful human propensity to pervert and distort the truth of God's revelation which becomes a basis for further judgement rather than a *praeparatio evangelica*."

1601. Strange, *Their Rock*, 113: "my more modest aim is to highlight the theoretical theological existence of the *prisca theologia* and comparative mythology to demonstrate that they have some precedent in Reformed historical theology." As Strange notes there are some supporters. He does not engage with the critics. One of the foremost of these would be Francis Turretin. In his *Institutes of Elenctic Theology*, volume 1, section 1.3.4, he flatly rejected the *prisca theologia* tradition:

> Third question—Whether natural theology may be granted. Our controversy here [over the place of natural theology] is with the Socinians who deny the existence of any such natural theology or knowledge of God and hold that what may appear to be such has flowed partly from tradition handed down from Adam, and partly from revelations made at different times. . . . The orthodox *on the contrary* uniformly teach that there is a natural theology, partly innate (derived from the book of conscience by means of common notions) . . . and partly acquired (drawn from the book of creatures discursively) [emphasis mine].

1602. Strange, *Their Rock*, 113.

1603. Strange, *Their Rock*, 84, 104.

1604. Strange, *Their Rock*, 257.

1605. As noted in chapter 5, Edwards did not view the light of nature as revelation. See *WJE* 19, 710. At the same time, Edwards believed that the light of nature teaches, "many truths concerning God and our duty to him," in *WJE* 20, 52–53.

1606. *WJE* 9, 445: "The light of nature shows that the religion of heathens, consisting in the worship of idols, and sacrificing their children to them, and obscene and abominable rites and ceremonies, is wickedness. And the superstitions and idolatries and usurpations of the church of Rome, are no less contrary to the light of nature." See also *WJE* 16, 442: "And we have also this advantage, that our religion would recommend itself more to their reason and to the light of nature in 'em than the religion of the French."

1607. Strange, *Their Rock*, 104.

1608. *Variegated* suppression of revelation is mentioned in Strange, *Their Rock*, 232–34.

1609. Strange, "Not Ashamed!," 255: "Given the sinful suppression and exchange of truth, a 'naked' natural law would seem no basis on which to build a society." This can be contrasted with the view of Donald Macleod, who stated that "strong ethical structures" in secular states result from an awareness of God's law known from nature. See Macleod, *Behold Your God*, 121.

1610. Strange, "Perilous Exchange," 218: "Concerning the relationship between Christianity and all other religions, the relationship is one of structural continuity in systemic discontinuity." See Strange, "Interview with Strange"—Response to Q.8: "*Thatness* provides the point of contact and so is 'positive' in this sense."

1611. Strange, *Their Rock*, 224–26. I say cursorily here, given the considerable amount of historical engagement with *Logos* enlightenment/illumination within the history of the Church on this subject.

1612. Strange, *Their Rock*, 225 (questioning Adam Sparks's interpretation).

1613. Strange, *Their Rock*, 255, states, "While I continue to defend both general revelation and the *imago Dei*, is this what John is referring to in his prologue?" The implication is that it is not. Some Reformed theologians have made such a connection. For example, Hughes, *True Image*, 3, stated, "The question regarding the significance of man's creation in the divine image is raised on the opening page of the Bible, but it is not clearly resolved until we come to the revelation in the New Testament that Christ himself, the Son, is the Image of God (2 Cor 4:4; Col 1:15)." On page 40 of the same book, he wrote, "Man's formation in the true Image is his formation in the divine Word."

1614. Strange, *Their Rock*, 319.

1615. Miller, "True Light Which Illumines."

1616. Strange, *Possibility of Salvation*, 237.

1617. Strange, *Possibility of Salvation*, 237.

1618. Strange, *Possibility of Salvation*, 242.

1619. Strange, *Possibility of Salvation*, 243n55: "While it is true to say that the work of the Trinity in creation is distinct from that of re-creation, it is not entirely separate and discontinuous because firstly it is the same Persons who accomplish their appropriate roles in both works, and secondly, because the background of re-creation is creation, as it is creation that is renewed."

1620. Strange, "Interview with Strange"—Response to Q.9: "My earlier work on soteriological inclusivism, and what I perceived as the misuse of The Logos (particularly in the work of my subject Clark Pinnock, but also in terms of legitimatizing prevenient grace and how Vatican II, Lux Mundi use it), meant that when I came to my theology of religions I didn't explore it in more detail seeing it as a something of a theological dead end. Maybe this was premature."

1621. Strange, "Interview with Strange"—Response to Q.10.

1622. Strange, *Their Rock*, 225n36.

1623. Bavinck, *Church between Temple and Mosque*, 127.

1624. Strange, "General Revelation," 59.

1625. Visser notes a number of areas where he believed Bavinck to have been influenced by Augustine and Calvin (*Heart for the Gospel*, 85–87). Regarding Calvin's influence, Visser believes this to be in the area that religion is a theological phenomenon (not a human invention), the idea that an indestructible awareness of God is stimulated by revelation and also in arriving at a negative evaluation of religion because what is known is "always immediately smothered or corrupted," 86. He states Bavinck was influenced by Augustine in the areas of the divine attributes, the fundamental human consciousness of God and the centrality of the revelation of God to understand human existence. Visser suggests Bavinck's view of *Logos* enlightenment to have been borrowed from Herman Bavinck (121n98). Visser also sees an influence of F. W. A. Korff concerning the idea of continuity between general and special revelation (on page 133). Kraemer seems to link the prologue and Romans 1 in *Religion*, 341. It is worth noting that Carl Henry also connects Romans 1 with the *Logos* in "Is It Fair?," 248.

1626. Bavinck rejects what he understands the apologists to refer to as *Logos* enlightenment (believing they equated this with human reason) in *Introduction to the Science of Missions*, 223–24. He states:

> The apologists of the first centuries were already of the opinion that human reason, the logos, was the powerful weapon with which they could attack the heathendom of their day.... The philosophers had ... withdrawn from

the bewitching influence of myth, and through the logos they had come to the insight that there was only a single divine nature or essence. The philosophers had experienced the logos, and the logos was a reflection of the great Logos, the Word that became flesh in Christ. For this reason, the apologists thought that some pagan philosophers, especially those such as Socrates, ought to be called Christians, even though they never knew the Incarnate Logos. We ought not to reproach the early apologists too much for having taken this tack. . . . The apologists had not sufficiently understood that the Logos, spoken of in the first chapter of John's Gospel, is actually quite different from the logos experienced by Socrates. They had no clear insight into the fact that the idea of God of late Greek philosophy had little to do with the preachings of the Lord, Jahveh, the living God, encountered in the Bible. . . . This course taken by the early apologist did much harm. Reason, regarded as, the great ally of faith, was viewed as a powerful weapon in the struggle against heathendom.

See also Bavinck, "Religious Consciousness in History," 249–50.

1627. Bavinck, *Church between Temple and Mosque*, 127.

1628. Bavinck, "Religious Consciousness in History," 247.

1629. In "Religious Consciousness in History," 249–50, in the context of critically reviewing Justin, and Clement of Alexandria, Bavinck states:

Meanwhile, these developments in theological thought clearly posed serious threats. In the first place, one can register serious objections to expressions like "the seed of the Logos implanted in the entire human race." In it, the Logos is made into a principle that is embedded in human nature and that is one with human nature. It no longer is the divine Word that stands over against humanity or that calls humanity to responsibility, but it is a power implanted in human nature. The "seed of the logos" lives in philosophers and poets. A poet is able, at least in part, to "possess" the Logos. And here the Logos becomes part of a person, something that a person has. By this the Logos is dragged down to the human level, and the human being is at the same time deified, at least in some of his or her capacities. A second objection must be found in the fact that in these and similar expressions the concept of "Logos" is weakened and reduced to reason and the highest wisdom. But the concept Logos as it appears in the Gospel of John, has a clear Old Testament background. But here it is increasingly pulled into the Greek world of thought and conflated with the universal reason dwelling in all things. Through such expressions as just noted, theological thought turned down a dangerous road.

In *Religions and World Views in Our Day* as cited in Visser, *Heart for the Gospel*, 121, Bavinck believed that John 1:9 indicates that "in the life of every human person a conversation takes place, whether noticed or heard or not between the person and the Word which is present everywhere around him, which always accompanies him, which embraces his entire life." In "Religious Consciousness in History," 238, Bavinck states:

Theology has certainly often understood it [general revelation] much too abstractly, too often as an impersonal idea. But in the Bible, particularly in the Old Testament, general revelation is intended to be much more personal. God's majesty is certainly revealed throughout the entire world. But in each instance that it is, whenever a given person begins to see that majesty, when his or her eyes are open to it and he or she is overwhelmed by it, general revelation takes on the character of a very individual intervention. . . . [he gives the example of an individual challenged by conscience] In other words, that so-called general revelation is depicted for us in the Bible as a much more personal involvement of God with each person than we in our theology once understood it to be.

In *Church between Temple and Mosque*, 120, Bavinck writes, "General revelation must be seen less as a philosophical instinct lodged in human superiority and more as a force that people encounter in their life-relationships. In other words, it must be understood more existentially." In "Religious Consciousness and Christian Faith," 296, he says, "The Greek word *nooumena*, literally 'being intelligently observed,' does not refer to seeing with the eyes in this case, but neither does it mean that 'seeing God's everlasting power and godhead' is attained by a process of reasoning. It is not a logical conclusion, but a flash that comes in a moment of vision. It comes suddenly to man, it overwhelms him." On the same page he goes on to state:

> The point of departure for all of our considerations needs to be God's self-disclosure or the general revelation that nonetheless bears the nature of a very personal engagement of God with each person separately. This general revelation is so real, so concrete, so inescapable, and so compelling that no person can escape it. It grips every person and renders him or her someone who knows in 'whom the unseen seen things are revealed.' In so doing, it defines the life of every person as a dialogue or a struggle with God. That is at the deepest core of every person's existence.

Bavinck, *Church between Temple and Mosque*, 124, writes:

> If we wish to use the expression "general revelation" we must not do so in the sense that one can logically conclude God's existence from it. This *may* be possible, but it only leads to a philosophical notion of God as the first cause. But that is not the biblical idea of 'general revelation.' When the Bible speaks of general revelation it means something quite different. There it has a much more personal nature. It is divine concern for men collectively and individually. God's deity and eternal power are evident; they overwhelm man; they strike him suddenly, in moments when he thought they were far away. They creep up on him; they do not let go of him, even though man does his best to escape them.

1630. Bavinck, "Religious Consciousness and Christian Faith," 296.

1631. Bavinck, "Religious Consciousness and Christian Faith," 297: "But people's religious consciousness—that product of illumination, repression and replacement—simply stands over against the gospel and is contradicted by the gospel." On the same page he states:

> That religious awareness is not to be construed as an act that flows from human nature. It does not belong to the structure of human nature as such. Rather, it should only be understood as the response or reaction to the voiceless speech of God's self-revelation. . . . The gospel of Jesus Christ breaks through human religious consciousness. It may never be put on the same level with the various manifestations of human religious consciousness as expressed in different religions, since it in fact exists on a different level. No continuity exists between the gospel and human religious consciousness, although definite continuity does exist between

the gospel and what lies behind human religious consciousness, namely God's general revelation.

See also n209

1632. Bavinck, "Religious Consciousness and Christian Faith," 297: "No continuity exists between the gospel and human religious consciousness, although definite continuity does exist between the gospel and what lies behind human religious consciousness, namely God's general revelation." On the same page he continues: "God's general and His special revelation are to be thought of as connected, and they continuously affect one another. Both of them are all about Jesus Christ. The Logos of John 1:14 who became flesh and dwelled among us is the same Logos who "enlightens all people" (John 1:9)." In "Religious Consciousness and Christian Faith," 291, he states:

> From the gospel of Jesus Christ, people gain an entirely new vision of the world in which they live and to which they are tied with every fiber of their beings. This is not to say that the gospel of Jesus Christ says something completely different from what general revelation has been saying to them already for a long time in its language without speech. On the contrary, continuity exists between that voiceless language and the gospel; They have an inner connection with each other.

In "Religious Consciousness and Christian Faith," 290, Bavinck writes:

> In the darkness of human existence, where repressing and replacing focus their empty work day and night, only the proclamation of the gospel of Jesus Christ can bring light. Truth is found in him. This is the complete and living power for people, the power long repressed and rejected. Contained in his words is always something of the "I was always with you, but you were not with me." "I am the Christ whom you have repressed." "I am the one with whom you have struggled and whom you have assaulted." "It is hard for you to kick against the pricks."

Visser, *Heart for the Gospel*, 132, comments, "Owing to the unity of God, the content of general revelation is formally identical to that of special revelation in Christ, though materially it differs from the latter," and also "Due to the fact that God is one, there exists both a material and an essential unity between the two forms of revelation: both are Christologically qualified." It should be stressed that Visser goes on to talk about differences too (133–35); however, these are not my focus here.

1633. Bavinck, "Religious Consciousness and Christian Faith," 297.

1634. Strange considers the grounding of common grace in *Possibility of Salvation*, 241–42n53, and its christological basis. However, he does not develop this. In the same volume (on page 262), he states, "General revelation speaks of God's nature and His demands but offers no knowledge as to how humanity can be saved." In *Their Rock*, 222, Strange seems to stress discontinuity more than continuity between general and special revelation, and suggests that general revelation is not revelation of Christ:

> Unlike special revelation, general revelation simply does not contain the truth content necessary for saving faith, and so is not an appropriate vehicle for the Spirit's saving work of regeneration. Faith cannot maintain its fully orbed character of *notitia*, *fiducia* and *assensus* if the object changes from Christ to God (or even Reality), as it is a knowledge of who Christ is and what he has done that defines saving faith. Looking outside ourselves to the objective work of Christ tells us also something of the role of faith and its efficacy.

1635. Bavinck "Religious Consciousness and Christian Faith," 297.

1636. Strange, "Interview with Strange"—Response to Q.10.

1637. Strange, "Interview with Strange"—Response to Q.10: "I would affirm the presence of the eternal Son but am cautious about 'revelatory' presence because I don't know what this means in terms of knowledge." "In terms of Bavinck, I think you are right that I don't emphasize the Christological groundedness of revelation as much as he does, mainly because I was a little uncertain to what he means by it."

1638. Strange, *Their Rock*, 90.

1639. Strange, *Their Rock*, 90: "The synthesis that, to my mind, best 'holds together' and 'captures' these different elements [i.e., creature-creator distinction, imago Dei, antithesis, common grace] is the theological anthropology underpinning the Reformed apologetic methodology known as 'presuppositionalism', associated with Cornelius Van Til and his students, especially Greg Bahnsen and John Frame."

See also Strange, "Exclusivisms," 45, and Strange's use of the acronym REPE—*Reformed Evangelical Presuppositional Exclusivism*.

1640. As noted by Henry Van Til, *Calvinistic Concept of Culture*, 180: "Calvinists, especially under the leadership of A. Kuyper in the 19th century, have maintained that the biblical concept of the antithesis refers to the enmity that God has set between the Seed of the woman, (the incarnate Word and all those who are incorporated by faith into his church) and the seed of the Serpent (all those who live in enmity with God, and who persist in their apostasy outside of the covenant.)"

1641. Van Til, *Common Grace*, 38, 40, critiques Kuyper as not being consistent, and he is also critical of H. Bavinck (on page 49) whom he argues has Roman Catholic and Natural theology leanings. See also page 54.

1642. Frame, *Cornelius Van Til*, 43. See also Wallace, "Antithesis Revisited."

1643. Frame, *Cornelius Van Til*, 188.

1644. For critical views of Van Til from reformed theologians, see Sproul et al., *Classical Apologetics*, 183–338, and the Reformed engagements with Frame in *Five Views on Apologetics*.

1645. Van Til, *Common Grace*, 68, 92, 165.

1646. Van Til, *Common Grace*, 173: "But I have argued at length, particularly against Barth, that the image of God in man consists of actual knowledge content."

1647. Van Til, *Common Grace*, 54.

1648. Van Til, *Common Grace*, 168–69.

1649. Strange, *Their Rock*, 85, 240. See also Strange, "Perilous Exchange," 115: "In terms of our analysis, the antithesis can be seen between those who worship YHWH, the self-contained ontological Trinity of the Bible, and those who worship idols."

1650. Strange, *Their Rock*, 39.

1651. Strange, *Their Rock*, 83.

1652. See Bahnsen, *Van Til's Apologetic Readings*, 274–75, on the antithesis and the eschaton. See also Van Til, *Common Grace*, 68, 92, and 165, on the eschatological aspect. At the same time, balancing this, is the stress on the principial compared to the practical in Strange's work.

1653. Strange, *Their Rock*, 83, 86.

1654. Strange, *Their Rock*, 86.

1655. Strange, *Their Rock*, 86.

1656. Farnham, "Postfoundational Epistemology," 216. He argues that Strange follows Van Til in the following areas: False religion being idolatrous, 258; being a "refashioning of divine revelation," 258; the antithesis in the area of Christian and non-Christian religions, 260; and the idea of subversive fulfilment, 262.

1657. Henry Stob was a professor at Calvin College from 1939 to 1975.

1658. Stob, "Observations."

1659. Stob, "Observations," 242: "From the Sacred Scriptures they [Christians from Apostolic times] had learned that there is a real and uncompromising, although uneven, contest being waged between God and Satan, between Christ and antichrist, between the seed of the woman and the seed of the serpent, between the church and the world."

1660. Stob, "Observations," 244–45:

> The good creation is God's thesis. The Satan-provoked fall of our first parents is humanity's antithesis to God's thesis. The gift of Christ and the gospel of redemption is God's move, not toward a Hegelian synthesis of thesis and antithesis but towards a re-assertion and reestablishment of an historically enriched original thesis. From a consideration of its origin it may therefore be concluded that the antithesis is for Christians less a principle to be applauded than a factor to be banished. To be with God is to be at bottom thetic, and to seek to remove from the world all that is antithetic. The antithesis, in short, is what the gospel is out to destroy.

1661. Stob, "Observations," 245. This positioning is similar to Henry Van Til's, *Calvinistic Concept of Culture*, 81, view of Augustine: "The two cities [in Augustine's thinking] are metaphysical entities: that is to say, one cannot find them on land or sea in concrete things. They have a spiritual existence, they are spiritual forces in opposition." Note also his comment on page 83 of the same volume:

> Although Augustine is not always clear on this matter, yet on the whole, we may say that the Church may not be identified with the kingdom of God. Church and kingdom cannot be equated because the former has many hypocrites in it, members of *civitas terrena*. But although the two may not be identified, nevertheless, in the church the appearance of the Kingdom is concentrated. In like manner the Kingdom of this world (*civitas terrena*) is revealed in political states, but it may not be identified with them.

This interpretation is also similar to that of Richard Mouw, *He Shines in All That's Fair*, 25: "the antithesis is not an opposition that holds between the church and the world as such, but between the cause of God and the cause of Satan, each of which can be seen at work in the lives of Christians and non-Christians alike."

1662. Stob, "Observations," 246.

1663. Stob, "Observations," 246.

1664. Stob comments in "Observations," 251:

> In the society of men it [the antithesis] is contextually conditioned by a residual solidarity . . . it takes place within a common humanity, and . . . it is articulated within a shared universe of discourse. The fact is that the antithesis, at bottom, is between sin and grace. But sin and grace are

adjectival; they modify creation. And the structures of creation persist. It is only as these structures remain intact and support and accommodate the clash of rival forces, that these forces can possess both the room and the instruments to exercise themselves against each other.

1665. Stob, *Theological Reflections*, 120.

1666. Stob, *Theological Reflections*, 121. Tiessen, "God's Work of Grace," 189, comments similarly, "It is as agents of special grace that the religions which are not based upon the revelation of God in Christ fail disastrously but, as agents of common grace, they may sometimes exceed some Christian communities."

1667. Stob, *Theological Reflections*, 121–22.

1668. Stob, *Theological Reflections*, 122:

> There is only one way to God, the way laid by God himself—his only begotten Son, the Saviour of the world—the way upon which Christians walk, the way which, if one walks upon it, makes one a Christian, an adherent of the Christian religion, a member of the Christian church. The Christian way is therefore unique, absolute, incomparable, for it is Christ himself, very God of very God. This, then, is what we mean when we say that Christianity is absolute, and opposed antithetically to all other religions.

1669. Stob, *Theological Reflections*, 124.

1670. Stob, *Theological Reflections*, 123.

1671. Stob, *Theological Reflections*, 124: "It is contrary to both fact and Scripture to regard the ethnic faiths as (simplistically) *nothing but* the out workings of sin, *nothing but* the work of Satan. There is grace in them too—not saving grace, and there is no salvation in them—but grace nevertheless, the presence of which is, of course, not an occasion to congratulate the sinner, but to magnify the Lord."

1672. Strange, *Their Rock*, 319: "Because of the common grace order worked by the Holy Spirit, a work that is external and in opposition to the essential nature of idolatrous religion and fallen humanity, non-Christian religions are instrumental in accomplishing the purposes given to common grace in restraining sin and exciting to civic righteousness." See also Strange, *Their Rock*, 246.

1673. Bavinck, *Impact of Christianity*, 55, 57.

1674. Bavinck, *Impact of Christianity*, 77, states:

> The culture of a nation is an indivisible unity: it is a system of tenets, principles, customs which are all interdependence. That is true, but it is not absolutely true. The culture of a nation tried to become an indivisible unity but it never succeeds. Somewhere in its structure there is a hidden crack. The culture of a nation is a product of human work, but there is an untraceable influence in its that cannot be scrutinized because it has its origin in the mercy of God.

On this point see also Djung, *Revelation and Grace*, 217, 219. Strange is clearly aware of this aspect of Bavinck's thinking: see *Their Rock*, 282–83.

1675. Kraemer, "Continuity," 4, makes it clear that he believes the Spirit to be working outside religions.

1676. Newbigin, *Gospel in a Pluralist Society*, 172.

1677. Klapwijk, "Antithesis and Common Grace," 181. Herman Bavinck, *Reformed Dogmatics, Prolegomena*, 319, stated:

> An operation of God's Spirit and of his common grace is discernible not only in science and art, morality and law, but also in the religions. Calvin rightly spoke of a "seed of religion," a "sense of divinity." . . . Founders of religion, after all, were not impostors or agents of Satan but men who, being religiously inclined, had to fulfill a mission to their time and people and often exerted a beneficial influence on the life of peoples.

1678. E.g., Bavinck, "General Revelation and the Non-Christian Religions (1955)," 54:

> Everything depends on what we mean by an element of 'truth'. If taken in a vague and general sense, it must be admitted that such elements are found in the non-Christian religions. If taken in a special and defined meaning, then it will be hardly tenable. All central ideas involved in Christian belief . . . are found in most religions, but they are all understood in a fundamentally different sense, and applied in a quite different connection. The deeper one enters into them, the more one grows aware that all is different in non-Christian religions.

1679. Bavinck, *Church between Temple and Mosque*, 200, writes, "Every religion contains, somehow, the silent work of God." In the same book, on page 112, he states, "Religion [not man's experience of God outside religion] is the way in which man experiences the deepest existential relations and gives expression to this experience." Visser, *Heart for the Gospel*, 167, translated Bavinck from *Het Christendom als absolute religio*, page 130, as follows: "There are in fact many beautiful and true thoughts of deep wisdom in pagan [holy] books. . . . We need not look upon the prophets of paganism as imposters; indeed we may freely acknowledge that they, too, may well have heard something of God's voice."

1680. Bavinck, *Church between Temple and Mosque*, 203.

1681. Bavinck, *Church between Temple and Mosque*, 28–29.

1682. I believe Strange occasionally speaks of differences, but as far as I can see he does not put religions on any kind of continuum (cf. Augustine).

1683. Bavinck, *Church between Temple and Mosque*, 111, states:

> We see that the history of religion depicts a great variety of divine forms and myths. That is why it is such a remarkable history. Again and again the same ideas crop up. Also, this history repeats itself many times. When examining its searching and groping we encounter so many different ideas that we are confused. They are sometimes bizarre, unbelievably childlike and foolish; yet sometimes they strike us as being sublime and imposing.

See also Bavinck, *Church between Temple and Mosque*, 126:

> This shows that there are gradations in the history of religion. We always encounter the powers of repression and exchange, but that does not mean that they were always of the same nature and strength. We meet figures in the history of the non-Christian religions of whom we feel that God wrestled with them in a very particular way. We still notice traces of that process of suppression and substitution in the way they responded, but occasionally we observe a far greater influence of God there than in many other human religions. The history of religion is not always and everywhere the same. It does not present monotonous picture of only folly and degeneration. There are culminating points in it, not because certain

human beings are much better than others, but because every now and then Divine compassion interferes, compassion, which keeps man from suppressing and substituting the truth completely.

Bavinck in *Church between Temple and Mosque*, 125, writes, "The great moments in the history of religion are the moments when God wrestled with man in a very particular way." See also Bavinck, "General Revelation and the Non-Christian Religion (2013)," 108: "In the modern world, people's spiritual condition is worse than those within the non-Christian religions."

1684. Bavinck, *Church between Temple and Mosque*, 20–21.

1685. For example, as argued by D'Costa, "Gavin D'Costa Responds," 150. D'Costa, after citing Strange's comment, "God through his Spirit does not strive with religious traditions and systems but with individuals made in his image," (page 121 of the same book) states, "But if the person in question writes texts that are taken as authoritative, cannot the action of the Spirit also be discerned in religious structures (for example in caring for widows)? What is the logic of isolating the Spirit in the personal inner subjectivity of the person, and not the structures which persons shape and form?"

1686. See for Example, Bavinck, *Impact of Christianity*, 102: "In the heart of the gentile dwells a mysterious knowledge of God that never becomes a real knowledge because it is always suppressed and superseded by his ungodliness and unrighteousness. In his ignorance there is always a trace of knowledge." See also Bavinck, "Defining Religious Consciousness," 183:

> The world in which we live is a double-sided world. Something of a divine smile is present over the world, but at the same time the demonic work of mysterious forces aimed at our destruction is also palpable. From moment to moment, the human race lives with the deep mystery of all existence. People feel that they are in God's presence, but at the same time they are aware of the power of demons. Our lives are bound by that mystery. Thus, we find a universal development in human history of the awareness that this world and all that happens in it is intimately connected to the mysterious, supernatural world of the gods. Something of that mystery, of that divine force, is found in everything that exists.

In *Church between Temple and Mosque*, 19, Bavinck writes, "The history of mankind is more than just a long account of what man has done, created and invented; its deepest mystery is the story of God's concern with man and man's response to God's revelation. Religion is by its very nature a communion, in which man answers and reacts to God's revelation." See also Bavinck, *Impact of Christianity*, 106–7: "But the question rises if it was possible to deprive them [Christian Ideas] absolutely of their original strength . . . here we suddenly feel ourselves confronted with the deepest of mysteries, the mystery of the power of God." In "God and the World," 319, Bavinck states, "It is not easy to respond to all these observations, especially because we sense that, against our will, we are standing here before one of the greatest of all mysteries. Nothing is more difficult for a person to understand than the riddle of God dwelling in the creature, of the presence of eternity in time." See also "I do not wish to deny that the Spirit of God has worked among the heathen more than we often suspect," as stated by Bavinck, cited in Visser, "Introduction," 47n215.

1687. Bavinck, *Impact of Christianity*, 95: "The history of religion is a strange mixture of beauty and ugliness. He who reads the sacred books of the various peoples of the world finds himself confronted with a great many interesting problems."

1688. Though not using the actual word antithesis—with one exception—*Introduction to the Science of Missions*, 137 (there referring to the work of Kraemer, *Christian Message*, 139).

1689. Bavinck, *Introduction to the Science of Missions*, 126–27:

> As long as we are annoyed by the stupidity of the "natives," at their primitive behaviour, at their deceit and pride, and as long as we only laugh at their foolish superstition, the path to an encounter in love is blocked. Not until I see all things such as stupidity, primitiveness and deceit as the elements constituting the structure of their flight from God and responsibility, can I begin to have room for love. For then I realise that apart from God's grace, this same flight from God is also the deepest motive of my own life. I try to flee in an infinitely more subtle manner, but I nevertheless flee, until Christ draws me out of my darkness and opens my eyes.

Bavinck, *Church between Temple and Mosque*, 200:

> Every Christian knows that he is always apt to hide the truth by his own unrighteousness, and that only God's grace has taught him to acknowledge and confess this as sin. With such humility the Church can give its testimony in the world of the other religions. As I have said elsewhere, "As long as I laugh at what I regard as being foolish superstition in other religions, I look down upon the adherents of them." Then I have not yet found the key to his [another religion's adherent's] soul. As soon as I understand that what he does in a noticeably naive and childish manner, I also do and continue to do again and again in a different form; as soon as I actually stand next to him, I can in the name of Christ stand in opposition to him and convince him of sin, as Christ did with me and still does each day. With these basic acknowledgments we can start the conversation.

Calvin spoke similarly of the antithesis within the Christian heart: *Institutes* 1.3.9.

1690. This being so, I do not think it could be *primary* in his theology of religions either.

1691. Strange, *Their Rock*, 39: "However, while I recognize the finitude, failures and inconsistencies of God's people, together with the terrible truth that judgment begins within God's household (1 Peter 4:17), I am still able to say that there is a fundamental, indeed antithetical, difference in principle between the regenerated and Spirit-enabled confession that Jesus is Lord."

1692. In *Their Rock*, 40, Strange states:

> Finally, and as a corollary to the previous point, while I intend this study to be a positive piece of theological construction, my conclusions concerning the nature of non-Christian religions are often negative. I hope such pronouncements do not give rise to the charge that I am guilty of the sins of malice or vainglory: it is imperative that the context for Christians engaging with religious traditions be one of grace. First, a constant acknowledgment that we ourselves as Christians have been saved by grace through faith and not because of any ethical or intellectual superiority.

Interestingly, Van Til seemed to argue for the importance of standing alongside, at least in terms of missional approach. In *Common Grace*, 168, he stated: "It is not in accordance with fact to say that the absolute ethical antithesis, even when taken as being such *in principle only*, is for me the starting point when dealing with the relation of the believer and the non-believer. As the preceding quotations imply, my starting point is always the fact that God originally made man in His image and that He placed him in an exhaustively revelational context."

1693. Strange is keenly evangelistic in his motivation and this is clearly present in his books *Plugged in* and *Making Faith Magnetic*. Here, I simply suggest that a book focusing on developing a theology of religions may, because of its methodology, not really treat theology of mission. I suggest that Bavinck was more aware of the symbiotic relationship between the two, allowing mission to more clearly inform his theology of religions.

1694. Belgic: 13, 14, 36; Canons of Dort II 5, 6, III and IV: 4,8,9; Westminster Confession V: 6

Van Leeuwen in the Translator's Introduction to "Herman Bavinck's 'Common Grace,'" 36n3, states, "The Reformed creeds do not deal with common grace as such, but in several of their pronouncements on sin and virtue, on the loss of the *imago Dei*, and on the authority of the state, they give expression to views that presuppose common grace."

1695. Van Til, *Common Grace* 91, writes, "Positively, common grace is the necessary correlative to the doctrine of total depravity." Berkhof, *Systematic Theology*, 432, states, "The origin of the doctrine of common grace was occasioned by the fact that there is in the world, alongside of the course of the Christian life with all its blessings, a natural course of life, which is not redemptive and yet exhibits many traces of the true, the good, and the beautiful." Dennison, "Christian Academy," 113n8, comments, "The Reformed tradition has had a particular interest in the concept of common grace in light of its view of total depravity." Herman Kuiper, *Calvin on Common Grace*, 229–30, believes: "The doctrine of common grace as propounded by Calvin enables us to do full justice to all the good found with unregenerate men and at the same time to cling to the Scriptural teaching on the total depravity of fallen man."

1696. I would suggest wrongly—see the reference to Paul Helm's interpretation of Calvin and natural law below, with which my own interpretation concurs (see also chapter 4 of this book).

1697. Herman Bavinck, "Common Grace," 39, wrote, "This principle [the reformed doctrine of common grace] was discovered in the Reformation, notably by Calvin." Van Til, *Common Grace*, 12, stated: "No one, we believe, can be seriously concerned with the question of common grace unless he seeks to be truly Reformed in his interpretation of life. Calvin, called the originator, and Kuyper, the great modern exponent, of the doctrine of common grace, were primarily concerned, in the whole thrust of their endeavor, to bring men face to face with the sovereign God." Murray, "Common Grace," 94, states,

> In this field of inquiry no name deserves more credit than that of the renowned reformer, John Calvin. No one was more deeply persuaded of the complete depravation of human nature by sin and of the consequent inability of unaided human nature to bring forth anything good, and so he explained the existence of good outside the sphere of God's special and saving grace by the presence of a grace that is common to all, yet enjoyed by some in special degree.

1698. Hoeksema, Engelsma, and Cammenga reject the word "grace" as an attitude of God to unbelievers, being outside of Christ. See Hoeksema, *God's Goodness Always Particular*; Engelsma, *Common Grace Revisited*; Cammenga, "Another Look at Calvin and Common Grace." Douma, *Common Grace*, 391, notices how Schilder rejected the idea of common grace. Richard Mouw, in *All That God Cares About*, 111, also discusses Schilder's dislike of the term and idea. See also Van Til, *Calvinistic Concept of Culture*, 141, concerning Schilder's rejection of the idea of common grace. Hoeksema's rejection is documented by Van Til, in *Common Grace*, 23. Strange provides a brief summary of twentieth century Reformed disagreements in *Possibility of Salvation*, 302n52. Strange does not relate common grace to two kingships, or two roles of Christ, as has been argued in some other Reformed common grace theologies—for example Herman Bavinck's. See John Bolt, "Herman Bavinck on Natural Law and Two Kingdoms," 69: "Bavinck explained common grace in connection with the various two kingdoms themes. He specifically associated the distinction between common and special grace with the twofold kingship of Christ, and he connected the Noahic covenant of nature with the work of the Logos in distinction from the work of Christ as mediator of the covenant of grace."

1699. Strange, "Perilous Exchange," 118: "This variegated non-salvific work of the Holy Spirit restrains sin and the consequences of sin in the non-Christian and excites non-Christians to perform acts of 'civic righteousness' and culture-building."

1700. Murray, as cited in Strange, *Their Rock*, 89.

1701. Macleod, as cited in Strange, *Their Rock*, 89.

1702. Van Til, as cited in Strange, *Their Rock*, 92.

1703. E.g., Strange, *Their Rock*, 94, 319.

1704. See Strange, *Possibility of Salvation*, 241n52. Strange links common grace to Christ, referring to Reformed debate over whether this is rooted in creation or in the atonement.

1705. Strange, *Their Rock*, 92.

1706. Strange, *Their Rock*, 92. The quotation is from Van Til, *Introduction to Systematic Theology*, 65.

1707. Strange, *Their Rock*, 94, citing with approval Van Til, *Common Grace and the Gospel*, 174: "Common grace is the means by which God keeps man from expressing the *principle* of hostility to its full extent, thus enabling man to do the 'relatively good.'"

1708. Strange, *Their Rock*, 288; See also Strange, "Perilous Exchange," 133: "because of the inconsistency of non-Christian worldviews (due to God's common grace and the imago Dei), other faiths may agree with a Christian stance on a certain ethical or political issue, because they are using the 'borrowed capital' of the Christian worldview."

1709. Strange, *Their Rock*, 86.

1710. Strange, "Perilous Exchange," 121: "God through his Spirit does not strive with religious traditions and systems but with individuals made in his image." See also Strange, *Their Rock*, 319: "Because of the common grace order worked by the Holy Spirit, a work that is external and in opposition to the essential nature of idolatrous religion and fallen humanity, non-Christian religions are instrumental in accomplishing the purposes given to common grace in restraining sin and exciting to civic righteousness."

1711. Strange, *Their Rock*, 246:

> Although at the principial or "root" level of religious presuppositions, the antithesis between Christian and non-Christian is stark: the practical and "lived" worldviews built upon these fundamental commitments are often

inconsistent at the level of "fruit." Within the unbeliever the theological explanation for this inconsistency is the nonsalvific work of the Holy Spirit who, in his common grace, restrains sin and excites to a civic righteousness.

1712. Van Til, *Common Grace*, 118–19. See also Bahnsen, *Van Til's Apologetic*, 433: "Skilled workmanship is often, by God's common grace, found more abundantly in the camp of the antitheists than in the camp of the theists."

1713. Strange, *Their Rock*, 213. Note that Strange refers to Bahnsen's quotation, above.

1714. See Visser, *Heart for the Gospel*, 167.

1715. Kraemer recognizes wisdom in pagan thought in the OT in *Religion*, 262.

1716. VanDrunen, "Wisdom," 162–63. See also VanDrunen, "Wisdom," 164:

Through the natural moral order non-Israelites did indeed know something about the ways of wisdom of the true God, the maker of heaven and earth, even if they did not know his name or experience his acts of redemption as Israel did; but Israel had the privilege of knowing this God more fully through a salvific covenant relationship, and their wisdom was to be sought only through this lens. Israel was to learn wisdom from others, but only as viewed through the fear of YHWH.

1717. VanDrunen, "Wisdom," 161, states, "there are numerous similarities between Amenemope, an ancient Egyptian wisdom document, and Proverbs 22:17–24:22.29. Most scholars today believe that the author of 22:17–24:22 used Amenemope. Although direct reliance is impossible to prove, their points of similarity are remarkable, and close parallels also exist between Amenemope and other sections of Proverbs."

1718. VanDrunen, "Wisdom," 160.

1719. VanDrunen, "Wisdom," 161–62, differentiates this wisdom from the knowledge of Yahweh in the following way:

Through observing, experiencing, and reflecting upon the world, people gain true knowledge that provides faithful guidance for living well. A corollary is that God and God's will are communicated through nature, and therefore wisdom ought to be pursued through the fear of the Lord. Wisdom and the Natural Moral Order therefore, provides no support for a natural law theory grounded in notions of religious neutrality or seeking a means for doing ethics without God.

1720. As Bennema notes, among the five possible backgrounds to the introduction to John's gospel, one of them is "the Jewish wisdom traditions." In his view this particular understanding "remains the most fertile environment to explain the claims made in the Logos hymn," according to Bennema, "Christology of the Johannine Prologue."

1721. Strange, "Perilous Exchange," 221.

1722. Strange, *Their Rock*, 322.

1723. Mouw, "Discerning the Spirit in World Religions," 203.

1724. Mouw is more appreciative of Strange's work in *All That God Cares About*, 42—especially the theft imagery present in *Their Rock*, 246. He also recognizes Strange to have followed the idea of a threefold function of common grace: bestowal of gifts, restraint from sin, and enabling unbelievers to engage in valuable civic acts in *All That God Cares About*, 45.

1725. Macleod, *Behold your God*, 121.

1726. Strange, "Co-belligerence and Common Grace," 3:

> The instrumentality of God's common grace is many and varied. God's general revelation of himself externally in creation (Acts 14:17; Romans 1:20, 32) and internally, the "law written on their hearts" (Romans 2:14, 15) means that "even where there is no gospel and no spiritual enlightenment there are those things which 'nature teaches' so that even specifically secular states and avowedly atheistic societies still possess strong ethical structures."

Strange's position regarding the blessings of common grace seems to be considerably reduced in a later paper: "Not Ashamed," 255: "Given the sinful suppression and exchange of truth, a 'naked' natural law would seem no basis on which to build a society."

1727. Masselink, "New Views of Common Grace," 196: "By God's common grace, the disposition of the natural man is still receptive to the external and internal witness of the Holy Spirit. So it is with the natural heart. The principle of absolute corruption is curbed by God's common grace to such a degree that natural man can become a recipient of the testimony of God's Spirit."

1728. Bavinck, *Church between Temple and Mosque*, 126: "every now and then divine compassion interferes, compassion which keeps man from suppressing and substituting the truth completely." In the same volume, 203, Bavinck writes, "We may say that by the grace of God repression and substitution do not always succeed. Time and again we notice things in the history of religion which show that God has really concerned Himself with these people."

1729. Strange, *Possibility of Salvation*, 242, comments, "Common grace enables human beings to see God's revelation in creation and in this sense this revelation is itself a fruit of common grace as it gives human beings a rationality and makes understanding possible." Strange, "For Their Rock Is Not as Our Rock" 392, states, "Because we are metaphysically all made in God's image, because of God's variegated common grace which restrains the depth of our suppression and substitution, because idols are parasites and counterfeits of the God—YHWH, there is a "thatness" to our humanity."

1730. Strange, *Their Rock*, 276.

1731. Strange, *Their Rock*, 246:

> Although at the principial or "root" level of religious presuppositions, the antithesis between Christian and non-Christian is stark: the practical and "lived" worldviews built upon these fundamental commitments are often inconsistent at the level of 'fruit'. Within the unbeliever the theological explanation for this inconsistency is the nonsalvific work of the Holy Spirit who, in his common grace, restrains sin and excites to a civic righteousness.

1732. Helm, *John Calvin's Ideas*, 384: "Calvin's attitude to natural law is by no means negative or dismissive. He does not draw attention to natural law and equity simply to eliminate them; rather he has a positive view of them."

1733. Helm, *Calvin at the Centre*, 333. Immediately preceding this, on the same page, Helm states:

> On Calvin's position, to say that a human ability or activity is the effect of common grace or that it is the working of nature, human nature, are

thus two ways of saying the same thing, or almost the same thing. What the phrase "common grace" brings out is that these abilities and activities, found in fallen and unregenerate human nature, are the result of undeserved, divine goodness. The effects of the Fall on human nature could have been worse than they are, and why they are not worse than they are is due to "common grace." The concept of nature looks at the same phenomenon from another angle, focusing on the persisting structures of human life. How are the gifts of common grace expressed? In the workings of human nature, created in the image of God and now fallen and suffering loss and perversion as a consequence. The Fall has resulted in loss and perversion but, due to divine goodness, not in obliteration.

See also McNeill, "Natural Law in the Teaching of the Reformers."

1734. Bavinck, *Introduction to the Science of Missions*, 227: "It must first be noted that each person, no matter how deeply fallen and how far departed, still is within the reach of God's common grace. God has not left himself without a witness. 'Because that which may be known of God is manifest in them,' says Paul in Romans 1: 19, they are without excuse."

1735. Kraemer, *Christian Message*, 118: "Revelation is an act of God, an act of divine grace for forlorn man and a forlorn world by which He condescends to reveal His Will and His Heart, and which, just because it is revelation, remains hidden except to the eye of *faith*, and even then remains an incomprehensible miracle."

1736. Bavinck, *Church between Temple and Mosque*, 19: "The history of mankind is more than just a long account of what man has done, created and invented; its deepest mystery is the story of God's concern with man and man's response to God's revelation. Religion is by its very nature a communion, in which man answers and reacts to God's revelation." See also Bavinck, *Impact of Christianity*, 106-7: "But the question rises if it was possible to deprive them [Christian Ideas] absolutely of their original strength. . . . Here we suddenly feel ourselves confronted with the deepest of mysteries, the mystery of the power of God." On page 77 of the same volume he writes, "There is God's mercy which shines through human wretchedness and misery. God has not surrendered us to the evil passions of our souls."

1737. H. Bavinck, *Reformed Dogmatics*, 1: 318: "But, however severely Scripture judges the character of paganism, it is precisely the general revelation it teaches that enables and authorizes us to recognize all the elements of truth that are present also in pagan religions." Macleod, *Person of Christ*, 239-40:

> The belief that Jesus Christ is universal Lord and the only saviour does not imply that Christianity has a monopoly of truth. It shares many of its values (for example, love of one's neighbour, concern for the poor and belief in the sanctity of life) with other world faiths. It also shares with some of those faiths a significant body of theological belief. . . . [B]elief in one personal creator and life after death is not confined only to religions which derive from the Bible . . . the invisible things of God are revealed through the things that are made (Rom. 1:20). This explains the overlap between Christianity and world religions . . . creation is revelatory precisely because the aeons were made through the divine Son (Heb 1:2). We may even, possibly, go further. John speaks of 'the true light that gives light to every man', and many theologians of unobjectionable orthodoxy have taken this to refer to a work of Christ, the eternal Logos in the heart of Everyman. . . . The presence of this light gives a perfectly coherent

explanation, from the standpoint of Christian exclusivism, for all that is true and valuable in the religions of the world.

Netland, *Encountering Religious Pluralism*, 333, states, "Given God's general revelation and the fact that all people bear the divine image, we should not be surprised to find elements of truth and value in other religions. There is no reason to maintain that everything taught by non-Christian religions is false or that there is nothing of value in them. Not only is this not demanded by Scripture but in fact it is not consistent with what we see in other traditions." Ferguson, *Holy Spirit*, 246, says, "It is appropriate to believe, with Calvin and many others, that all truth is God's truth, even when it is found in the mouth of the ungodly." Corduan, *Neighboring Faiths*, 57, writes:

> Are other religions true? I am now looking at the belief systems as a whole and have to conclude that this is not possible. If any religion is true, even if it does not make exclusive truth claims, any religion that is inconsistent with it must be false. This is simple logic. Earlier in the chapter we talked about how people, rather than simply submitting to God, wanted to have more of a hand in controlling their lives and so fell away from monotheism into other forms of religion. They filled the capacity that God has given us to have fellowship with him with fictions, speculations and counterfeits. . . . Do other religions contain truths? Of course they do. As you will see as you study the various religions in this book, other religions may contain simple factual truths (for example, people want to know what happens after they die), spiritual truths (for example, there is a God), and even wisdom (for example, by putting our own interests ahead of caring for others we are ultimately harming ourselves). Still, containing truths does not mean that the entire set of beliefs is true.

See also Corduan, "Budha, Shiva, and Mohammed," 130; Corduan, *Tapestry of Faiths*, 70–71.

1738. Strange, *Their Rock*, 306. In "Daniel Strange Re-responds," 218, Strange states, "Concerning the relationship between Christianity and all other religions, the relationship is one of structural continuity in systemic discontinuity." Although Strange writes this, at the same time, he very occasionally speaks of truth (in an unqualified sense) being present in non-Christian religions: See Strange, *Their Rock*, 321: "As God fulfils these creational purposes it is to be expected that even false religion will display the marks of God's creative work in the world: truth, beauty and order will all be evident in other religions and cultures." In the context of remnantal and influential revelation he states that "revelatory evidence is found in non-Christian religious traditions. Indeed, we would expect to see it," (*Their Rock*, 258). I assume this revelatory evidence could be termed "truth" here.

1739. Strange, *Their Rock*, 306.

1740. Strange, "Interview with Strange"—Response to Q.3: "Examples of 'suppressed truth' would be Paul's quotations of the pagan poets in Acts 17, through to the 'suppressed truth' of doctrine of transcendence and immanence in say Islam or other so-called 'world religions'. Again the doctrine of common grace means there are different levels of suppression."

1741. Strange, "Interview with Strange"—Response to Q.3.

1742. Strange, "Interview with Strange"—Response to Q.3.

1743. Strange, "Interview with Strange"—Response to Q.3.

1744. See Wallace, "Antithesis Revisited," 2.

1745. Van Til, *Common Grace*, 115: "But how can any fact in this world be a fact, and be the kind of fact it is, except as revelational of the will of God to man? A fact in this world is what it is according to the function that it has to perform in the plan of God. Every fact *is* its function, and therefore every fact contains, in conjunction with all other facts, the covenantal claims of God upon man."

1746. Farnham, "Postfoundational Epistemology," 56.

1747. Groothuis, an advocate of the correspondence theory, in *Truth Decay*, 109, states, "The theological statement 'Jesus is Lord of the universe' is either true or false. Whether it is coolly uttered or it is proclaimed with great emotion, it has only one truth value: either true or false. It either honors reality or it does not. This is because truth is a quality of propositions and beliefs. It is not ratified by any subjective response or majority vote or cultural fashion." Note also the comment of Stob in "Observations," 255: "Facts constitute the currency of the realm of knowledge, and they are both distinguishable from and separable from the interpretative context, in which, in any concrete instance they are inserted. I suspect that this escapes Van Til's notice because he consistently thinks in terms of a total system and neglects or depreciates the role of scientific abstractionism."

1748. Bavinck, *Introduction to the Science of Missions*, 228.

1749. Visser, *Heart for the Gospel*, 172, also quoted in Strange, *Their Rock*, 243.

1750. Strange, *Their Rock*, 86, states:

> If the above description is correct, the "seed of the woman" and the "seed of Satan" entail two antithetical and incommensurable worldviews, fundamentally oriented in the presuppositions of the heart, which are all encompassing and hermetically sealed interpretations of reality. As such they do not allow for any epistemological or ethical neutrality, and in theory are organic, interrelated and inseparable "systems" where, to use the illustration, as Jesus himself does, tree and fruit are related to one another (Matt. 7:15 20). As such, in principle these worldviews are "seamless garments" that demand "systemic" rather than "atomistic" analysis.

1751. Visser, *Heart for the Gospel*, 173, interprets Bavinck to argue that truth does actually remain in religions: "Thanks to the overwhelming power of God's revelation, certain components of pseudo religion can contain elements of veracity."

1752. Bavinck, *Impact of Christianity*, 98: "A Christian who anxiously tries to understand what heathenism essentially is will never shut his eyes to the sparks of truth and devotion which he certainly will see, although he will be deeply aware of the power of darkness which fascinates and captivates the hearts of the nations of the earth."

1753. Bavinck, *Impact of Christianity*, 108.

1754. In "Religious Consciousness and Christian Faith," 290, Bavinck writes, "In the darkness of human existence, where repressing and replacing focus their empty work day and night, only the proclamation of the gospel of Jesus Christ can bring light. Truth is found in him. This is the complete and living power for people, the power long repressed and rejected." In *Church between Temple and Mosque*, 203, Bavinck says, "We may say that by the grace of God, repression and substitution do not always succeed. Time and again we notice things in the history of religion which show that God has really concerned Himself with these people."

1755. Suggesting total suppression in "This Rock Unmoved," 73, Strange comments, "The point that I stress in various places in the book, which Kyle picks up on, and which

I reiterate again here, is that because of the idolatrous impulse, such revelatory material is immediately corrupted and distorted in sin and so is not salvific." Later on, he states, "I do not agree with Kyle that the establishment of remnantal revelation 'opens the door wide for speculation on its salvific possibilities', because we are dealing with suppressed truth which is counterfeit and not genuine." In *Their Rock*, 104, he says, "such revelatory material [i.e., remnantal] is always sinfully corrupted, distorted and degenerates to the point of being salvifically useless." On the other hand, his commitment to incomplete suppression is also stated. For example, in *Their Rock*, 270: "Because we are metaphysically all made in God's image, because of God's variegated common grace, which restrains the depth of our suppression and substitution, because idols are parasites and counterfeits of the God, Yahweh, there is a thatness to our humanity," and also in *Their Rock*, 232: "Secondly, the variegated nature of this suppression in human beings. In some the impact of revelation hardly makes a ripple, while others are overwhelmed by it. . . . The reason for such variation is not the 'goodness' of humans but rather the restraining grace of God through the operation of the Holy Spirit."

1756. The reader may consider related material in chapter 3, and the discussion there of the existence of knowledge and mis-knowledge in Augustine's thinking.

1757. Strange, "Interview with Strange"—Response to Q.3.

1758. Tension is mentioned a number of times in the works translated into English. I provide two examples, below. In "Religious Consciousness and Christian Faith," 285, Bavinck states, "People have been resisting, suppressing. They have done so unconsciously. But they do so all the time, moment by moment, always unaware that they are doing so. But at the same time, there is always a definite unsettledness deep within them as a consequence of that suppression. This amounts to a definite dissatisfaction and tension." On talking of religious consciousness, in *Church between Temple and Mosque*, 30, Bavinck writes, "it is a complicated thing, full of tensions and contrasts."

1759. Dennison, "Christian Academy," 114–15, states:

> When analyzing the Christian worldview in relationship to a non-Christian worldview, the two systems, holistically conceived, are antithetical to each other. Herein, the universal frameworks of two holistic systems of thought are thoroughly distinct and at odds with one another. Nevertheless, although this holistic antithesis exists, such a position does not restrict a non-Christian from affirming a truth in compliance with what has been revealed by God, for example, 2+2=4. In other words, the holistic character of one's system of unbelief is antithetical to Christianity, whereas a particular element in that system may be a common grace insight, one which can be shared by believer and unbeliever alike.

1760. Bahnsen, *Van Til's Apologetic*, 169, citing Van Til, writes, "It is our contention that only the Christian can obtain real coherence in his thinking. If all of our thoughts about the facts of the universe are correspondence with God's ideas of these facts, there will naturally be coherence in our thinking because there is a complete coherence in God's thinking."

1761. Van Til, *Introduction to Systematic Theology*, 65:

> As the Christian sins against his will, the natural man "sins against" his own essentially Satanic principle. As the Christian has the incubus of his "old man" weighing him down and therefore keeping him from realizing the 'life of Christ' within him, so the natural man has the incubus of the sense of Deity weighing him down and keeping him from realizing the life

of Satan within him. *The actual situation is therefore always a mix of truth with error* [emphasis mine].

Frame, "Van Til on Antithesis," states, "On the basis of common grace, Van Til maintains that unbelievers know some truth despite their sin and that's a fact." And, "On the basis of common grace, Van Til maintains that unbelievers know some truth despite their sin and its effects."

1762. In his own version of presuppositionalism, Frame, "Presuppositional Apologetics," 212, has stated that truth and error may exist side by side, the consequence being contradiction. In contrast to Strange's comment above, concerning the total absence of truth in the non-Christian thought, he writes (in Cowen, *Five Views*, 360), "I do think that the unregenerate have some true knowledge, and I am quite willing ... to attribute this fact to God's common grace." Frame, "Presuppositional Apologetics," 213, acknowledges that the pharisees held "many true ideas," and believes the key issue differentiating one's position vis a vis truth is the state of the heart. This viewpoint is implicitly present in Bavinck's comment, noted above, differentiating subjective and objective reality.

1763. Bavinck, *Impact of Christianity*, 103.

1764. Strange, *Their Rock*, 321: "As God fulfils these creational purposes it is to be expected that even false religion will display the marks of God's creative work in the world: truth, beauty and order will all be evident in other religions and cultures."

1765. Strange, "Daniel Strange Re-responds," 218, writes, "concerning the relationship between Christianity and all other religions, the relationship is one of structural continuity in systemic discontinuity."

1766. Strange, *Their Rock*, 323–24: "God's power is expressed as non-Christian religions are forced to provide a framework within which God's saving revelation might be expressed." In *Their Rock*, 281, he states, "First, even though the thatness of a universal religious consciousness is almost immediately 'filled' by the whatness of the sinful suppression and substitution of this knowledge of God, thatness is still missiologically essential."

1767. Visser, *Heart for the Gospel*, 171, speaking of Bavinck's thought says, "the 'thatness' of religion also manifests shades of depth and breath." Note also Bavinck's comment in *An Introduction to the Science of Missions*, 228: "That they believe in a God is an element of truth."

1768. Kraemer, *Religion and the Christian Faith*, 179

1769. Dhavamony, *Phenomenology of Religions*, 22, citing Boas, "History and Science in Anthropology," 137.

1770. I use the image employed by Kraemer, while recognizing that Scripture is, for the Christian believer, God's truth.

1771. The light of nature is very important for Edwards as a kind of foundation for Christian knowledge, whereas for Strange common grace is responsible for inconsistent worldviews among unbelievers.

1772. Note the comment of Kraemer, *Christian Message*, 63: "The ethical is always in the Bible submerged in, derived from, and subordinated to, the religious, because the Bible is radically theocentric." See also page 87 of the same volume.

1773. See Hacker, "Religions of the Gentiles," 257.

1774. Justin's demonic mimesis theory finds its origin not on earth but in heaven (the demons overhear what is going on in heaven): they do not corrupt existing revelation on earth.

1775. I believe Edwards would probably concur with Strange's view on this matter.

1776. Klapwijk, "Antithesis, Synthesis," 144.

1777. Both Strange and I would, I believe, argue this.

1778. Calvin, *Treatise on Relics*, 281.

1779. VanDrunen, "Wisdom," 162: "Perhaps the wisdom shared by Israelites and their pagan neighbors could be called a "common" or "proximate" wisdom, while that attained through knowledge of YHWH could be called a "sanctified" or "ultimate" wisdom."

1780. See Bennema, "Christology of the Johannine Prologue." See also Keener, *Gospel of John*, 1:363: "John's choice of the Logos (embracing also Wisdom and Torah) to articulate his Christology was brilliant." Schnackenburg, *Gospel according to St. John*, 1:228, writes, "it is a recurrent theme in the Wisdom literature that Wisdom met with rejection when it came among men. . . . Hence, it is quite possible and intelligible that the Christian community should also give more place to the activity of the pre-existent Logos who takes the place of Wisdom."

1781. As argued by Hermann Bavinck, *Prolegomena*, 319.

1782. Bavinck, *Impact of Christianity*, 62, 181.

1783. For Bavinck, christological general revelation is behind religious consciousness, and the message of the Gospel is connected to the revelation. False Religion, sitting between the two revelations, is generally viewed as idolatrous confusion.

1784. I acknowledge that the three-fold focus used in this book may not necessarily be adequate for studying other figures. I believe that it has been a helpful one for the theologians examined in this study.

1785. Bavinck, "Religious Consciousness and Christian Faith," 245: "A knowledge of God exists also among those who in their practice of their religion profess not to know him."

1786. Newbigin, *Gospel in a Pluralist Society*, 172: "The contemporary debate about Christianity and the world's religions is generally conducted with the unspoken assumption that 'religion' is the primary medium of human contact with the divine. When the New Testament affirms that God has nowhere left himself without witness, there is no suggestion that this witness is necessarily to be found in the sphere of what we call religion."

1787. Kraemer, "Continuity or Discontinuity," 4–5:

> This fundamental discontinuity of the world of spiritual reality, embodied in the revelation in Christ, to the whole range of human religion, excludes the possibility and legitimacy of a theologia naturalis in the sense of a science of God and man, conceived as an imperfect form of revelation, introductory to the world of divine grace in Christ. This rejection of a theologia naturalis as affording the basic religious truths on which the realm of the Christian revelation rises as the fitting superstructure, does not, however, include denying that God has been working in the minds of men outside the sphere of the Christian revelation and that there have been, and may be now, acceptable men of faith who live under the sway of non-Christian religions—products, however, not of these non-Christian religions but of

the mysterious workings of God's spirit. God forbid that we mortal men should be so irreverent as to dispose of how and where the Sovereign God of grace and love has to act.

1788. Clooney, *Comparative Theology*.

1789. Kraemer, *Religion and the Christian Faith*, 377.

Bibliography

Abdelnour, Mohammed Gamal. *A Comparative History of Catholic and Aš'arī Theologies of Truth and Salvation: Inclusive Minorities, Exclusive Majorities.* Leiden: Brill, 2021.

Allert, Craig D. "Revelation, Truth, Canon, and Interpretation: Studies in Justin Martyr's Dialogue with Trypho." PhD diss., University of Nottingham, 2001.

———. "What Are We Trying to Conserve? Evangelicalism and Sola Scriptura." *Evangelical Quarterly* 76 (2004) 327–48.

Anderson, Owen. *Reason and Worldviews: Warfield, Kuyper, Van Til, and Plantinga on the Clarity of General Revelation and Function of Apologetics.* Lanham, MD: University Press of America, 2008.

Ando, Clifford. "Pagan Apologetics and Christian Intolerance in the Ages of Themistius and Augustine." *Journal of Early Christian Studies* 4 (1996) 171–207.

Andresen, Carl. *Logos und Nomos: die Polemik des Kelsos wider das Christentum.* Berlin: de Gruyter, 1955.

Ash, Carisa A. *A Critical Evaluation of the Doctrine of Revelation in Evangelical Theology.* Eugene, OR: Pickwick, 2015.

Aucoin, Mary Aloysius. "Augustine and John Chrysostom: Commentators on St. John's Prologue." *Sciences Ecclesiastiques* 40 (1963) 123–31.

Augustine. *Augustine on Romans: Propositions from the Epistle to the Romans and Unfinished Commentary on the Epistles to the Romans.* Translated by Paula Landes. Scholars Press: Chico, CA, 1982.

———. *The City of God against the Pagans.* Edited and translated by R. W. Dyson. Cambridge: Cambridge University Press, 1998.

———. *Confessions.* Translated by Henry Chadwick. Oxford: Oxford University Press, 1998.

———. *The Confessions and Letters of St. Augustine, with a Sketch of his Life and Work.* Edited by Philip Schaff. Nicene and Post Nicene Fathers 1. Grand Rapids: Eerdmans, 1956.

———. *Expositions on the Book of Psalms.* Edited by Philip Schaff. Nicene and Post Nicene Fathers 8. New York: Christian Literature, 1888.

———. *Homilies on the Gospel of John 1–40.* Translated by Edmund Hill. The Works of Saint Augustine. Hyde Park, NY: New City, 2009.

BIBLIOGRAPHY

———. *Letters 211–270, 1*–29**. Translated by Roland Teske. The Works of Saint Augustine. Hyde Park, NY: New City, 2005.

———. *On Christian Belief*. Edited by Boniface Ramsey. The Works of Saint Augustine. New York: New City, 2005.

———. *The Retractions*. Translated by Mary Inez Bogan. The Fathers of the Church 60. Washington, DC: Catholic University of America Press, 1968.

———. *Saint Augustine on Genesis: Two Books on Genesis against the Manichees and on the Literal Interpretation of Genesis: An Unfinished Book*. Translated by Roland J. Teske. The Fathers of the Church 84. Washington, DC: Catholic University of America Press, 1991.

———. *Saint Augustin on Sermon on the Mount, Harmony of the Gospels, Homilies on the Gospels*. Edited by Philip Schaff. Nicene and Post Nicene Fathers 6. Grand Rapids: Eerdmans, 1956.

———. *Sermons*. Translated by Edmund Hill. 5 vols. The Works of Saint Augustine. New York: New City, 1997.

———. *Tractates (Lectures) on the Gospel of John*. https://www.newadvent.org/fathers/1701.htm.

Babcock, William S. "The Human and the Angelic Fall: Will and Moral Agency in Augustine's *City of God*." In *Augustine from Rhetor to Theologian*, edited by Joanne McWilliam, 133–50. Waterloo, ON: Wilfrid Laurier University Press, 1992.

Backus, Irena. "Calvin and the Greek Fathers." In *Continuity and Change: The Harvest of Late Medieval and Reformation History*, edited by Robert J. Bast and Andrew C. Gow, 253–76. Leiden: Brill, 2000.

———. "Calvin's Concept of Natural and Roman Law." *Calvin Theological Journal* 38 (2003) 7–26.

Baechle, Carl Francis. "A Reappraisal of the Christology of St. Justin Martyr." PhD diss., Fordham University, 2009.

Bahnsen, Greg L. *Van Til's Apologetic: Readings and Analysis*. Phillipsburg, NJ: P&R, 1998.

Balserak, Jon. *John Calvin as Sixteenth-Century Prophet*. Oxford: Oxford University Press, 2014.

Barnard, L. W. *Justin Martyr: His Life and Thought*. Cambridge: Cambridge University Press, 1967.

———. "Justin Martyr in Recent Study." *Scottish Journal of Theology* 22 (1969) 152–64.

———. "The Logos Theology of St. Justin Martyr." *Downside Review* 89 (1971) 132–41.

Barnett, S. J. *The Enlightenment and Religion: Myths of Modernity*. Manchester: Manchester University Press, 2003.

Barth, Karl. *Church Dogmatics*. Translated by G. W. Bromiley et al. London: T&T Clark, 2009.

Bates, Matthew W. "Justin Martyr's Logocentric Hermeneutical Transformation of Isaiah's Vision of the Nations." *Journal of Theological Studies* 60 (2009) 538–55.

Bavinck, Herman. "Common Grace." *Calvin Theological Journal* 24 (1989) 38–65.

———. *The Philosophy of Revelation*. Grand Rapids: Baker Book House, 1979.

———. *Reformed Dogmatics*. Vol. 1, *Prolegomena*. Edited by John Bolt. Translated by John Vriend. Grand Rapids: Baker Academic, 2003.

Bavinck, J. H. *The Church between Temple and Mosque*. Grand Rapids: Eerdmans, 1981.

———. *The Church between Temple and Mosque: A Study of the Relationship between Christianity and Other Religions*. Glenside, PA: Westminster Seminary Press, 2023.

BIBLIOGRAPHY

———. "Debating Religious Consciousness: Natural Religion." In *The J. H. Bavinck Reader*, edited by John Bolt et al., 199–232. Grand Rapids: Eerdmans, 2013.
———. "Defining Religious Consciousness: The Five Magnetic Points." In *The J. H. Bavinck Reader*, edited by John Bolt et al., 145–98. Grand Rapids: Eerdmans, 2013.
———. "General Revelation and the Non-Christian Religions." In *The J. H. Bavinck Reader*, edited by John Bolt et al., 95–109. Grand Rapids: Eerdmans, 2013.
———. "General Revelation and the Non-Christian Religions." *FUQ* 4 (1955) 43–55.
———. "God and the World." In *The J. H. Bavinck Reader*, edited by John Bolt et al., 303–29. Grand Rapids: Eerdmans, 2013.
———. "Human Religion in God's Eyes: A Study of Romans 1:18–32." *Scottish Bulletin of Evangelical Theology* 12 (1994) 44–52.
———. *The Impact of Christianity on the Non-Christian World*. Grand Rapids: Eerdmans, 1948.
———. *An Introduction to the Science of Missions*. Translated by David H. Freeman. Philadelphia: P&R, 1960.
———. "Religious Consciousness and Christian Faith." In *The J. H. Bavinck Reader*, edited by John Bolt et al., 277–99. Grand Rapids: Eerdmans, 2013.
———. "Religious Consciousness in History." In *The J. H. Bavinck Reader*, edited by John Bolt et al., 233–96. Grand Rapids: Eerdmans, 2013.
Beale, Gregory K. "Other Religions in New Testament Theology." In *Biblical Faith and Other Religions: An Evangelical Assessment*, edited by David W. Baker, 79–105. Grand Rapids: Kregel, 2004.
Bebbington, David W. *Evangelicalism in Modern Britain*. London: Hyman, 1989.
Bedouelle, Guy. "Attacks on the Biblical Humanism of Jacques Lefèvre d'Etaples." In *Biblical Humanism and Scholasticism in the Age of Erasmus*, edited by Erika Rummel, translated by Anna Machado-Matheson, 117–42. Leiden: Brill, 2008.
Bennema, Cornelis. "The Christology of the Johannine Prologue." In *T&T Clark Handbook of Christology*, edited by Daren Sumner and Chris Tilling. London: Bloomsbury T&T Clark, forthcoming.
Berkhof, Louis. *Systematic Theology*. Grand Rapids: Eerdmans, 1939.
Berkouwer, G. C. *General Revelation*. Grand Rapids: Eerdmans, 1955.
Beyerhaus, Peter P. "My Pilgrimage in Mission." *International Bulletin of Mission Research* 24 (2000) 172–74.
Block, Daniel I. "Other Religions in Old Testament Theology." In *Biblical Faith and Other Religions: An Evangelical Assessment*, edited by David W. Baker, 43–78. Grand Rapids: Kregel, 2004.
Boice, James Montgomery. *Genesis: An Expositional Commentary*. 3 vols. Grand Rapids: Zondervan, 1982.
Bolt, John. "Herman Bavinck on Natural Law and Two Kingdoms: Some Further Reflections." *Bavinck Review* 4 (2013) 64–93.
Bolt, John, et al., eds. *The J. H. Bavinck Reader*. Grand Rapids: Eerdmans, 2013.
Bolt, Peter G., et al. "The Legacy of Paul's Epistle to the Romans: From Augustine to Agamben." In *Romans and the Legacy of Saint Paul: Historical, Theological, and Social Perspectives*, edited by Peter G. Bolt and James R. Harrison, 455–518. Macquarie Park: SCD, 2019.
Bombaro, John Joseph. "Beautiful Beings: the Function of the Reprobate in the Philosophical Theology of Jonathan Edwards." PhD diss., King's College, University of London, 2001.

———. "Dispositional Peculiarity, History, and Edwards's Evangelistic Appeal to Self-love." *Westminster Theological Journal* 66 (2004) 121–57.
Bonaventure. *The Soul's Journey into God, The Tree of Life, The Life of St. Francis*. Translated by E. Cousins. New York: Paulist, 1978.
Bonnington, Stuart. "Calvin and Islam." *Reformed Theological Review* 68 (2009) 77–87.
Bouquet, A. C. "Revelation and the Divine Logos." In *The Theology of the Christian Mission*, edited by Gerald H. Anderson, 183–98. London: SCM, 1961.
Bouwsma, William J. *John Calvin: A Sixteenth-Century Portrait*. Oxford: Oxford University Press, 1988.
———. *A Usable Past: Essays in European Cultural History*. Berkeley: University of California Press, 1990.
Boyle, Marjorie O'Rourke. *Christening Pagan Mysteries: Erasmus in Pursuit of Wisdom*. Toronto: University of Toronto Press, 1981.
Braaten, Carl E. *No Other Gospel! Christianity among the World's Religions*. Eugene, OR: Wipf & Stock, 2000.
Brachtendorf, Johannes. "Augustine on the Glory and the Limits of Philosophy." In *Augustine and Philosophy*, edited by Phillip Cary et al., 3–21. Lanham, MD: Lexington, 2010.
Bradnick, David. *Evil, Spirits, and Possession: An Emergentist Theology of the Demonic*. Leiden: Brill, 2017.
Bray, Gerald. "Explaining Christianity to Pagans: The Second-Century Apologists." In *The Trinity in a Pluralistic Age: Theological Essays on Culture and Religion*, edited by Kevin J. Vanhoozer, 9–25. Grand Rapids: Eerdmans, 1997.
Breen, Quirinus. *John Calvin: A Study in French Humanism*. 2nd ed. Archon, 1968.
Brown, Brian, et al., eds. *Augustine and World Religions*. Lanham, MD: Lexington, 2008.
Brown, Peter. *Augustine of Hippo: A Biography*. New ed. Berkeley: University of California Press, 2000.
Brown, Robert E. *Jonathan Edwards and the Bible*. Bloomington: Indiana University Press, 2002.
Brunner, Emil. *Revelation and Reason*. London: SCM, 1947.
Buck, P. Lorraine. "Justin Martyr's *Apologies*: Their Number, Destination, and Form." *Journal of Theological Studies* 54 (2003) 45–59.
Burns, J. Patout. "Augustine on the Origin and Progress of Evil." *Journal of Religious Ethics* 16 (1988) 9–27.
Butler, Diane. "God's Visible Glory: The Beauty of Nature in the Thought of John Calvin and Jonathan Edwards." *Westminster Theological Journal* 52 (1990) 13–26.
Byrne, James M. *Religion and the Enlightenment from Descartes to Kant*. Louisville: Westminster John Knox, 1997.
Byrne, Peter. *Natural Religion and the Nature of Religion*. London: Routledge, 1989.
Calvin, John, *Commentaries*. 22 vols. Grand Rapids: Baker Book House, 1989. https://www.ccel.org/ccel/calvin/commentaries.i.html.
———. *Institutes of the Christian Religion*. Edited by John T. McNeill. Louisville: Westminster John Knox, 2006.
———. *A Treatise on Relics*. Edinburgh: Johnston and Hunter, 1854.
Cameron, Michael. "Augustine and John's Gospel from Conversion to Confessiones." *Augustinian Studies* 48 (2017) 263–78.

Cammenga, Ronald. "Another Look at Calvin and Common Grace." *Protestant Reformed Theological Journal* 41 (2008) 3–25.
Campi, Emidio. "Early Reformed Attitudes towards Islam." *Theological Review of the Near East School of Theology* 31 (2010) 131–51.
Canlis, Julie. *Calvin's Ladder: A Spiritual Theology of Ascent and Ascension*. Grand Rapids: Eerdmans, 2010.
Capetz, Paul E. "'A Seed of Religion': A Study in the Theologies of Calvin and Schleiermacher." PhD diss., University of Chicago, 1996.
Cavadini, John C. *Visioning Augustine*. Chichester: Wiley-Blackwell, 2019.
Carson, D. A., ed. *The Enduring Authority of the Christian Scriptures*. Nottingham: Apollos, 2016.
Chadwick, Henry. *Early Christian Thought and the Classical Tradition*. Oxford: Clarendon, 1966.
———. "The Gospel a Reduplication of Natural Religion in Justin Martyr." *Illinois Classical Studies* 18 (1993) 237–47.
———. "Justin Martyr's Defence of Christianity." *BJRL* 7 (1965) 275–97.
Chandler, William Terrell, III. "The Contribution of Karl Barth toward the Formulation of an Evangelical Theology of Religions." PhD diss., Southern Baptist Theological Seminary, 2010.
Cherry, Conrad. "Symbols of Spiritual Truth: Jonathan Edwards as Biblical Interpreter." *Interpretation* 34 (1985) 263–71.
———. *The Theology of Jonathan Edwards: A Reappraisal*. New York: Anchor, 1966.
Chesnut, Glenn F. "The Ruler and the Logos in Neopythagorean, Middle Platonic, and Late Stoic Political Philosophy." In *Band 16/2. Teilband Religion* in *Aufstieg und Niedergang der römischen Welt (ANRW) / Rise and Decline of the Roman World*, edited by Wolfgang Haase, 1310–32. Berlin: de Gruyter, 1978.
Chrysostom, St. John. *Commentary on Saint John the Evangelist, Homilies 1–47*. Translated by Aquinas Goggin. New York: Fathers of the Church, 1957.
Clooney, Francis X. "Augustine, Apuleius, and Hermes Trismegistus: The City of God and Advice on How (Not) to Read Hindu Texts on Augustine's Mediator Focus in the City of God." In Brian Brown et al., *Augustine and World Religions*, 141–72. Lanham, MD: Lexington, 2008.
———. *Comparative Theology: Deep Learning across Religious Borders*. Chichester: Wiley-Blackwell, 2010.
Contreras, Carlos A. "Christian Views of Paganism." *Aufstieg und Niedergang der Römischen Welt* 23 (1980) 974–1022.
Copeland, E. Luther. "Nomos as a Medium of Revelation—Paralleling Logos—in Ante-Nicene Christianity." *Studia Theologica* 27 (1973) 51–61.
Corduan, Winfried. "Budha, Shiva, and Mohammed: Theistic Faith in Other Religions." In *Who Will Be Saved? Defending the Biblical Understanding of God, Salvation, and Evangelism*, edited by Paul R. House, and Gregory A. Thornbury, 129–43. Wheaton, IL: Crossway, 2000.
———. *In the Beginning God: A Fresh Look at the Case for Original Monotheism*. Nashville: Broadman & Holman, 2013.
———. *Neighbouring Faiths: A Christian Introduction to World Religions*. Downers Grove, IL: IVP Academic, 2013.
———. *A Tapestry of Faiths*. Downers Grove, IL: InterVarsity, 2002.

Corey, Judith L. *Light from Light: Cosmology and the Theology of the Logos*. Minneapolis: Fortress, 2016.

Cowen, Steven B., ed. *Five Views on Apologetics*. Grand Rapids: Zondervan, 2000.

Crisp, Oliver D., and Kyle C. Strobel, *Jonathan Edwards: An Introduction to His Thought*. Grand Rapids: Eerdmans, 2018.

Cruess, Gregory Michael. "Augustine's Biblical Christology: A Study of the *In Iohannis Evangelium Tractatus CXXIV*." PhD diss., University of Notre Dame, 2019.

Cumin, Paul. *Christ at the Crux: The Mediation of God and Creation in Christological Perspective*. Eugene, OR: Pickwick, 2014.

Cushman, Robert E. "Faith and Reason in the Thought of St. Augustine." *Church History* 19 (1950) 271–94.

Cyril of Alexandria. *Ancient Christian Texts, Commentary on John*. Vol. 1, *Cyril of Alexandria*. Edited by Joel C. Elowsky. Translated by David R. Maxwell. Grand Rapids: IVP Academic, 2013.

Daley, Brian E. *God Visible: Patristic Christology Reconsidered*. Oxford: Oxford University Press, 2018.

Daniélou, Jean. *Gospel Message and Hellenistic Culture*. London: Darton, Longman, & Todd, 1973.

Davey, D. M. "Justin Martyr and the Fourth Gospel." *Scripture* 17 (1965) 117–22.

Davids, A. "Justin Martyr on Monotheism and Heresy." *Nederlands archief voor kerkgeschiedenis / Dutch Review of Church History* 56 (1975) 210–34.

D'Costa, Gavin. *Christianity and World Religions: Disputed Questions in the Theology of Religions*. Chichester: Wiley-Blackwell, 2009.

———. "Gavin D'Costa Responds to Paul Knitter and Daniel Strange." In Gavin D'Costa et al., *Only One Way?*, 139–52. London: SCM, 2011.

———. "Gavin D'Costa Re-responds to Paul Knitter and Daniel Strange." In Gavin D'Costa et al., *Only One Way?*, 185–98. London: SCM, 2011.

———. "Revelation and Revelations: Discerning God in Other Religions: Beyond a Static Valuation." *Modern Theology* 10 (1994) 165–83.

D'Costa, Gavin, et al. *Only One Way? Three Christian Responses on the Uniqueness of Christ in a Religiously Plural World*. London: SCM, 2011.

De Jonge, Henk Jan. "The Sibyls in the Fifteenth and Sixteenth Centuries, or Ficino, Castellio, and 'The Ancient Theology.'" *Bibliothèque d'Humanisme et Renaissance* 78 (2016) 7–21.

Demarest, Bruce A. *General Revelation: Historical Views and Contemporary Issues*. Grand Rapids: Zondervan, 1982.

Dennison, William D. "The Christian Academy: Antithesis, Common Grace, and Plato's View of the Soul." *Journal of the Evangelical Theological Society* 30 (2011) 109–31.

Dermer, Scott. "Magna Gratiae Commendatio: Augustine's Teaching on Grace in the Tractates on the Gospel of John." PhD diss., Saint Louis University, 2018.

Dhavamony, Mariasusai. *Phenomenology of Religions*. Rome: Gregorian University Press, 1973.

Djung, Phillip. *Revelation and Grace*. Carlisle: Langham Monographs, 2021.

———. Review of *For Their Rock Is Not as Our Rock*, by Daniel Strange. *Calvin Theological Journal* 52 (2017) 419–21.

Douma, J. *Common Grace in Kuyper, Schilder, and Calvin*. Translated by Albert H. Oosterhoff. Ontario: Lucerna, 2017.

Dowey, Edward A., Jr. *The Knowledge of God in Calvin's Theology*. 3rd ed. Grand Rapids: Eerdmans, 1994.
Droge, Arthur J. "Justin Martyr and the Restoration of Philosophy." *Church History* 56 (1987) 303–19.
Drummond, Richard Henry. *Toward a New Age in Christian Theology*. Maryknoll, NY: Orbis, 1985.
Du Preez, J. "John Calvin's Contribution to a Theologia Religionum." *Missionalia* 16 (1988) 69–78.
Duce, Philip, and Daniel Strange, eds. *Getting Your Bearings: Engaging with Contemporary Theologians*. Nottingham: Apollos, 2003.
Dufault, Olivier. "Augustine and the Invention of Magical Dissent." In Brian Brown et al., *Augustine and World Religions*, 3–20. Lanham, MD: Lexington, 2008.
Dulles, Avery. *A History of Apologetics*. San Franciso: Ignatius, 1999.
Dunn, James D. G. *Christianity in the Making*. Vol. 3, *Neither Jew nor Greek: A Contested Identity*. Grand Rapids: Eerdmans, 2015.
Dupont, Anthony. "The Position of Gentiles and Pagans and Their Relation to Grace in Augustine's *Sermones ad Populum*." In *Studia Patristica: St. Augustine and His Opponents*, edited by J. Baun et al., 181–96. Leuven: Peeters, 2010.
———. "The Relation between *Pagani, Gentes*, and *Infideles* in Augustine's *Sermones ad Populum*: A Case Study of Augustine's Doctrine of Grace." *Augustiniana* 58 (2008) 95–126.
Dupuis, Jacques. *Toward a Christian Theology of Religious Pluralism*. Maryknoll, NY: Orbis, 1997.
Edelheit, Amos. *Ficino, Pico, and Savonarola: The Evolution of Humanist Theology 1461/2–1498*. Leiden: Brill, 2008.
Edmondson, Stephen. *Calvin's Christology*. Cambridge: Cambridge University Press, 2004.
Edwards, Jonathan. "Apocalyptic Writings (1723)." In *Works of Jonathan Edwards Online, Volume 5*, edited by Stephen J. Stein.
———. "The Blank Bible (1730)." In *Works of Jonathan Edwards Online, Volume 24*, edited by Stephen J. Stein.
———. "Catalogues of Books (1743)." In *Works of Jonathan Edwards Online, Volume 26*, edited by Peter J. Thuesen.
———. "Controversies Notebook (1743)." In *Works of Jonathan Edwards Online, Volume 27*, edited by Jonathan Edwards Center.
———. "Ecclesiastical Writings (1737)." In *Works of Jonathan Edwards Online, Volume 12*, edited by David D. Hall.
———. "Ethical Writings (1749)." In *Works of Jonathan Edwards Online, Volume 8*, edited by Paul Ramsey.
———. "Freedom of the Will (1754)." In *Works of Jonathan Edwards Online, Volume 1*, edited by Paul Ramsey,
———. "History of Redemption Notebooks (1743)." In *Works of Jonathan Edwards Online, Volume 31*, edited by Jonathan Edwards Center.
———. "A History of the Work of Redemption (1739)." In *Works of Jonathan Edwards Online, Volume 9*, edited by John F. Wilson.
———. "Man's Natural Blindness in the Things of Religion." In *The Works of Jonathan Edwards, Volume 2*, edited by Edward Hickman. Carlisle, PA: Banner of Truth Trust, 1974.

---. "Notes on Scripture (1722)." In *Works of Jonathan Edwards Online, Volume 15*, edited by Stephen J. Stein.

---. "The Miscellanies Entry Nos. 1153-1360 (1740)." In *Works of Jonathan Edwards Online, Volume 23*, edited by Douglas A. Sweeney.

---. "The Miscellanies Entry Nos. a-z, aa-zz, 1-500 (1722)." In *Works of Jonathan Edwards Online, Volume 13*, edited by Harry S. Stout.

---. "The Miscellanies 501-832 (1731)." In *Works of Jonathan Edwards Online, Volume 18*, edited by Ava Chamberlain.

---. "The Miscellanies 833-1152 (1740)." In *Works of Jonathan Edwards Online, Volume 20*, edited by Amy Plantinga Pauw.

---. "Original Sin (1758)." In *Works of Jonathan Edwards Online, Volume 3*, edited by Clyde A. Holbrook.

---. "Religious Affections (1754)." In *Works of Jonathan Edwards Online, Volume 2*, edited by Paul Ramsey.

---. "Sermons and Discourses 1720-1723 (1720)." In *Works of Jonathan Edwards Online, Volume 10*, edited by Wilson H. Kimnach.

---. "Sermons and Discourses 1723-1729 (1723)." In *Works of Jonathan Edwards Online, Volume 14*, edited by Kenneth P. Minkema.

---. "Sermons and Discourses, 1730-1733 (1730)." In *Works of Jonathan Edwards Online, Volume 17*, edited by Mark Valeri.

---. "Sermons and Discourses, 1734-1738 (1734)." In *Works of Jonathan Edwards Online, Volume 19*, edited by M. X. Lesser.

---. "Sermons and Discourses, 1739-1742 (1739)." In *Works of Jonathan Edwards Online, Volume 22*, edited by Harry S. Stout.

---. "Sermons and Discourses, 1743-1758 (1743)." In *Works of Jonathan Edwards Online, Volume 25*, edited by Wilson H. Kimnach.

---. "Sermons Series II 1739 (1743)." In *Works of Jonathan Edwards Online, Volume 54*, edited by Jonathan Edwards Center.

---. "Sermons Series II 1743 (1743)." In *Works of Jonathan Edwards Online, Volume 61*, edited by Jonathan Edwards Center.

---. "Sermons Series II, 1733 (1743)." In *Works of Jonathan Edwards, Volume 48*, edited by Jonathan Edwards Center.

---. "Sermons, Series II, 1728-1729 (1743)." In *Works of Jonathan Edwards Online, Volume 43*, edited by Jonathan Edwards Center.

---. "Sermons, Series II, 1729-1731 (1743)." In *Works of Jonathan Edwards Online, Volume 45*, edited by Jonathan Edwards Center.

---. "Sermons, Series II, 1731-1732 (1743)." In *Works of Jonathan Edwards Online, Volume 46*, edited by Jonathan Edwards Center.

---. "Sermons, Series II, 1737 (1743)." In *Works of Jonathan Edwards Online, Volume 52*, edited by Jonathan Edwards Center.

---. "Typological Writings (1744)." In *Works of Jonathan Edwards Online, Volume 11*, edited by Wallace E. Anderson et al.

---. "Writings on the Trinity, Grace, and Faith (1740)." In *Works of Jonathan Edwards Online, Volume 21*, edited by Sang Hyun Lee.

---. *The Works of Jonathan Edwards Online*. Jonathan Edwards Center at Yale University. http://edwards.yale.edu/.

---. *The Works of Jonathan Edwards*. Vol. 2. Revised and corrected by Edward Hickman. Edinburgh: The Banner of Truth Trust, 1974.

———. *The Works of President Edwards*. Vol. 8. New York: Converse, 1830.

Edwards, Mark. "Books 8–10: Augustine and Platonism." In *The Cambridge Companion to Augustine's City of God*, edited by David Vincent Meconi, 122–44. Cambridge: Cambridge University Press, 2021.

———. *Image, Word, and God in the Early Christian Centuries*. London: Routledge, 2016.

———. "Justin's Logos and the Word of God." *Journal of Early Christian Studies* 3 (1995) 261–80.

———. "Socrates in the Early Church." In *Socrates from Antiquity to the Enlightenment*, edited by Michael Trapp, 127–42. London: Routledge, 2016.

Ehrhardt, Arnold. "Justin Martyr's Two Apologies." *Journal of Ecclesiastical History* 4 (1953) 1–12.

Eire, Carlos M. N. "John Calvin, Accidental Anthropologist." In *John Calvin and Roman Catholicism: Critique and Engagement, Then and Now*, edited by Randall C. Zachman, 145–63. Michigan: Baker Academic, 2008.

———. *War against the Idols: The Reformation of Worship from Erasmus to Calvin*. Cambridge: Cambridge University Press, 1989.

Elwood, Douglas J. *The Philosophical Theology of Jonathan Edwards*. New York: Columbia University Press, 1960.

Engelsma, David J. *Common Grace Revisited*. Grandville, MI: Reformed Free, 2003.

Ensminger, Sven. *Karl Barth's Theology as a Resource for a Christian Theology of Religions*. London: Bloomsbury T&T Clark, 2014.

Erdt, Terence. "The Calvinist Psychology of the Heart and the 'Sense' of Jonathan Edwards." *Early American Literature* 13 (1978) 165–80.

Evans, G. R. *Augustine on Evil*. Cambridge: Cambridge University Press, 1982.

Fabiney, Tibor. "Edwards and Biblical Typology." In *Understanding Jonathan Edwards: An Introduction to America's Theologian*, edited by Gerald R. McDermott, 91–108. Oxford: Oxford University Press, 2009.

Faircloth, Kyle. "Daniel Strange on the Theological Question of the Unevangelized: A Doctrinal Assessment." *Themelios* 41 (2016) 59–70.

Farnham, Mark. "Postfoundational Epistemology and Christian Uniqueness: Coherentism in the Theology of Stanley J. Grenz." PhD diss., Westminster Theological Seminary, 2015.

Farrar, Thomas J. "The Intimate and Ultimate Adversary: Satanology in Early Second-Century Christian Literature." *Journal of Early Christian Studies* 26 (2018) 517–46.

Ferguson, Everett. *Demonology of the Early Christian World*. New York: Mellen, 1984.

Ferguson, Sinclair B. *The Holy Spirit*. Downers Grove, IL: InterVarsity, 1996.

Fitzgerald, Allan D., ed. *Augustine through the Ages*. Grand Rapids: Eerdmans, 1999.

Fowden, Garth. *The Egyptian Hermes: A Historical Approach to the Late Pagan Mind*. Princeton: Princeton University Press, 1986.

Frame, John. *Cornelius Van Til: An Analysis of His Thought*. Phillipsburg, NJ: P&R, 1995.

———. "Presuppositional Apologetics." In Steven B. Cowen, *Five Views on Apologetics*, 208–31. Grand Rapids: Zondervan, 2000.

———. "Van Til on Antithesis." *The Works of John Frame & Vern Poythress*, June 7, 2012. https://frame-poythress.org/van-til-on-antithesis/.

Fredriksen, Paula. *Augustine and the Jews: A Christian Defense of Jews and Judaism*. New Haven: Yale University Press, 2010.

Gale, Theophilus. *Court of the Gentiles*. Oxford: Hall, 1672.

Garin, Eugenio. "Gian Francesco Pico Della Mirandola: Savonarolan Apologetics and the Critique of Ancient Thought." In *Christianity and the Renaissance: Image and Religious Imagination in the Quattrocento*, edited by Timothy Verdon and John Henderson, 523–32. Syracuse: Syracuse University Press, 1990.

Garnsey, Peter. "Augustine and Lactantius." In *Representations of Empire: Rome and the Mediterranean World*, edited by Alan K. Bowman et al., 153–80. Oxford: Oxford University Press, 2002.

Gassman, Mattias. "An Ancient Account of Pagan Origins: Making Sense of Filastrius, Diuersarum hereseon liber 111*." *Revue d'études Augustiniennes et Patristiques* 67 (2021) 83–105.

Geehan, E. R., ed. *Jerusalem and Athens: Critical Discussions on the Philosophy and Apologetics of Cornelius Van Til*. Phillipsburg, NJ: P&R, 1971.

Gerstner, John H. *The Rational Biblical Theology of Jonathan Edwards*. Vol. 1. Orlando: Ligonier Ministries, 1991.

Gibson, James Edward. "The Development of the *Sensus Divinitatis* and Its Application to the Propagation of the Christian Gospel: Case Studies of the Divine Sense in Western Christian History." PhD diss., Macquarie University, Sydney, 2014.

Gilbert, Greg D. "The Nations Will Worship: Jonathan Edwards and the Salvation of the Heathen." *Trinity Journal* 23 (2002) 53–76.

Gill, David W. J. "Behind the Classical Façade: Local Religions of the Roman Empire." In *One God, One Lord in a World of Religious Pluralism*, edited by Andrew D. Clarke and Bruce W. Winter, 72–87. Cambridge: Tyndale House, 1991.

Gilson, Etienne. *The Christian Philosophy of Saint Augustine*. New York: Random House, 1960.

Gioia, Luigi. *The Theological Epistemology of Augustine's "De Trinitate."* Oxford: Oxford University Press, 2008.

Goodenough, Ernest R. *The Theology of Justin Martyr*. Jena: Verlag Frommannsche Buchhandlung, 1923.

Gootjes, H. "The Sense of Divinity: A Critical Examination of the Views of Calvin and Demarest." *Westminster Theological Journal* 48 (1986) 337–50.

Goudriaan, Aza. "Reformed Theology and the Church Fathers." In *The Oxford Handbook of Reformed Theology*, edited by Michael Allen and Scott R. Swain, 9–23. Oxford: Oxford University Press, 2020.

Graf, Fritz. "Augustine and Magic." In *The Metamorphosis of Magic from Late Antiquity to the Early Modern Period*, edited by Jan N. Bremmer and Jan R. Veenstra, 87–104. Leuven: Peeters, 2002.

Grant, Robert M. *Greek Apologists of the Second Century*. Philadelphia: Westminster, 1988.

Green, R. P. H., ed. and trans. *De Doctrina Christiana*. Oxford: Clarendon, 1995.

Grillmeier, Aloys. *Christ in Christian Tradition*. Vol. 1, *From the Apostolic Age to Chalcedon*. 2nd rev. ed. Translated by John Bowden. Atlanta: Knox, 1975.

Groothuis, Douglas. *Truth Decay: Defending Christianity against the Challenges of Postmodernism*. Downers Grove, IL: InterVarsity, 2000.

Hacker, Paul. "Religions of the Gentiles as Viewed by Fathers of the Church." *Zeitschrift für Missionswissenschaft und Religionswissenschaft* 54 (1970) 253–78.

Hadas, Daniel. "Christians, Sibyls, and Eclogue 4*." *Recherches Augustiniennes et Patristiques* 37 (2013) 51–129.

Haines, David. *Natural Theology*. Landrum, SC: Davenant, 2021.
Hanegraaff, Wouter J. "Hermetism." In *The Oxford Guide to the Historical Reception of Augustine*, edited by Karla Pollmann and Willemien Otten, 1135–39. Oxford: Oxford University Press, 2014.
Hanson, Carol. *Rethinking Augustine's Early Theology: An Argument for Continuity*. Oxford: Oxford University Press, 2006.
Hanson, R. P. C. "The Christian Attitude to Pagan Religions up to the Time of Constantine the Great." In *Band 23/2 Halbband Religion Vorkonstantinisches Christentum: Verhältnis zu römischem Staat und heidnischer Religion, Fortsetzung*, edited by Hildegard Temporini and Wolfgang Haase, 910–73. Berlin: de Gruyter, 1980.
Harakas, Stanley S. "Eastern Orthodox Perspectives on Natural Law." *American Journal of Jurisprudence* 24 (1979) 86–113.
Hardy, Richard P. "The Incarnation and Revelation in Augustine's Tractatus in Iohannis Evangelium." *Eglise et Theologie* 3 (1972) 193–200.
Harnack, Adolf. *History of Dogma*. Vols. 1–2. Boston: Little, Brown, and Co., 1899.
Harrison, Peter. *"Religion" and the Religions in the English Enlightenment*. Cambridge: Cambridge University Press, 1990.
Hayes, A. D. R. "Justin's Christian Philosophy: New Possibilities for Relations between Jews, Graeco-Romans and Christians." *Studies in Church History* 51 (2015) 14–32.
Hayes, Andrew. *Justin against Marcion: Defining the Christian Philosophy*. Minneapolis: Fortress, 2017.
Hedges, Paul M. "A Reflection on Typologies: Negotiating a Fast-Moving Discussion in Christian Approaches to Other Faiths." In *Christian Approaches to Other Faiths*, edited by Alan Race and Paul M. Hedges, 17–33. London: SCM, 2008.
Heintz, Michael. "The Immateriality and Eternity of Word in St. Augustine's Sermons on the Prologue of John's Gospel." In *Collectanea Augustiniana*, edited by Roland J. Teske and Earl C. Muller, 395–402. New York: Lang, 1993.
Helleman, Wendy Elgersma. "Justin Martyr and the Logos: An Apologetical Strategy." *Philosophia Reformata* 67 (2002) 128–47.
Helm, Paul. *Calvin at the Centre*. Oxford: Oxford University Press, 2010.
———. *Human Nature from Calvin to Edwards*. Grand Rapids: Reformed Heritage, 2018.
———. *John Calvin's Ideas*. Oxford: Oxford University Press, 2004.
Henry, Carl. "Is It Fair?" In *Through No Fault of Their Own?*, edited by William V. Crockett and James G. Sigountos, 245–56. Grand Rapids: Baker Book House, 1991.
Hesselink, I. John. *Calvin's Concept of the Law*. Eugene, OR: Pickwick, 1992.
———. "Christ, the Law, and the Christian in Readings in Calvin's Theology." In *Readings in Calvin's Theology*, edited by Donald McKim, 179–91. Grand Rapids: Baker, 1984.
———. "Law and Gospel or Gospel and Law? Karl Barth, Martin Luther, and John Calvin." *Dutch Reformed Theological Journal* 53 (2012) 62–80.
Hexham, Irving. *Understanding World Religions: An Interdisciplinary Approach*. Grand Rapids: Zondervan, 2011.
Hick, John. *A Christian Theology of Religions: The Rainbow of Faiths*. Louisville: Westminster John Knox, 1995.

BIBLIOGRAPHY

Hillar, Marian. *From Logos to Trinity: The Evolution of Religious Beliefs from Pythagoras to Tertullian.* Cambridge: Cambridge University Press, 2012.

Hoeksema, Herman. *God's Goodness Always Particular.* 2nd ed. Jenison, MI: Reformed Free, 2015.

Hoitenga, Dewey J., Jr. "Faith and Reason in Calvin's Doctrine of the Knowledge of God." In *Rationality in the Calvinian Tradition*, edited by Hendrik Hart et al., 17-39. Eugene, OR: Wipf & Stock, 2011.

Holbrook, Clyde A. *The Ethics of Jonathan Edwards: Morality and Aesthetics.* Ann Arbor, MI: University of Michigan Press, 1973.

———. "Jonathan Edwards Addresses Some 'Modern Critics' of Original Sin." *Journal of Religion* 63 (1983) 211-30.

Holder, R. Ward. "Calvin as Commentator on the Pauline Epistles." In *Calvin and the Bible*, edited by Donald K. McKim, 224-56. Cambridge: Cambridge University Press, 2006.

Holifield, E. Brooks. *Theology in America.* New Haven: Yale University Press, 2003.

Holmes, Michael W. "The Biblical Canon." In *The Oxford Handbook of Early Christian Studies*, edited by Susan Ashbrook Harvey and David G. Hunter, 406-26. Oxford: Oxford University Press, 2008.

Holmes, Stephen R. *God of Grace and God of Glory.* London: T&T Clark, 2000.

Holte, Ragnar. "Logos Spermatikos Christianity and Ancient Philosophy according to St. Justin's Apologies." *Studia Theologica* 12 (1958) 109-68.

Hooker, Mischa André. "The Use of Sibyls and Sibylline Oracles in Early Christian Writers." PhD diss., University of Cincinnati, 2007.

Horbury, William. *Jews and Christians in Contact and Controversy.* Edinburgh: T&T Clark, 1998.

Horner, Timothy J. "The Problem with Abraham: Justin Martyr's Use of Abraham in the Dialogue with Trypho a Jew." *Churchman* 110 (1996) 230-50.

Horowitz, Maryanne Cline. "The Stoic Synthesis of the Idea of Natural Law in Man: Four Themes." *Journal of the History of Ideas* 35 (1974) 3-16.

Horton, Michael S. "Calvin and the Law-Gospel Hermeneutic." *Pro Ecclesia* 6 (1997) 27-42.

Howlett, Sophia. *Marsilio Ficino and His World.* New York: Palgrave Macmillan, 2016.

Hudson, Wayne. *The English Deists.* London: Pickering & Chatto, 2009.

Hughes, P. E. *The True Image.* Grand Rapids: Eerdmans, 1989.

Idel, Moshe. "Prisca Theologia in Marsilio Ficino and in Some Jewish Treatments." In *Marsilio Ficino: His Theology, His Philosophy, His Legacy*, edited by Michael J. B. Allen and Valery Rees, 137-58. Leiden: Brill, 2002.

Ivanovska, Inta. "The Demonology of Saint Augustine of Hippo." PhD diss., Saint Louis University, 2011.

Jackson-McCabe, Matt A. *Logos and Law in the Letter of James: The Law of Nature, the Law of Moses, and the Law of Freedom.* Koln: Brill, 2000.

Jeffreys, Derek S. "How Reformed Is Reformed Epistemology? Alvin Plantinga and Calvin's *Sensus Divinitatis*." *Religious Studies* 33 (1997) 419-31.

Jenson, Robert W. *America's Theologian: A Recommendation of Jonathan Edwards.* New York: Oxford University Press, 1988.

Johnson, Keith E. "Christian Theology of Religions." In *Missiology: An Introduction to the Foundations, History, and Strategies of World Missions*, edited by John Mark Terry, 365-76. Nashville: B&H Academic, 2015.

BIBLIOGRAPHY

———. *Rethinking the Trinity and Religious Pluralism*. Downers Grove, IL: InterVarsity, 2011.

Jones, Kevin. "*Religio* and *Res Publica* in Augustine and Aquinas." PhD diss., The Catholic University of America, 2018.

Jones, Serene. *Calvin and the Rhetoric of Piety*. Louisville: Westminster John Knox, 1995.

Juchno, Andrew J. "Beyond Salem and Secularism: Jonathan Edwards and Satan in Early America." *Jonathan Edwards Studies* 11 (2021) 73–94.

Justin Martyr. *Writings of Saint Justin Martyr*. Translated by Thomas B. Falls. The Fathers of the Church 6. Washington, DC: The Catholic University of America Press, 1948.

Kahlos, Maijastina. *Debate and Dialogue: Christian and Pagan Cultures c. 360–430*. Hampshire: Ashgate, 2007.

Kärkkäinen, Veli-Matti. "Calvin and Religions." In *John Calvin and Evangelical Theology: Legacy and Prospect*, edited by Sung Wook Chung, 266–83. Milton Keynes: Paternoster, 2009.

———. *An Introduction to the Theology of Religions*. Downers Grove, IL: InterVarsity, 2003.

Karlowicz, Dariusz. *Socrates and Other Saints: Early Christian Understandings of Reason and Philosophy*. Translated by Artur Sebastian Rosman. Eugene, OR: Cascade, 2017.

Keener, Craig S. *The Gospel of John: A Commentary*. Vol. 1. Grand Rapids: Baker Academic, 2003.

Keith, Graham. "Justin Martyr and Religious Exclusivism." *Tyndale Bulletin* 43 (1992) 57–80.

Kelly, J. N. D. *Early Christian Doctrines*. 2nd ed. London: Adam and Charles Black, 1968.

Kimnach, Wilson H., et al. "Editors' Introduction." In *The Sermons of Jonathan Edwards: A Reader*, edited by Wilson H. Kimnach et al., ix–xlviii. New Haven: Yale University Press, 1999.

King, Peter, ed. and trans. *On the Free Choice of the Will, On Grace and Free Choice, and Other Writings*. Cambridge: Cambridge University Press, 2010.

Klapwijk, J. "Antithesis and Common Grace." In *Bringing into Captivity Every Thought*, edited by J. Klapwijk et al., 169–90. Lanham, MD: University Press of America, 1991.

——— "Antithesis, Synthesis, and the Idea of Transformational Philosophy." *Philosophia Reformata* 51 (1986) 138–52.

Klein, Elizabeth. *Augustine's Theology of Angels*. Cambridge: Cambridge University Press, 2018.

Knight, Janice. "Typology." In *The Princeton Companion to Jonathan Edwards*, edited by Sang Hyun Lee, 190–209. Princeton: Princeton University Press, 2005.

Knitter, Paul F. *No Other Name? A Critical Survey of Christian Attitudes towards the World Religions*. London: SCM, 1985.

Kok, Joel Edward. "The Influence of Martin Bucer on John Calvin's Interpretation of Romans: A Comparative Case Study." PhD diss., Duke University, 1993.

Koskenniemi, Erkki. "Forgetting an Epic Battle: Did the Early Church Understand the Debate between Paul and His Judaistic Opponents? Preliminary Notes on the Role of the Torah in the Early Church." In *The Challenge of the Mosaic Torah in Judaism, Christianity, and Islam*, edited by Antti Laato, 143–68. Leiden: Brill, 2021.

Kraemer, Hendrik. *The Christian Message in a Non-Christian World*. 2nd ed. London: Edinburgh House, 1947.

———. "Continuity or Discontinuity." In *The Authority of the Faith*, edited by G. Paton, 1–21. London: International Missionary Council, 1939.

———. *Religion and the Christian Faith*. Philadelphia: Westminster, 1956.

———. *Why Christianity of All Religions?* London: Lutterworth, 1962.

Kreitzer, Mark. *The Concept of Ethnicity in the Bible: A Theological Analysis*. London: Mellen, 2008.

Kristeller, Paul Oskar. *Eight Philosophers of the Italian Renaissance*. London: Chatto & Windus, 1965.

Kuiper, Herman. *Calvin on Common Grace*. Goes: Oosterbaan & Le Cointre, 1928.

LaChance, Paul Joseph. "A Christian *Aeneid*: Pagan and Christian Education in the Confessions." In Brian Brown et al., *Augustine and World Religions*, 71–96. Lanham, MD: Lexington, 2008.

Lane, Anthony N. S. *John Calvin: Student of the Church Fathers*. Edinburgh: T&T Clark, 1999.

Larsson, Tord. *God in the Fourth Gospel: A Hermeneutical Study of the History of Interpretations*. Coniectanea Biblica, New Testament Series 35. Stockholm: Almqvist & Wiksell, 2001.

Latourelle, René. *Theology of Revelation*. New York: Alba, 1966.

Lee, Constance Y. "The Spark That Still Shines: John Calvin on Conscience and Natural Law." *Oxford Journal of Law and Religion* 8 (2019) 615–40.

Lee, Sang Hyun. *The Philosophical Theology of Jonathan Edwards*. Expanded ed. Princeton: Princeton University Press, 2000.

Leith, John H. "John Calvin's Polemic against Idolatry." In *Soli Deo Gloria*, edited by J. McDowell Richards, 111–24. Richmond, VA: Knox, 1968.

Leithart, Peter J. "That Eminent Pagan: Calvin's Use of Cicero in Institutes 1.1–5." *Westminster Theological Journal* 52 (1990) 1–12.

———. "Stoic Elements in Calvin's Doctrine of the Christian Life, Part I: Original Corruption, Natural Law, and the Order of the Soul." *Westminster Theological Journal* 55 (1993) 31–54.

Levi, Anthony. "Ficino, Augustine, and the Pagans." In *Marsilio Ficino: His Theology, His Philosophy, His Legacy*, edited by Michael J. B. Allen et al., 99–114. Leiden: Brill, 2002.

Levitin, Dmitri. *Ancient Wisdom in the Age of the New Science: Histories of Philosophy in England, c. 1640–1700*. Cambridge: Cambridge University Press, 2015.

Lilla, Salvatore R. C. *Clement of Alexandria: A Study in Christian Platonism and Gnosticism*. Oxford: Oxford University Press, 1971.

Litfin, Bryan M. *Getting to Know the Church Fathers: An Evangelical Introduction*. Grand Rapids: Baker Academic, 2016.

Little, Dale William. "The Significance of Theology of the Holy Spirit for Theology of Religion and for Theology of Mission in the Writings of Lesslie Newbigin and Clark Pinnock." PhD diss., Trinity Evangelical Divinity School, 2000.

Lohr, Winrich. "The Theft of the Greeks." *Revue d'histoire Ecclésiastique* 95 (2000) 403–26.

Macleod, Donald. *Behold Your God*. Ross-shire: Christian Focus, 1990.

———. *The Person of Christ*. Downers Grove, IL: InterVarsity, 1998.

Madec, Goulven. "Augustin et le Neoplatonisme." *Revue de l'Institut Catholique de Paris* 19 (1986) 41–52.

Malherbe, Abraham J. "Towards Understanding the Apologists: Review Article." In *Light from the Gentiles: Hellenistic Philosophy and Early Christianity, Collected Essays, 1959–2012*, edited by Carl R. Holladay et al., 1:797–805. Leiden: Brill, 2014.

Malusa, Luciano. "Renaissance Antecedents to the Historiography of Philosophy." In *Models of the History of Philosophy: From Its Origins in the Renaissance to the "Historia Philosophica,"* by Francesco Bottin et al., 3–65. Dordrecht: Springer Science and Business Media, 1993.

Mangum, R. Todd. "Is There a Reformed Way to Get the Benefits of the Atonement to 'Those Who Have Never Heard?.'" *Journal of the Evangelical Theological Society* 47 (2004) 121–36.

Manuel, Frank E. *The Eighteenth Century Confronts the Gods*. New York: Athenuem, 1967.

Marenbon, John. *Pagans and Philosophers: The Problem of Paganism from Augustine to Leibniz*. Princeton: Princeton University Press, 2015.

Marsden, George M. *Jonathan Edwards: A Life*. New Haven: Yale University Press, 2003.

Martens, John W. *One God, One Law: Philo of Alexandria on the Mosaic and Greco-Roman Law*. Leiden: Brill, 2003.

Masselink, William. "New Views of Common Grace in the Light of Historic Reformed Theology." *Calvin Forum* 19 (1954) 194–203.

McClymond, Michael J., and Gerald R. McDermott. *The Theology of Jonathan Edwards*. New York: Oxford University Press, 2012.

McDermott, Gerald R. *Can Evangelicals Learn from World Religions?* Downers Grove, IL: IVP Academic, 2000.

———. *God's Rivals: Why Has God Allowed Different Religions—Insights from the Bible and the Early Church*. Downers Grove, IL: InterVarsity, 2007.

———. "Jonathan Edwards and Islam." *Jonathan Edwards Studies* 6 (2016) 93–106.

———. *Jonathan Edwards Confronts the Gods*. New York: Oxford University Press, 2000.

———. "Jonathan Edwards, John Henry Newman, and Non-Christian Religions." In *Jonathan Edwards: Philosophical Theologian*, edited by Oliver Crisp and Paul Helm, 127–37. Aldershot: Ashgate, 2003.

———. "A Possibility of Reconciliation: Jonathan Edwards and the Salvation of Non-Christians." In *Jonathan Edwards in Our Time: Jonathan Edwards and Contemporary Theological Issues*, edited by Sang Hyun Lee and Allen Guelzo, 173–202. Grand Rapids: Eerdmans, 1999.

———. "Response to Gilbert: The Nations Will Worship: Jonathan Edwards and the Salvation of the Heathen." *Trinity Journal* 23 (2002) 77–80.

———. "Was Jonathan Edwards an Evangelical? Scripture and Tradition in America's Theologian." In *Jonathan Edwards and Scripture: Biblical Exegesis in British North America*, edited by Douglas A. Barshinger and Douglas A. Sweeney, 233–48. New York: Oxford University Press, 2018.

———. "What If Paul Had Been from China?" In *No Other Gods before Me*, edited by John G. Stackhouse, 17–35. Grand Rapids: Baker Academic, 2001.

McDermott, Gerald R., and Harold A. Netland. *A Trinitarian Theology of Religions: An Evangelical Proposal*. Oxford: Oxford University Press, 2014.

BIBLIOGRAPHY

McGee, Iain. "An Interview with Daniel Strange on His Christian Theology of Religions." https://www.academia.edu/113943191/An_Interview_with_Daniel_Strange_on_his_Christian_Theology_of_Religions

———. "John Calvin: Logos-Centric Theologian of Religions." *Journal of Reformed Theology* 17 (2023) 3–28.

———. "Reconsidering the *Sensus Divinitatis* in the Light of the *Semen Religionis*: John Calvin and Non-Christian Religion." *European Journal of Theology* 31 (2022) 215–39.

———. "Revelation and Religions: Towards a More 'Harmonious' Jonathan Edwards." *Themelios* 46 (2021) 620–40.

McGrath, Alister. *Evangelicalism and the Future of Christianity*. London: Hodder and Stoughton, 1993.

McLelland, Joseph C. "Calvin and Philosophy." *Journal of Canadian Theology* 11 (1965) 42–53.

McNeill, John T. "Natural Law in the Teaching of the Reformers." *Journal of Religion* 26 (1946) 168–82.

Miles, Todd. *A God of Many Understandings? The Gospel and a Theology of Religions*. Nashville: B&H Academic, 2010.

Miller, Ed L. "The True Light Which Illumines Every Person." In *Good News in History*, edited by L. Miller, 63–83. Atlanta: Scholars, 1993.

Miller, Ike. "Conceiving Knowledge: The 'Economy of Divine Light' in Augustine's and Karl Barth's Readings of the Gospel and Letters of John." PhD diss., Trinity Evangelical Divinity School, 2016.

Minkema, Kenneth P. "'If Thou Reckon Right': Angels from John Calvin to Jonathan Edwards via John Milton." In *The Oxford Handbook of Calvin and Calvinism*, edited by Bruce Gordon, and Carl Trueman, 393–407. Oxford: Oxford University Press, 2021.

Minns, Denis, and Paul Parvis. *Justin, Philosopher, and Martyr: Apologies, Edited with Commentary on the Text*. Oxford: Oxford University Press, 2009.

Mody, Rohintan. *Evil and Empty: The Worship of Other Faiths in 1 Corinthians 10:18–22 and Today*. Latimer Studies 71. London: Latimer Trust, 2010.

———. "The Relationship between Powers of Evil and Idols in 1 Corinthians 8:4–5 and 10:18–22 in the Context of the Pauline Corpus and Early Judaism." PhD diss., Aberdeen University, 2008.

Moll, Sebastian. *The Arch-Heretic Marcion*. Tübingen: Mohr Siebeck, 2010.

Moon, Byung-Ho. "Lex Dei Regula Vivendi et Vivificandi: Calvin's Christological Understanding of the Law in the Light of his Concept of Christus Mediator Legis." PhD diss., University of Edinburgh, 2003.

Morali, Ilari. "Catholic Theology vis-à-vis Religions and Dialogue Fifty Years after Vatican II." In *The Past, Present, and Future of Theologies of Interreligious Dialogue*, edited by Terrence Merrigan and John Friday, 81–92. Oxford: Oxford University Press, 2017.

Mori, Giuliano. "Natural Theology and Ancient Theology in the Jesuit China Mission." *Intellectual History Review* 30 (2020) 187–208.

Morris, William. *The Young Jonathan Edwards: A Reconstruction*. Brooklyn: Carlson, 1991.

Mouw, Richard. *All That God Cares About*. Grand Rapids: Brazos, 2020.

———. "Discerning the Spirit in World Religions: A Neocalvinist Approach." In *The Spirit Is Moving: New Pathways in Pneumatology: Studies Presented to Professor Cornelis van der Kooi on the Occasion of His Retirement*, edited by Gijsbert van den Brink et al., 200–214. Leiden: Brill, 2019.

———. *He Shines in All That's Fair: Culture and Common Grace*. Grand Rapids: Eerdmans, 2001.

Muller, Richard A. *Post-Reformation Reformed Dogmatics*. Vol. 1, *Prolegomena to Theology*. Grand Rapids: Baker Book House, 1987.

———. *The Unaccommodated Calvin: Studies in the Foundation of a Theological Tradition*. New York: Oxford University Press, 2000.

———. "Was It Really Viral? Natural Theology in the Early Modern Reformed Tradition." In *Crossing Traditions: Essays on the Reformation and Intellectual History in Honour of Irena Backus*, edited by Maria-Cristina Pitassi and Daniela Solfaroli Camillocci, 507–31. Leiden: Brill, 2018.

Murray, John. "Common Grace." In *Collected Writings of John Murray*, 2:93–122. Edinburgh: Banner of Truth Trust, 1977.

Nahm, Charles. "The Debate on the 'Platonism' of Justin Martyr." *Journal of Early Christian Studies* 9 (1992) 129–51.

Nash, Ronald H. "Illumination Divine." In *Augustine Through the Ages*, edited by Allen D. Fitzgerald, 438–40. Grand Rapids: Eerdmans, 1999.

———. *The Light of the Mind: St. Augustine's Theory of Knowledge*. Lima, OH: Academic Renewal, 2003.

Netland, Harold A. *Encountering Religious Pluralism: The Challenge to Christian Faith and Mission*. Downers Grove, IL: InterVarsity, 2001.

———. "Theology of Religions, Missiology, and Evangelicals." *Missiology* 33 (2005) 141–58.

Newbigin, Lesslie. *The Gospel in a Pluralist Society*. Grand Rapids: Eerdmans, 1989.

Nichols, Stephen J. "'An Absolute Sort of Certainty': The Holy Spirit and the Apologetics of Jonathan Edwards." PhD diss., Westminster Theological Seminary, 2000.

Niesel, Wilhelm. *The Theology of Calvin*. Translated by Harold Knight. Philadelphia: Westminster, 1956.

Nilson, Jon. "To Whom Is Justin's Dialogue with Trypho Addressed?" *Theological Studies* 38 (1977) 538–46.

Noll, Mark A. *America's God: From Jonathan Edwards to Abraham Lincoln*. Oxford: Oxford University Press, 2002.

Nongbri, Brent. *Before Religion: A History of a Modern Concept*. New Haven: Yale University Press, 2013.

Norris, John M. "The Theological Structure of St. Augustine's Exegesis in His *Tractus Iohannis Euangelium*." PhD diss., Marquette University, 1990.

Norris, Richard A., Jr. "The Apologists." In *The Cambridge History of Early Christian Literature*, edited by Frances Young et al., 36–44. Cambridge: Cambridge University Press, 2004.

Nuovo, Victor Lawrence. "Calvin's Theology: A Study of Its Sources in Classical Antiquity." PhD diss., Columbia University, 1964.

Nyström, David E. *The Apology of Justin Martyr: Literary Strategies and the Defence of Christianity*. Tübingen: Mohr Siebeck, 2018.

O'Collins, Gerald. *Salvation for All God's Other Peoples*. Oxford: Oxford University Press, 2008.

———. *The Second Vatican Council: Message and Meaning.* Collegeville, MN: Liturgical, 2014.

———. *The Second Vatican Council on Other Religions.* Oxford: Oxford University Press, 2013.

O'Daly, Gerard. *Augustine's City of God: A Reader's Guide.* 2nd ed. Oxford: Oxford University Press, 2020.

Oliphint, K. Scott. "Historical and Theological Studies: Using Reason by Faith." *Westminster Theological Journal* 73 (2011) 97–112.

———. *Reasons for Faith: Philosophy in the Service of Theology.* Phillipsburg, NJ: P&R, 2006.

Ortlund, Gavin. *Theological Retrieval for Evangelicals: Why We Need Our Past to Have a Future.* Wheaton, IL: Crossway, 2019.

Osborn, Eric. *The Beginning of Christian Philosophy.* Cambridge: Cambridge University Press, 1981.

———. *Justin Martyr.* Tübingen: Mohr Siebeck, 1973.

———. "Justin Martyr and the Logos Spermatikos." *Studia Missionalia* 42 (1993) 143–59.

Otto, Bernd-Christian, and Michael Stausberg. "Augustine of Hippo." In *Defining Magic: A Reader*, edited by Bernd-Christian Otto and Michael Stausberg, 33–40. London: Routledge, 2014.

Owen, John. *Selected Works of John Owen.* Vol. 3. Edited by C. Bradley. London: Tegg, 1831.

Parker, T. H. L. *Calvin: An Introduction to his Thought.* London: Continuum, 1995.

Partee, Charles. *Calvin and Classical Philosophy.* Leiden: Brill, 1977.

———. "The Soul in Plato, Platonism, and Calvin." *Scottish Journal of Theology* 22 (1969) 278–95.

———. *The Theology of John Calvin.* Louisville: Westminster John Knox, 2008.

Pauw, Amy Plantinga. "The Trinity." In *The Princeton Companion to Jonathan Edwards*, edited by Sang Hyun Lee, 44–58. Princeton: Princeton University Press, 2005.

———. "'Where Theologians Fear to Tread.'" *Modern Theology* 16 (2000) 39–59.

Pelikan, Jaroslav. *The Emergence of the Catholic Tradition (100–600).* Chicago: University of Chicago Press, 1971.

Pelkonen, J. Peter. "The Teaching of John Calvin on the Nature and Function of the Conscience." *Lutheran Quarterly* 21 (1969) 74–88.

Perry, Tim S. *Radical Difference: A Defence of Hendrick Kraemer's Theology of Religions.* Waterloo: Wilfrid Laurier University Press, 2001.

Pickett, Mark. "Hard Rock Theology." *Foundations* 64 (2014) 78–91.

Pinnock, Clark H. *A Wideness in God's Mercy.* Grand Rapids: Zondervan, 1992.

Pitkin, Barbara. "Erasmus, Calvin, and the Faces of Stoicism in Renaissance and Reformation Thought." In *The Routledge Handbook of the Stoic Tradition*, edited by John Sellars, 145–59. London: Routledge, 2016.

———. "The Spiritual Gospel? Christ and Human Nature in Calvin's Commentary on John." *Dutch Review of Church History* 85 (2005) 187–204.

———. *What Pure Eyes Could See: Calvin's Doctrine of Faith in Its Exegetical Context.* New York: Oxford University Press, 1999.

Plantinga, Alvin. *Warranted Christian Belief.* New York: Oxford University Press, 2000.

Poston, Larry. "The Bible and the Religions." Unpublished manuscript.

Potgieter, P. C. "Calvin and Other Religions." *Acta Theologica* 24 (2004) 147–67.

Pretila, Noël Wayne. "'Re-appropriating 'Marvelous Fables': Justin Martyr's Strategic Retrieval of Myth in 1 Apology." PhD diss., Saint Louis University, 2012.
Preus, J. Samuel. "Zwingli, Calvin, and the Origin of Religion." *Church History* 46 (1977) 186–202.
Price, R. M. "Are There Holy Pagans in Justin Martyr?" *Studia Patristica* 31 (1997) 167–71.
Purves, George T. *The Testimony of Justin Martyr to Early Christianity*. New York: Randolph, 1889.
Race, Alan. *Christians and Religious Pluralism: Patterns in the Christian Theology of Religions*. London: SCM, 1983.
Rajak, Tessa. "Talking at Trypho: Christian Apologetic as Anti-Judaism in Justin's *Dialogue with Trypho the Jew*." In *Apologetics in the Roman Empire*, edited by Mark Edwards et al., 58–80. Oxford: Oxford University Press, 1999.
Reaske, Christopher R. "The Devil and Jonathan Edwards." *Journal of the History of Ideas* 33 (1972) 123–38.
Reed, Annette Yoshiko. "The Trickery of the Fallen Angels and the Demonic Mimesis of the Divine: Aetiology, Demonology, and Polemics in the Writings of Justin Martyr." *Journal of Early Christian Studies* 12 (2004) 141–71.
Richardson, Cyril C., ed. *Early Christian Fathers*. Louisville: Westminster John Knox, 2006.
Ricketts, Allyn Lee. "The Primacy of Revelation in the Philosophical Theology of Jonathan Edwards." PhD diss., Westminster Theological Seminary, 1995.
Richie, Tony L. "Hints from Heaven: Can C. S. Lewis Help Evangelicals Hear God in Other Religions?" *Evangelical Review of Theology* 32 (2008) 38–55.
Roberts, Alexander, and James Donaldson, eds. *Lactantius, Venantius, Asterius, Victorinus, Dionysius, Apostolic Teaching and Constitutions, Homily, and Liturgies*. Ante-Nicene Fathers 7. New York: Christian Literature, 1896.
Rokeah, David. *Justin Martyr and the Jews*. Leiden: Brill, 2002.
Roth, Norman. "The 'Theft of Philosophy' by the Greeks from the Jews." *Classical Folia* 32 (1978) 53–67.
Rubiés, Joan Pau. "Theology, Ethnography, and the Historicization of Idolatry." *Journal of the History of Ideas* 67 (2006) 571–96.
Runia, David T. "Philo and the Early Christian Fathers." In *The Cambridge Companion to Philo*, edited by Adam Kamesar, 210–30. Cambridge: Cambridge University Press, 2009.
Russell, Robert. "The Role of Neoplatonism in St. Augustine's *de Civitate Dei* (160–170)." In *Neoplatonism and Early Christian Thought: Essays in Honour of A. H. Armstrong*, edited by H. J. Blumenthal and R. E. Markus, 160–70. London: Variorum, 1981.
Sakamoto, Kuni. *Julius Caesar Scaliger, Renaissance Reformer of Aristotelianism: A Study of His Exotericae Exercitationes*. Leiden: Brill, 2016.
Salaman, Clement. "Echoes of Egypt in Hermes and Ficino." In *Marsilio Ficino: His Theology, His Philosophy, His Legacy*, edited by Michael J. B. Allen and Valery Rees, 115–36. Leiden: Brill, 2002.
Saldanha, Chrys. *Divine Pedagogy: A Patristic View of Non-Christian Religions*. Rome: LAS, 1984.
Salih, Sarah. "Idol Theory." *Preternature* 4 (2015) 13–36.

Salminen, Joona. "The City of God and the Place of Demons—City Life and Demonology in Early Christianity." In *Spaces in Late Antiquity: Cultural, Theological, and Archaeological Perspectives*, edited by Juliette Day et al., 106–17. London: Routledge, 2016.

Salzman, Michele Renee. "Christian Sermons against Pagans: The Evidence from Augustine's Sermons on the New Year and on the Sack of Rome in 410." In *The Cambridge Companion to the Age of Attila*, edited by Michael Maas, 344–57. New York: Cambridge University Press, 2015.

Sanders, John. *No Other Name*. Grand Rapids: Eerdmans, 1992.

Schmitt, Charles B. "Perennial Philosophy: From Agostino Steuco to Leibniz." *Journal of the History of Ideas* 27 (1966) 505–32.

Schnackenburg, Rudolf. *The Gospel According to St. John*. Vol. 1. New York: Crossroad, 1982.

Schumacher, Lydia. *Divine Illumination: The History and Future of Augustine's Theory of Knowledge*. Chichester: Wiley, 2011.

Schweitzer, William M. "Interpreting the Harmony of Reality: Jonathan Edwards' Theology of Revelation." PhD diss., University of Edinburgh, 2008.

———. "Rage against the Machine: Jonathan Edwards versus the God of Deism." *Scottish Bulletin of Evangelical Theology* 25 (2007) 61–79.

Screech, Michael A. *Laughter at the Foot of the Cross*. Chicago: University of Chicago Press, 2015.

Seay, Scott. "Satan and His Maleficium in the Thought of Jonathan Edwards." In *The Contribution of Jonathan Edwards to American Culture and Society*, edited by Richard A. S. Hall, 259–80. Lewiston, NY: Mellen, 2008.

Sheather, Mary. "The Apology of Justin Martyr and the Legatio of Athenagoras: Two Responses to the Challenge of Being a Christian in the Second Century." *Scrinium* 14 (2018) 115–32.

Sholl, Brian Keith. "The Excellency of Minds: Jonathan Edwards's Theological Style." PhD diss., University of Virginia, 2008.

Sigountos, James D. "Did Early Christians Believe Pagan Religions Could Save?" In *Through No Fault of Their Own? The Fate of Those Who Have Never Heard*, edited by William V. Crockett and James D. Sigountos, 229–41. Grand Rapids: Baker Book House, 2009.

Simonson, Harold Peter. *Jonathan Edwards: Theologian of the Heart*. Grand Rapids: Eerdmans, 1974.

Skarsaune, Oskar. "The Conversion of Justin Martyr." *Studia Theologica* 30 (1976) 53–73.

———. "Judaism and Hellenism in Justin Martyr, Elucidated from His Portrait of Socrates." In *Geschichte-Tradition-Reflexion: Festschrift für Martin Hengel zum 70. Geburtstag, Band III: Frühes Christentum*, edited by H. Cancik et al., 585–611. Tübingen: Mohr, 1996.

Smith, Claude A. "Jonathan Edwards and 'The Way of Ideas.'" *Harvard Theological Review* 59 (1966) 153–73.

Smith, Gordon T. "Religions and the Bible: An Agenda for Evangelicals." In *Christianity and the Religions: A Biblical Theology of World Religions*, edited by Edward Rommen and Harold Netland, 9–29. Littleton, CO: Carey, 1995.

Smith, John E. "Jonathan Edwards as Philosophical Theologian." *Review of Metaphysics* 30 (1976) 306–24.

Smith, Shawn C. "Was Justin Martyr an Inclusivist?" *Stone-Campbell Journal* 10 (2007) 193–211.

Sparks, Adam. *One of a Kind: The Relationship between Old and New Covenants as the Hermeneutical Key for Christian Theology of Religions*. Eugene, OR: Pickwick, 2010.

———. "Was Justin Martyr a Proto-Inclusivist?" *Journal of Ecumenical Studies* 43 (2008) 495–510.

Sproul, Robert Charles, et al. *Classical Apologetics: A Rational Defense of the Christian Faith and a Critique of Presuppositional Apologetics*. Grand Rapids: Zondervan, 1984.

Statham, Todd. Review of *Their Rock Is Not Like Our Rock: A Theology of Religions*, by Daniel Strange. *European Journal of Theology* 26 (2017) 82–84.

Stefano, Frances. "Lordship over Weakness: Christ's Graced Humanity as Locus of Divine Power in Augustine's Tractates on the Gospel of John." *Augustinian Studies* 16 (1985) 1–19.

Stengel, Friedemann. "Reformation, Renaissance, and Hermeticism: Contexts and Interfaces of the Early Reformation Movement." *Reformation & Renaissance Review* 20 (2018) 103–33.

Stob, Henry. "Observations on the Concept of the Antithesis." In *Perspectives on the Christian Reformed Church: Studies in Its History, Theology, and Ecumenicity*, edited by Peter de Clerk and Richard R. De Ritter, 241–58. Grand Rapids: Baker Book House, 1983.

———. *Theological Reflections*. Grand Rapids: Eerdmans, 1981.

Strand, Daniel Deforrest. "The Gods of the Nations: St. Augustine's Apocalyptic Political Theology." PhD diss., University of Chicago, 2015.

Strange, Daniel. "Co-belligerence and Common Grace: Can the Enemy of My Enemy Be My Friend?" *Cambridge Papers* 14 (2005) 1–4.

———. "Daniel Strange Re-responds to Gavin D'Costa and Paul Knitter." In Gavin D'Costa et al., *Only One Way?*, 213–28. London: SCM, 2011.

———. "Exclusivisms: 'Indeed Their Rock Is Not Like Our Rock.'" In *Christian Approaches to Other Faiths*, edited by Alan Race and Paul M. Hedges, 36–62. London: SCM, 2008.

———. "For Their Rock Is Not as Our Rock: The Gospel as the 'Subversive Fulfillment' of the Religious Other." *Journal of the Evangelical Theological Society* 56 (2013) 379–95.

———. *For Their Rock Is Not as Our Rock*. Nottingham: Apollos, 2014.

———. "General Revelation: Sufficient or Insufficient?" In *Faith Comes by Hearing: A Response to Inclusivism*, edited by Christopher W. Morgan and Robert A. Peterson, 40–77. Downers Grove, IL: InterVarsity, 2008.

———. "An Interview with Daniel Strange on His Christian Theology of Religions." https://www.researchgate.net/publication/377628096_An_Interview_with_Daniel_Strange_on_his_Christian_Theology_of_Religions.

———. *Making Faith Magnetic*. Surrey: Good Book, 2021.

———. "Not Ashamed! The Sufficiency of Scripture for Public Theology." *Themelios* 36 (2011) 238–60.

———. "Perilous Exchange, Precious Good News: A Reformed 'Subversive Fulfilment' Interpretation of Other Religions." In Gavin D'Costa et al., *Only One Way?*, 91–136. London: SCM, 2011.

———. *Plugged In*. Surrey: Good Book, 2019.

———. *The Possibility of Salvation among the Unevangelised: An Analysis of Inclusivism in Recent Evangelical Theology*. Carlisle: Paternoster, 2002.

———. "The Secret Diaries of Jonathan Edwards Aged 54 1/2: A Reconstruction (and Deconstruction?) of the New England Theologian—A Review Article." *Themelios* 47 (2001) 32–43.

———. "This Rock Unmoved: A Rejoinder to Kyle Faircloth." *Themelios* 41 (2016) 71–75.

Strange, Daniel, and David Gibson, eds. *Engaging with Barth*. Nottingham: Apollos, 2008.

Strange, Daniel, and Michael Ovey. *Confident: Why We Can Trust the Bible*. Ross-shire: Christian Focus, 2015.

Strobel, Kyle C. *Jonathan Edwards's Theology: A Reinterpretation*. London: Bloomsbury T&T Clark, 2013.

Studebaker, Steven M. "Jonathan Edwards' Pneumatological Concept of Grace and Dispositional Soteriology: Resources for an Evangelical Inclusivism." *Pro Ecclesia* 14 (2005) 324–39.

Studebaker, Steven M., and Robert M. Caldwell III. *The Trinitarian Theology of Jonathan Edwards: Text, Context, and Application*. Farnham: Ashgate, 2012.

Studer, Basil. *The Grace of Christ and the Grace of God in Augustine of Hippo: Christocentrism or Theocentrism?* Translated by Matthew J. O'Connell. Collegeville, MN: Liturgical, 1997.

Sudduth, Michael. "Pico della Mirandola's Philosophy of Religion." In *Pico della Mirandola: New Essays*, edited by M. V. Dougherty, 61–80. Cambridge: Cambridge University Press, 2008.

Sweeney, Douglas A. "Jonathan Edwards and the World Religions: A Response to Gerald McDermott." Unpublished lecture notes.

Tennent, Timothy C. "An Evangelical Theology of Religions." *Asbury Journal* 76 (2021) 246–82.

Teselle, Eugene. "Augustine and Augustinianism." In *Encyclopedia of the Reformed Faith*, edited by Donald McKim, 17–18. Louisville: Westminster John Knox, 1992.

Teske, Roland J. "'Homo Spiritualis' in the Confessions of Saint Augustine." In *Augustine from Rhetor to Theologian*, edited by Joanne McWilliam, 67–76. Waterloo: Wilfrid Laurier University Press, 1992.

Thomas, Joe M. *Christ and the World of Religions: Lesslie Newbigin's Theology*. Eugene, OR: Wipf & Stock, 2020.

Thomas, John Newton. "The Place of Natural Theology in the Thought of John Calvin." *Journal of Religious Thought* 15 (1958) 107–36.

Thomas, Owen C. "Introduction." In *Attitudes toward Other Religions: Some Christian Interpretations*, edited by Owen C. Thomas, 1–28. London: SCM, 1969.

Thorsteinsson, Runar M. "Justin and Stoic Cosmo-theology." *Journal of Theological Studies* 63 (2012) 533–71.

———. "Justin's Debate with Crescens the Stoic." *Zeitschrift für antikes Christentum* 17 (2013) 451–78.

———. "The Literary Genre and Purpose of Justin's *Second Apology*: A Critical Review with Insights from Ancient Epistolography." *Harvard Theological Review* 105 (2012) 91–114.

BIBLIOGRAPHY

Thuesen, Peter J. "Edwards' Intellectual Background." In *The Princeton Companion to Jonathan Edwards*, edited by Sang Hyun Lee, 16–33. Princeton: Princeton University Press, 2005.

Thyssen, Henrik Pontoppidan. "Philosophical Christology in The New Testament." *Numen* 53 (2006) 133–76.

Tidball, Derek. *Who Are the Evangelicals? Tracing the Roots of Today's Movement*. London: Pickering, 1994.

Tiessen, Terrance. "God's Work of Grace in the Context of the Religions." *Didaskalia* (2007) 165–91.

———. *Who Can Be Saved? Reassessing Salvation in Christ and World Religions*. Downers Grove, IL: InterVarsity, 2004.

Toland, John, *Christianity Not Mysterious*. London, 1696.

Troxel, Craig. "'All Things to All People': Justin Martyr's Apologetical Method." *Fides et Historia* 27 (1995) 23–43.

Turretin, Francis. *Institutes of Elenctic Theology*. Vol. 1. Edited by James T. Dennison Jr. Translated by George Musgrave. Phillipsburg, NJ: P&R, 1997.

Ulrich, Jörg. "Justin Martyr." In *Early Christianity in the Context of Antiquity*, edited by Jakob Engberg et al., 51–66. Frankfurt am Main: Lang, 2014.

Van der Kooi, Cornelis. *As in a Mirror: John Calvin and Karl Barth on Knowing God: A Diptych*. Leiden: Brill, 2005.

Vandici, Gratian. "Reading the Rules of Knowledge in the Story of the Fall: Calvin and Reformed Epistemology on the Noetic Effects of Original Sin." *Journal of Theological Interpretation* 10 (2016) 173–91.

VanDrunen, David. "Wisdom and the Natural Moral Order: The Contribution of Proverbs to a Christian Theology of Natural Law." *Journal of the Society of Christian Ethics* 33 (2013) 153–68.

Van Gelder, H. A. Enno. *The Two Reformations in the 16th Century*. The Hague: Nijhoff, 1961.

Van Herwaarden, Jan. "Erasmus and the Non-Christian World." *Erasmus of Rotterdam Society Yearbook* 32 (2012) 69–83.

Van Houten, David Jon. "Earthly Wisdom and Heavenly Wisdom: Reason in the Theology of John Calvin." PhD diss., University of Chicago, 1993.

Van Leeuwen, Raymond C., trans. "Translator's Introduction to Herman Bavinck's 'Common Grace.'" *Calvin Theological Journal* 24 (1989) 35–37.

Van Oort, Johannes. "Augustine and Hermes Trismegistus: An Inquiry into the Spirituality of Augustine's Hidden Years." *Journal of Early Christian History* 6 (2016) 55–76.

Van Til, Cornelius. *Common Grace and the Gospel*. Philadelphia: P&R, 1974.

———. *An Introduction to Systematic Theology*. Edited by William Edgar. 2nd ed. Phillipsburg, NJ: P&R, 2007.

Van Til, Henry R. *The Calvinistic Concept of Culture*. Philadelphia: P&R, 1959.

Venema, Cornelis P. "The 'Twofold Knowledge of God' and the Structure of Calvin's Theology." *Mid-America Journal of Theology* 4 (1988) 156–82.

Visser, Paul Jan. *Heart for the Gospel, Heart for the World: The Life and Thought of a Reformed Pioneer Missiologist Johan Herman Bavinck, 1895–1964*. Eugene, OR: Wipf & Stock, 2003.

———. "Introduction: The Life and Thought of Johan Herman Bavinck (1895–1964)." In *The J. H. Bavinck Reader*, edited by John Bolt et al., 1–92. Grand Rapids: Eerdmans, 2013.

———. "Religion in Biblical and Reformed Perspective." *Calvin Theological Journal* 44 (2009) 9–36.

———. "Religion, Mission, and Kingdom: A Comparison of Herman and Johan Herman Bavinck." *Calvin Theological Journal* 45 (2010) 117–32.

Von Bredow, Benjamin. "The Superbia of the Platonists in St. Augustine's *Confessions*." *Pseudo-Dionysius* 18 (2016) 73–80.

Vorster, Nico. "Calvin on the Created Structure of Human Nature: The Influence of His Anthropology on His Theology." *Journal of Theology for Southern Africa* 151 (2015) 162–81.

Waddington, Jeffrey C. "Must We Believe? Jonathan Edwards and Conscious Faith in Christ." *Confessional Presbyterian* 6 (2010) 11–21.

———. "The Unified Operations of the Human Soul: Jonathan Edwards' Theological Anthropology and Apologetic." PhD diss., Westminster Theological Seminary, 2013.

Wainwright, William J. "Jonathan Edwards and the Hiddenness of God." In *Divine Hiddenness: New Essays*, edited by Daniel Howard-Snyder and Paul K. Moser, 98–119. New York: Cambridge University Press, 2002.

———. *Reason and the Heart*. Ithaca, NY: Cornell University Press, 1995.

Walker, D. P. *The Ancient Theology*. London: Duckworth, 1972.

———. "The Prisca Theologia in France." *Journal of the Warburg and Courtauld Institutes* 17 (1954) 204–59.

Wallace, Dewey D., Jr. *Shapers of English Calvinism, 1660–1714: Variety, Persistence, and Transformation*. Oxford: Oxford University Press, 2011.

Wallace, Jeremy. "Antithesis Revisited: The Nature and Development of 'Antithesis' in Van Tillian Presuppositionalism." Paper presented to the Evangelical Theological Society, Multnomah University Portland, Oregon, March 4, 2016. https://www.kerygma21.com/uploads/1/0/8/4/108403703/antithesis_revisited.paper.pdf.

Warfield, Benjamin Breckinridge. *Calvin and Calvinism*. New York: Oxford University Press, 1931.

Wendel, Susan J. *Scriptural Interpretation and Community: Self-Definition in Luke-Acts and the Writings of Justin Martyr*. Leiden: Brill, 2011.

Westerholm, Martin. "The Work of the Trinity and the Knowledge of God in Augustine's *De Trinitate*." *International Journal of Systematic Theology* 15 (2013) 5–24.

Whitehead, Philip. "A Pauline Approach to the Theology of Religions." PhD diss., University of Nottingham, 2017.

Widdicombe, Peter. "Justin Martyr, Allegorical Interpretation, and the Greek Myths." *Studia Patristica* 31 (1997) 234–39.

Wiebe, Gregory D. "Demons in the Theology of Augustine." PhD diss., McMaster University, 2015.

Wilken, Robert Louis. "Religious Pluralism and Early Christian Theology." *Interpretation* 40 (1986) 379–91.

———. *The Spirit of Early Christian Thought*. New Haven: Yale University Press, 2003.

Williams, A. N. *The Divine Sense: The Intellect in Patristic Theology*. Cambridge: Cambridge University Press, 2007.

BIBLIOGRAPHY

Williams, D. H. *Defending and Defining the Faith: An Introduction to Early Christian Apologetic Literature*. Oxford: Oxford University Press, 2020.

Williams, Donald T. "John Calvin: Humanist and Reformer: The Influence of Calvin's Early Humanism on his Work as a Christian Theologian." *Trinity Journal* 5 (1976) 67–78.

Williams, George Huntston. "Erasmus and the Reformers on Non-Christian Religions and *salus extra ecclesiam*." In *Action and Conviction in Early Modern Europe*, edited by Theodore Rabb and Jerrold Seigel, 319–70. Princeton: Princeton University Press, 1969.

Willis, E. David. *Calvin's Catholic Christology: The Function of the So-called Extra Calvinisticum in Calvin's Theology*. Leiden: Brill, 1966.

Winslow, Lisanne D'Andrea. "A Great and Remarkable Analogy: A Trinitarian Theology of Nature." PhD diss., University of Aberdeen, 2018.

Wolfson, Harry Austryn. *The Philosophy of the Church Fathers*. Cambridge: Harvard University Press, 1956.

Wolterstorff, Nicholas. "The Reformed Tradition." In *A Companion to Philosophy of Religion*, edited by Charles Taliaferro et al., 204–9. Chichester: Wiley-Blackwell, 2010.

Woolford, Thomas. "Natural Theology and Natural Philosophy in the Late Renaissance." PhD diss., University of Cambridge, 2011.

Wright, David F. "Christian Faith in the Greek World: Justin Martyr's Testimony." *Evangelical Quarterly* 54 (1982) 77–87.

Wyatt, Peter. *Jesus Christ and Creation in the Theology of John Calvin*. Eugene, OR: Pickwick, 1996.

Zakai, Avihu. "The Age of Enlightenment." In *The Cambridge Companion to Jonathan Edwards*, edited by Stephen J. Stein, 80–99. Cambridge: Cambridge University Press, 2007.

———. *Jonathan Edwards's Philosophy of History: The Reenchantment of the World in the Age of Enlightenment*. Princeton: Princeton University Press, 2003.

———. "The Theological Origins of Jonathan Edwards's Philosophy of Nature." *Journal of Ecclesiastical History* 60 (2009) 708–24.

Zarotiadis, Nikolaos. "Religious Conflict with the Demons according to St. Augustine." *Theology & Culture* 3 (2021) 27–34.

Zhu, Victor. *America's Theologian beyond America: Jonathan Edwards, Israel, and China*. Oxford: Oxford University Press, 2022.

Ziegler, Roland. "Natural Knowledge of God and the Trinity." *Concordia Theological Quarterly* 69 (2005) 133–58.

www.ingramcontent.com/pod-product-compliance
Lightning Source LLC
Chambersburg PA
CBHW071148300426
44113CB00009B/1132